ANTHONY MATTINA

Beginning
English
Grammar

Beginning English Grammar

SAMUEL JAY KEYSER
University of Massachusetts

PAUL M. POSTAL
Thomas J. Watson Research Center
IBM

HARPER & ROW, Publishers
New York Hagerstown San Francisco London

Sponsoring Editor: *George A. Middendorf*
Project Editor: *Renée E. Beach*
Designer: *Frances Torbert Tilley*
Production Supervisor: *Francis X. Giordano*
Compositor: *Santype International Limited*
Printer: *Halliday Lithograph Corporation*
Binder: *Halliday Lithograph Corporation*

Library of Congress Cataloging in Publication Data

Keyser, Samuel Jay, 1935-
    Beginning English grammar.

    Bibliography: p.
    Includes index.
    1. English language—Grammar, Generative.
2. English language—Grammar—1950-   I. Postal,
Paul Martin, 1936-   joint author. II. Title.
PE1112.K45   425   76-2542
ISBN 0-06-045254-4

We dedicate this work to our parents:
Abraham and Sabina Keyser
and
Bernard and Margaret Postal.

CONTENTS

PART II ON THE NATURE OF THE GRAMMAR

PART III SOME FUNDAMENTAL GRAMMATICAL OPERATIONS

PART IV SOME ASPECTS OF THE VERBAL SYSTEM

PART V CONCLUSION

PROLOGUE

This book is intended for readers with no background in linguistics but with an interest in studying English grammar and in finding out what modern linguistics can reveal about it. It lies within the tradition of transformational grammar, which has developed during the last twenty years and which continues to flourish as of this writing.

This is, of course, not the first introductory book to be offered within this tradition, nor is it likely to be the last. This raises the question, Why this book? In presenting various aspects of English grammar, the authors have stressed the justification of claims made about grammar. This is, of course, impossible in every case in an introductory book. But we have devoted a considerable portion of the alloted space not to mere assertions about English but to argumentation in support of the claims advanced. While this approach in an introductory book on grammar may not be unique, it is relatively rare.

Moreover, stress on justifying claims is no small virtue. Without an effective method for evaluating claims about the subject matter, students are left at the mercy of competing analyses. They have no way to bring their critical powers to bear on the statements about language which are offered. Without some stress on techniques of acquiring and justifying purported knowledge about English, an introductory book can inadvertently give the impression of presenting a degree of understanding which, in fact, does not exist. There is, however, every reason to avoid giving the impression that linguistics today can provide the student of English with a fixed, well-worked out systematic description of the grammar of the language. Dogmatism is dogmatism, whether wrapped in the concepts and terminology of an outmoded Latin tradition or in those of what claims to be modern science.

This book, then, seeks to accomplish two different things. First, it attempts to present various fragments of English grammar, some well-worked out, others less so. Second, it attempts to introduce and exemplify a method of inquiry into English grammar. Of these, the former is likely to be the more evanescent contribution. While a great deal is now known about English grammar, there is far more that is not known. New insights, new facts, and the concomitant revisions of previous views they require are now the everyday norm. Therefore, the authors would not be surprised to find that analyses put forward in this manual had become at least partially outmoded within the next few years.

Many readers may be perturbed at not being given a complete and solid analysis of English. The fragmentary and tentative character of the grammatical analyses presented in their manual may seem a defect. Our own feeling is that nothing more than a fragmentary account of English grammatical patterns can now be given, once one gets beyond the more superficial regularities (articles precede nouns, etc.). To present a technically complete set of rules would be misleading and misguided. For, in fact, there is simply not the available understanding to construct such a system at the moment. Elaborate bodies of formal rules are thus, at this stage, necessarily doomed to be artificial and arbitrary to a great degree.

On the other hand, the analytic *methods* presented implicitly in this book will, hopefully, wear better than particular analyses. Indeed, this manual will have done a great deal if readers succeed in grasping something of techniques which linguists use today in the study of grammatical patterns. For, in doing so, they will begin to equip themselves to judge what is questionable in the analyses put forth not only in the present book but in other works on English grammar as well.

We would like to express our debt to the many scholars whose contributions underlie much of the work presented here. In any such acknowledgment, first place goes to Noam Chomsky, whose pioneering perspective on language brought about a revolution in linguistic theory. Our thanks also go to Charles Fillmore, Edward Klima, Robert Lees, Stanley Peters, Peter Rosenbaum, and John Ross. We have profited greatly from their insightful studies of various aspects of English. There are others too numerous to mention to whom we also owe a debt. We beg their indulgence for this silent acknowledgment. What we present is a complex fabric woven out of the ideas of all of these investigators. Naturally, though, they are not responsible for what we have made of their work nor are they to blame for what we have ignored or changed.

Finally, each of the authors would like to state that any shortcomings and flaws that may have crept into this manual are due to the other.

SAMUEL JAY KEYSER
PAUL M. POSTAL

NOTE TO TEACHERS

The material in this book is to a large extent organized in a step-by-step fashion. Thus, each successive chapter builds on the preceding chapters. Maximal benefit will be obtained by making use of the whole. However, the manual is written in such a way that those instructors who wish to present less material, or material of lesser complexity, can with no real difficulty teach only a portion of the book.

It would, for example, be entirely natural to base a course only on Chapters 1–23, that is, to terminate after Part III is completed. A natural course could also be based on Chapters 1–24, or on Chapters 1–25. However, if Chapter 26 is used, it is strongly advised to continue to Chapter 27.

It would also be possible to use Chapters 1–25 and Chapter 29, or Chapters 1–27 and Chapter 29. That is, Chapter 28 is relatively self-contained, and Chapter 29 does not depend on it. Other possible courses would include Chapters 1–23 and Chapter 28, or Chapters 1–24 and Chapter 28. Chapter 29, though intimately connected to much earlier discussion, is highly theoretical in comparison to most of the rest. Possibly some instructors will wish to skip this discussion, or only make use of part of it.

S.J.K.
P.M.P.

CHAPTER I **INTRODUCTION**

We take English grammar to be a field of empirical study. By this, we mean it is a domain of investigation in which claims must have the support of observed fact. English grammar is a subject matter which, though studied from numerous points of view for years by many scholars in different traditions, remains for the most part uncharted territory. We approach it as explorers who find the tip of some unknown object buried in the sand. Those facts about English which are known correspond to the visible tip. But the substance of the inquiry consists of discovering what lies below the surface.

We have just asserted that not much is known about English grammar. This may seem ridiculous or even offensive. We have not meant, of course, to deny the existence of a certain level of understanding. It is known that in English articles precede nouns, that subjects agree with their verbs, etc. A considerable body of such information is available in the mass of careful and extensive manuals and handbooks. It is easy, however, to exaggerate the degree of understanding which this kind of information provides. It takes no great labor to show that even the most banal and ordinary sentences reveal properties that nothing in traditional grammatical doctrine accounts for.

Consider, for instance, the following:

(1) a   All of them are $\begin{Bmatrix} \text{difficult} \\ \text{likely} \end{Bmatrix}$ to understand.

    b   They all are $\begin{Bmatrix} \text{difficult} \\ \text{likely} \end{Bmatrix}$ to understand.

c They are all $\begin{Bmatrix} \text{difficult} \\ \text{likely} \end{Bmatrix}$ to understand.

d They are $\begin{Bmatrix} \text{*difficult} \\ \text{likely} \end{Bmatrix}$ to all understand.

Here we introduce the device, which will be used throughout, of marking those examples which violate genuine English grammatical rules with a star (*). They will be referred to as *ungrammatical* or *ill-formed*. There are eight examples represented in (1), containing the quantifying word *all*. This word occurs in four different positions. In three of these positions, the well-formedness of the examples with *difficult* is not distinguished from that of the examples with *likely*. But positioning *all* directly in front of the verb *understand* (in (1d)) yields a contrast in well-formedness.

We predict that readers will look in vain in standard grammars for a statement of facts like those in (1). Still less will they find a general description of *all* from which the distribution in such sentences follows.[1] This is a genuine, and quite typical, case where straightforward facts about English sentence formation are not well understood. Past grammarians were probably not even aware of the existence of the problem illustrated in (1). A case like (1) thus illustrates simultaneously the limitations of past linguistic insight and the possibility of an interesting inquiry into English grammar. Scholars sometimes draw a distinction between known and unknown languages. By the latter, they normally refer to the languages of some obscure and isolated group. Facts like (1) reveal, however, that in a more interesting sense, English is an unknown language once one delves beneath the surface.

The scope of the mystery manifested in (1) enlarges when it is realized that, in ordinary grammatical terms, the various pairs in (1) have the same grammatical structure. Take those in (1b). Each consists of a pronoun subject, the word *all*, the copula verb *are*, an adjective, and an infinitive based on the verb *understand*. Nothing in such a description predicts the difference in (1d). Still less does it predict the sharp difference in the way the parts of an example like (1b) are related to each other. When it occurs with the adjective *difficult*, the pronoun *they* refers to things which are understood, while with the adjective *likely*, *they* refers to beings who understand. Put differently, in the first case, *they* is interpreted as the object of *understand*, while in the second it is interpreted as the subject of *understand*.

It is not hard to elaborate masses of cases like (1). The possibility of doing so makes clear that the level of understanding about English sentence formation so far achieved is relatively primitive. The present work is designed to introduce the reader to an approach to grammar which seeks to provide an account of facts like those in (1), that is, which seeks to discover principles of sentence construction which underlie our knowledge of the endless number of cases like (1). In Chapters 24, 25, and 29, we provide an account of the distribution of words like *all*, which goes a long way toward explaining the facts manifested in (1). This account lies toward the end of this work for a good reason. It turns out that the principles and generalizations which are involved in cases like (1) can only be formulated in terms of a rather particular and richly articulated conception of grammatical structure. And it is only after a considerable elaboration of such a framework that it is possible to approach examples like (1) successfully.

The approach we adopt in this manual contrasts markedly with a different orientation toward grammar which has dominated a great deal of grammatical discussion within the framework of liberal education. The latter approaches language from a rather hygienic point of view. In this view, language is not so much a subject for study as an object in need of repair and constant preventive maintenance. Grammatical scholarship in this framework tends to shade off into a kind of social engineering, whose goal is to preserve and even improve the language. No better example of this attitude could be found than the statement of John Adams, one of the signers of the Declaration of Independence and second President of the United States. In a letter to Congress dated 1780, Adams proposed an Academy to fix and improve American English: "The honor of forming the first public institution for refining, correcting, improving, and ascertaining the English language, I hope is reserved for congress; they have every motive that can possibly influence a public assembly to undertake it. It will have a happy effect upon the union of the States to have a public standard for all persons in every part of the continent to appeal to both for the signification and pronunciation of the language."[2]

The hygienic approach is much concerned with minor differences between different varieties or dialects of the language. It tends to pick one variant as the norm and to regard deviations as "errors." It is preoccupied with "proper English," by which it usually means conformity with some prestigious dialect. It tends to equate normal linguistic change with decay, and is often in the position of attempting to maintain or to impose archaic usages. These interests preclude a serious concern with the fundamental principles of sentence formation common to different varieties of the language and condemn such discussion for the most part to the level of superficialities.

In this work, we are not concerned with hygienic considerations. We are concerned with the linguistic properties speakers do have, not with those others think they ought to have. For the most part, we deal with facts which differ little from one dialect to another. Where we are aware of differences, we point them out. But we make no invidious distinctions.

We can now consider the overall organization of this book. The remaining twenty-eight chapters are divided into five parts, each connected by a persistent theme. Part I is concerned to lead the reader to an understanding of the fundamental theoretical concept of transformational grammar: underlying grammatical structure. We use the term *remote structure* to refer to this notion. The ten chapters of Part I begin with very elementary aspects of English grammar, but are progressively expanded in scope and depth of analysis. The reader is led to see the near inevitability of the theoretical proposals made. It is seen how certain phenomena require certain rules, how further facts lead to modifications of these rules, how these modifications require certain theoretical assumptions, etc. Ultimately, the reader is shown how individual rules, each recognized to handle a certain range of relatively elementary cases, interact in the formation of complex examples. At the end of this part, the reader will hopefully have been led to see the need for, and some of the basic features of, what is now generally referred to as a transformational grammar. However, no serious characterization of this approach is presented in Part I. Thus the reader is introduced to the substance and problems of English grammatical description in a way which makes minimal appeal to technical devices and which only gradually leads away from elementary and well-known facts.

It is only in Part II that we attempt a sketch of the theoretical framework in which a transformational description of English must be embedded. We approach this by making use of the knowledge gained in Part I. We begin to consider in greater detail the kind of theory which the facts previously gone over show to be required. Part II explores the fact that the set of sentences in English is infinite and establishes the basic conclusions that can be drawn from this. It outlines the fundamental division of a transformational grammar between base rules and transformational rules. It shows how such a grammar accounts for the unbounded or infinite aspect of sentence formation. It considers the nature of the lexicon that must be associated with the rules and shows how items from the lexicon are inserted into sentence structures. It analyzes the content of the lexicon and argues that many English words are productively formed by rule from phrases. Finally, it sketches briefly a way of representing transformational rules.

At the end of Part II, the reader is assumed to have an elementary grasp of the overall features of a transformational description. Then in Part III, we turn to describing four basic grammatical processes crucial to an understanding of English clause structure. Only one of these, passivization, is really familiar from traditional descriptions. Considerable care is taken to empirically motivate several new rules, which underlie what may be surprising analyses of a wide range of constructions. Part III thus begins to put to work the body of understanding built up in Parts I and II.

Part IV is the most novel aspect of the present work. Starting with the description of a revealing but traditionally neglected phenomenon, the distribution of the quantifier words *all*, *both*, and *each* when these are not attached to nominal phrases, it leads naturally to some relatively radical but well-motivated and formally simple analyses of the basics of the English verbal system. In particular, it provides new insights into the relations between the traditional categories of adjective and verb and to the character of so-called auxiliary verbs. This part concludes with a description of basic interrogative clause structures and their characteristic word order.

Part V contains only one chapter. It introduces a general principle of rule application. It is shown how this principle interacts with a number of rules considered earlier to provide explanations for a variety of clear facts and to solve certain apparent anomalies. The generalization presented in this chapter differs qualitatively from those presented in earlier chapters. The latter took the form of particular rules of English grammar. The former has the status of a linguistic universal which is hypothesized to govern certain rules in all languages.

Each of the twenty-eight chapters of Parts I–V has the following overall organization. There is a brief Preview section, a long text section, and a final brief Summary. The previews indicate the scope of the material to be covered in the main text section. The summaries recapitulate the most important points covered. Each chapter contains several problems based on the material covered. Answers to all problems are provided. Most of the problems in this manual are designed in such a way that their fomulation and answer expands the coverage of the material they relate to. They are not simply mechanical regurgitations of previous material. Thus, working through the problems is an important part of using the book productively, and should not be neglected. Most chapters also contain a number of notes. These provide much descriptive material related to that covered in the text. They also provide an important perspective on many of the claims and descriptions in the text proper. Often, certain limiting conditions, special constraints, or unexplained phenomena are described only in the notes. The reader will inevitably go astray if this material is ignored.

The book ends with a list of suggested readings. These will help the reader fit the present work into the intellectual traditions of which it is a part. They will also provide, in many cases, more complete and more detailed descriptions of areas of grammar only touched on here. The reader must recognize, however, that the description of English grammar is a basically open subject matter about which much disagreement exists. He should not be disturbed or distracted by a lack of congruence between some of the descriptions and terminology of this manual and studies mentioned in the Bibliography. The day when there is a fixed, agreed-upon description and uniform terminology for the grammatical description of English lies in the far-off future.

Despite the fact that, for most aspects of English grammar covered here, one or more competing solutions are available in the literature, we have made no attempt to weigh relative merits in such cases. In fact, we have not generally even mentioned alternative solutions. Our feeling is that the proper place for the student to encounter alternative viewpoints is in the literature indicated in the Bibliography and in the further texts that will be found when that literature is consulted. Without attempting to minimize the existence of controversy in the field today, an introductory manual of this sort does not seem to be the proper forum to discuss it. We have therefore limited ourselves to presenting and motivating those analyses of the topics dealt with which seem to us most promising on the basis of current evidence.

We would like to conclude this introduction with an important clarification. Our overriding interest in this book is to present and justify a number of generalizations about the formation of English sentences. It turns out that the grammar of a human language is a highly complex, abstract, and technical kind of thing. Therefore, it is inevitable that a serious and accurate description of the generalizations underlying such a system must involve a certain amount of technical descriptive apparatus. This fact is unquestionably unpleasant or even disturbing to many. We want to stress, therefore, that we have made every effort to keep such apparatus to an absolute minimum in this manual. We have presupposed absolutely no knowledge of technical linguistic literature, no familiarity with particular linguistic theories or particular ideas about the form and nature of grammars. That degree of technical detail we have introduced is motivated solely by the need to express those generalizations which the facts reveal. We hope that those readers who approach this work from backgrounds unfamiliar with technical domains will not be put off. While the discussion in this manual is not necessarily easy or trivial, and demands close attention, it requires no special technical expertise or talent. We feel that students who apply themselves will follow the arguments and quickly master those elements of theoretical apparatus which are introduced. In proceeding, the user may even gain some interest in the technical matters and be led to go beyond the elementary account of this work to the now rich and expanding literature on English grammar and grammatical theory, which offers a fascinating variety of puzzles, mysteries, proposals, insights, and even solutions. We hope, therefore, that in the end the reader will see this book as a window on a new world of investigation.

NOTES

1. It would be a valuable exercise for the reader to try and learn something about facts like those in (1) by searching in the works of such encyclopedic grammarians as Curme, Jespersen, and Poutsma, cited in the bibliographical references at the end of this book.

2. The citation from Adams appears in George Philip Krapp, *The English Language in America*, vol. 1 (New York: Ungar, 1960), pp. 6–7. Krapp notes that Adams mentions in the same letter that projects similar to the one he proposed had failed in Britain. It is noteworthy that Jonathan Swift in 1711 sent a letter to the Lord High Treasurer of Great Britain entitled "Proposal for Correcting, Improving and Ascertaining the English Tongue." The title of Swift's letter and the goals in Adams' letter are strikingly alike; that is, both mention specifically "correcting, improving and ascertaining."

PART I THE ROAD TO REMOTE STRUCTURES

CHAPTER 2 **A FIRST ENCOUNTER WITH GRAMMAR**

PREVIEW

In this chapter, the beginnings of a rule which accounts for the facts about
words of speaker self-reference are introduced. The discussion considers
three words, *I*, *me*, *myself*, which are used by the speaker of a sentence
to refer to himself. The word *myself* differs from the other two in that it
can occur only when there are at least two self-references in the sentence
in which it occurs. The words *I* and *me*, on the other hand, occur where
there is only a single self-reference. Attention is then directed toward
distinguishing the conditions favoring *I* as against *me*. The rule offered here
will be modified as the discussion proceeds.

A sentence in any language involves the perspective of the individual
who utters it. That is, a particular sentence in English is related to a
unique individual, its *speaker*. The relation between a sentence and the
speaker of that sentence is of such importance that it is not surprising that
the language contains certain words and rules which directly relate to the representation of the speaker's role in sentences.

Thus English has two words, *me* and *myself*, which we see and hear con-
stantly in our use of the language. They seem familiar enough. We might say
that these words are used by the speaker of a sentence to refer to himself.[1,2]
This familiarity is deceptive. The use of these words is governed by principles
and constraints which are not at all familiar. When, for instance, is it appro-

priate to refer to oneself by the use of *me*, and when by the use of *myself*?
Me is clearly appropriate in sentences such as:

(1) a   Max likes me.
    b   Harry wouldn't talk to me.
    c   She bought me a cake.

However, it is obviously not right to use *me* in:

(2) a   *Me like George.
    b   *Harry said that me was wrong.

Here we use a new kind of punctuation: we place a star (*) before examples
which are not *well-formed*. These are examples which anyone who speaks
English natively (*native speakers*) can tell have something wrong with their
construction. Such examples will be referred to equivalently as *ill-formed* or
ungrammatical. One can make out what (2a,b) mean. If a foreigner or little
child said either of them[3] to us, we could understand him. We would recognize, however, that the speaker did not know English perfectly (or else, was
deviating from known rules for some special effect). Some rule or principle
of English has not been followed in the formation of (2a,b). If so inclined,
we might *correct* the user of these. We would point out that (2a,b) should be
replaced by:

(3) a   I like George.
    b   Harry said that I was wrong.

That is, there are at least three[4] words used for speaker self-reference. Of these,
only *I* is appropriate in place of the blanks in:

(4) a   _____ like George.
    b   Harry said that _____ was wrong.

Myself cannot occur here:

(5) a   *Myself like George.
    b   *Harry said that myself was wrong.[5]

One may conclude that English has a *rule* which requires that, in cases of
speaker self-reference, one picks *I* and not *me* or *myself* in contexts like (4).
To say that there is a rule is not to say what the rule is, that is, not to formulate it accurately or precisely. This is a task which turns out to involve a surprising amount of difficulty. But we can see already that an understanding of
what English grammar is will certainly require the specification of such a rule.
The foreigner or little child who does not master this rule cannot be said to
know English properly. He reveals this lack of knowledge by saying things
like (2a), when speakers of English know one must say (3a).
    Look again at sentences (1a–c). These are well-formed and contain the

word *me*. If one replaces *me* by the word *I* in these, one obtains ill-formed results:

(6) a *Max likes I.
   b *Harry wouldn't talk to I.
   c *She bought I a cake.

Thus, just as there are positions (for example, those in (4)) where *I* is required, there are those like

(7) a Max likes _____.
   b Harry wouldn't talk to _____.
   c She bought _____ a cake.

where *I* cannot occur but where *me* is appropriate. *Myself* is also impossible in contexts like (7):

(8) a *Max likes myself.
   b *Harry wouldn't talk to myself.
   c *She bought myself a cake.

Consequently, English must contain some rule or rules which require that, for self-reference, a speaker must use *me* and not *I* or *myself* in contexts like (7).

So far, we have presented no well-formed examples containing *myself*. Proper sentences with this word are:

(9) a I like myself.
   b I forced myself to do it.
   c Joe spoke to me about myself.

In these sentences, not only is *myself* appropriate, but neither of the forms *I* or *me* can replace it:

(10) a *I like I.
    b *I like me.[6]
    c *I forced I to do it.
    d *I forced me to do it.
    e *Joe spoke to me about I.
    f *Joe spoke to me about me.

We can observe that the sentences in (9) have a special property. Each contains *two* words from the set (*I*, *me*, *myself*). That is, in these sentences *there are at least two separate references by the speaker to himself*. This is no accident. It turns out to be a regularity of English that a form like *myself* is only used in sentences with more than one self-reference. This distinguishes *myself* from both *I* and *me*, which are not subject to this restriction (as many of the examples before (9) show). A traditional way of saying this is that *myself* requires an *antecedent* (literally, "something coming before"). We shall say more about this important though unclear notion below. Here it suffices to say that the relevant property of *myself* yields a division of the three forms under discussion as follows:

(11) Form   Requires an Antecedent?
       I   No
       me   No
       myself   Yes

We might thus redescribe the facts gone over so far as follows:

(12) Rule 1A
   In cases of speaker self-reference,
   a   The form *myself* is used if there is an antecedent reference to the speaker;
   b   Otherwise, either the form *I* or the form *me* is used, depending on conditions yet to be specified.

Rule 1A breaks down the three-way distinction between *I, me, myself* into two parts. Subrule (a) picks out *myself* when there is an antecedent. Subrule (b) distinguishes between *I* and *me* when no antecedent is present. Neither of these subrules is yet formulated adequately. However, the regularity observed with *myself*—that it requires an antecedent—already seems to explain why it cannot occur as the initial element in:

(13) a   *Myself is sick.
       b   *Myself wants a drink.

For, interpreting *antecedent* literally,[7] we see that initial occurrence excludes the possibility of there being an antecedent reference to the speaker.

Let us now consider briefly the conditions which determine the occurrence of *I* or *me*; that is, let us try to say something more definite about subrule (b) of Rule 1A. To do this, it is necessary to say something about the types of words in English, traditionally called the *parts of speech*. We shall say more about these in Chapter 4. One of the parts of speech is, of course, *Verb*. Verbs include *like, force, is, paralyze, squirm*, and *concern*. In terms of the notion verb, one can *roughly* describe the different positions of *I* and *me* as follows (remembering we are speaking only of cases without antecedents):

(14) Rule 1B
   a   Speaker self-reference requires *I* in positions directly before a verb.
   b   Speaker self-reference requires *me* elsewhere.

Elements like *boy, dog, car, truth*, etc., are traditionally assigned to the part of speech called *Noun*. *I, me*, and *myself* are assigned to *Pronoun*. Let us refer to *phrases*, that is, sequences of words[8] based upon nouns or pronouns, as *Nominals* or *Noun Phrases*. We abbreviate this by *NP*. NPs then include the italicized expressions in:

(15) a   *Harry* was hunting for *a gorilla.*
     b   *You* shouldn't talk like *that* to **your** *father.*
     c   *The captain over there* is married to **somebody's** *sister.*
     d   *People who eat* **gravel** tend to be strange.

NPs are one of the fundamental building blocks out of which English sentences are constructed. The bold-face in (15b,c,d) illustrate the interesting and important fact that some NPs can occur *inside of* or *contained in* others. Thus, the NP *your* is contained in the larger NP *your father* in (15b); the NP *somebody's* is contained in the larger NP *somebody's sister*; and the NP *gravel* is contained in the larger NP *people who eat gravel* in (15d).

It is traditional to speak of the NP which occurs directly before a verb as a *subject* or as the *subject of* that verb.

(16) a   Harry knows Betsy.
     b   I miss my friend.
     c   Those people should learn French.

Harry, I, and *Those people* in (16a,b,c) are traditionally considered subjects (of *knows, miss,* and *should,* respectively.) Making use of this term, one can formulate Rule 1B in a new way:

(17) Rule 1C
     a   A subject NP which involves reference to the speaker takes the form *I.*[9,10]
     b   Other NPs making reference to the speaker take the form *me.*

Which formulation is superior, Rule 1B or Rule 1C? To see that Rule 1C is superior, consider:

(18) a   I really like apples.
     b   Should I now leave?
     c   Must I then surrender my license?

These cases are not accounted for by Rule 1B. In (18), the word *I* occurs either separated from a following verb or postverbally, which violates subrule (a) of Rule 1B. Yet all of the examples in (18) are perfectly grammatical. Moreover, substitution of *me* for *I* in such examples yields badly ill-formed structures:

(19) a   *Me really like apples. .
     b   *Should me now leave?
     c   *Must me then surrender my license?

Thus Rule 1B, which specifies that *I* occurs only directly in front of a verb, is too restricted. Rule 1C, on the other hand, offers hope of accounting both for those examples for which Rule 1B is adequate and those for which it is not. It does so if the notion *subject* on which it is based is characterized in such a way that, in all of the examples of (18), *I* is a subject even though not directly in front of any verb. This is of course the standard view. That is, *I* is traditionally considered the subject of *did* in all of these sentences:

(20)   a I did such a thing.
       b I really did such a thing.
       c At no time did I do such a thing.

In other words, traditionally, subjects are not directly linked to *immediate* preverbal position in the strings of words which make up sentences. Sentences like (18) and (20b,c) thus lead to the view that Rule 1C is a closer approximation to the truth than Rule 1B.[11]

SUMMARY

To begin to account for some of the grammatical behavior of words of speaker self-reference, we have stated two rules. The first, Rule 1A, specifies that if there is an antecedent reference to the speaker, the word *myself* is used for subsequent references. The second, Rule 1C, makes crucial reference to the notion *subject* and deals only with those cases not covered by Rule 1A. It states that *I* is the form for an NP of speaker self-reference when that NP is a subject, and that *me* is the form for speaker self-reference in the remaining cases, that is, for nonsubject NPs of speaker self-reference.

NOTES

1. *Reference* is fundamental to language. It is a relation between some of the elements of sentences (those we call *Nominals,* or *Noun Phrases*) and elements in various worlds, real or hypothetical. Typically, to refer to an object X in some world, one will use a nominal containing either *a name of* X or some *descriptive expression* identifying X. Thus, to refer to some person, one can utilize a nominal of the form *Max Jones* if his name happens to be that, or else one can say *the guy standing over there*, if the person in question is a guy and is standing over there.

However, in English and most other natural languages, it is not normal for the speaker of a sentence to refer to himself in that sentence with either names or descriptive expressions. A person whose name is Mary Calahan and who is the tallest girl in her class does not normally say either:

  (i)   Mary (Calahan) is hungry.
  (ii) The tallest girl in this class is hungry.

Rather, English has various forms, just those under consideration in this chapter, which have the special function of referring to the speaker. Instead of (i) or (ii), Mary will, of course, say:

(iii) I am hungry.

In sentences like (iii), the word *I* refers not to some one particular individual fixed for all time but rather contextually to whoever utters (iii). Anyone is free to use (iii), and in so doing makes use of *I* to refer to himself. *I* is one of the special elements used by speakers of English to refer to themselves.

2. Recently, an asymmetry in English has been pointed out. Namely, in sentences like the one in the text to which this note refers, where the antecedent (in the text sentence: *the speaker*) of a pronoun is sexually undetermined, one uses *masculine* pronoun forms (*he, him, his, himself*), not *feminine* ones (*she, her, hers, herself*). Some persons tend to correlate this asymmetry in pronoun usage with the social asymmetry in American society, to see the former as a reflection of the latter. They find this aspect of English usage discriminatory and offensive, a linguistic marking of social inferiority. In other cases, there are asymmetries which select feminine forms. Thus countries (at least when partially personified) can be referred to with feminine pronouns

(i) France refuses to divulge the extent of her military expenditures.

But never masculine ones:

(ii) *The United States insists on his right to bomb those countries.

Similarly, vehicles can be referred to as *she/her* but never as *he/him*:

(iii) Fill her up.
(iv) She has an 800 horsepower V-48 engine.
(v) *Fill him up.
(vi) *He has an 800 horsepower V-48 engine.

It is doubtful that anyone will see in usages like those in (i), (iii), and (iv) reflections of psychological assumptions or social positions.

3. In fact, the use of *me* in examples like (2a) seems to be standard for small children.

4. Of course, there are more, namely, *my* and *mine*. These so-called *genitive* or *possessive* forms will not be considered in this manual. But see note 4 of Chapter 6.

5. We have starred (5b) because it is ill-formed if *myself* is interpreted as a form of speaker self-reference. However, the string of words in (5b) does form a proper English sentence, as can be seen from the following dialogue:

(i) Is myself the right word to use in that context?
(ii) No. Harry said that myself was wrong.

Both (i) and (ii) illustrate that the word *myself* can be used not only to refer to the speaker, but also to refer to the word *myself*. That is, (ii) is, in the latter usage, an abbreviated form of:

(iii) Harry said that the word myself was wrong.

It is common but not invariable for such uses to be placed between double quotes; an alternate convention is to place words which refer to themselves in italic type (or underscored in script):

(iv) Harry said that "myself" was wrong.
(iv) Harry said that *myself* was wrong.

Such usages are in no way peculiar to *myself*. *Any* word can be used to refer to itself.

(v) Harry said that { to / of / tonsilitis / disenchant / enormous / erstwhile / than / but } was wrong.

The difference between a word being used to refer to itself and to what it normally refers to is clearly brought out by such contrasts as:

(vi) *Gorillas* has eight letters.
(vii) Gorillas have two arms.

Note that the verb in (vi), whose subject refers to a word, is not interchangeable with that in (vii), whose subject refers to animals. Nor can that in (vii) be replaced by that in (vi). The difference in reference thus correlates with a difference in what is traditionally called *verb agreement*.

One moral of this discussion is that it makes no real sense to star or fail to star an orthographic representation like (5b). For such representations correspond only crudely to the sentential elements of the English language. They often confound separate sentences in a single representation. This is the case with (5b). Nonetheless, given the convenience of the standard orthography, we will generally confine ourselves to it, guarding against problems with occasional warnings and explications like this one.

6. We have starred examples like (10b,d,f). Such claims of ungrammaticality require important restrictions involving *stress*, that is, involving which syllables in a particular stretch are more prominent than others. A discussion of this occurs in note 3 of Chapter 3.

7. That is, interpreting 'A is an antecedent of B' in such a way that A must always precede B in the string of words. Such an interpretation cannot be maintained. For instance, it can be argued that in

(i) If he comes late, Bob will be fired.

Bob is the antecedent of *he*, although the former follows the latter.

8. We shall consider that a single word can be a special case of a sequence of words, allowing for the many one-word nominals and one-word phrases of other types.

9. This ignores those cases where reference to the speaker is combined with reference to other individuals, yielding the plural forms *we, us, ourselves*, etc. We return to these in Chapter 6. The discussion in the text is concerned with *exclusive* references to the speaker.

10. Strangely enough, in a unique usage, *I* can also occur freely in a variety of sentence positions as one member of a *coordinated* NP (those strung together with the conjunctions *and* or *or*):

  (i)   Harry and I are related.
  (ii)   They interviewed Harry and I.
  (iii)   Marsha spoke to Harry and I.
  (iv)   They loaned Harry and I a book about alligator distribution.

Thus *I* within a conjoined NP is not subject to the *subject* condition. The conjoined NP containing *I* does not have to be a subject (though it can be one). Correspondingly, in more colloquial usage, *me* can occur in conjoined NPs in a variety of positions, including subject position:

  (v)   Me and him are good friends.
  (vi)   They called me and him.
  (vii)   They gave me and him a ticket.

For many speakers, the occurrence of *me* and *I* in coordinated NPs does not follow the rules for independent *me* and *I* but is subject to peculiar rules of its own. When so used, *I* must be the last element of the coordinated sequence, while *me* must be the first element:

(viii)   *I and Harry are related.
  (ix)   *Joan, (and) I and Harry are related.
  (x)   Joan, Harry and I are related.
  (xi)   Me and him are related.
  (xii)   *Joan, me and him are related.
(xiii)   Me, Joan and him are related.

Prescriptive (hygienic) grammar encourages the use of *I* rather than *me* in such cases. This may account for our feeling that forms like (xiii), etc., are "uneducated." Finally, the difference between (ix) and (x) is much sharper than that between (xii) and (xiii), etc. This correlates with the fact that nearly everyone has the constraint requiring *I* to be final, but not everyone requires *me* to be initial.

11. Rule 1C is still rough. It does not, for instance, cover cases where, in some dialects, *I* may also occur in still other (than those in note 10) nonsubject positions:

  (i) a It was _____ who saved the horse.
        b Harry is taller than _____.

Moreover, *I* is impossible in the contexts of the italicized forms in

  (ii) a For $\left\{{me \atop *I}\right\}$ to do that would be immoral.

        b He resented $\left\{{my \atop *I}\right\}$ kissing his wife.

although there are many reasons, as we shall see later (see note 6 of Chapter 6), showing that these are subject positions. Rule 1C predicts certain occurrences of *I* which are not possible, and does not predict certain occurrences which are. Thus it is far from the last word on the distribution of *I*. However, the rule suffices for present purposes and will be refined later in this manual.

PROBLEMS

1. Which occurrence of *myself* is responsible for the ungrammaticality of:

(i) *Myself likes myself.

Why?

2. Dictionaries often define *antecedent* as meaning something which goes before. Recall that only pronouns have antecedents. What are the antecedents of the pronouns in the following sentences?

  (i) John said that he would bring the ice.
 (ii) Mary told John that he would be sorry when she died.

Now consider:

(iii) Near his house, John built a swimming pool.

What is the antecedent of *his*?

    If you answered that *John* is the antecedent, what does this say about the dictionary definition of *antecedent* as something which goes before a pronoun?

CHAPTER 3 **MORE ON** *myself*

PREVIEW

In this chapter we show that Rule 1A(a) of the preceding chapter fails for an important set of English sentences. We then show that the traditional notion of *clause* plays a role in the problem set by such sentences. By taking the notion of clause into account, it becomes possible to reformulate Rule 1A(a) more adequately. Specifically, the concept of *minimal clause* is defined. The rule for choosing the form of self-referential pronouns is then restated in terms of this notion. Although the notion of minimal clause furthers our understanding of the grammar of pronouns, serious problems still remain.

In Chapter 2, we formulated informally two explicit and one implicit rule governing the occurrence of the three forms *I, me, myself.* The implicit rule is that one uses some one of these forms when making a reference to one-self.[1] The explicit rules are that one uses *myself* when there is an antecedent self-reference, *I* or *me* when there is not. The latter choice is based on the principle that one uses *I* in subject position, *me* elsewhere. We now turn to some of the facts which show that this description is inadequate. In particular, the principle specifying that *myself* is used when there is an antecedent speaker self-reference requires considerable amendment.

This can be seen by considering:

(1)   a   I told Fred that he couldn't beat me.
        b   Mary asked me if I would help her.

These are perfectly well-formed. However, they contain *me* or *I*. But there are antecedent speaker self-references, that is, antecedent occurrences of *I* or *me*. Moreover, if the second speaker self-reference form in each of these is replaced by *myself*, ill-formedness results:

(2) a   *I told Fred that he couldn't beat myself.
    b   *Mary asked me if myself would help her.

There are two choices. First, one could conclude that Rule 1A(a) of Chapter 2 (requiring use of *myself* when there is an antecedent speaker self-reference) is simply incorrect. Or, one could conclude that, while essentially correct, this principle requires some further restriction. It turns out that the second course is the correct one. Rule 1A(a) is basically correct, but in a limited domain. The rightness of this conclusion can be demonstrated by discovering exactly where Rule 1A(a) is valid. We need to discover some property which distinguishes contexts like those in (2), for which Rule 1A(a) of Chapter 2 breaks down, from those which led us to formulate Rule 1A(a) in the first place.

Consider the difference between:

(3) a   I criticized myself.
    b   I thought (that)² Betty criticized me.

In (3a), speaker self-reference with an antecedent must take the form *myself*.³ In (3b), such a self-reference must take the form *me*. This form contrast is associated with another difference. Sentence (3b) seems to have a more complicated structure than (3a). Where (3a) is a simple sentence, (3b) is complex. It is complex in one very definite sense. It has *embedded* or contained in it a subpart which could itself be an independent sentence, namely, the subpart *Betty criticized me*. Suppose, in a more or less traditional manner, one refers to such subparts as *clauses*.⁴ Then one might say that (3b) is a sentence which contains two clauses. One clause is coextensive with the whole sentence. That is, we shall use the term *clause* in such a way that an independent sentence is itself regarded as a clause. The other is the subpart just mentioned. Both sentences in (3) thus have *clause boundaries* at their beginnings and ends. However, (3b) differs from (3a) in that it has an extra clause boundary, the one just before the word *Betty*. Clause boundaries occurring between other clause boundaries will be called *internal clause boundaries*. We need to examine these more closely.

Internal clause boundaries are, of course, extremely common in more complex sentences. This is illustrated in the following examples, where we mark clause boundaries by the symbol # :

(4) a   #The lady #*who called me* # didn't know me #.
    b   #I didn't know the lady #*who called me* #, unfortunately #.
    c   #John, #*who hates me* #, attacked me #.
    d   #I, #*who am impartial* #, attacked John, #*who hates me* # #.

e # #*Jack ignored me* # *and so* #*I ignored him* # #.
f #*If* #*Barbara helps me* #, #*I can win easily* # #.
g #*I was surprised when* #*Betty called me* # #.
h # #*That I passed the exam* # *shocked me* #.

In some of the examples in (4), more than a single # appears adjacent to some word. This is because more than a single clause terminates after some particular word. For example, in (4d), two #'s appear to the right of the word *me*; the clause #*who hates me*# terminates after *me*. But so does the clause which comprises the entire sentence, #*I, who am impartial, attacked John, who hates me*#. We indicate the number of clauses which terminate after a word by the number of #'s which occur there. Similarly, we indicate with more than one # the number of clauses which initiate before a given word. Thus, in (4h) the two #'s to the left of *That* indicate the beginning of the clause #*That I passed the exam*# as well as the beginning of the clause that coincides with the entire sentence, #*That I passed the exam shocked me*#. The distribution of internal clause boundaries in (4) is not mysterious or arbitrarily imposed. Every speaker can see the naturalness of the distribution in (4) as opposed to a truly arbitrary distribution, such as that obtained by moving each internal clause boundary in (4) one word to the right. For example, if one were to claim that the clause boundaries were not as in (4a) but rather as in

(5) #The lady who #called me didn't # know me #.

a reader would rightly be mystified. In other words, native speakers somehow know where internal clause boundaries are. So all (4) does is to indicate with explicit symbols what we all implicitly recognize anyway.

But there is an important gain from beginning to formalize this aspect of linguistic knowledge. One can explicitly define certain relevant notions which will deepen our understanding of what knowledge of English is. In particular, these notions will serve as a foundation for formulating more valid rules. For example, given the notions of clause and clause boundary, one can initially define the idea of *minimal* clause as follows:

(6) A *minimal clause* is a clause which contains no internal clause boundaries.

Accordingly, the minimal clauses in (4), for example, are:

(7) a #who called me #
     b #who called me #
     c #who hates me #
     d #who am impartial #; #who hates me #
     e #Jack ignored me #; #I ignored him #
     f #Barbara helps me #; #I can win easily #
     g #Betty called me #
     h #That I passed the exam #

The sentences in (3) are repeated here with all clause boundaries marked:

(8) a #I criticized myself #.

  b #I thought (that) #Betty criticized me # #.

The entire sentence in (8a) is a minimal clause, as is the smaller clause in (8b). But the larger clause in (8b) is not a minimal clause. It contains a clause boundary before the word *Betty* (as well as after *me*). Given the notion of minimal clause, one can reformulate Rule 1A(a) of Chapter 2 more adequately. Observe that in (8a) the form *myself* is in the same sentence with its antecedent and also necessarily in the same minimal clause. In (8b), on the contrary, while *me* is in the same sentence with its antecedent, and in the same larger clause, it is *not* in the same minimal clause. This suggests that the difference between sentences like (8a,b) with respect to the correct use of *myself* has to do with the occurrence of the antecedent *in the same minimal clause*. This will turn out to be basically right. Hence a more correct formulation of Rule 1A of Chapter 2 might be:

(9) Rule 1D
  In cases of speaker self-reference,
  a The form *myself* is used (i) if there is an antecedent reference to the speaker in the sentence, and (ii) if the form expressing this antecedent reference is in the same minimal clause as the form expressing the second reference.
  b Otherwise, one uses *I* or *me* as described in Rule 1C of Chapter 2.

We have arrived at Rule 1D(a) on the basis of examples like (1), (2), and (8). There are many other constructions for which Rule 1D predicts, correctly, that speaker self-references with antecedents do not take the form *myself*. Notable are those in (4), which we repeat below:

(10) a #The lady #who called me # didn't know ${me \atop *myself}$ #.

  b #I didn't know the lady #who called ${me \atop *myself}$ #, unfortunately #.

  c #John, #who hates me #, attacked ${me \atop *myself}$ #.

  d #I, #who am impartial #, attacked John, #who hates ${me \atop *myself}$ # #.

  e # #Jack ignored me # and so # ${I \atop *myself}$ ignored him # #.

  f #If Barbara helps me #, # ${I \atop *myself}$ can win easily # #.

  g #I was surprised when #Betty called ${me \atop *myself}$ # #.

  h # #That I passed the exam # shocked ${me \atop *myself}$ #.

In each of these, the second occurrence of a speaker self-reference does not take the form *myself.* This follows from Rule 1D(a), since in each there is at least one clause boundary between the second occurrence and its antecedent. In (10a), there is a clause boundary before the word *who* and after the first occurrence of the word *me.* In (10b), there are such boundaries before *who* and after *me.* Clauses like those in (10a,b) are called *restrictive relative clauses,* a key feature of which is the occurrence of a *relative pronoun* (*who, which, that,*[5] *where, when, why*) in initial or near initial position. In (10c,d), there are clause boundaries at the points indicated by commas. These clauses are referred to as *appositive* or *nonrestrictive relative clauses.* They are partially similar to restrictive relative clauses. In (10e), there is a clause boundary before the word *and* and another after the word *so.* This is the first case of a *coordinate construction* we have encountered. In (10f), there is a clause boundary between *me* and *I,*[6] in (10g) between *when* and *Betty,* and in (10h) between *exam* and *shocked.* The clauses following *if* in (10f), *when* in (10g) and *that* in (10h) are traditionally referred to as *subordinate clauses,* along with many others following such words as *because, since, after, so, why,* etc. Sentences (10f,g,h) illustrate that such clauses can occur in either sentence-initial or sentence-final position.

Thus, nowhere in (10a–h) is the second form representing a speaker's reference to himself in the same minimal clause as an antecedent reference. In each case, antecedent and pronoun are separated by at least one clause boundary. For example, in (10b) the antecedent pronoun referring to the speaker, *I,* is separated from the second speaker self-reference by an internal clause boundary between the words *lady* and *who.* Hence the two occurrences are not in the same minimal clause. The choice of *me* as against *myself* is correctly predicted by Rule 1D. The situation in (10b) can be represented graphically as follows:

(11)   # I didn't know the lady # who called me #, unfortunately #.

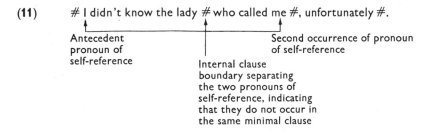

The preceding facts support the reformulation of Rule 1A of Chapter 2 as Rule 1D(a). That is, they support the idea that the domain of the word *myself* is to be partially specified as follows: *myself* must have an antecedent form expressing speaker self-reference *within the same minimal clause.*

Analysis of sentence structure in terms of clauses is, of course, traditional. We have been directly led to it by an attempt to specify accurately the distributions of *I, me,* and *myself* in well-formed English sentences. Our unusual approach provides support for the traditional view that clause structure is fundamental to sentence structure. It also clarifies an important theoretical point about grammar, namely, that the attempt to state accurate grammatical rules is closely tied to a certain conceptual framework. The latter involves assumptions about what sort of things sentences are, what kinds of parts make them up, etc.

The discussion of clause structure so far is vague and imprecise. We have not specified clearly what it means to say that sentences have clause structure. We deal with this problem in the next chapter. It begins to make itself felt here, however. The account in Rule 1D seems to fail for certain sentences of the following sort:

(12) a #*I*, #who am from Chicago#, understand *myself*#.
  b # #Bob's kissing the girl# made *me* talk to *myself*#.
  c #*I*, and #everyone knows #how serious I am # # have outdone *myself* this time#.

Speaker self-reference obviously requires *myself* in the rightmost member of the italicized pairs in (12). Replacement of *myself* by *me* yields ill-formed results:

(13) a * #*I*, #who am from Chicago#, understand *me*#.
  b * # #Bob's kissing the girl# made *me* talk to *me*#.
  c * #*I*, and #everyone knows #how serious I am # # have outdone *me* this time#.

The following difficulty confronts us. Rule 1D predicts that the examples in (13) should be well-formed, while those in (12) should be ill-formed. The reason is that none of the overall word sequences in (12) or (13) are, by the earlier definition, minimal clauses. The italicized *I* and *me* in (13a) are members of the clause consisting of the entire sentence. But this is not a minimal clause, since it contains internal clause boundaries after *I* and before *understand*. This situation is illustrated graphically in (14):

(14) #*I*, #who am from Chicago#, understand myself#.

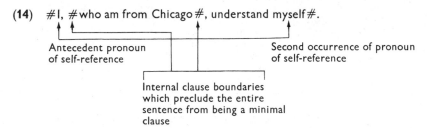

It can be argued that the difficulty is in the notion of minimal clause rather than in Rule 1D itself. For there is a clear contrast between cases like (12), where *myself* is required, and earlier examples, like (10c,d), where it is impossible. Consider, for example, (12a). In this sentence, neither the word *I* nor the word *myself* is inside of the relative clause *who am from Chicago*. Both are parts of the traditionally so-called *main clause*. In (10c,d), however, one or the other of the elements representing a speaker self-reference is inside of a relative clause:

(15) a #John, #who hates me#, attacked me#.

b #I, #who am impartial#, attacked John, #who hates me# #.

Contrast (14), which represents (12a), with the following representation of (15a):

(16)   #John, #who hates me#, attacked me#.

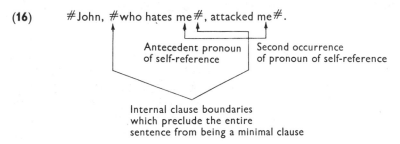

Antecedent pronoun | Second occurrence
of self-reference | of pronoun of self-reference

Internal clause boundaries
which preclude the entire
sentence from being a minimal clause

Although the structures seem superficially the same, there are differences. From a *linear* point of view, antecedent and pronoun are separated by internal clause boundaries in both (14) and (16). But this linear fact covers up deeper differences.

Notice what happens if one removes the relative clause from both (14) and (16). In (14), this will leave *I understand myself*, a structure without internal clause boundaries and containing both pronoun and antecedent. In (16), however, what will be left is *John attacked me*, where *me* has no antecedent. This suggests that there is a sense in which *I* and *myself* are in the same minimal clause in (14) but where *me* and *me* are not, in (16). This correlates with the need for *myself* in the former and its impossibility in the latter. This sense of *minimal clause* is not represented by the definition of minimal clause given in (6) above. According to that definition, *I* and *myself* in examples like (12a) are not in any minimal clause. This suggests that the first definition, though valid for certain cases, is not correct. A more correct account can be given by making more explicit the notions involved in talking about clause structure. These notions are also involved in talking about phrases, parts of speech, etc. All of these concepts are based on a set of common underlying assumptions, which linguists call *constituent structure*. We turn next to an introductory discussion of this topic.

SUMMARY

In this chapter, counterexamples to Rule 1A of Chapter 2 were dealt with by taking into account the fact that sentences have clause structure. In particular, the notion of *minimal clause* was defined. The domain of distribution for the form *myself* was then restricted in terms of this notion. That is, Rule 1A was replaced by Rule 1D(a). Still further examples incompatible even with the newer formulation were found. We concluded that nonetheless Rule 1D(a) was correct, but that the definition of minimal clause on which it was based required refinement.

NOTES

1. This can be described in somewhat traditional terms as follows. Traditionally, NPs are categorized into various types along the dimension of *person*, distinguishing *first person* NPs, *second person* NPs, and *third person* NPs according as these designate the speaker, the person(s) spoken to, or others. The implicit rule mentioned in the text is that first person (singular) NPs, that is, those which refer to the speaker alone, take one of the shapes *I*, *me*, *myself* (ignoring *my*, *mine*).

2. This example introduces the useful convention of enclosing *optional* elements in parentheses. In this way, a single sequence can illustrate several distinct examples. Sentence (3b) is an abbreviation for:

(i) I thought that Betty criticized me.
(ii) I thought Betty criticized me.

We use this abbreviatory notation freely in this manual.

The word *that* here is sometimes called a *complementizer*. These introduce many subordinate clauses in English. It is often omissable in object positions like (i), but not always:

(iii) We have established that they have nuclear weapons.
(iv) *We have established they have nuclear weapons.

It is *never* omissable in subject position:

(v) That they have nuclear weapons was reported by the *Tribune*.
(vi) *They have nuclear weapons was reported by the *Tribune*.

3. This claim is not true without important qualifications involving stress. It only holds without exception where the pronoun in examples like (3a) is unstressed and the verb is stressed. Where the object NP is stressed and the verb destressed, there is a possible variation:

(i) I criticized mé.
(ii) I criticized mysélf.

The accent mark indicates very strong stress. In general, contrastively stressed forms have many poorly understood properties. We ignore them in this introductory manual. Consequently, our regularities, like Rule 1D, only deal with ordinarily stressed forms.

It is worth pointing out that cases like (i) and (ii) differ in meaning from sentences like (3a) in the text. Example (3a) is a simple assertion about an act of criticism. It presupposes nothing in particular. Both (i) and (ii) presuppose that the individual designated by *I* criticized someone and assert that the one so criticized was the speaker. Both (i) and (ii) are suitable *answers* to the *question*:

(iii) Who did you criticize?

Example (3a) is not, because the question context specifies the presupposition. Thus (i) and (ii) are synonymous with, respectively,

(iv) The one who I criticized was mé.

(v) The one who I criticized was mysélf.

and with:

(vi) It was mé who I criticized.

(vii) It was mysélf who I criticized.

Note also that (3a), (i), and (ii) contrast in meaning with:

(viii) Í criticized me.

The latter is a paraphrase of

(ix) The one who criticized me was $\begin{Bmatrix} \text{Í} \\ \text{mé} \end{Bmatrix}$.

and of:

(x) It was $\begin{Bmatrix} \text{Í} \\ \text{mé} \end{Bmatrix}$ who criticized me.

4. We ultimately use the term *clause* for somewhat deformed structures which cannot stand alone as independent sentences. These have most of the other crucial properties of clauses which do stand alone. Examples include the italicized sequences:

(i) *For Bob to quit* would be tragic.
(ii) *Your leaving Sandra* would be scandalous.
(iii) *Tony having disappeared*, Joan began dating Ed.

5. It may be a mistake to consider *that* a relative pronoun in cases like:

(i) The machine that I bought is broken.

Possibly, it is the complementizer *that* discussed in note 2.

6. There is a contrast between (10f) and (10g) in this regard. In (10f), the words *me* and *I* are separated by two clause boundaries, while in (10g) the words *when* and *Betty* are separated by only one. This is because *I* in the former not only begins one clause but occurs just after the end of another. But *I was surprised when* in (10g) is not a clause.

PROBLEMS

1. Which of the following sentences is compatible with Rule 1D and which is not?

  (i)   Gregory, and I think you know him better than Melvin does, wouldn't do such a thing to me.
 (ii)   I put the question of whether it is better to die for one's country than to live forever in ignominy to myself.

2. See if you can construct a sentence whose final word concludes at least four separate clauses. Can you construct one with more?

3. Construct a sentence which contains two consecutive occurrences of the word *is*. Why was it possible to do this? Can you construct a sentence with three consecutive occurrences of the word *is*?

CHAPTER 4 REPRESENTING SENTENCE PARTS

PREVIEW

In this chapter, a notational system is developed for representing the possible relations between sentence parts. This system does three things to achieve this goal. First, it shows what portions of sentences constitute genuine subparts and what portions do not. Second, it shows what categories the recognized subparts belong to. Third, it shows how these categorized subparts interrelate to make up the structural wholes called sentences. Certain traditional grammatical terms such as *phrase* and *part of speech* are shown to be restricted notions subsumed by the more general concepts developed here.

In the previous chapter we stated that sentences like

(1) a I thought (that) Betty criticized me.
     b Joan thinks (that) bats are clever birds.

contain clauses as subparts. In particular, (1a) contains the clause *# Betty criticized me #* and (1b) contains *# bats are clever birds #* as clausal sub-parts. It is important to consider what it means to say that a sentence can have a clause as a subpart. There are at least two distinct notions involved. One is that sentences are composed of parts. The second is that these parts are of different types. Thus, we have stated that *# Betty criticized me #* is a part of

(1a). Moreover, we have assigned that part to a certain category, namely, *Clause* (henceforth abbreviated C). Sentence (1b) contains a similar subpart, the clause #*bats are clever birds*#. There are other parts to the sentences in (1). These parts belong to categories other than clause. Recall that in Chapter 2 we spoke of a category of *Nominal* or *Noun Phrase* (abbreviated NP). To this category belonged phrases based on nouns or pronouns. Examples of the category NP were given in (15) of Chapter 2. NPs are the sorts of things which can occur as subjects, direct objects, and objects of prepositions. It is evident that the sentences in (1) contain many parts belonging to the category NP:

(2) NP in (1a)   NP in (1b)
   I   Joan
   Betty   bats
   me   clever birds

We also spoke of a category *Verb* in Chapter 2, to which words like *like*, *forced*, *is*, *paralyze*, and *squirm* belong. There are parts of the sentences in (1) which belong to this category (henceforth abbreviated V):

(3) V in (1a)   V in (1b)
   thought   thinks
   criticized are

The categories named so far, with one important exception, largely exhaust those to which the parts of these sentences belong. The major exception is the word *clever*, which is a subpart of (1b). This word is traditionally said to belong to the category *Adjective* (Adj), containing words like *tall, blue, persistent, morbid, beautiful*, etc. In Chapters 25 and 26, we argue that the category *Adjective* is not really on a par with a category like V but should rather be regarded as one of several *subtypes* of V.

The sentences in (1) are made up of parts and these parts belong to various categories including NP, V, Adj, and C.

This does not exhaust what we can say about the sentences in (1). Among the first observations made about a sentence like (3b) in Chapter 3 was that it contains a clause embedded as a subpart. We have identified the subpart, namely #*Betty criticized me*#. We have also labeled it a C. We have not, however, clarified the notion *embedded*. That is, we have not managed to be explicit about how this clause subpart is contained in the larger clause coincident with the entire sentence (1a) above. More generally, merely talking about the division of sentences into parts and the assignment of these parts to categories does not fully deal with the question of how sentences are formed out of the parts in question. It neglects the way these parts are organized into larger wholes. To deal with this problem, we must consider sentence parts and the categories to which they are assigned within an explicit system for describing sentence structure. Such a system must provide a precise method for expressing various kinds of structural information.

The latter must include the ways in which sentence parts are organized. A *notational system* for representing the possible relationships between sentence parts is needed.

Such a notational system must do at least three things. First, it must show what portions of a sentence constitute subparts and what portions do not. Second, it must indicate what categories these subparts belong to. Third, it must specify the interrelations between these categorized subparts. Only the combination of all of this information can characterize the structural wholes which are sentences.

Let us consider each function of the notational system in turn. We begin with the demarcation of subparts.

It has been noted that there must be some way of indicating that # *Betty criticized me* # is a bonafide subpart, while the sequence *thought Betty* is not. A notational system can indicate that some sequence is a genuine subpart of a sentence by enclosing that sequence in a pair of brackets—[   ]. The left (or opening) bracket, [, indicates where the subpart begins. The right (or closing) bracket,], indicates where the subpart ends. Each left bracket is associated with a right bracket. Thus, we can represent the clausal component of (1a) as:

(4)   I thought [Betty criticized me]

We are assuming that full sentences are also clauses. So a left and right bracket will not only surround *Betty criticized me*, but also the entire sentence in (4):

(5)   [I thought [Betty criticized me]]

The two right brackets at the end are associated with different left brackets. The outermost right bracket is associated with the outermost left bracket, namely, that before the word *I*. The innermost right bracket is associated with the innermost left bracket, namely, that before the word *Betty*. *I*, *Betty*, and *me* are nominal subparts of (1a). Therefore, they too must be bracketed within the notational system:

(6)   [[I] thought [[Betty] criticized [me]]]

While a bit more complicated, it is still possible to keep the left and right brackets sorted out. Three right brackets close off (6). The two outermost right brackets are paired as they were in (5). The innermost right bracket has been added. It is paired with the left bracket occurring before the word *me*. There are still other subparts of (1a) which need to be indicated: the verbs *thought* and *criticized*:

(7)   [[I] [thought] [[Betty] [criticized] [me]]]

Although this method of indicating subparts is explicit, it is obviously difficult to read. The more subparts a sequence has the harder it becomes to match up left and right brackets. The diagram in (8) indicates by connecting lines the linked brackets. Any sequence contained within any given pair of brackets is a subpart of the sentence. No other sequences are:

(8) [[I] [thought] [[Betty] [criticized] [me]]]

For example, the sequence *thought Betty* is not enclosed between brackets. This corresponds to our intuition that this sequence is not a subpart of (1a).

The second function of a notational system is to indicate the categories subparts belong to. This can be accomplished by labeling the paired brackets. The labels stand for the categories already isolated, like NP, V, and C. Such labels can be attached to the brackets in (8) as follows:

(9) [c [NP I NP] [vthoughtv] [c [NP BettyNP] [vcriticizedv] [NPmeNP] c] c]

In (9), the subscripted symbols indicate the category and the brackets indicate the domain of the category. For example, the notation which indicates that *I* is a subpart belonging to the category NP in (9) *I* is *I*:

(10) [NP I NP]

Since it has become apparent that diagrams like (7), (8), and (9) are difficult to read, the reader may not be overjoyed at the prospect of reading far more complicated diagrams in the chapters to follow. There is, though, another way of displaying precisely the same information. Instead of (10), one can represent the membership of *I* in the category NP as:

(11)   NP

                                                         |

                                                          I

The NP symbol represents the category and the line is attached to what lies within the brackets. Both (10) and (11) then state that *I* is a subpart of (1a) and in particular, a subpart belonging to the category NP. Representing just the NPs and Vs of (9) in this fashion gives:

(12)   NP   V   NP   V   NP

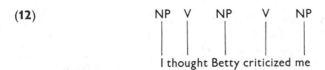

I thought Betty criticized me

In (12), the portion assigned to each category consists of a single word. Therefore only one line has been drawn from each category label. However, as is evident in (9), there are categories whose members are not always single words. For example, consider the subpart of (9) consisting of the entire clause *Betty criticized me*. In the bracket notation, it appears as:

(13)   [c [NP Betty NP] [v criticized v] [NP me NP] c]

In terms of the label and line notation, (13) would have to be represented as:

(14)

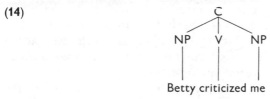

Betty criticized me

Diagram (14) indicates not only that *Betty*, *criticized*, and *me* are members of the categories NP, V, and NP, respectively. It also specifies that those words in that order form an additional subpart, which is a member of the category C.

A line and label notation for the entire sequence (9) would be:

(15)

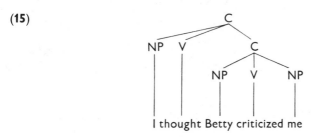

I thought Betty criticized me

Line and label diagrams like that in (15) are called *trees*, although from one point of view they are upside down. Such tree diagrams are entirely equivalent to labeled bracket diagrams like those in (9), but have the obvious advantage of being far easier to read.

Thus, a glance at (15) shows that the entire sequence *I thought Betty criticized me* is an instance of the category C, that this category is composed of subparts NP V C in that order, that the lower C is made up of NP V NP in that order, and, finally, that *I*, *thought*, *Betty*, *criticized*, and *me* belong to the categories NP, V, NP, V, and NP, respectively. Moreover, since the grammatical information expressed by (9) and (15) is equivalent, the choice between labeled bracket notation and tree notation can be based on the superior readability of the latter. For this reason, we use tree notation throughout this book.

The third function of a notational system is to specify the interrelations between categorized subparts of grammatical structures. Consider the tree diagram for (lb):

(16)

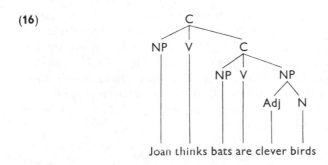

Joan thinks bats are clever birds

This tree, like all others, is made up of four different types of element. There are the lines in the trees, the points where the lines intersect (call them *nodes*), the category labels affixed to the nodes, and the words which occur at the end of the lines. The words are the elements from which no lines emanate downward. Lines are drawn to them only from above.

A concept crucial to show how subparts of trees are interrelated is the notion of *constituent*. A certain sequence of words (or subparts of words) in a tree is a constituent *of that tree* if and only if that sequence makes up all and only the structure attached to some individual node. Thus, in the tree in (16), the sequence *bats are clever birds* is a constituent because this string of words is attached to a single node, the lower of the two nodes labeled C:

(17)

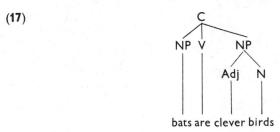

Similarly in (17), *clever birds* is a constituent, since that word sequence is traceable back to a single node (labeled NP):

(18)

Just so, each of the words in (17) is a constituent since each one is traceable back to a single node:

(19)

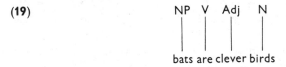

To determine whether a particular sequence of elements in a tree is a constituent, it is necessary to consider not only the sequence but also the structure above it. Only by consideration of this structure is it possible to determine whether the sequence makes up all and only the structure that dangles from an individual node. A word sequence together with its structure is called a *subtree*. Thus, the diagrams in (17), (18), and (19) are all subtrees of (16). Each is composed of the four types of elements that make up trees: lines, nodes, category labels, and words. The four subtrees in (19) are minimal. Each consists of only one node, one line, one category label, and one word.

Consider once again (16), which we repeat:

(20)

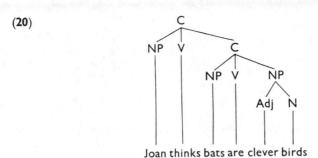

Excluding the entire sentence, the constituents in (20) are:

(21) a Joan (NP)
    b thinks (V)
    c bats are clever birds (C)
    d bats (NP)
    e are (V)
    f clever birds (NP)
    g clever (Adj)
    h birds (N)

Associated with each of the constituents listed in (21) are, respectively, the following subtrees:

(22) a NP

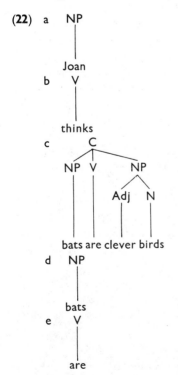

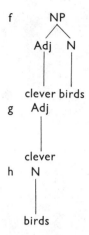

Comparison of the subtrees in (22) with their corresponding constituent word sequences in (21) reveals the relationship which exists between constituents and subtrees. Constituents are the word sequences (including word sequences made up of single words) which occur at the bottoms of subtrees.

It remains to specify how subtrees and their constituents interrelate to form full trees for particular sentences. This requires specification of two relationships between subtrees. Return to the tree in (20). Of the subtrees which make it up, some *precede* (that is, occur to the left of) others. Thus, the subtree of which *Joan* is the associated constituent and of which NP is the highest label *precedes* the subtree of which *clever birds* is the associated constituent. The subtree whose associated constituent is *Joan* thus *precedes* every other subtree in (20). However, the subtree which occurs immediately to its right has a special relationship to it. It will be said to *immediately precede* that subtree. Thus, the subtree (22a) immediately precedes subtree (22b); the latter immediately precedes (22c). But (22c) does not immediately precede any other subtree in (20).

The notions of *precedence* and *immediate precedence* do not exhaust the kinds of relations which exist between subtrees in (20). Consider, for example, the subtree for the constituent *bats are clever birds*, whose highest node label is C, and the subtree for the constituent *clever birds*, whose highest node label is NP. Neither of these subtrees can be said to precede the other. What is their relation to each other? Consider the portion of structure labeled C minus the subtree labeled NP:

(**23**) a   C   b   NP

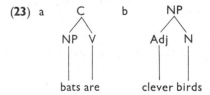

How must (23a) be connected to the subtree in (23b)? The answer is that a line must be drawn connecting the highest node label of (23b) with the highest node label of (23a):

(24)

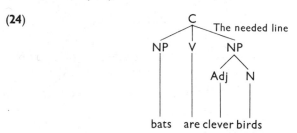

Nodes which are connected to one another by a line drawn from one to the other without passing through any other node are said to be *immediately connected*. The higher node is said to *immediately dominate* the lower of the immediately connected nodes. Now consider two subtrees which are immediately connected, C in (24) and the NP subtree associated with the constituent *clever birds*. We say·that the constituent *clever birds* is an *immediate constituent* of C. And, in general, we say that any word sequence which is a constituent is an immediate constituent of the subtree which immediately dominates the subtree associated with that word sequence. For example, returning to (24), *bats* is an immediate constituent of C since the highest node of its subtree (labeled NP) is immediately dominated by C. Similarly, *are* is an immediate constituent of C and *clever* is an immediate constituent of NP, as is *birds*. In the case of *clever*, the highest node of its subtree (labeled Adj) is immediately dominated by NP. In the case of *birds*, the highest node of its subtree (labeled N) is immediately dominated by the same NP. (Moreover, the subtree Adj immediately precedes the subtree N.) Returning to the full tree in (20), the immediate constituents of the highest C are *Joan*, *thinks*, and *bats are clever birds*. Of the two C nodes in (20), only one is the highest node of a subtree, namely, the C which is a subtree of the higher C. The higher C, on the other hand, is not the highest node of a subtree. It is the highest node of a full tree. C nodes which are the highest nodes of full trees are sentence nodes. Thus, sentences are clauses which are not subtrees.[1]

This completes the discussion of the ways in which the grammatical parts of sentences interrelate. Now consider some relations between the notational system just described and some concepts of traditional grammar. The term *phrase* plays a great role in traditional grammar books. To see how this was used, let us look at:

(25) a *That John is sick is sad.*
      b *John is sad.*
      c *The sick boys are sad.*
      d *Boys can be sad.*
      e *That man is sad.*

Of the italicized sequences in (25), only two would traditionally be called phrases:

(26) a The sick boys
b That man

What do these share that sets them apart from the remaining combinations in (25)? These sequences are constituents of their respective sentences. In fact, both are NPs:

(27) a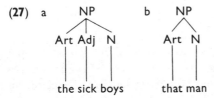

However, this cannot distinguish them from the other italicized constituents in (25). The others are constituents and members of the category NP as well:

(28) a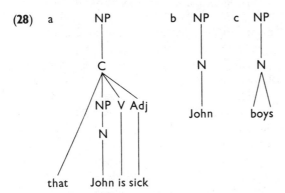

Thus, being a constituent (of the NP type) does not distinguish the subtrees in (27) from those in (28). Further examination reveals another property of relevance. The constituents in (27) are both composed of more than one word. This distinguishes them from (28b,c), which contain only single words. The traditional usage of the term *phrase* was restricted to constituents made up of more than one word.

But what of (28a)? This constituent also contains more than one word. However, traditional grammarians would not have referred to it as a phrase but rather as a clause. Apparently then, the term *phrase* is used to pick out just those constituents which are "larger" than single words but "smaller" than clauses.[2] Phrases are constituents which are in a sense "intermediate" between words and clauses.

As further evidence of this, there are other constructions in English which have constituent structure but which are also not traditionally considered members of the class of phrases. Consider a word like *anti-integrationist*. An approximation to its complex structure is:

(29)

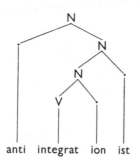

anti   integrat   ion   ist

The unlabeled nodes in (29) represent the affixes, *anti-*, *-ion*, and *-ist*, which combine with the stem *integrat*[3] to make up the complex word. However, no traditional grammar would consider the constituent in (29) a phrase for the same reason that (28b,c) are not considered phrases—namely, (29) does not consist of more than one word.

The reader might well think that traditional approaches are peculiar. Why give a name to just those nonclausal constituents consisting of more than one word? However, this usage is consistent with the existence of the term *part of speech*. This term was reserved for those classes of constituents labeled N, V, Adj, Preposition, etc. These share the property that their members are single words and only single words.[4] Thus sequences like *clever birds*, which we regard as NPs, were not members of any traditional part of speech. There is no traditional part of speech corresponding to our NP, as there is to our N.

Similarly, the affixes *anti-*, etc., are not members of any traditional part of speech, since they are not words. They always function as parts of words. Both the notions of phrase and part of speech are based on a view which attributes fundamental importance to the word. This view sees the grammar of the sentence as fundamentally divided into two different types of process. One builds up words out of stems, affixes, etc.; the other forms sentences out of words. We do not accept this view in its entirety (see especially Chapter 15, where certain processes forming words out of phrases are considered). Therefore, we attribute no special importance to the notions of phrase or part of speech.

From our point of view, phrase and part of speech are restricted concepts. They are easily definable in terms of the more general concepts of constituent structure allowed by the present system of grammatical representation. The particular subclasses of constituents picked out by the traditional terms are of limited interest. We shall have little occasion to speak of them from this point on. Instead we utilize the more general, and therefore more useful terminology. We are not denying the reality or application of the traditional terms. We merely stress that they are useful only for describing a portion of constituent structure properties, where what is needed is a system for describing this domain in its entirety.

SUMMARY

This chapter began with the observation that many sentences contain clauses as subparts. This means that sentences are composed of parts, some complex, and that these parts belong to various categories. Therefore, one needs an explicit statement of the ways in which clausal and other subparts are contained in sentences.

To clarify the ways in which the parts of sentences combine, an explicit system of grammatical representation was developed. In this system, the relations between the subparts of sentences are precisely expressible. The chief notions of relevance are *dominance*, the relation between a node and other nodes which are part of it; *precedence*, the linear ordering of elements; and *labeling*, used to assign categories to various types (C, NP, V, etc.). In terms of these basic notions, certain others were defined, including *tree*, *subtree*, *constituent*, and *immediate constituent*. The set of general concepts developed for grammatical representation can be used to explicate traditional grammatical terms like *phrase* and *part of speech*. These turn out to be special cases of the more general constituent structure framework which we developed.

Given the notational system introduced in this chapter, it is now easy to state what it means to say that one constituent is embedded in another. This will permit us to deal with the problem raised for Rule 1D by sentences like (12) of Chapter 3. We turn to this issue in the following chapter.

NOTES

1. This represents a terminological departure from most recent work, which has taken *Sentence* as the primitive concept and has defined clauses as those sentences other than that represented by the highest node. In that approach, the nodes we label C are labeled S, and one speaks of embedded sentences, etc. Although there is no empirical difference between these, our present approach is more in accord with tradition. The key point is that *Sentence* and *Clause* are not independent notions. Given one, the other is derivatively definable.

2. This is not literally true in all cases. For instance, in

(i) Jack told me that it was raining.

the sequence *told me that it was raining* is a constituent, and one which would traditionally be called a phrase. However, it contains a clause as one of its immediate constituents. Thus, the sense in which a phrase is "smaller" than a clause precludes a phrase from being coextensive with a clause but not from containing clauses as subparts.

3. At a still deeper level, it might be argued that this stem itself is complex and composed of the root *integr*, found also in *integral*, and the affix *-at/ate* found in such words as *floatation* (compare *float*), *habitation* (compare *inhabit*), etc.

4. Other categories, like NP, sometimes have members which are single words:

(i) *Men* are happy.
(ii) *John* left.

The italicized forms are single-word NPs. However, this is not an invariant property of NPs. The second clause of the sentence in the text thus excludes them from the class of parts of speech.

PROBLEMS

1. Convert the following labeled bracket notation to tree notation:

(i) [c[NP[NP[N Jack's N]NP] [N mother N] NP] [V is V]
[AdjP[Adj fond Adj] [PP[P of P] [NP[N rice N]NP]PP]AdjP] c]

2. Construct a tree diagram for the following sentence:

(i) Charlie went to France.

3. Construct a tree using the node labels A,B,C,D, and E and the "words" 1, 2, and 3 according to the following instructions:

(i) The highest node is labeled A.
(ii) A immediately dominates the nodes labeled B and C.
(iii) B immediately dominates the nodes labeled D and E.
(iv) C immediately dominates a node labeled F.
(v) The subtree whose highest node is labeled C precedes the subtree whose highest node is labeled B.
(vi) The subtree whose highest node is labeled D precedes the subtree whose highest node is labeled E.
(vii) 1 is a member of E; 2 is a member of D; 3 is a member of F.

CHAPTER 5 THE MINIMAL CLAUSE PROBLEM

PREVIEW

In this chapter we turn to the problem of refining the notion of minimal clause, which arose at the end of Chapter 3. We delayed dealing with this matter until the notions of constituent structure could be made more precise. The system of grammatical representation for constituency worked out is here brought to bear on the minimal clause question. The greater precision afforded by tree notation leads to an adequate redefinition of minimal clause. Given this definition, the apparent exceptions to Rule 1D are seen to be regular.

The redefinition of minimal clause is based on a new concept, *clause mate*. This important notion plays a central role in the distribution of *myself* and related phenomena in English. It is shown how a modification of Rule 1D in terms of the concept of clause mate successfully deals with the earlier difficulty.

At the end of Chapter 3, we confronted a problem concerning the proper formulation of the notion *minimal clause*, which was defined as a clause containing no internal clause boundaries. This was the critical concept in Rule 1D:

(1) Rule 1D
In cases of speaker self-reference,
a   The form *myself* is used (i) if there is an antecedent reference to the

speaker In the sentence, and (ii) if the form expressing this antecedent reference is in the same minimal clause as the form expressing
the second reference.

b Otherwise, one uses *I* or *me* as described in Rule 1C of Chapter 2.

Recall that in sentences like

(2) a #I called Bob, #who knows$\left\{\begin{array}{l}\text{me}\\ \text{*myself}\end{array}\right\}$#.

b #John, #who hates me #, attacked$\left\{\begin{array}{l}\text{me}\\ \text{*myself}\end{array}\right\}$#.

the minimal clause definition correctly rules out *myself*, since an internal
clause boundary intervenes between each pair of self-referring pronouns:

(3) a #I called Bob, #who knows me#.

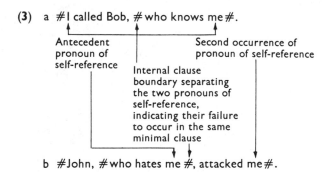

b #John, #who hates me #, attacked me#.

The minimal clause notion as previously defined accounts for the distribution
of pronominal forms in (2). That is, it predicts the impossibility of *myself*.
However, it fails to work for:

(4) #I, #who am from Chicago, #understand$\left\{\begin{array}{l}\text{myself}\\ \text{*me}\end{array}\right\}$#.

In (4) the self-referential pronouns are separated by an internal clause
boundary, that directly after the word *Chicago*. Therefore, according to
Rule 1D, the second pronoun should *not* be *myself*. Yet *myself* is not only
possible but required. Thus our notion of minimal clause seems to be faulty.

Another way in which the minimal clause definition fails is illustrated by:

(5) #Bob's kissing the girl #made *me* talk to$\left\{\begin{array}{l}\text{myself}\\ \text{*me}\end{array}\right\}$#.

In this sentence too, the minimal clause notion fails to make the correct
prediction. No clause boundary intervenes between the italicized elements.
Nonetheless, these do not appear in a minimal clause, since the string #*made
me talk to myself*# is not a clause. And while *me* and *myself* are part of the
overall clause coextensive with (5), this is not a *minimal* clause. It contains
the internal clause boundary after *girl*. Thus, our earlier account of minimal
clauses fails in a second way.

It was suggested in Chapter 3 that a more precise account of the minimal clause notion was possible, but only after a more explicit account of constituent structure was available. In Chapter 4, we devoted considerable space to developing an explicit system of grammatical representation.

Armed with this theoretical machinery, let us then reconsider the constituent structure of (4):[1,2]

(6)

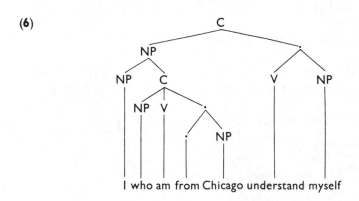

I who am from Chicago understand myself

This tree represents a sentence for which the earlier minimal clause definition makes the wrong prediction. Contrast it with the tree structure of (2a), for which the previous account makes a correct prediction:

(7)

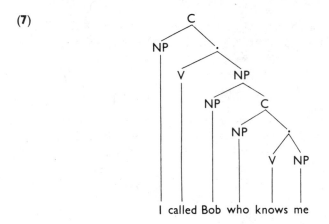

I called Bob who knows me

These two trees suggest a way to reformulate the minimal clause notion so that the right predictions are made for both trees. To see what is required, take a pencil and place it on the word *I* in the diagram in (7). Now trace the *shortest*[3] possible path along the branches of the diagram to the second word of self-reference, *me*. To move from *I* to *me*, your pencil inevitably passes through *two* nodes labeled C, the topmost node in (7) and the lower C node. Now turn back to diagram (6). Trace the shortest path from *I* to *myself*.

Significantly, in (6) this path passes through only a single node labeled C, the topmost node in the tree. It does not pass through the lower C node (representing the nonrestrictive relative clause). We have discovered an interesting and unexpected fact. The contrast between the necessity for *me* in (7) and *myself* in (6) is correlated with differences in the number of nodes crossed in tracing the paths between these pronouns and antecedent references to the speaker.

This suggests that one can revise the minimal clause notion along the following lines, taking advantage of the discovery just noted:

(8) Two or more constituents A_1, A_2, ..., A_n, are all members of some minimal clause (defined by a particular node labeled C) if (and only if) (i) they are dominated by a node labeled C, and (ii) it is possible to trace a path between them without going through any other node labeled C. Elements which meet this condition will be known as *minimal clause mates*, or *clause mates* for short.

Replacing the original minimal clause definition (which was assumed in Rule 1D) by (8), return to the tree in (6). The new definition says that *I* and *myself* in (6) are clause mates. This is so because it is possible to trace a path from one to the other without traversing more than one C node, in this instance, the topmost C in (6). Since *I* and *myself* are in the same minimal clause, Rule 1D now predicts that the correct form for the second is *myself*.

Consider again tree (7). According to the definition in (8), *I* and *me* are not clause mates, because there is no way to pass from one to the other without passing through two C nodes. Therefore, Rule 1D now correctly predicts that the second member of the pair should not have the form *myself*.

Return now to sentence (5), also inconsistent with an account based on the first notion of minimal clause; (5) has the constituent structure:

(9)

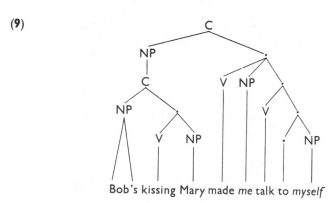

Bob's kissing Mary made *me* talk to *myself*

In terms of the first definition of minimal clause, the italicized forms in (9) do not meet the conditions of Rule 1D. They are not within a minimal clause in the earlier sense because the string #*made me talk to myself*# is not a clause. Thus the only clause containing these two pronouns of speaker self-reference is the overall sentence. But this is not a minimal clause either, because it contains a clause as subject. In terms of the new definition of minimal clause in (8), two forms are members of a minimal clause if they are connectable without tracing through more than one C node which dominates them both. This condition is met in (9) since the shortest path between *me* and *myself* traverses no C nodes whatever.[4] This is consistent with the claim that *me* and *myself* are clause mates in (9) because the definition refers to paths which do not go through more than one C node. The definition therefore includes as a special case situations where one constituent is reachable from another without passing through *any* node labeled C. The revised account of the distribution of *myself*, based on the notion *clause mate*, correctly predicts the necessity of *myself* in (9), where the earlier definition of minimal clause fails.

Another instance of the clause mate condition holding without the path between constituents passing through any C node is

(10) The doctor talked to me about myself.

(11)

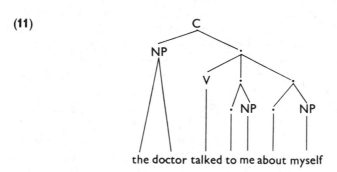

the doctor talked to me about myself

In passing from *me* to *myself* no nodes labeled C are intersected. The new account predicts that *me* and *myself* are clause mates. Hence, it correctly predicts the necessity for *myself*:

(12) *The doctor talked to me about me.

It is possible to offer a revised, somewhat simplified version of the rule for pronouns of self-reference. This makes explicit reference to the clause mate condition:

(13) Rule 1E
In cases of speaker self-reference,
a The form *myself* is used (i) if there is an antecedent reference to the speaker in the sentence, and (ii) if the forms expressing the antecedent and secondary reference(s) are clause mates.
b Otherwise, one uses *I* or *me* as described in Rule 1C of Chapter 2.

SUMMARY

The more precise system of grammatical representation introduced in Chapter 4 makes it possible to redefine the concept of minimal clause and to introduce the notion of clause mate. Several of the problem sentences at the end of Chapter 3 were reexamined. The notion of clause mate deals appropriately with the apparent exceptions to Rule 1D and with those cases which worked regularly. This in itself provides interesting initial justification for the various concepts introduced in Chapter 4. That is it supports the explicit notational system for representing constituent structure information.

The chapter ended with the introduction of a replacement for Rule 1D, Rule 1E, which incorporates explicit reference to the clause mate condition to overcome the limitations of the original formulation.

NOTES

1. In (6) and below, use is made of unlabeled nodes in trees. These are *not* to be thought of as representing claims about sentences, that is, that there are nodes without labels. They are a discursive technique permitting us to avoid claims which are either irrelevant to the points at issue or else unsettled.

2. In (6) and below, it is indicated for the first time that the verb and object NP of a simple clause form a constituent, a fact hitherto ignored. This unlabeled node has often been called Verb Phrase (VP). We leave the question of labeling to one side for the present. Intuitively, however, there is no doubt that an English clause like

(i) Harry knows French.

has a superficial division into two immediate constituents, *Harry* and *knows French*, rather than a ternary division into *Harry*, *knows*, and *French*, or a binary division into *Harry knows* and *French*. We indicate this for the present by recognizing an unlabeled node in the relevant cases. In Chapter 27, we consider the origin of this binary bracketing and our reasons for believing that it does *not* offer a genuine basis for recognizing a special category type VP.

3. The length of the path between two nodes is determined by counting the number of nodes passed through. For instance, in (7), to get from *Bob* to *who* the path intersects four nodes, while to get from *knows* to *me* the path only intersects three nodes.

4. This assumes that none of the unlabeled nodes are properly labeled C in fuller representations.

PROBLEMS

1. Consider the sentence:

(i) I said I would shoot myself.

Of the three words of self-reference, *I*, *I*, and *myself*, which are clause mates and why?

2. Explain the need for *me* and not *myself* in the italicized position in the sentence:

(i) People who live near me are not the people who like $\left\{ \begin{array}{l} me \\ *myself \end{array} \right\}$.

CHAPTER 6 GENERALIZATION OF THE RULES FOR *I, me, myself* AND THE NOTION OF COREFERENCE

PREVIEW

In this chapter, we show that the rules set up earlier for *I, me, myself* hold for at least twenty-two other pronominal forms. Thus earlier formulations must be generalized. In moving toward such a generalization, we introduce the relation of *coreference*, which holds between NPs designating the same objects. We propose a simple orthographic device for representing this relation. It is shown how earlier rules can be reformulated to cover the full variety of pronominal forms involving coreference. These matters lead to an unexpected conception of grammatical structure in which the actual form of a sentence is connected by definite steps or stages to an abstract underlying structure. This is a foretaste of things to come.

The discussion at the end of the previous chapter may have left many questions in the mind of the reader. It is all very well, one might complain, to give a rule for choosing *myself* as against *I/me* based on a notion of clause mate defined in terms of tree structures. But how does one determine what the proper tree for a given sentence is? How does one determine the right bracketing structure, the right labels? Where are the clause boundaries, and so on? These are serious questions, which have received no real answers. But they will be dealt with as we continue.

In the three previous chapters, we have dealt with some of the principles governing the proper occurrence of the forms *I, me, myself* in well-formed

English sentences and the relation between these principles and more general aspects of sentence formation (that is, clause structure). It was implicitly assumed that the distinctions between these three forms were unique. The principles given were so formulated. But this is not the case. The rules which distinguish *myself* from *I/me* and the latter two forms from each other are each more general. They cover various other forms as well. Consider the three forms *we, us, ourselves*. These refer to the speaker and one or more other individuals. Their distributions are, however, governed by the same principles as those involved with *I, me, myself*. Thus *ourselves* can only occur in positions where there is a clause mate antecedent referring to the speaker and one or more other individuals:

(1) a *Ourselves are very happy.
     b *Jimmy explained that to ourselves.
     c *I discussed ourselves.
     d   We dressed ourselves.
     e *We said that Bill dressed ourselves.
     f *The man who insulted ourselves is going to visit us.
     g *We are going to visit John, who insulted ourselves.
     h *If he asks us, ourselves will tell him what to do.
     i   John thinks (that) we should surrender ourselves to the police.

This parallelism between the grammatical behavior of *ourselves* and *myself* brings out the fact that there is only one rule operating here. That is, the rule which determines that (1a) is ill-formed is the same as that which rules out:

(2) *Myself is very happy.

The parallelism in grammatical *distribution* between *myself* and *ourselves* is correlated with a similarity in *form*. Like *myself*, *ourselves* is divisible into two major parts (called *morphemes*).[1] These are an initial element, which occurs elsewhere, and a special *stem*.[2] This stem, *self/selve*, has two variant forms, depending on whether the noun (or pronoun) it forms is singular or plural. Since most English noun stems do not have this property, the stem in question is said to be *irregular*. Other irregular noun stems include *wife/wive* and *knife/knive* (compare the regular *laugh, puff, cliff*). The stem underlying the words *myself* and *ourselves* is called the *reflexive* element. Compound forms based on it are called *reflexive forms*, or just *reflexives*. Hence *myself* and *ourselves* are reflexives. Sometimes we will refer to them as *reflexive pronouns*.

Just as the condition for *myself* is needed to specify the correct position of *ourselves*, the condition specifying the environments where *I* can occur (as against *me*) also specifies where *we* can occur (as against *us*). That is, *we* occurs as subject, *us* elsewhere (ignoring *our, ours*):

(3) a   We are happy.
     b   Maxwell knows we are happy.

    c *Harry won't talk to we.
    d *He told we that Betty was coming.
    e *John likes we.
    f Harry won't talk to us.
    g He told us that Betty was coming.
    h John likes us.

Thus the rules worked out for *I, me, myself* must be generalized to cover *we, us, ourselves.* But this is not the end of it. The same principles are also involved in the following triples:

(4) a he, him, himself
     b she, her, herself
     c they, them, themselves
     d it, it, itself
     e you, you, yourself
     f you, you, yourselves
     g one, one, oneself

Several observations can be made. First, the reflexive element occurs in the last member of each triple. Second, in the last four triples, the first two members are identical. In these cases the same form is used in both subject and nonsubject positions:

(5) a It is heavy.
     b I like it.
     c They dug the hole with it.
     d You are silly.
     e I know you.
     f I will give it to you.

Third, the first members of two sets of triples are the same. This is due to the fact that, except for reflexive words, *plurality* is not marked in second person forms:

(6) a You have annoyed your husband.
     b You have annoyed your husbands.

(7) a Your husband has insulted you.
     b Your husbands have insulted you.

But in general, subject and object forms are different, and singular and plural forms contrast.

    The last member of the triples in (4), like *myself* and *ourselves,* are called reflexives. It is also useful to have names for the first and second members of such groups. Let us call the members of the first position in these triples *subject forms* and the members of the second position *object forms.* Hence, *I, we, he, she, they, it, you,* and *one* are subject forms; *me, us, him, her, them, it, you,* and *one* are object forms. Some words fall into both classes. Traditionally, the words discussed so far are members of the part of speech called *Pronoun.* This is in turn subsumed under the more general category NP. Thus pronouns are a subtype of NP. So far we have really determined a fundamental pair of hierarchical distinctions among pronouns, establishing three classes of such forms:

(8)

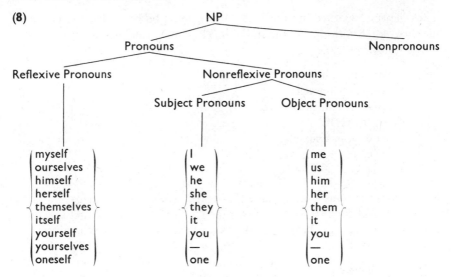

Pronouns are the only subtype of NP in English that participate in the three-way distinction of form illustrated. Most NPs cannot enter into antecedent relations like the reflexive forms can, and most NPs do not have contrasting subject and object shapes. Thus, NPs like *a nice boy, the nurse who loves Harry,* etc., occur equally appropriately as subjects or nonsubjects:

(9) a A nice boy called Harriet.
   b Harriet called a nice boy.
   c The nurse who loves Harry talked to the teacher.
   d The teacher talked to the nurse who loves Harry.

Differences between subject and object forms in various languages are often discussed in terms of the notion of *case.* One speaks of the *case marking* of NP. Some languages have complicated systems of case markings, in which *inflectional endings*[3] on nouns distinguish not only subjects from nonsubjects but other differences as well. English has, however, only a limited system of case distinctions and then, with the exception of the genitive forms,[4] only in pronouns.[5] Nouns in English (unlike those in German, Latin, Japanese, and Russian, for example) do not have different case forms for subject and nonsubject positions.

There is an important fact which goes against the implications of the terminology that has been introduced. As noted at the end of Chapter 2, subject forms are not always appropriate in subject positions. In particular there are good reasons[6] to take the italicized forms in the following examples to be in subject position within their clauses. But in no case are the subject forms of pronouns permissible:

(10) a $\#\#\begin{Bmatrix} His \\ *He \end{Bmatrix}$ catching a cold $\#$ upsets our plans $\#$.

b $\#\#$ For $\begin{Bmatrix} me \\ *I \end{Bmatrix}$ to leave $\#$ would be rude $\#$.

c $\#$I am for $\#\begin{Bmatrix} us \\ *we \end{Bmatrix}$ leaving right now $\#\#$.

d $\#$ The necessity $\#$ for $\begin{Bmatrix} them \\ *they \end{Bmatrix}$ to remain here $\#$ is obvious $\#$.

This shows that the potential rule

(11) The choice among nonreflexive pronoun forms within sets like those in (8) is made according to the principle:
  a Subject forms occur in subject positions.
  b Object forms occur elsewhere.

is not completely acceptable.

Compare clauses like those in (10), where either genitive forms like *his* or object forms are found, with clauses requiring subject forms in subject position. An additional correlated difference emerges. Clauses of the latter sort regularly have *main verbs*[7] which *inflect* for *tense.*[8] That is, they have present or past tense forms. Clauses like those in (10), however, either have main verbs with no inflectional endings at all, or with a *participial* ending *-ing,* which does not mark tense. Compare:

(12) a He $\begin{Bmatrix} has \\ had \\ *have \end{Bmatrix}$ a book.

b For him to $\begin{Bmatrix} have \\ *has \\ *had \end{Bmatrix}$ a book (would be nice).

c His $\begin{Bmatrix} having \\ *has \\ *had \end{Bmatrix}$ a book (was surprising).

Suppose one refers to clauses with tense-inflected main verbs as *tensed clauses.* Then one can improve the formulation in (11):

(13) Rule 1F
  a Subject forms occur in the subject positions *of tensed clauses.*
  b Object forms occur elsewhere.

The italicized qualification is the improvement.

It was claimed earlier that the rules for *I, me, myself* needed to be generalized to cover the other sets of pronominal forms mentioned. We have done this only in part, however. Before proceeding further toward this goal, recall the earlier discussion of *myself* and the notion of antecedent. In sentences like

(14) a *I* criticized *myself.*
      b *We* criticized *ourselves.*
      c *You* criticized *yourself.*
      d *You* criticized *yourselves.*
      e *He* criticized *himself.*
      f *She* criticized *herself.*
      g *They* criticized *themselves.*
      h *One* must criticize *oneself.*
      i *It* paid for *itself.*

a special relation holds between the pair of italicized NPs in each. Whatever entities are *referred to* by one NP are also referred to by the other. Thus in (14a), *I* refers to the speaker of (14a) and so does *myself.* The person criticizing and the one being criticized are the same. In (14b), *we* refers to the speaker of (14b) together with some other particular (unspecified) individuals X (Y, Z), etc. But *ourselves* must refer to the speaker and exactly X (Y, Z), etc. And so on in the other cases.[9] This relation between NPs is so important in grammar that it is useful to have a name for it. Such NPs are said to be *coreferential,* or to be *coreferents.* Thus, *I* and *myself* are coreferents in (14a), *she* and *herself* are coreferents in (14f), etc.

So far, we have only illustrated coreferentiality with pairs of NPs, at least one of which is a reflexive pronoun. However, two NPs, neither of which is a reflexive, can be coreferential:

(15) a *John* thinks *he* is intelligent.
      b When *the soldiers* arrived, *they* were met by the mayor.
      c *The plane* would have burned if *its* gas tank had been punctured.

However, such sentences reveal a contrast between reflexive and nonreflexive pronouns in spite of the fact that both can be terms of the relation of coreference. When a reflexive pronoun occurs in a sentence, it must have a fixed antecedent NP or range[10] of antecedent NPs in that sentence, with which it is coreferential. But this is not the case for nonreflexive pronouns. While in (15a), *John* and *he* can be coreferential, they need not be. That is, *he* in (15a) can refer to an individual different from that referred to by *John.* This difference between reflexive and nonreflexive pronouns shows up clearly in:

(16) a Mary thinks Barbara is talking about herself.
      b Mary thinks Barbara is talking about her.

In (16a), *herself* must be coreferential with *Barbara.* But in (16b), *her* can be coreferential with *Mary* or not. That is, *her* in (16b) need not be coreferential with any other NP in (16b).

GENERALIZATION OF RULES FOR *I, ME, MYSELF,* AND COREFERENCE

The principal function of pronouns is to express the relation of coreferentiality. In speaking of the antecedents of reflexive forms like *myself*, we have been referring to some previously occurring NP with which the reflexive form was coreferential. We argued in the previous paragraph that reflexive pronouns have the property of only occurring as one term of a relation of coreference.[11] In this respect they are unlike the nonreflexive pronouns we have considered,[12] and are even more unlike NPs which are not pronouns.

Given the technical concept of coreference and the principle distinguishing between subject and object forms, one can reformulate Rule 1D of Chapter 3 to incorporate the entire discussion of pronouns to this point:

(17) Rule 1G
The choice between the subject, object, and reflexive[13] forms of a triple of pronouns is determined as follows:
a   The reflexive form is used (i) if there is an antecedent coreferent NP in the sentence, and (ii) also if the antecedent and pronoun are clause mates.
b   Otherwise, (i) one uses subject forms in the subject positions of tensed clauses, and (ii) object forms elsewhere.

Rule 1G now covers not only the triple *I, me, myself* but the other triples as well. The coverage of Rule 1G is greater than previous rules. They referred to *I, me, myself*, where Rule 1G refers more generally to pairs of NP which are coreferential. It thus includes sets like *I, me* and *I, myself*, etc., as special cases.

An observation can be made about pronominal forms and their coreferential antecedents. Consider reflexives. Given the antecedent of a reflexive, one can generally specify the form of the reflexive. That is, the particular shape of the reflexive word does not carry information not present in the antecedent. Hence, one might represent sentences like

(18)   a   My father supports himself.
          b   You should study yourself.

as:

(19)   a   [My father supports self]
          b   [You should study self]

Such a notation indicates that the initial parts of reflexive words are redundant. The traditional way of expressing this is to say that reflexives *agree with* their antecedents. That is, the shape of the reflexive word is determined by certain properties (traditionally called *gender, number,* and *person*) of the antecedent NP. This says that, in addition to Rule 1G, there is a rule of (Reflexive) Pronoun Agreement. Such a rule determines the appropriate shape of reflexive pronouns in terms of the above-mentioned properties of their antecedent NPs.[14]

Further, there is a sense in which nonreflexive pronouns also agree with their coreferential antecedents. The following are well-formed:

(20) a *Jack's brother* said *she* was sad.

    b The car which struck *Bob* was owned by *their* tenant.

But in neither case can the italicized elements be coreferential. Coreference thus requires agreement for nonreflexive as well as reflexive forms.

There is an interesting gap in the devices sketched for the description of sentence structure. In discussions of constituent structure in preceding chapters, we were able to propose formal notational devices for the representation of the relevant concepts, namely, labeled brackets and labeled trees of certain sorts. We have now proposed that, in addition to these elements, sentences manifest the fundamental relation of coreference. However, no method for the representation of this property has been offered. Among other things, this gap prevents us from distinguishing the two distinct meanings of sentences like:

(21) a *Jack* thinks *he* is clever.

    b *Marsha* is visiting the lady who helped *her*.

There is one reading in which the italicized NPs are coreferents, another in which they are not.

The gap in our notational devices is related to the question of agreement, touched on above. On the readings in which the italicized NPs in (21a) are coreferents, the pronoun has the form *he* due to the agreement rule. The same is true in (21b) with *her*. Suppose one introduces the device of arbitrary *subscripts* on NPs[15] as a way of indicating coreference. NPs *with the same subscript* will be regarded as coreferential. The two readings of (21a) can then be naturally distinguished:

(22) a Jack$_i$ thinks he$_i$ is clever.

    b Jack$_j$ thinks he$_k$ is clever.

The notation in (22a) indicates the coreferential reading. By saying the subscripts are arbitrary, we mean that the choice of letter makes absolutely no difference beyond the question of whether distinct occurrences of subscripts are identical.

However, it was noted that in (22a) *he* has the shape it does because of the Pronoun Agreement rule. The representation in (22a) is redundant. This suggests that a more appropriate representation for (22a) might be:

(23) Jack$_x$ thinks x is clever

This represents the coreferentiality directly with no indication of the ultimate shape of the pronoun. This is an account of a real feature of such sentences because the shape of the pronoun which occurs in the position of x in a structure like (23) is predictable from the properties of the antecedent, *Jack*. Hence (23) is a structure which is "abstract" from the actual form of the sentence.

Nonetheless it represents the coreferentiality relations (independently of the shapes of the pronouns determined by Pronoun Agreement). We shall have more to say about such abstract structures. Abstract representations are equally appropriate for reflexive sentences. Thus one can represent (24a) as (24b):

(24) a Harry understands himself.
    b Harry$_x$ understands x

For the fact that *him*- shows up in such cases is predictable from the properties of the antecedent. The fact that *-self* shows up is predictable from the fact that the antecedent and the secondary NP, which are coreferential, are clause mates.

Hence, everything about the shape of *himself* is predictable from the properties given in (24b).[16] Therefore, reflexive and nonreflexive pronouns are equally describable by Pronoun Agreement. But reflexives are subject to a special statement specifying the occurrence of the stem *self/selve*.

One might express the relations between reflexive pronoun agreement and nonreflexive pronoun agreement somewhat differently as follows. A coreferential pronoun has a morphological structure consisting of an element added by Pronoun Agreement (*he/him, they/them,* etc.) and a stem. The reflexive stem has the shape *self/selve*. The nonreflexive pronoun stem has the null shape, that is, no pronunciation at all.[17] This means that Rule 1G(a) is actually concerned with the determination of the proper shape of the stem of coreferential pronouns (*self/selve* versus null), while Rule 1G(b) is actually concerned with the shapes of the markers added by Pronoun Agreement.[18]

Over the last few pages our discussion has surreptitiously taken an unexpected turn. For in these passages, as well as in note 16, we have moved toward a new way of looking at sentence structure. Hitherto, we had, as is traditional, restricted ourselves to analyzing sentences by dividing them into parts, characterizing these parts in terms of categories, etc. We have now begun to think of a sentence as if it were only the superficial realization of some more abstract structure, a realization connected to this more abstract structure by rules. For example, the description of the last few paragraphs might be made more explicit as follows. Consider:

(25) Joan understands herself.

This sentence has as its essential structure a representation of the form:[19]

(26)

This representation is turned into the structure

(27)

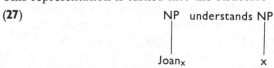

by a Pronominalization rule. Such a rule says, in effect, that in the case of two clause mate coreferent NPs, the antecedent NP must precede. In turn, the representation in (27) is converted into:

(28)

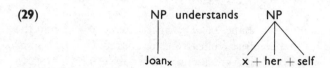

by an interpretation of Rule 1G(a). This structure is then converted to

(29)

by a rule of Pronoun Agreement. Finally, (29) is turned into the final form of the sentence (25) by a general principle which suppresses all coreference indices.

Within these terms, the grammatical rules we have been talking about informally (Rule 1G, the Pronominalization rule, Pronoun Agreement, etc.) are regarded as rules *which connect different levels or stages of representation of sentences*. Note that Rule 1G, as is, does *not* really fit into this framework. It would have to be restated to fulfill this function.

We do not pursue this theoretical treatment of pronouns. It suffices to stress that this form of description seems revealing for these elements. We will in following chapters argue that this conception of grammar, in which many grammatical rules connect superficial representations of sentences to abstract structures, is required on other grounds.

SUMMARY

In this chapter, regularities governing the distribution of *I, me, myself* were shown to operate for the whole set of twenty-five pronouns (*we, us, you, him, themselves, one,* etc.). We reformulated earlier rules in a more general way to cover all these forms. The reformulation was presented in Rule 1G. This made crucial reference to the notion of coreference. We described the notational device of identical subscripts on NPs to indicate coreference. As the discussion developed, we considered how pronouns agree with their antecedents and the interaction of this agreement with coreference. This led to a new outlook on grammar. We viewed certain grammatical rules as describing the relations between the actual string of words making up the superficial form of a sentence and more abstract stages of structure. Although these are not directly manifested in the string of words, they provide relevant information (e.g., coreference) for the description of certain regularities. This introduced a new theory of sentence structure. Grammatical organization is now regarded as more complicated than bracketing and categorizing strings of words and their parts. In the mode of description hinted at toward the end of this chapter, sentence structure is seen to consist in part of a statement of how the superficial string of words is "derived" through successive stages from a more abstract representation. This theory will be elaborated more fully in the chapters that follow.

NOTES

1. Roughly, morphemes are the grammatically significant parts of words. Thus, if we mark boundaries between morphemes by the sign +, the words

(i)   a   pickles
       b   antifeminist
       c   murdered
       d   overweight
       e   realization

would have the following analyses:

(ii)   a   pickle + s
       b   anti + femin + ist
       c   murder + ed
       d   over + weigh + t
       e   realiz + at + ion

Morphemes tend to recur in other combinations. For example, the final morpheme in (iia), normally called the plural, occurs in thousands of other words, including:

(iii)   a   dogs   c   traumas
        b   bananas   d   eclipses

The first morpheme in (iib) occurs in such other words as:

(iv)   a   antisocial
       b   anticommunist

The final morpheme in (iie) occurs in such other words as:

(v)   a   promotion
      b   revision
      c   contraction

Although the term is new, the concept involved in the discussion of morphemes is elementary. This concept is a reflection of the fact that words are not grammatically unanalyzable wholes. Rather, they are formed of more primitive elements. That is, they can be. There are, of course, words consisting of single morphemes, like the first and third words of this sentence. This is inherently no more puzzling than the fact that there are one-word sentences (Duck!).

2. *Stem* is one of several terms used in forming a rough typology of types of morphemes. Other parallel terms in such a typology include *inflection* (and *inflectional ending*), *derivational affix, particle,* etc. We shall not attempt precise definitions of these. Roughly though, stems refer to the stock of lexical morphemes in a language. These form the huge open classes underlying nouns, verbs, and adjectives. We can recognize one stem in the italicized words:

(i) a He *bored* me.
    b He was *bored*.
    c He was *boring*.
    d He was a *bore*.

Notice that this common stem occurs in several different traditional parts of speech; in (a) it is a verb, in (b,c) it functions as an adjective, and in (d) it is a noun.

3. These are another one of the elements of the typology mentioned in note 2. Inflectional endings occur obligatorily as parts of nouns, verbs, or adjectives, marking certain grammatical categories in certain positions. They are always drawn from a finite, fairly small list for each language. In English the inflectional endings for nouns are the plural morpheme and the genitive morpheme (see note 4); for verbs they are the tense markers and the so-called participial endings, *-ing* and *-ed*:

(i) a John is sing*ing*.
    b They have insult*ed* Sally.

4. Genitive forms are the so-called possessive NP, whose ending is typically *'s* (although this is suppressed in speech after the plural in *s*):

 (i) a Jack's car
     b Jack's kissing Betty annoyed me.
     c a friend of Jack's

 (ii) a *the boys's toys
      b the boys' toys
but:
      c the men's toys

That is, only a few irregular plurals like *men* have audible genitive endings.

Pronouns typically have irregular genitive shapes:

(iii) a my (*me's)
    b your (*you's)
    c our (*us's)
    d his (*him's)
    e her (*her's)
    f their (*them's)

One is, for a pronoun, exceptionally regular, since it has a genitive like *Jack*. There is a further contrast between genitive forms like those in (iii) and

(iv) a mine
    b yours
    c ours
    d his
    e hers
    f theirs

But we will not study these forms.

5. Case distinctions are much discussed in school grammar with respect to two types of pronouns we have so far ignored: *relative pronouns* and *question* or *interrogative pronouns* like *who, whom, whose*, etc. The traditional rule was that *who* was used in subject positions (parallel to *I*) and *whom* elsewhere (parallel to *me*). Much effort has been expended in schools to enforce the usage of sentences like (a) as against (b):

(i) a Whom did you see?
    b Who did you see?

This amounts, for the most part, to an attempt to prescribe anachronistic forms. American English has changed in such a way that for a vast number of speakers, including the present writers, (a) is now marginal.

6. We have space to point out only one. There is an adverbial expression in English of the form *on X's own*. This expression is semantically connected to subject NP and must agree with the subject of its clause:

(i) a Jack called Betty on $\left\{ \begin{array}{l} \text{his} \\ \text{*her} \\ \text{*my} \\ \text{*your} \end{array} \right\}$ own.

    b Jack left on $\left\{ \begin{array}{l} \text{his} \\ \text{*my} \\ \text{*her} \end{array} \right\}$ own.

However, this expression occurs with the requisite agreement in all of the clause types illustrated in (10) in the text, where subject forms are not permissible:

(ii) a *His* doing it on his own upsets our plans.
  b For *me* to do it on my own would be rude.
  c I am for *your* doing it on your own.
  d The necessity for *them* to do it on their own is obvious.

A large number of phenomena in English parallel the expression type *on X's own*, which require reference to subjects and which treat italicized NPs like those in (ii) as subjects. Therefore, complications ensue if one denies subject status to NPs in the italicized positions. We must thus conclude that such NPs are subjects.

7. Generally, it is possible to isolate a single verbal element which is the pivot around which a clause is built. This is called the *main verb* of that clause. In English, the main verb is (i) normally the leftmost verb in the clause, and (ii) the verb which can *agree with* the subject NP, if the clause is tensed. In the following examples, we italicize the main verbs of the clauses whose boundaries are indicated:

(i) a #Harry *attacked* me #.
  b #I *was* attacked by Harry #.
  c #Why *have* you been crying # ?
  d Jack thinks #I *tried* to call you #.
  e If #you *were* clever # you could win.

8. One systematic exception involves clauses functioning as the complements of verbs like *demand*, *insist* and adjectives like *mandatory*, whose main verbs must be uninflected:

(i) a I demanded that $\left\{ \begin{array}{l} \text{he} \\ \text{*him} \end{array} \right\}$ be arrested.

  b He $\left\{ \begin{array}{l} \text{was} \\ \text{*be} \end{array} \right\}$ arrested.

(ii) a I insist that $\left\{ \begin{array}{l} \text{they} \\ \text{*them} \end{array} \right\}$ be warned.

  b They $\left\{ \begin{array}{l} \text{are} \\ \text{*be} \end{array} \right\}$ warned.

(iii) a It is mandatory that $\left\{ \begin{array}{l} \text{she} \\ \text{*her} \end{array} \right\}$ leave.

  b She $\left\{ \begin{array}{l} \text{leaves} \\ \text{*leave} \end{array} \right\}$.

Somehow or other the grammar must say that these behave like tensed clauses even though superficially without tense. They behave like tensed clauses not only with respect to pronoun shape but in other respects. For example, the clauses in (i–iii), unlike other superficially untensed clauses in English (such as those in (10) in the text), occur with the element *that*, typical of tensed (Subordinate) clauses. Further, unlike other untensed clauses, those in (i–iii) occur with adverbial modifiers before the subject:

(iv) a I demand that at this time he be recalled.
 b It is mandatory that at least once a year each car be inspected.

Contrast:

(v) a *It is necessary for at this time him to be recalled.
 b It is necessary for him to be recalled at this time.
 c *I am for at least once a year each car being inspected.
 d I am for each car being inspected at least once a year.

9. There is a semantic contrast between the forms *one* and *oneself* in (14) and all of the other pronominal forms. The others will, in any particular usage, refer to a specific set of individuals or objects. This is not the case with *one/oneself.* These words resemble what logicians refer to as *variables.* The other forms resemble what logicians call *constants.* However, the relation of coreference is defined between occurrences of *one* and *oneself* just as it is between NPs which function as constants. Many other NPs also function as variables, including those italicized in:

(i) a *Anyone who eats mercuric dioxide* will regret it.
 b *Most southerners* are polite.
 c *Few congressmen* understand Swahili.

10. This qualification is necessary because in certain cases a reflexive NP can have two or more possible antecedents within a single sentence:

(i) Jack spoke to Larry about himself.

Himself can be coreferential to either *Jack* or *Larry*, and must be coreferential with one of them.

11. It can be argued, however, that all pronouns, reflexive and nonreflexive alike, must be terms of coreferential relations. This can be maintained in the face of sentences like:

(i) He is sick.

In (i) a pronoun occurs with no antecedent. But, one can extend the notion of antecedent so that it describes elements related in different sentences of a discourse, or even a pronoun in one sentence related to an abstract element which has never shown up in a particular sentence. These matters go beyond the scope of an introductory work.

12. This ignores reflexive words like those in:

(i) a Harry himself is honest.
 b That is in itself sufficient reason to reject that proposal.

These are often called *emphatic reflexives.* They seem to have nothing to do with coreference. Such reflexive words are not covered by our discussion.

13. Reference to reflexive forms is misleading in that the rule stated only accounts for a subset of reflexive usages. Moreover, the class of reflexives not handled by the rule is larger than is suggested by note 12 above. Reflexive words manifest coreferential linkages in a variety of environments distinct from those characterized in Rule 1G:

   (i)   a   Harry thinks there is a picture of himself in the post office.
          b   Harry knows that students like himself are obnoxious.
          c   Harry said that as for himself he was not interested in a movie career.

We say little about reflexives like those in (i). It is important though to clarify the logical relation between such examples and our rule. For this illustrates a basic and often overlooked or confused distinction which is important in the study of grammar.

One can think of any rule, including Rule 1G, as saying:

   (ii)   Certain forms, A, in the environment X_____Y, have the properties P.

From this point of view, a rule is shown to be literally incorrect if one finds occurrences of A in the environment X_____Y which do *not* have the properties P. Such occurrences are *counterexamples* to the rule. For example, in the case of Rule 1G(a), a counterexample would be a pair of coreferential NPs which are clause mates but such that neither is a reflexive, that is, a sentence like:

   (iii)   *Harry$_i$ likes him$_i$

However, no such examples are really known (but see note 3 of Chapter 3). On the other hand, there can be (and frequently are) *exceptions* to rules. These are different from counterexamples. With respect to (ii), they involve occurrences of A with the properties P which are not in the environment X_____Y. Examples like (i) are exceptions to Rule 1G(a). They reveal reflexives in a set of environments distinct from that specified in the rule in the text.

Exceptions have a different status than counterexamples. Genuine counterexamples to a rule show that the formulation is incorrect. Exceptions as such only show that a rule is not a full and complete account of a certain class of forms. But unless a formulation has claimed completeness, this is not necessarily of great import. Exceptions are of real interest only when comparing two distinct formulations. If neither has known counterexamples, and one properly explains a class of cases which are exceptions in the other formulation, then one chooses that formulation with fewer exceptions.

Our assumption is that English *has more than one rule determining reflexive shape for pronouns* and that (i) illustrates the action of rules distinct from that (Rule 1G) responsible for the reflexives discussed in the text. This assumption might be wrong. But it cannot be shown to be such until someone formulates a single rule predicting both those reflexives covered by Rule 1G(a) and others like those in (i).

14. Things are more complicated. The grammatical structure of the antecedent sometimes does not uniquely determine the agreement. Thus the identical antecedent can determine different agreements:

(i)　a　My neighbor considers himself patriotic.
　　　b　My neighbor considers herself patriotic.

The user of (a) assumes that the subject NP designates a male, while the user of (b) assumes that this NP designates a female. The agreement rule must ultimately be sensitive to assumptions of this sort, which are not explicitly marked in the antecedent NP.

15. We limit subscript indices to *nouns*, writing

(i)　the plane$_i$ which exploded

and not:

(ii)　the plane which exploded$_i$

It is arbitrary to have the subscript follow the noun rather than precede it, just as it is arbitrary to have subscripts and not superscripts, etc. None of these features involve claims about linguistic structure.

16. There is still one kind of information represented in structures like (24b) which is governed by laws or rules. Given a pair of clause mate coreferential NPs, the antecedent *precedes* the pronoun. However, this is governed by rule, since the opposite order is impossible:

(i)　*Himself understands Harry.

Hence, an even more revealing notational structure for (24a) might be:

(ii)
$$\begin{array}{l} \text{x understands x} \\ \quad\lfloor\underline{\quad\text{Harry}\quad}\rfloor \end{array}$$

A structure like (ii) indicates that the clause consists of two coreferential elements, whose reference is determined by the name *Harry*. But it does not indicate the relative order in the actual sentence of the NP *Harry* and the NP *himself*. This order must be predicted by a further Pronominalization rule. This determines the possible relative configurations of pronouns and their antecedents. The study of this domain is an interesting one but we will not be able to deal with it.

17. Morphemes which are unpronounced in some positions are not so rare. For instance, the plural morpheme is null in some cases:

(i)　a　one duck
　　　b　two ducks

c   one sheep
d   two sheep
e   *two sheeps

18. This is just as true of first and second person NPs as for third person NPs. Along the lines of note 16, one can represent a sentence like

(i)   I think I am clever.

as:

(ii)   x thinks x is clever

The second x takes on the ultimate shape *I* because of Pronoun Agreement in conjunction with Rule 1G(b). The latter would pick the agreement marker *I* instead of *me* because the second x is the subject of a tensed clause.

19. In this and following representations in this chapter, we suppress unnecessary information, that the whole is a C, that *understands* is a V, etc.

PROBLEMS

1. Using the subscript notation described in this chapter, represent all possible coreferential relationships in the following sentences:

(i)   She told Mary that her mother was sick.
(ii)   The possibility that Bob has cancer doesn't worry him, but it does worry his mother.
(iii) The realization that Bob has cancer doesn't worry him, but it does worry his mother.

2. What accounts for the *they/them* contrast in the following sentences?

(i)   I argued that $\begin{Bmatrix} \text{they} \\ \text{*them} \end{Bmatrix}$ were arrested.

(ii)   I argued for $\begin{Bmatrix} \text{they} \\ \text{*them} \end{Bmatrix}$ to be arrested.

CHAPTER 7 MORE ON REFLEXIVES: REMOTE STRUCTURES

PREVIEW

In this chapter, a set of apparent exceptions to Rule 1G is examined. These involve imperative clauses like *Stop yourself from yawning* and *Give yourself a break*. These appear to be exceptions because they contain reflexive pronouns, in spite of the fact that there is no antecedent clause mate coreferent. Such examples are exceptions only from the point of view of certain unstated assumptions about the nature of grammatical structure and the kinds of things rules must refer to. These assumptions are made explicit and examined. The view that examples like these above are exceptions to Rule 1G is a function of these hidden assumptions.

An alternative set of assumptions is proposed and examined briefly. The imperative clauses in question are then seen to follow from Rule 1G, with no modification or addition. This result suggests that the revised set of assumptions reveals something important about the nature of language. It also illustrates the general methodological principle that exceptions, counterexamples, apparent irregularities, etc., may show that underlying theories of grammar are wrong rather than that particular rule formulations are incorrect.

There is a class of sentences traditionally called *imperatives*:

(1) a Weigh the meat.   d Give me a drink.
       b Stop talking.   e Sleep well.
       c Open the door.   f Stop.

These have *no subject NPs*.[1] Compare the examples of (1) with the *declarative* sentences:

(2) a Harry weighed the meat.   d He gave me a drink.
       b They stopped talking.   e All of us slept well.
       c You will open the door.   f The train stopped.

In these, the subject NPs are *Harry, they, you, he, all of us*, and *the train*, respectively. Given the appropriate antecedents, declarative sentences manifest the full range of reflexive forms, *myself, ourselves, himself*, etc., as we saw earlier, where all of the examples were declaratives.

Consider then what Rule 1G of Chapter 6 predicts about imperative sentences. Observe that in many (in fact, most) cases in declaratives, the antecedent of a reflexive form *is a subject NP*:

(3) a You have cut yourself.
       b Harry hurt himself.
       c John and Mary didn't criticize themselves.

Rule 1G requires that a reflexive form have an antecedent which is a clause mate. Therefore, this rule predicts that imperative clauses, which have no subjects, should contain no reflexive elements whose antecedents in the analogous declarative clauses would be subjects. Thus, Rule 1G allows imperatives like:

(4) a Talk to me about myself.
       b Don't argue with me about myself.

Here the antecedents of the reflexives are *non*subjects. However, Rule 1G should predict that there are no imperative sentences analogous to declarative sentences in which the antecedents of reflexive forms are subjects. But this is false:

(5) a John shaved himself.
       b Shave yourself.

(6) a I criticized myself.
       b Criticize yourself.

(7) a The girl dressed herself.
       b Dress yourself.

(8) a The boys amused themselves.
       b Amuse yourselves.

Thus imperative clauses manifest reflexives which do not have antecedents within the sentence. This violates[2] Rule 1G.

There are now two choices. Reformulating the rule for reflexives might seem to be the only choice. But there is a second choice. This involves providing a description of imperative sentences such that the rule for reflexives can be maintained without revision or extension. On the face of it, this seems impossible. The rule says that a reflexive must have an antecedent coreferent within the clause, and there are no such antecedents in the (b) sentences of (5)−(8). Thus, as *exception* is defined in note 13 of Chapter 6, these reflexives are genuine exceptions to the rule we gave for reflexive choice. That is, they are instances of reflexive usage which do not follow from the rule.

The belief that it is impossible for Rule 1G to cover exceptions like those in the (b) sentences of (5)−(8) reveals an interesting assumption implicitly made about rules:

(9) Every rule must be characterized in terms of the actual strings of words which make up sentences.

This view might seem so obvious as to be beyond question. In reality, it is a contingent claim about language. One can imagine many possible linguistic systems for intelligent creatures not having the property in (9). Consequently, it is matter of empirical fact whether (9) is true of English. Logically, it could be false. No open-minded inquiry into the nature of grammar can, therefore, accept (9) as unchallengeable.

Principle (9) is closely connected to another assumption:

(10) The only structure which sentences have is that provided by the strings of words which make them up, together with the analysis of these into categories, parts of speech, clauses, etc. That is, grammatical structure is exhausted by constituent structure in the sense of Chapter 4.

If, contrary to (10), sentences had aspects of structure beyond that directly represented by their bracketed and categorized strings of words, it would be irrational to insist on (9), that is, to insist that no rule could refer to other aspects of structure. Principle (9) only makes sense if (10) is true. Principles (9) and (10) together form a single common theory of sentences. They can be referred to jointly as the *principle of superficial grammar*, for reasons which will become clear as we progress.

If this principle is correct, Rule 1G must either be changed or supplemented by special statements to handle reflexives in imperative sentences such as (5b). If this principle is not correct, there is the possiblity that Rule 1G can predict all of the reflexives of imperative sentences if it is embedded within a description of English which provides more "abstract" structures for sentences. The reflexive rule would then be regarded as referring to these abstract structures rather than to actual strings of words.

At one point earlier, we deviated from the view that the structure of a sentence is exhausted by the analysis of its string of words. This was in the discussion of coreference and its relation to the agreement between antecedent and pronoun toward the end of Chapter 6. Coreference is a relation between NPs not directly manifested in the morphological properties of strings of words. Beginning with the introduction of the identical subscript notation (for representing coreference) and proceeding to a new interpretation of Rule 1G as involving links between abstract stages of sentences, we recognized that sentences have structure more abstract than that directly given by their word strings.

A first ground for indicating that English imperative sentences have a more abstract structure than that manifested by their strings of words is provided by an apparently curious restriction on the type of reflexives which can occur in sentences like the (b) ones in (5)—(8) above. Only *second person* reflexives, the singular *yourself* and the plural *yourselves*, are found in sentences like these:

(11)
a	Wash yourself.	f	*Wash themselves.
b	Wash yourselves.	g	*Wash itself.
c	*Wash myself.	h	*Wash ourselves.
d	*Wash himself.	i	*Wash oneself.
e	*Wash herself.		

Given that reflexive pronouns must be coreferential with and agree with their antecedents, the occurrence of only *yourself* and *yourselves* in contexts like (11) can still be predicted. To do so, imperative clauses must be restricted to second person subjects, that is, to subjects of the type which normally show up as the word *you*.

Is there any sense in which imperative sentences have such subjects? Consider:

(12) a You washed the car.
b You washed yourselves.

These declaratives have visible subjects. These subject NPs have a particular property of *interpretation*. They designate the *agents* of the activity determined by the verb *washed*, that is, the subject NPs in (12) designate the entities which do the washing:

(13) With verbs like *wash*, subjects of declarative, active sentences are interpreted as agents, the "doers".[3]

Thus, in (12b), the subject of *washed* is interpreted as the doer of the relevant act of washing. Since this subject is *you*, it is interpreted as referring to the individual (or individuals) to whom the speaker addresses his utterance.[4]

Consider again imperative sentences such as:

(14) Wash yourself.

What do we know about the agent of the washing in this case? Speakers of English know that the agent of the activity in (14) is the person to whom (14)

Is addressed; (14) is a request, command, etc.,[5] for that person to perform the activity described. English imperative clauses are regularly interpreted as having second person agents. Traditional grammar makes partial note of this by saying that such sentences have "understood" second person pronouns in them. This is to say that they have second person agents but no subject NPs of the form *you* in their strings of words.

We have noted the following generalizations:

(15) a Declarative (active) clauses containing verbs like *wash* have their subjects interpreted as agents.
    b Imperative clauses are interpreted as having second person agents.
    c Imperative clauses do not contain subjects.[6]
    d Imperative clauses can contain apparently antecedentless reflexive forms, but only of the second person variety.

Generalizations (15c,d) comprise a set of apparent exceptions to Rule 1G(a), which determines the appropriate contexts for reflexive pronouns. Generalization (15b), in context with (15a), is an exception to the possibility of saying for all active clauses containing verbs like *wash* that the agent of the action is the individual or individuals designated by the subject of the clause. Thus, (15b,c) prevent a fully general account of the relation between subject and agent, apparently requiring separate statements for imperatives and declaratives.

Imperative clauses yield exceptions to regularities involving the antecedents of reflexives and the relation between subjects and agenthood. This correlation between exceptions to regularities is suspicious. One seeks some treatment which can maintain both generalizations. Such an account is available. One need only make precise the traditional statement that imperatives have "understood" second person subjects. The import of this traditional view is that *imperatives have at least two levels rather than one level of grammatical structure.* One level, the ordinary and everywhere accepted and understood one, is the level of the actual string of words which make up a sentence. At this level, imperatives have no subjects. We henceforth refer to this level as *surface structure.* But the remark about "understood" subjects provides sentences with an additional level of structure. At this level, elements may be present which are not present in surface structure. We refer to any such level as *remote structure.* And let us represent remote structures for the moment in square brackets to distinguish them from our ordinary orthographical representations of surface structures. In this notation, (14) has a remote structure of the form:

(16) [you wash yourself]

Remote structures, unlike surface structures, do *not* directly describe what words a sentence contains, their order, bracketing, etc. Rather, they give more subtle and less obvious information. For example, they indicate how notions like *agent* play a part in their interpretation. Thus (16) serves to indicate that (14), though subjectless in surface structure, is interpreted as having a second person agent. It does this, however, only if one specifies that remote structures, like surface structures, can have subjects, and if one replaces (15a,b) by the generalization:

(17) In remote structures like (16), the subjects of verbs like *wash* are interpreted as agents.

Structures like (16) provide the basis for general statements about properties like agenthood, covering at once declaratives and imperatives. At the same time, structures like (16) permit the original rule for reflexive distribution to cover reflexives like those in the (b) sentences of (5)−(8) and in (14). This is true *if* this rule is reinterpreted to apply not to the level of surface structure but rather to some[7] level of remote structure like (16). For in (16), sentence (14) is provided with a structure in which the reflexive element has a clause mate coreferent antecedent.

To explain the restriction of imperative clauses to second person reflexives (ignoring those like (4)), one must impose on imperative remote structures (like (16)) the requirement that their subjects be exclusively second person. This fact cannot, as far as we know, be predicted from any independently needed syntactic principle.[8] However, once this provision is assumed, it explains why there is a restriction to antecedentless *second person* reflexives and also why there are restrictions like:

(18) a *Protect you.   d *Take care of you.
      b *Shave you.   e *Defend you.
      c *Talk to me about you. f *Treat you.

If remote structures like (16) contain exclusively second person subjects, restrictions like (18) are a function of the same rule which blocks *declarative* sentences like:

(19) a *You protect you.   d *You should take care of you.
      b *You shave you.   e *You were defending you.
      c *You talked to me about   f *You are treating you.
        you.

That is, within structures where the clause mate condition holds, an NP with a coreferent antecedent must take on reflexive form. Remote structures like (16) have extended the range of the generalization about agents. They have also accounted for reflexives in imperative clauses. Now we see that they are relevant for extending the generalization about examples like (19) to imperatives.

We begin to understand how a rule which is valid for a wide range of data, say Rule 1G(a), can be shown to cover a set of apparent exceptions *by adopting a more sophisticated, abstract, and complex theory of grammar.* Moreover, the strategy of extending grammatical theory serves not only to resolve apparent exceptions, but also apparent counterexamples in many cases. Both exceptions and counterexamples to particular rules may thus be due to different factors: (i) the incorrectness of the rule; and (ii) the inadequacy of certain theoretical assumptions underlying, and essentially independent of, the formulation of the rule. Anomalies to rules may show, therefore, not that particular rules are incorrect, but rather that the theoretical principle (or principles) on which they depend are partially mistaken.

For instance, if our approach to imperative clauses is correct, then the second person reflexives of imperative clauses do not show anything about the inadequacy of Rule 1G(a). Rather, they are the first evidence indicating the inadequacy of the principle of superficial grammar. Thus, the error in the earlier discussion was not an incorrect formulation of Rule 1G(a) but rather the implicit and unjustified assumption that Rule 1G(a) was to be interpreted within the terms of the principle of superficial grammar.

We have concluded that sentences whose surface structures are subjectless can contain remote structures which possess subjects. Generalizing, we have concluded that sentences whose surface structures do not have certain kinds of elements can have remote structures which do contain them. One of the most obvious implications of such a view is that there must be rules connecting remote to surface structures. There must be a rule which *deletes* the second person subjects of imperative sentences. We call this rule I Deletion. This is a rule which relates two different levels of sentence structure. Operating on a remote structure of the form

(20)   [you wash yourself]

it yields the surface structure:

(21)   wash yourself.

Rules of this type are called *transformations*. We shall have much to say about them throughout. The existence of this deletion rule accounts for the fact that imperatives, like a restricted-set of other sentence types, are more or less alone among English *main clauses*[9] in being subjectless in surface structure. That is, it accounts for why they have "understood" subjects in the traditional terminology. In general, "understood" elements refer to elements present in remote structures which have been deleted by one or another rule, and which are, therefore, absent from the relevant surface strings of words. Correspondingly, deletion rules are one of the major subtypes of transformational operations linking surface structures to remote structures.

SUMMARY

In this chapter, we adopted a more abstract and conceptually more complex theory of grammar. According to this view, the full structure of sentences involves remote structures as well as surface structures. Certain apparent exceptions to Rule 1G then disappeared. This is a positive benefit of a more complex theory. However, such a grammatical theory raises new and difficult questions. A sceptical reader might complain that it would be easier and more "realistic" to suppose that rules relate only to surface structures. If this makes imperative clauses exceptional, then it is simply a fact that they *are* exceptional. This sort of scepticism is not to be cavalierly dismissed.

In positing structures for sentences that are only indirectly connected to actual strings of words, the possibility arises of purely fanciful, entirely arbitrary or unmotivated constructions. Means must be found for distinguishing justifiable abstract structures from others. But this is not really a surprising conclusion. The same issue arises in any serious field of inquiry. The problem of distinguishing valid from invalid theoretical constructions must always be faced. Justification for remote structures is approached in detail in the following chapter. There we argue that there are rational methods for dispelling genuine scepticism.

NOTES

1. This view can be defended against the possible objection that in examples like (1a,c) etc., the postverbal NP *is* the subject by noting the requirement of object pronominal forms in parallel cases:

(i) Help $\left\{ \begin{array}{l} \text{me} \\ \text{*I} \end{array} \right\}$.

(ii) Help $\left\{ \begin{array}{l} \text{him} \\ \text{*he} \end{array} \right\}$.

If postverbal NPs were subjects, we would expect to find the starred forms grammatical.

Similarly, in note 6 of Chapter 6, it was pointed out that only subject NPs can be the antecedents in cases like:

(iii) John called Betty on $\left\{ \begin{array}{l} \text{his} \\ \text{*her} \end{array} \right\}$ own.

If postverbal NPs were subjects, we would expect them to be possible antecedents for *own*. But this is not possible:

(iv) *Help me on my own.
(v) *Write to me on my own.

2. The terms *violation*, *violate*, etc., will be used ambiguously to cover both counterexamples and exceptions. In this case, we are dealing with exceptions.

3. There are three remarks to be made about the statement in (13).

First, with verbs such as *know, believe, like,* etc., subjects of declarative active sentences are interpreted as *experiencers,* that is, as possessors of the *minds* which experience or have the states described by the verb and its complements. Verbs with experiencer subjects form a subset of verbs which are often called *stative.* These are opposed to *active* verbs, which take agents. One characteristic which distinguishes these two subsets is that stative verbs cannot occur in *progressive* aspect configurations:

(i) a   Joan is washing her face.
    b   *Joan is knowing French.
    c   *Joan is understanding her daughter.

Second, *Active* sentences are not *passive* in form. Most *transitive* verbs, those taking both subjects and objects, occur in both active and passive clauses:

(ii) a   Joan washed the bowl.   (Active)
    b   The bowl was washed by Joan.   (Passive)

In passives, the subjects are not interpreted as agents with verbs like *wash.* In (iib) it is *Joan,* a nonsubject, that is the agent NP, just as in (iia). An explanation for this will be provided in Chapter 18.

Third, the identification of agents with "doers" is inadequate. The notion of agent involves an entity with a mind which, in addition to doing the action, *wills* the action involved. Thus in sentences like

(iii) a   The crane knocked over the building.
    b   The wind drove the rain against the house.
    c   The dead body fell through the skylight.

there are "doers" but no agents.

4. This is not quite right since, in the case of plural *you,* it is only necessary that the individuals designated by the NP *include* at least one person who is addressed:

(i) You both should get married.

This can be addressed to a single person, although the subject NP designates two individuals.

5. Normally, the meaning of imperatives is unspecified with respect to the parameter of entreaty, request, command, order, threat, etc.

6. Rather, this should say that it is *possible* for them not to contain subjects:

(i)   You open that window.
(ii) You get out of here right now.

Semantically these are imperatives. Examples like (i) and (ii) are not simply *free variants* of the analogous sentences with the subjects missing. Associated with the retention of the subject is a specific aspect of meaning. Examples (i) and (ii) can only be used appropriately when the speaker and addressee are in a hierarchical relationship, with the speaker superior. Hence (i) can be naturally used by parent to child, master to servant, person with gun to victim, etc. But not conversely. Correspondingly, while *politeness emphasizers* like *please* and *kindly* can occur with subjectless imperatives, they are impossible with those retaining subjects:

(iii)   a   Please open that window.
       b   Kindly open that window.
       c   *You please open that window.
       d   *Please you open that window.
       e   *You open that window please.

This follows, we think, since the essence of politeness is an expression of the *lack* of subservience of hearer to speaker. Therefore, retention of the subject and the use of politeness particles clash semantically.

7. We shall see in following chapters that there are many levels of remote structure. Thus, exactly which levels are relevant for the reflexive rule is an open question. This topic is considered in detail in Chapter 29.

8. It is an open question, however, whether it can be predicted from general characteristics of the meaning of imperatives, for example, from the fact that they involve an injunction to act. However, the claim that the individuals enjoined to act are necessarily identical to the individuals addressed is vitiated by the fact that many languages have imperative sentences not restricted to second person subjects, with meanings like 'let him go', 'may they die', etc.

9. Other examples of subjectless main clauses include:

  (i)   Why not criticize yourself.
  (ii)   Praise yourself just once and everybody thinks you're an egomaniac.

We return to these in Chapters 8 and 9. There it is argued that they support the view that subjectless imperatives have remote structures containing subjects. Similarly there are subjectless curses:

(iii)   Damn those guys!

(iv)   Damn $\left\{ \begin{matrix} \text{him} \\ \text{*he} \end{matrix} \right\}$!

And there are such exclamations as:

  (v)   How wonderful to live in a place without bats!
  (vi)   Oh to be able to read minds!

Main clauses contrast with *subordinate clauses*, those embedded in other clauses. Subordinate clauses in English occur much more commonly without subjects, as we see later.

PROBLEMS

1. Try to explain why the example

 (i) *Talk to me about you.

is ill-formed, while the example

(ii) Sandra talked to me about you.

is not.

2. What does the account of imperatives given in this chapter suggest about curses like:

 (i) Damn $\left\{ \begin{array}{l} \text{you} \\ \text{*yourself} \end{array} \right\}$!

(ii) Darn $\left\{ \begin{array}{l} \text{you} \\ \text{*yourself} \end{array} \right\}$!

3. Explain the difference between

 (i) I argued with Sally about myself.

and

(ii) *Argue with Sally about myself.

CHAPTER 8 JUSTIFICATION
FOR REMOTE STRUCTURES

PREVIEW

In the preceding chapter, it was claimed that superficially subjectless imperative sentences were associated with remote structures containing necessarily second person subjects. The justifications for this claim involved regularities concerning agenthood and true reflexives. In this chapter, four distinct phenomena which interact with imperatives are examined: the element *own*, idioms like *crane one's neck*, predicate nominals, and adverbial reflexives like *by oneself*. If viewed exclusively from the point of view of surface structures, these present anomalies for otherwise valid generalizations just when found in subjectless imperative clauses. We then show how each anomaly vanishes under exactly the set of assumptions about remote structures made for imperative clauses in the previous chapter.

It is not uncommon for those faced with remote structures for the first time to view their postulation with considerable scepticism. They are apt to view remote structures as a trick designed to save wrong rules and false generalizations rather than as a step toward more accurate specification of sentence structure. Such a lack of credulity is not out of place. Since it is a relatively new theoretical idea, the notion of remote structure deserves close scrutiny. Moreover, if no constraints are placed on the postulation of remote structures, almost any proposed rule can be saved from counterexamples. Thus a grammatical description could lose the capability of being empirically disconfirmed. Only claims which can be wrong can be right. Invulnerable descriptions are necessarily contentless.

However, postulation of remote structures is subject to serious constraints. These preclude arbitrary or unreal structures posited for dogmatic or whimsical reasons. The structures postulated for one sort of sentential property must be adequate for others. Thus, in the analysis of subjectless imperatives, we posited remote structures containing second person subjects. This was based on the distribution of reflexives and other pronouns and on the relation between subject NP and agent interpretation. If, however, such *underlying* subjects are a real aspect of the structure of subjectless imperative sentences, one should find that they automatically account for facts not originally invoked as justification.

Consider the form *own*, which occurs in contexts like:

(1) a Joseph lost his own dog.
   b I met my own mother.
   c Charlotte was mean to her own sister.
   d I talked to them about their own careers.

It occurs directly after a pronominal NP which has the genitive case marking,[1] mentioned in Chapter 6 (see note 4 there). This marker normally appears in writing as *'s*. But, as noted earlier, the *pronominal* genitive forms are irregular, consisting of *my*, *your*, *his*, etc.

While occurrence after a genitive NP is a *necessary condition* for the occurrence of *own*, it is by no means *sufficient*:

(2) a *I think that Jack met *my own mother*.
   b *The baron who met you called *your own sister*.
   c *Mary smiled and so *her own mother* laughed.
   d *Harry's own mother* is outside.[2]
   e *If Jack comes late, call *his own office*.

These restrictions on *own* are reminiscent of those governing reflexives. If one substitutes an appropriately agreeing reflexive form for the italicized *own*-containing NP in (2), an ill-formed structure results:

(3) a *I think that Jack met myself.
   b *The baron who met you called yourself.
   c *Mary smiled and so herself laughed.
   d *Herself is outside.
   e *If Jack comes late, call himself.

This might suggest that *own* is also governed by a clause mate condition, that is, that the antecedent of the genitive pronoun in front of *own* must be a clause mate of that genitive pronoun. While generally valid, this does not quite seem to be the case. Many speakers accept as well sentences like:

(4) a Jimmy thinks that his own mother reported him.
   b Joan arranged for her own dog to be sold.

In these, antecedent and genitive pronoun are not clause mates, since there are internal clause boundaries after the verbs *thinks* and *arranged*. Note the impossibility of substituting appropriate reflexives for the *own*-containing NPs here.

We are not at present able to specify the conditions for *own* as sharply as those for reflexives. Nonetheless, in declarative examples the pronoun in front of *own* must agree with[3] its coreferent antecedent:

(5) a   I talked to my own brother.
      b   *I talked to your own brother.
      c   You talked to your own brother.
      d   *You talked to his own brother.

Consider *own* in imperative sentences and nonsentences like:

(6) a   Help your own mother.
      b   Don't talk to your own friends.
      c   *Visit my own father.
      d   *Ask his own uncle.
      e   *Shave their own cat.

Here, *own* occurs *only after second person pronouns*. Given (5), the examples in (6) follow from the previously needed restriction that the only subjects possessed by imperatives in remote structures are second person ones. Just as this restriction explains the limitation of imperatives to second person reflexives, it explains facts like those in (6) involving *own*. Of course, these comments only refer to forms with subject antecedents; compare:

(7) a   Talk to me about myself.
      b   Talk to me about my own problems.

The postulation of deleted subjects for imperatives not only explains facts about agenthood and facts about reflexives. It also accounts for facts about the behavior of the word *own*. This *dovetailing* of explanatory consequences provides one kind of empirical check on postulations of remote structures. In itself it guards against the introduction of arbitrary or fanciful abstract structures.

Moreover, we have not exhausted the facts which follow from the claim that subjectless imperatives have exclusively second person subjects in remote structures. If one considers expressions like

(8) a   Harry craned his neck.
      b   Mary blinked her eyes.
      c   You stubbed your toe.

a special restriction is noticed. The genitive pronoun after the verb *must agree with the subject NP*:

(9) a   *Harry craned my neck.
      b   *Mary blinked your eyes.
      c   *You stubbed his toe.

There are many expressions subject to this peculiar agreement constraint. Such forms can occur in imperatives:

(10) a Crane your neck.
     b Blink your eyes.
     c Don't stub your toe.

However, the only genitive pronouns which occur postverbally in these sentences are second person ones:

(11) a *Crane his neck..
     b *Blink my eyes.
     c *Don't stub her toe.

This follows automatically from the agreement restriction revealed by (8) and (9), *if* imperatives like (10) have second person subjects in their remote structures and if only such subjects are possible in the remote structures of imperatives. Again, our assumptions explain facts of a kind which did not figure in the original motivations for them.

A further argument of the same kind can be given. Sentences of the form

(12) a John is the kid who called Louise.
     b I am the one who found the evidence.

manifest a special restriction. The NP after the verb *be* (here, in the inflected forms *is*, *am*), traditionally referred to as a *predicate nominal*, cannot contain a coreferent of the subject NP:

(13) a *I am the boy who called me.
     b *She is the one who called her.

Example (13a) is ill-formed because it violates this constraint. Example (13b) is well-formed. But *she* and *her* cannot refer to the same person. Contrast (13b) in this regard with:

(14) She saw the one who called her.

Here, as we expect, *she* and *her* may or may not refer to the same person. Observe further:

(15) a *You are the one who describes you.
     b *You are the one who criticizes you.

Now, sentences like (12) have imperative analogues:

(16) a Don't be the one who describes the body.
     b Don't be the one who criticizes him.

But second person pronouns cannot occur in the predicate nominals of such imperatives:

(17) a *Don't be the one who describes you.
     b *Don't be the one who criticizes you.

This fact is *not* general for pronouns:

(18) a Don't be the one who describes me.
       b Don't be the one who criticizes him.

That second person pronouns cannot occur in such imperatives follows automatically from the constraints noted for sentences like (12), *if*, again, imperatives have deleted subjects which must be second person. That is, the facts in (17) follow from the restriction that sentences like (12) cannot have a coreferent of the subject NP in the predicate nominal. This provides further evidence for the reality of deleted second person subjects in subjectless imperatives.

Additional evidence comes from the properties of a certain class of reflexives. Earlier it was noted that reflexives can be used for emphasis. One case involves the sequence of *by* plus reflexive in the sense of "alone" or "without aid":

(19) a Mary wrote that by herself.
       b He blew up the house by himself.

In this construction, the reflexive must agree with its antecedent:

(20) a *My father did that by themselves.
       b *He ate the whole thing by myself.
       c *She ran away by ourselves.

Within declaratives and interrogatives, the antecedent for this *by* phrase type of reflexive *must be a subject*:

(21) a *I sawed the log by itself.
       b *Joan annoyed Jack by himself.
       c *The policeman threatened them by themselves.
       d *I talked to Bob by himself.
       e *I bought that for Joan by $\begin{Bmatrix} \text{herself} \\ \text{itself} \end{Bmatrix}$.

The rule for the *by* phrase (or, adverbial) reflexive is that it must agree with an antecedent subject NP. Such *by* phrases are found in superficially subjectless imperatives:

(22) a Do it by yourself.
       b Write the letters by yourselves.
       c Go there by yourself.

But only second person reflexives are possible in such clauses:

(23) a *Do it by himself.
       b *Write the letters by themselves.
       c *Go there by herself.

Again, otherwise peculiar facts follow from the single pair of assumptions originally made on different grounds.

The facts gone over do not exhaust those which can be advanced to justify the view that subjectless imperatives have remote structures containing second person subjects. But it is already clear that a large set of otherwise aberrant facts fall naturally into place under this assumption. If the postulation of remote structures were merely an act of desperation to save an incorrect reflexive rule, how could it properly account for several other sets of apparently exceptional facts?

The correlation of correct explanatory consequences can justify assumptions that particular sentences have remote structures distinct from their surface structures. Moreover, it can show what specific properties these remote structures have.

SUMMARY

In this and the preceding chapter, we have seen how five distinct phenomena involve regularities which treat superficially subjectless imperative clauses as if they had exclusively second person subjects. Such grammatical features were used to provide a formal reconstruction of the traditional insight that imperative clauses have "understood" second person subjects. This reconstruction took the form of a claim that imperative clauses have associated with them remote structures which contain second person subjects. These remote structures are related to the subjectless surface structures by a deletion rule. Such an analysis can only be offered within the context of a theory of grammar which rejects the principle of superficial grammar and which allows sentences to have remote structures distinct from their surface structures. The *methodological* insight of the last two chapters is that the postulation of such remote structures is subject to significant confirmation. This is provided when a remote structure posited on a restricted basis of facts explains a variety of anomalies in several independent domains.

NOTES

1. There are further positional requirements. Genitive NPs occur in at least two distinct positions within a larger NP:

(i) a Jack's house was disgusting.
    b A man's home is his castle.

(ii) a The house of my father's (which burned down) was disgusting.

      b A friend of that preacher's was arrested.

Such NPs occur in both *prenominal* and *postnominal* environments within larger NPs. But *own* can only occur in general when the genitive NP is prenominal:

(iii) a Jack's own house was disgusting.

      b *The own house of my father's which burned down was disgusting.

      c *The house of my father's own (which burned down) was disgusting.

Marginal apparent exceptions include:

(iv) I want a barn of my own.

2. Examples like (2d) (cf. (iiia) in note 1) are well-formed when there is strong stress on *own*. This construction, in which the NP before *own* need not be a pronoun and hence need not have an antecedent, is probably distinct from that discussed in the text. It is usable only in contexts where the possessor NP is contrasted with some other NP. One would not begin a discourse with (iiia). But it would be natural in context with:

(i) The house Jack worked in was spotless.

3. This agreement may also be described by the same rule, Pronoun Agreement, which serves for reflexive pronouns and nongenitive, nonreflexive pronouns. It would take us beyond the scope of this manual to explore this question.

PROBLEMS

1. Notice that the phrase *on X's own* requires that the pronoun which fills the X position agree with the subject of a sentence. The following sentences illustrate this fact:

(i) John sent Mary a letter on $\left\{ \begin{array}{l} \text{his} \\ \text{*her} \end{array} \right\}$ own.

(ii) I visited the prince on $\left\{ \begin{array}{l} \text{my} \\ \text{*his} \end{array} \right\}$ own.

Make use of this fact to support the existence of second person subjects in the remote structures of imperatives.

2. The following sentences are well-formed:

(i) $\left\{ \begin{array}{l} \text{I} \\ \text{Fred} \\ \text{The nurse} \\ \text{Those doctors} \end{array} \right\}$ analyzed you patients.

However, the following is ill-formed:

(ii) *You analyzed you patients.

How does the ill-formedness of (iii) support our remote structure analysis of imperatives?

(iii) *Analyze you patients.

3. Consider the following sentences:

(i) Did John do $\left\{\begin{array}{l}\text{his} \\ \text{*your} \\ \text{*my} \\ \text{*their} \\ \text{*our}\end{array}\right\}$ best?

(ii) Did Sally do $\left\{\begin{array}{l}\text{her} \\ \text{*his} \\ \text{*your} \\ \text{*my} \\ \text{*their} \\ \text{*our}\end{array}\right\}$ best?

(iii) Did you do $\left\{\begin{array}{l}\text{your} \\ \text{*my} \\ \text{*his} \\ \text{*her} \\ \text{*their} \\ \text{*our}\end{array}\right\}$ best?

How can the regularity illustrated in (i)–(iii) be used to support the remote structure analysis of imperatives as containing a second person subject?

4. In the text we have illustrated a variety of idiomatic expressions like *crane X's neck, stub X's toe, blink X's eyes* which have a special property; namely, part of the idiom (that part in the *X* position) must be a pronoun which agrees with the subject of the idiomatic expression. Try to find at least ten other such expressions distinct from those in the text.

CHAPTER 9 FURTHER SPECIALIZED DELETION RULES

PREVIEW

In the preceding two chapters, we showed how the presence in remote structure of subjects of imperative clauses interacts with a variety of phenomena including reflexivization, *own*, etc., to explain several otherwise peculiar and anomalous distributions. We suggested that an imperative deletion rule (called I Deletion) accounts for the absence of such subjects in the superficial structure of various imperative clauses. The explanation follows because this type of deletion rule permits such clauses to have (particular kinds of) subjects in remote structure, even though they lack them in their actual strings of words. In the present chapter, we indicate how a formally identical analysis, recognizing two deletion rules parallel to I Deletion, has identical consequences with respect to the same phenomena. Thus, the theoretical approach to subjectless imperative clauses, involving subject-containing remote structures and a deletion rule, is shown to be independently justifiable.

We have seen in Chapters 7 and 8 how apparently exceptional phenomena are regularized if one assumes that superficially subjectless imperative clauses have remote structures containing (exclusively second person) subjects. This requires the postulation of a rule to delete such subjects. More fundamentally, it requires adoption of a conception of grammatical structure in which sentences have remote structures as well as surface structures.

Is the deletion relevant for imperative sentences—call it *Imperative Deletion* (I Deletion)—a unique sort of grammatical process? It is not. Consider:

(1) a Praise yourself once and everyone says you are an egomaniac.
b Try to improve yourself and they kick you out.

Once more we find reflexive forms with no antecedents in surface structure. Sentences like (1) involve a pair of clauses linked by the word *and*, with the initial clauses subjectless. Here again is a phenomenon seemingly linked to second person forms. However, while sentences like (1) involve forms which are *morphologically* the same as second person forms, these words are not *semantically* second person. Such sentences do not involve statements about the particular person(s) addressed. Rather they express lawlike regularities whose range of applicability includes the person addressed. Sentences like (1) are essentially[1] paraphrases of, and more colloquial variants of:

(2) a Praise oneself once and everyone says one is an egomaniac.
b Try to improve oneself and they kick one out.

These contain the explicitly third person forms *oneself* and *one*.[2] Notice the agreement form of *be* in (2a) is *is* instead of the *are* of (1a). In colloquial styles, there is a standard substitution of *you* for *one*, *yourself* for *oneself*, *your* for *one's*, etc. From this point of view, sentences like (1) are really variants of those like (2). They do not involve semantically second person elements at all. Put differently, the so-called second person pronouns in English are homonymous representatives of two different sorts of elements.

The sentences in (1) and (2) involve reflexives with no visible antecedents. One can regularize the account of these examples of the *one/you* type. This requires postulating a rule which, in this class of sentences, deletes such subjects from the initial clauses. Since *one/you* is a kind of *general* pronoun, let us call this rule *General Deletion*.

Our analysis of sentences like (1) and (2) is now formally almost identical to that offered for subjectless imperative clauses earlier. Just as imperative sentences must be restricted to underlying second person subjects, these sentences are restricted to underlying general subjects. If this is so, the only reflexives possible in positions like those in (1) and (2) would be general reflexives. And this is true:

(3) *Praise $\left(\begin{array}{l}\text{himself} \\ \text{themselves} \\ \text{yourselves}^3 \\ \text{ourselves} \\ \text{myself}\end{array}\right)$ once and everyone says that $\left(\begin{array}{l}\text{he} \\ \text{they} \\ \text{you} \\ \text{we} \\ \text{I}\end{array}\right)$ $\left(\begin{array}{l}\text{is} \\ \text{are} \\ \text{am}\end{array}\right)$ egotistical.

Just as a deletion analysis explained the restriction of imperative sentences to second person reflexives, similarly such an analysis can explain the restriction in these sentences to general reflexives.

In the discussion of imperatives, the treatment which regularized the reflexive pattern also regularized other restrictions, involving *own*, etc. This is also true in the case of the deletion analysis of sentences such as (1) and (2). *First*, they can contain *own*, but only with a general pronoun:

(4) a Praise $\left\{\begin{matrix} \text{one's} \\ \text{your} \end{matrix}\right\}$ own mother and everyone boos.

   b *Praise $\left\{\begin{matrix} \text{his} \\ \text{my} \\ \text{Jane's} \end{matrix}\right\}$ own mother and everyone boos.

Given remote structures for the first clause containing general subject NPs, the restriction in (4) is a consequence of the regularity that *own* must follow a pronoun which agrees with an antecedent.

Second, as noted earlier, there are idiomatic expressions like *crane X's neck*, etc., in which *X* must be a pronoun agreeing with an antecedent (subject) NP. Just as our analysis of sentences like (1) and (2) predicts, the only pronouns which can fill the *X* position in such idioms in these sentences are the general ones:

(5) a Stub $\left\{\begin{matrix} \text{one's} \\ \text{your} \end{matrix}\right\}$ toe and everyone laughs.

   b *Stub $\left\{\begin{matrix} \text{his} \\ \text{my} \\ \text{their} \\ \text{our} \end{matrix}\right\}$ toe(s) and everyone laughs.

(6) a Crane $\left\{\begin{matrix} \text{one's} \\ \text{your} \end{matrix}\right\}$ neck and everyone says $\left\{\begin{matrix} \text{one} \\ \text{you} \end{matrix}\right\}$ $\left\{\begin{matrix} \text{is} \\ \text{are} \end{matrix}\right\}$ nosy.

   b *Crane $\left\{\begin{matrix} \text{her} \\ \text{our} \\ \text{their} \end{matrix}\right\}$ neck(s) and everyone says $\left\{\begin{matrix} \text{she} \\ \text{we} \\ \text{they} \end{matrix}\right\}$ $\left\{\begin{matrix} \text{is} \\ \text{are} \end{matrix}\right\}$ nosy.

These apparently peculiar restrictions also follow directly from the kind of analysis advocated here, further supporting it. Once General Deletion is postulated, this range of facts is an automatic consequence of the restriction of the first clauses to general subjects.

Third, we saw that the *by* phrase reflexive (*by X self*) had to have the *X* slot filled by a pronoun which agreed with a subject. Hence the advocated analysis of the sentences of this chapter predicts that the only *by* phrases of this type possible in the initial clauses will be those in which *X* is a general pronoun. And this is true:

(7) a Sing by $\left\{\begin{matrix} \text{oneself} \\ \text{yourself} \end{matrix}\right\}$ and nobody applauds.

b *Sing by $\begin{cases} \text{himself} \\ \text{myself} \\ \text{ourselves} \\ \text{themselves} \end{cases}$ and nobody applauds.

An analysis of clauses like (1) and (2) involving remote structures whose initial conjuncts contain general subjects is supported by facts beyond reflexives, just as in the discussion of subjectless imperatives. The notions of remote structure and deletion rule, needed for imperative clauses without surface subjects, are necessary and supportable in the analysis of other sorts of constructions. These notions are not whimsical inventions designed to preserve an incorrect treatment of reflexives, *own*, etc., in the face of apparently exceptional imperative sentences.

Further evidence that the treatment of imperatives is not unique is furnished by another, formally parallel set of constructions. There is a way of making suggestions which utilizes the normally interrogative particle *why* with the negative:

(8) Why don't you go to the movies.

Example (8) can be either a question, requiring an answer specifying the reason, or a suggestion. Such sentences can, naturally, contain reflexives:

(9) a Why don't you improve yourself.
b Why doesn't Bob dress himself.
c Why don't they shoot themselves.

These require no comment at this point. They have proper antecedents, even from the point of view of surface structure. However, there are *why not* suggestion clauses which are subjectless:

(10) a Why not go to the movies.
b Why not call the FBI.

At least they are subjectless in surface structure. Sentences like (10), in contrast to those like (9), can *only* be read as suggestions. They have no interpretation as questions.[4] A further peculiarity of these, beyond the lack of surface subjects, is the absence of the verb *do*, found in (9):

(11) a *Why don't go to the movies.
b *Why do not go to the movies.

Sentences like (10) can contain reflexives:

(12) a Why not shoot yourself.
b Why not devote yourself to charitable works.

Given our previous accounts of imperative clauses and sentences with general subject NPs, we deal with subjectless *why not* suggestion clauses in the same way. We postulate that they also have remote structures containing subjects. This requires recognition of a further deletion rule, call it *Why Not Deletion*. The pronouns in (12) are true second person pronouns, not colloquial forms of general pronouns. It might be assumed that, parallel to imperatives, these *why not* sentences are restricted to second person forms.

This is not exactly the case, however. Most types of reflexives are banned in such sentences:

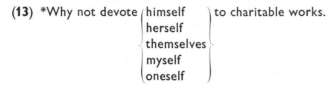

(13) *Why not devote
himself
herself
themselves
myself
oneself
to charitable works.

But it is not true that only second person reflexives can occur:

(14) Why not devote
yourself
yourselves
ourselves
to charitable works.

Initially, it seems strange that both singular and plural second person pronouns are acceptable, but nothing else except the plural *ourselves*. A closer scrutiny of *ourselves*, and more generally of all so called first person plural pronouns, *we, us, our*, etc., suggests that the grouping in (14) is not unnatural. Consider:

(15) a   We are happy.
      b   They criticized us.

Such sentences may seem to have only one meaning. But each is actually ambiguous. The *we, us* must in each case refer to the speaker and one or more other individuals. The ambiguity depends on whether these persons include the individual(s) addressed, or not. Taking (15a) for discussion, and assuming it is addressed to a single hearer, the *we* could refer either to:

(16) a   The speaker and the hearer alone
      b   The speaker and one or more individuals all distinct from the hearer
      c   The speaker, the hearer, and one or more individuals distinct from the hearer

Traditionally, first person plural pronouns with the meaning in (16b) are called *exclusive* first person plurals. Their reference excludes the hearer. Those with meanings like (16a, c) are called *inclusive* first person plurals. English does not mark this distinction morphologically. Many languages have distinct forms, that is, a form which designates the speaker and one or more hearers but not third persons, and another which includes third persons, or perhaps, more restrictively, only third persons.

The key fact about the grouping in (14) is that *ourselves* has a reference which excludes any third persons. It is of the most restrictive type of inclusive first person plural. It designates only the speaker and one or more intended hearers. Setting aside the explicit second person forms *yourself* and *your-selves*, the only pronouns in English with second person reference are the inclusive first person plurals. There is then a generalization which picks out the class of reflexives in (14) from the class of all reflexives. Example (14) contains just those whose referents *include* the second person domain.

Parallel to the treatment of imperatives and general subject NP sentences, one can describe superficially subjectless *why not* suggestion clauses by assuming that they also have remote structures containing subjects. Whereas imperatives had to have remote subjects, exclusively second person, and general subject NP sentences had to have general pronominal subjects, subjectless *why not* clauses must be restricted to remote subjects which include reference to second person. This means that there is a restriction to the remote subjects *you* (singular), *you* (plural) and *we* (inclusive).

Given these assumptions, the grammar will predict just the occurring class of reflexives. The subjects that serve as antecedents will disappear because of Why Not Deletion. Given what is known of the parallel (to reflexives) behavior of *own*, idioms, *by X self*, etc., an analysis involving remote structure and Why Not Deletion should (and does) also predict the following pattern of contrasts:

(17) a Why not call $\begin{Bmatrix} \text{your own wife} \\ \text{your own wives} \\ \text{our own wives} \end{Bmatrix}$.

　　 b *Why not call $\begin{Bmatrix} \text{his own wife} \\ \text{one's own wife} \\ \text{my own wife} \\ \text{their own wives} \end{Bmatrix}$.

(18) a Why not crane $\begin{Bmatrix} \text{your neck} \\ \text{your necks} \\ \text{our necks} \end{Bmatrix}$.

　　 b *Why not crane $\begin{Bmatrix} \begin{Bmatrix} \text{his} \\ \text{her} \\ \text{my} \\ \text{one's} \end{Bmatrix} \text{neck} \\ \text{their necks} \end{Bmatrix}$.

(19) a Why not go there by $\begin{Bmatrix} \text{yourself} \\ \text{yourselves} \\ \text{ourselves} \end{Bmatrix}$.

　　 b *Why not go there by $\begin{Bmatrix} \text{himself} \\ \text{herself} \\ \text{myself} \\ \text{oneself} \\ \text{themselves} \end{Bmatrix}$.

Let us emphasize some general properties of the patterns that have been discovered in imperatives, general subject NP sentences, and *why not* suggestion sentences. In all of these, we have found that certain superficially subjectless clauses behave with respect to various regularities as if they had subjects (of certain restricted types). Within a framework of grammar which restricts linguistic structure to surface structure, such patterns are irreducible anomalies. This hints at the enormous price to be paid for clinging to the principle of superficial grammar (see notes 7 and 9 of Chapter 7). Within a framework assigning sentences both remote structures and surface structures, however, they can be naturally accounted for by *deriving*[5] the subjectless clauses from remote structures containing specified types of subjects. Simultaneously, one will recognize that the regularities which seem to be violated are true of remote structures rather than of surface structures. The logic of this approach should be kept in mind and generalized. It must not be thought that remote structures differ from surface structures only in terms of the deletion of subject NP, or even of NP. We encounter in succeeding chapters other types of deletions. Moreover, we soon see that the relation between remote and surface structure is not identifiable with deletion alone. There are several other types of changes or processes which relate such structures.

SUMMARY

We have introduced General Deletion, Why Not Deletion, and I Deletion. These rules delete fixed types of subjects in limited classes of constructions. The postulation of these rules and the subject-containing remote structures on which they operate regularize otherwise anomalous distributions of elements involving coreferential antecedents and agreements. The line of discussion in this chapter supports the conclusions of the previous two chapters. It shows that deletion rules and surface/remote structure differences are an integral part of English grammar, rather than artificial devices designed to cover up the inadequacy of, for instance, Rule 1G.

NOTES

1. The word *essentially* is not redundant here. There seem to be subtle differences between the two types:

(i)   a In the Congo, you don't live in the same house as your wife.
       b In the Congo, one doesn't live in the same house as one's wife.

(ii) a ?It is said that in the Congo you don't live in the same house as your wife.

b It is said that in the Congo one doesn't live in the same house as one's wife.

The difference between (ia) and (ib) is, we believe, that in choosing the *you* forms the speaker claims direct knowledge underlying his statement of the law expressed. Hence (ia) is natural from one who is from the Congo, has lived there, has studied it intensely, etc., while (ib) is natural, if formal, for anyone under any conditions. Just so, (iia) but not (iib) is anomalous or odd, as indicated by the question mark, because this "direct knowledge" assumption conflicts with the meaning of *it is said*. The latter is used to state things not known directly as the result of experience, but through hearsay, etc.

2. These were the forms discussed in Chapter 6, note 9 in terms of the logical notion of variable.

3. Here the example with plural *yourselves* is ill-formed, unlike the one with the singular *yourself*. This follows because the only variant of general *one* with *you* is singular. Hence the form in the text must be interpreted as a true second person form. It is ill-formed for the same reason all of the other nongeneral forms are.

4. There is another class of subjectless clauses involving initial *why*. These are superficially like (10), except that they lack the negative element:

(i) Why go to the movies.
(ii) Why call the FBI.

One's first reaction may be that these are standard questions, peculiar only in lacking subjects. However, examples like (i) and (ii) do not function as questions. They express disagreement, doubt, or objection. Example (i), for example, is appropriately used only after someone has indicated an intention to go to the movies.

5. The notion of *deriving* one structure from another is a fundamental one in a theory which recognizes remote as well as surface structures. Most of the rest of this manual is devoted to elaborating and clarifying this idea.

PROBLEMS

1. Consider the following examples:

(i) How about criticizing ourselves.
(ii) It is time to dress yourself.
(iii) It is too hot to bake yourself in the sun.
(iv) It is a drag to have to shave myself.

Construct arguments showing that deleted subjects are involved in this range of constructions. In your answers, try to specify what type of subject is required for each case.

2. Consider the following sentences:

(i) Why go to the movies.
(ii) Why call the FBI.

These sentences are parallel to the *why not* constructions in the text. Construct arguments parallel to those in the text to show that these constructions also involve subject deletion.

3. Use the contrast illustrated by

(i)
$$\left\{ \begin{array}{l} \text{I} \\ \text{James} \\ \text{Sally} \\ \text{They} \\ \text{*You} \end{array} \right\} \text{analyzed you both.}$$

to construct an argument for the presence of subjects in the remote structure of subjectless *why not* suggestion clauses.

CHAPTER 10 **A NEW TYPE OF DELETION RULE**

PREVIEW

Up to now we have considered transformational rules which delete certain constituents irrespective of their relationship to other NP constituents in the structure. In this chapter, a new kind of deletion rule is encountered. This kind deletes a designated NP only if it is coreferential to another NP. These operations are called *controlled* deletions.

The specific controlled deletion rule presented in this chapter, *Conjoined Coreferential Subject Deletion* (CCS Deletion), enables a coherent account to be presented of certain sentences exhibiting reflexive pronouns but no apparent clause mate antecedents. The interaction of CCS Deletion and Rule 1G accounts for these facts. The interaction of CCS Deletion with *crane X's neck* type idioms and with the *by* phrase reflexive construction also automatically accounts for what would otherwise be exceptions to certain generalizations.

Finally, the interaction of CCS Deletion with I Deletion and with Why Not Deletion is examined. Given the remote structure analyses required by the postulation of CCS, many sentence types are regular which would otherwise have to be regarded as anomalous. The data examined provide independent justification for I Deletion and Why Not Deletion.

We have been considering deletion rules which obliterate designated NPs from the remote trees of certain constructions. These interact with a host of phenomena involving coreferent and agreement antecedents. I Deletion, General Deletion, and Why Not Deletion share the property that they delete the (remote) subjects of clauses. Furthermore, the NPs which are deleted need not necessarily be in any particular relation to any other NPs in the structure. Such deletion rules can be called *uncontrolled deletion rules*.

English also has deletion rules which erase NPs from remote structures only if these NPs are coreferential to certain other NPs in the same structure. The second or controlling NP is called the *controller*. Such rules are called *controlled deletion rules*.

The need for such rules appears from examples like:

(1) a   John$_i$ started out as a trumpet player and then he$_i$ learned piano.
     b   John started out as a trumpet player and then learned piano.

In (1a), *John$_i$* and *he$_i$* are coreferential. Example (1b) shows that there are sentences, parallel to (1a) differing only in the absence of the subject NP of the *then* clause. A natural suggestion would be that sentences like (1b) are derived from remote structures like (1a). The subject of the initial clause is the controller for the deletion. For such deletion to occur, both the controller and the NP to be deleted must be subjects:

(2) a   John hired Americans$_i$ and then Frank started hiring them$_i$.
     b   *John hired Americans$_i$ and then Frank started hiring.
     c   John hired Americans$_i$ and then they$_i$ started hiring Turks.
     d   *John hired Americans$_i$ and then started hiring Turks.

Despite the star, (2d) is well-formed. But only on a reading in which the deleted NP is a coreferent of *John*. The star indicates that (2d) is not derivable from a structure like (2c). The pair *Americans$_i$,they$_i$* in (2c) is not susceptible to deletion because *Americans$_i$* is not the subject of its clause.[1]

This controlled NP erasure rule applies when the second clause is introduced by the conjunction *and* or *but*, usually followed by an adverbial element like *then, immediately*, etc.:

(3) a   Jim hired Americans and then started hiring Turks.
     b   Jim hired Americans but then started hiring Turks.
     c   Jim hired Americans and immediately after started hiring Turks.

Let us refer to this operation as *Conjoined Coreferential Subject Deletion* (CCS Deletion).

Several facts would be inexplicable if one were unable to appeal to the interaction between CCS Deletion and other rules, such as that for reflexives. Reflexive marking does not take place between coreferents in distinct conjoined clauses:

(4)   a   John$_i$ helped Mary and then he$_i$ helped Sally.
     b   *John$_i$ helped Mary and then himself$_i$ helped Sally.
     c   John$_i$ helped Mary and then Sally helped him$_i$.
     d   *John$_i$ helped Mary and then Sally helped himself$_i$.

This follows from previous assumptions. The pairs *John$_i$,he$_i$* in (4a) and *John$_i$,him$_i$* in (4c) are not clause mates. This accounts for the ungrammaticality of the sequences (4b,d). But what of:

(5)   a   John$_i$ started out on piano and then taught himself$_i$ guitar.
     b   Margo$_i$ got her children off to school and then treated herself$_i$ to a
        beer.

In (5) the pairs *John$_i$,himself$_i$* and *Margo$_i$,herself$_i$* are apparent exceptions to the conditions required to determine reflexives. Although the members of each pair are coreferential, they are not clause mates. How is it possible to regularize a description in which (4d) is ill-formed but (5a) grammatical? The difficulty only arises if one takes the surface structure of (5a) to be the only structure relevant for the assignment of reflexive form. We suggest that examples like (5a) result from the operation of CCS Deletion on a structure like:

(6)   [John$_i$ started out on piano and then he$_i$ taught him$_i$ guitar]

From this structure, the subject pronoun of the second clause, *he$_i$*, has been deleted, with *John$_i$* the controller. But at this level, *he$_i$* can function as the antecedent coreferent clause mate of *him$_i$*, prior to its deletion. If Rule 1G operates not on (5a) but on the remote structure in (6), the apparent paradox engendered by the examples in (5) disappears. The fact that the object of *taught* in (6) must ultimately have reflexive form is predicted without abandoning the clause mate condition. Examples like (5) constitute regular instances of reflexive marking when one perceives that the relevant structure for such marking is a level of remote structure.

    Just as CCS Deletion plays a key role in regularizing apparent irregularities in the distribution of reflexives, it plays a similar role with idioms. Recall that there are idioms like *crane X's neck, blink X's eyes*, etc., in which the *X* takes the form of a genitive pronoun agreeing with the subject NP of the clause:

(7)   a   Harry craned his neck.
     b   Mary held her breath.
     c   *John blinked $\begin{Bmatrix} \text{her} \\ \text{their} \\ \text{my} \\ \text{your} \end{Bmatrix}$ eyes.

This agreement must be between clause mates:

(8) a *Harry$_i$ said that Mary craned his$_i$ neck.
  b *When Harry$_i$ arrives, I will crane his$_i$ neck.

On the face of it then, examples like

(9) Bill$_i$ asked the question and then held his$_i$ breath.

are apparent exceptions to these regularities. If the agreeing pair of NPs in (9) is taken to be $Bill_i$,his_i, then (9) does not fall under the regularities governing examples like (7). Moreover, if attention is restricted to surface strings of words, there is no choice but to take the relevant pair to be these two NPs. Given the notion of remote structures and the rule CCS Deletion, however, the relevant pair can be taken to be he_i,his_i in (10):

(10) [Bill$_i$ asked the question and then he$_i$ held his$_i$ breath]

Here, he_i will be deleted by CCS Deletion, with $Bill_i$ the controller. There is then nothing remarkable about the agreement which the idiom requires. CCS Deletion dissolves the apparent anomalies.

Consider the behavior of the sequence *by* plus reflexive. The antecedent of the reflexive pronoun must be a subject. In addition, the antecedent subject must be a clause mate of the reflexive word:

(11) a *John$_i$ wrote the first part with Mary and then she finished it by himself$_i$.
  b *John$_i$ thinks that Mary did it by himself$_i$.
  c *If Mary$_i$ decides to leave, John will leave by herself$_i$.

The following sentences are seeming exceptions to the regular behavior of the *by* phrase reflexive when only the surface structure is examined:

(12) a John$_i$ wrote the first part with Mary and then finished it by himself$_i$.
  b John$_i$ promised to go with Mary and then went by himself$_i$.

But these fall under the relevant regularities once it is seen that their remote structures are like:

(13) [John$_i$ promised to go with Mary and then he$_i$ went by himself$_i$]

These remote structures are suitable for the application of CCS Deletion.

The parallelism between the interactions of CCS Deletion and ordinary reflexives, idioms, and *by* phrase reflexives needs no stress. In each case, the same analysis involving CCS Deletion eliminates what would otherwise be an unexplained breakdown in generalizations.

The possibility exists that I Deletion, General Deletion, and Why Not Deletion might interact with the controlled deletion rule, CCS Deletion, to further buttress the approach to grammatical description introduced here. I Deletion relates remote structures like (14a) to surface strings like (14b):

(14) a [you find a house]
      b Find a house.

Consider then:

(15) a Find a house and then get yourself a bank loan.
      b Learn a trade and then make a name for yourself.
      c Close the door and then pour yourself a drink.

These have the look of sentences derived by CCS Deletion. But this rule will optionally delete the subject pronoun of the rightmost of two clauses conjoined by *and* or *but* only if that subject is coreferential with the subject of the preceding clause. The sentences in (15) have subjects in neither clause. This raises the question of how CCS Deletion could operate.

Examine the second clauses in (15). On the basis of their agenthood properties and because of the existence of the second person reflexives in them, their remote structures (subject to CCS Deletion) would have to be:

(16) a [and then you get you a bank loan]
      b [and then you make a name for you]
      c [and then you pour you a drink]

In all cases, the subject is second person. If sentences like (15) are derived by CCS Deletion, the subjects of the first clauses must also be second person. But this is important because in imperative clauses I Deletion will delete second person subjects. Hence, it causes no difficulty to posit for sentence (15a) an overall remote structure of the form:

(17) [you find a house and then you get you a bank loan]

The first clause subject acts as a controller for the deletion of the rightmost clause subject under CCS Deletion. The first clause subject will then be deleted by the independently needed I Deletion. These two rules dovetail perfectly. Thus CCS Deletion provides additional support for the existence of I Deletion. This follows since to make the derivation of (15a) from (17) work, CCS Deletion must apply. But for it to apply, one needs a structure like (17), containing an initial clause subject which does not show up in the surface structure. Therefore some rule must delete it. I Deletion is just what is needed.

Next recall Why Not Deletion, which is responsible for the missing subjects in:

(18) a Why not pour yourself a drink.
      b Why not pour yourselves drinks.
      c Why not pour ourselves drinks.

d *Why not pour $\begin{Bmatrix} \text{himself} \\ \text{herself} \\ \text{myself} \\ \text{themselves} \end{Bmatrix}$ $\begin{Bmatrix} \text{a drink} \\ \text{drinks} \end{Bmatrix}$.

We can find more complex sentences and nonsentences like:

(19) a   Why not buy a lot and then build $\begin{Bmatrix} \text{yourself} \\ \text{yourselves} \\ \text{ourselves} \end{Bmatrix}$ a house on it.

b   *Why not buy a lot and then build $\begin{Bmatrix} \text{himself} \\ \text{herself} \\ \text{myself} \\ \text{oneself} \\ \text{themselves} \end{Bmatrix}$ a house on it.

These examples provide an opportunity to construct a new argument for Why Not Deletion of the same sort just provided for I Deletion.

One wants to explain the lack of subjects in the *then* clauses in terms of CCS Deletion. This forces one to posit subjects in the first clauses. Since these have no surface structure realizations, they must be deleted by some rule. And Why Not Deletion is available to do the job. Further, we recall that Why Not Deletion can only delete subjects with second person reference. Therefore, if examples like (19a) are derived by a combination of CCS Deletion and Why Not Deletion, the fact that only second person reflexives can occur in such examples is explained, as follows. The reflexives must be coreferential with clause mate antecedents. The latter are the subjects deleted by CCS Deletion. These subjects must be coreferential with the CCS Deletion controllers. The latter are the subjects of the initial clauses. These must in turn be deleted by Why Not Deletion, which can only delete subjects with second person reference. Therefore, if the only subjects which can be deleted by Why Not Deletion must have second person reference, the reflexives which are necessarily linked to them by two chains of coreference must also have it. The facts in (19), involving CCS Deletion, thus provide additional support for Why Not Deletion, and for CCS Deletion as well.

The interactions of CCS Deletion with I Deletion and Why Not Deletion provide an illustration of the power and explanatory insight offered by an approach to grammar which goes beyond surface facts to a consideration of the remote structures underlying the superficial strings of words. Again we stress how analyses posited on the basis of one range of facts serve to explicate others. This further illustrates an earlier comment, namely, that such correlations limit the potential misuse of remote structures.

SUMMARY

This chapter introduced a controlled deletion rule named CCS Deletion. This transformation differs from previously examined deletion rules. It operates only when a controller NP is present. Both the controller and the NP to be deleted must be subjects of conjoined clauses. The leftmost is the controller.

Examples are presented containing conjoined clauses from which NPs have been deleted, apparently because of the operation of CCS Deletion. The presence of a controller NP in the appropriate position of the initial clause would trigger application of CCS Deletion in the final clause. The apparent difficulty is that in the actual surface structures, no controller NPs are present in the initial clauses. However, this difficulty is only apparent. Postulating controller NPs at a more remote level of structure satisfies the conditions for CCS Deletion. It requires no special statements since there are rules which operate independently to delete the CCS Deletion controller NP, namely, I Deletion and Why Not Deletion. Thus, the particular sentences discussed are not only shown to be regular consequences of the grammar rather than anomalies, but they provide independent evidence for I Deletion and Why Not Deletion.

The complex interactions between CCS Deletion, I Deletion, and Why Not Deletion illustrate the explanatory power of an approach to grammar involving the recognition of remote structures and rules relating these to actual strings of words.

NOTES

1. The controller must not only be a subject in the leftmost clause but must be the subject of that whole clause:

(**i**)   *Jack$_i$ told me that Joan$_j$ was sick and then criticized herself$_j$.
(**ii**)   *Jack$_i$ demanded that I leave and then justified myself.

Here *Joan$_j$* is a subject in (i), *I* in (ii), but *Jack$_i$* is the main clause subject and the only possible controller under CCS Deletion.

PROBLEMS

1. Why is the following example ill-formed?

(**i**)   *Throckmorton called Betty and then defended herself.

2. How would you account for the well-formedness of the italicized expression in this example,

(**i**)   Why not buy a shovel and then *do your best* to dig a proper grave.

taking into account the ill-formedness of:

(ii) *John bought a shovel and then did your best to dig a proper grave.

3. We have provided a CCS Deletion analysis for examples like:

  (i) Jack bought a gun and then shot himself.

How do the regularities illustrated in the following examples support such an analysis?

(ii) Jimmy bought a gun before shooting $\left\{\begin{array}{l}\text{himself}\\ \text{*myself}\\ \text{*yourself}\\ \text{*herself}\\ \text{*themselves}\\ \text{*ourselves}\end{array}\right\}$.

(iii) Francis went to Chicago and
then bought a gun before shooting $\left\{\begin{array}{l}\text{himself}\\ \text{*myself}\\ \text{*yourself}\\ \text{*herself}\\ \text{*themselves}\\ \text{*ourselves}\end{array}\right\}$.

CHAPTER 11 ANOTHER CONTROLLED DELETION RULE

PREVIEW

In this chapter, an apparent mystery concerning the infinitival complements which follow the verb *promise* is examined. Sentences like *I promised Bob to criticize myself* seem to suggest, given our earlier discussions, that *I* and *myself* are clause mates. This raises a problem for examples like **I promised Bob$_i$ to criticize himself$_i$*. If *I* and *myself* are clause mates in the former, then *Bob* and *himself* are clause mates in the latter, and the sequence should be well-formed. However, the well-formed version requires a nonreflexive: *I promised Bob$_i$ to criticize him$_i$*. This paradox dissolves in a theory of grammatical structure which appeals to remote structures. In the course of the discussion, another controlled deletion rule, called *Equi*, is introduced. This rule interacts in several ways with the deletion rules examined in previous chapters. These interactions provide independent evidence for the existence of remote structures and further support for the earlier deletion rules.

In the preceding chapter we encountered a deletion rule which removed a pronoun only if a coreferential NP (the controller) existed somewhere in the structure submitted to the rule. It is convenient to speak of such NPs as *triggering* deletion or as being the *trigger*. Henceforth, we use the terms *control(ler)* and *trigger* interchangeably.

There is another rule in English which involves the deletion of NPs subject to the existence of a controller. Consider:

(1) I promised Bob to criticize myself.

The reflexive pronoun *myself* in (1), with its coreferential antecedent *I* in subject position, suggests that (1) as a whole is a single clause. Suppose this were so. Then, if one were to substitute for *myself* the reflexive pronoun *himself*, the resultant sentence would also be well-formed. This would follow since *himself* would have *Bob* as a coreferential clause mate antecedent.

However, substitution of *himself* yields an ungrammatical sequence:

(2) *I promised Bob$_i$ to criticize himself$_i$.

To correct sequences like (2), the postverbal pronoun in the infinitive must be nonreflexive whenever that pronoun is not coreferential to the subject of the main verb:

(3) a I promised Bob$_i$ to help$\begin{Bmatrix} \text{him}_i \\ \text{*himself}_i \end{Bmatrix}$.

b Bob promised Mary$_u$ to help$\begin{Bmatrix} \text{her}_u \\ \text{*herself}_u \end{Bmatrix}$.

c Sheila promised the kids$_m$ to help$\begin{Bmatrix} \text{them}_m \\ \text{*themselves}_m \end{Bmatrix}$.

However, whenever the pronoun in the infinitive of sentences like (3) is coreferential with the subject of the main verb, it must have reflexive form:

(4) a I promised Bob to improve$\begin{Bmatrix} \text{*me} \\ \text{myself} \end{Bmatrix}$.

b Bob$_i$ promised Mary to improve$\begin{Bmatrix} \text{*him}_i \\ \text{himself}_i \end{Bmatrix}$.

c Sheila$_i$ promised the kids to improve$\begin{Bmatrix} \text{*her}_i \\ \text{herself}_i \end{Bmatrix}$.

We appear to be on the horns of a dilemma. The examples in (4) act as if the coreferential pairs were clause mates, while the apparently parallel examples in (3) act as if the coreferential pairs were not clause mates. Both can't be true. Earlier, recourse to remote structure provided explanations for certain paradoxes involving reflexives (see Chapter 7). Let us see if a similar theoretical move will regularize the facts of sentences like (3) and (4).

The facts in (3) preclude analyzing sentences like (3) and (4) as simple clauses. The only possibility is to treat (3) and (4) as *complex* clauses. To explore this idea, return to (3a):

(5) I promised Bob$_i$ to help$\begin{Bmatrix} \text{him}_i \\ \text{*himself}_i \end{Bmatrix}$.

Here the infinitival phrase *to help him$_i$* is understood as having an agent that is coreferential with the subject of the main verb, namely, *I*. This is completely general for infinitival phrases with the verb *promise*:

(6) a You promised Bob; to help him;.
      b He promised Bob; to help him;.

In (6) as in (5), the agent of the infinitive is understood to be the same as the individual designated by the subject of *promise*, that is, *you* in (6a) and *he* in (6b). Suppose we postulate a remote structure for such examples in which these understood agents actually appear as subject NPs. Then the remote structure of (5) would be:

(7)

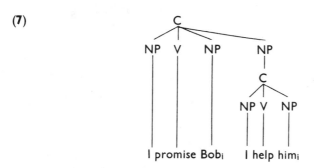

This structure claims that (5) is a complex sentence containing the embedded clause *I help him*. Sentences like (6) would be similarly structured, but with requisite changes in pronouns:

(8)

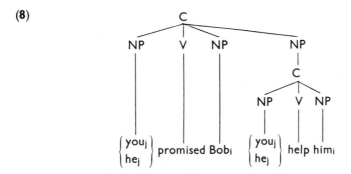

With such remote structures, the facts involving pronoun choice encountered in (3)–(6) can be accounted for. Take (5). Given that the remote structure of (5) is as in (7), the impossibility of a reflexive pronoun coreferential to *Bob* follows from the clause mate requirement in Rule 1G. The object of *promise*, *Bob*, and the object of *help*, *him*, are not clause mates. An analogous explanation holds for (3b,c), which would have trees parallel to (7). Recognition of an embedded clause explains the failure of reflexivization in examples like (3). But what then of those examples in (4), which not only permit but require reflexive form for the object pronoun of the embedded clause? These facts also follow from recognition of embedded clause structures. Consider (4a) above. It would have a remote structure of the form:

(9)

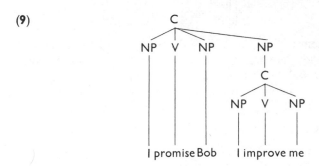

Rule 1G predicts reflexive form for the object of *improve*, since it appears with a coreferential clause mate. When we said earlier that sentences like (1) looked as if they were simple sentences, we did so on the *mistaken* assumption that the coreferential antecedent which triggered the reflexive pronoun, *myself*, was the subject of the main verb *promise*. Given (9), we can see how this is wrong. We now recognize that it is the subject of the embedded clause rather than the subject of the main clause which determines reflexivization in such cases.

Turning to (4b,c), it is easy to understand how the right choice of reflexive forms results from the assumption of remote structures parallel to (9). Consider (4b):

(10)   Bob$_i$ promised Mary to improve himself$_i$.

The understood subject of the infinitive is coreferential to *Bob*. Example (10) would have the remote structure representation:

(11)

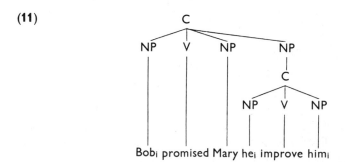

But in (11), the reflexive marking of the object of *improve* follows from the clause mate condition because of the coreferential subject. An analogous analysis holds for (4c).

There is an underlying regularity running through the examples we have been examining. In the remote structures postulated, the subject of the embedded clause has been a coreferent of the main clause subject. Moreover, in no case does the embedded clause subject have a surface structure realization. To account for this, then, it is necessary to postulate a further deletion rule. This will say that, under quite general conditions, the subject NP of an embedded clause is deleted when it is coreferential to the subject of the main clause in which it is directly embedded. Let us call this rule *Equivalent NP Deletion* (for short, Equi). Equi falls into the same class of deletion rules as CCS Deletion. Like the latter, the deletion is controlled by a coreferential antecedent elsewhere in the structure.[1]

One basis for postulating Equi with verbs like *promise* is that it regularizes the facts of reflexivization in examples like (4). It reveals that the reflexive marking is triggered by the embedded clause subject, which Equi deletes, rather than by the main clause subject. Given Equi, further facts about sentences based on *promise* fall under existing regularities. This is true of the behavior of idioms like *hold X's breath* or *crane X's neck*. In Chapter 8 we saw that these were subject to the condition that the pronoun in the position of *X* have an agreeing clause mate antecedent. Observe the following distributions:

(12)   a   I promised Bob to hold $\begin{Bmatrix} my \\ {*}his \\ {*}your \end{Bmatrix}$ breath.

   b   Jane$_i$ promised them to hold $\begin{Bmatrix} her_i \\ {*}their \\ {*}my \end{Bmatrix}$ breath.

The pronoun in the idiom must agree with the subject of the main clause. This distribution of data follows from the independently needed conditions on such idioms if examples like (12) are derived by Equi from remote structures of the sort suggested earlier. The structure relevant for (12a), for instance, would then be:

(13)

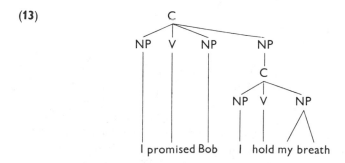

And the fact that the pronoun in the idiom seems to agree with the main clause subject follows from the fact that it really agrees with the subject of its own minimal clause. The latter subject is deleted by Equi because it is a coreferent of the main clause subject. Thus the ill-formed versions in (12a) are, under our Equi analysis of *promise* sentences, ill-formed for exactly the same reasons as clauses of the form:

(14) a *I held his breath.
       b *I held your breath.

They require no special statements or restrictions.

The same considerations apply to other construction types dealt with in Chapters 8 and 9. For example, *own* obeys constraints somewhat parallel to those of reflexives. It will thus follow from the embedding analysis of *promise* sentences that occurrences of *own* in infinitives must agree with the main clause subject, since this subject will have a coreferent in the subordinate clause:

(15) I promised Bob to buy $\begin{pmatrix} \text{my} \\ \text{*your} \\ \text{*his} \end{pmatrix}$ own ticket.

Given the full clause analysis of these infinitives (reduced by Equi), the facts in (15) follow from the independently needed constraints on *own* in simple clauses:

(16) I will buy $\begin{pmatrix} \text{my} \\ \text{*your} \\ \text{*his} \end{pmatrix}$ own ticket.

In Chapter 10, the interaction of CCS Deletion with other rules, in particular, the uncontrolled erasure operations I Deletion and Why Not Deletion, provided independent justification for the latter rules. It also supported the general concept of remote structure. Since Equi is a member of the same class of rules as CCS Deletion, it is worth considering how it interacts with uncontrolled deletions. Consider the interaction of I Deletion and Rule 1G with Equi:

(17) Promise Bob to take care of yourself.

In (17), the reflexive object of *take care of* is known to require an antecedent coreferent clause mate, that is, a *you*. Since no such word occurs in the surface structure, some deletion rule must have operated. The parallelism between examples like (17) and those considered earlier suggests that the rule in question is Equi. However, Equi requires a subject of *promise* to trigger the deletion of the embedded clause subject. Therefore, one must posit a *you* subject for *promise* in examples like (17). This raises a difficulty, since the surface structure reveals no such NP. A further deletion rule is needed. But there already is an appropriate rule, namely, I Deletion. Thus I Deletion deletes the *you* which is required to trigger the deletion of the embedded subject *you*, which is itself in turn required to trigger the reflexive object *yourself*. The fact that I Deletion enables Equi to apply in such sentences as (17) provides independent evidence for the existence of I Deletion. That is, one would have had to create I Deletion just in order to facilitate the operation of Equi in such cases.

Now let us reconsider Why Not Deletion. This too interacts with Equi:

(18) a Why not promise Bob to shoot $\left\{\begin{array}{l}\text{yourself}\\\text{yourselves}\\\text{ourselves}\end{array}\right\}$.

b *Why not promise Bob to shoot $\left\{\begin{array}{l}\text{himself}\\\text{herself}\\\text{myself}\\\text{oneself}\\\text{themselves}\end{array}\right\}$.

The reflexives in (18a) exist in surface structures which provide no co-referential antecedents for them. The antecedents required must be respectively *you* (singular), *you* (plural), and *we* (inclusive). If these forms were the subjects of *shoot* in remote structure, they would certainly give rise to the appropriate reflexive forms. However, since no such subjects exist on the surface, they must have been deleted. This deletion can be brought about by Equi. But this is possible only if the main verb *promise* has as its subjects *you* (singular), *you* (plural), or *we* (inclusive). Remote structures of the following forms would be required for the well-formed examples in (18a):

(19) [Why not $\left\{\begin{array}{l}\text{you (singular)}\\\text{you (plural)}\\\text{we (inclusive)}\end{array}\right\}$ promise Bob ($\left\{\begin{array}{l}\text{you (singular)}\\\text{you (plural)}\\\text{we (inclusive)}\end{array}\right\}$ shoot $\left\{\begin{array}{l}\text{you}\\\text{you}\\\text{us}\end{array}\right\}$)]

The subject NPs in the embedded clause will determine the object reflexives in the same clause. Then these subject NPs will correctly delete by Equi under coreference to the subject NPs of the main clause. However, the main clause subject NPs must themselves delete since they have no reflexes in surface structure. But we already have recognized a rule which can carry out the needed erasure, namely, Why Not Deletion. This will delete the correct set of main clause subject NPs, which are in turn needed to trigger the erasure of the embedded clause subject NPs under Equi. Thus Equi phenomena provide further support for Why Not Deletion.

The role of Why Not Deletion in the derivation of examples like (18a) helps to explain the ill-formedness of those like (18b). This follows because the embedded clause reflexives require embedded clause subject antecedents (*he, she, I, one,* and *they*). If these are coreferential to the main clause subjects, Equi will certainly delete them. However, the main clause subjects must also be deleted. And there is no rule to accomplish that, since these do not meet the conditions for Why Not Deletion.

A final example of the interaction between Equi and another deletion rule is revealed by:

(20) Promise your creditors to shoot yourself and everyone thinks you are crazy.

In the pre-*and* clause of (20), the reflexive requires a coreferent antecedent as a clause mate. This means that the subordinate clause in the first conjunct must have an underlying form like:

(21) [you shoot you]

Evidently, however, the subject NP of this clause must be deleted. The obvious candidate for this job is Equi. It requires as controller the subject of the immediately higher clause. Thus a remote structure containing *you* as subject of *promise* is necessary. This *you* will control the deletion of the subject of the embedded clause. But it too must be deleted, since it has no realization in the surface structure. Thus a rule is necessary to delete the general pronoun *you* in such sentences. Such a rule is already available, that called General Deletion in Chapter 9. This rule is needed independently of sentences involving *promise* to describe sentences like:

(22) Praise yourself once and everyone thinks you are an egomaniac.

Since General Deletion is needed to permit Equi to operate properly in (20), Equi further supports the existence of General Deletion as well as I Deletion and Why Not Deletion.

In this chapter, we introduced Equi exclusively on the basis of constructions involving the main verb *promise*. Once motivated, it is not hard to see that the same rule, deleting the subjects of subordinate clauses, operates with other main clause verbs and adjectives:

(23) a   Jack wanted Mary to go.
     b   *Jack$_i$ wanted him$_i$ to go. $\Longrightarrow$ Jack wanted to go.

(24) a   Jack arranged for Betty to stay.
     b   *Jack$_i$ arranged for him$_i$ to stay. $\Longrightarrow$ Jack arranged to stay.

(25) a   I am anxious for you to win.
     b   *I am anxious for me to win. $\Longrightarrow$ I am anxious to win.

(26) a   They intended for her to fail.
     b   *They$_i$ intended for them$_i$ to fail. $\Longrightarrow$ They intended to fail.

In all these cases, the controller is the subject of the main clause, just as with *promise*.

SUMMARY

Based upon the behavior of reflexive pronouns in the infinitival complements of verbs like *promise*, a new argument for postulating remote structures was given. This involved recognition of the rule Equi. We indicated how the assumptions relevant to properly predict reflexive facts also correctly deal with facts relating to the element *own* and to idioms like *hold X's breath*, when these occur in the infinitival complements of *promise*. Only a recognition of Equi operating on a level of remote structure makes it possible to relate the distribution of pronouns in these constructions to earlier discussions. Given Equi, the patterns uncovered with *promise* turn out to be automatic results of the same clause mate conditions needed for simpler clauses. Appeal to remote structure permits superficial anomalies to be reduced to underlying generalizations.

The argument for Equi and remote structures relating to Equi was further strengthened by studying how Equi constructions interact with previous deletion rules. Each such interaction points up how a superficially intricate distribution of forms is the predictable consequence of the operation of independently needed rules on the appropriate remote structures.

NOTES

1. The verb *promise* can occur with subordinate clauses containing subjects, but these are *that* clauses rather than infinitives:

(i) Jack$_i$ promised that he$_i$ would come early.

In such cases, the subordinate subject need not be a coreferent of the main clause subject (as it is in (i)):

(ii) Jack promised that Mary would come early.

Examples like (ii) point up the fact that the overall grammar must restrict the class of infinitival clauses with *promise* to just those which meet the co-reference conditions for Equi:

(iii) *Jack promised (for) Mary to come early.

The best method for accomplishing this kind of constraint is unclear. One possibility is to have Equi *optionally* apply to *that* clauses like those in (i). If it does not apply, well-formed structures still result. If it does apply, one can assume that, with *promise* and many other verbs, there is an obligatory rule specifying that a subjectless subordinate clause takes on infinitival form.

PROBLEMS

1. Account for the possible and impossible reflexive distribution in the following example:

(i) Sally won the lottery and then promised Martin to improve $\begin{Bmatrix} \text{herself} \\ \text{*himself} \\ \text{*yourself} \end{Bmatrix}$.

2. Explain the range of possible pronouns in the example:

(i) Vow to do $\begin{Bmatrix} \text{your} \\ \text{*my} \\ \text{*his} \\ \text{*her} \end{Bmatrix}$ best.

3. Consider the following example:

(i) Promise to vow to improve yourself.

Postulate a remote structure for this example and give as complete an account as you can of the deletion rules which must apply to form the surface structure.

PART II ON THE NATURE OF THE GRAMMAR

CHAPTER 12 INITIAL TREES

PREVIEW

A language can be depicted as a system for describing the set of sentences which make it up. Up to this point, various fragments and aspects of this system for English have been treated. We have considered pronoun distributions, considered the way constituent structure can be represented, seen the necessity for recognizing remote structures, and hence realized the need for rules which change or deform remote structures into surface forms. The discussion so far has suffered, however, from excessive attention to segments of the system and a lack of focus on the system as a whole. This and immediately following chapters will attempt to rectify this by sketching some of the general outlines of the grammatical system we assume underlies the grammar of English.

We begin with an inquiry into the question of the number of remote structures that are associated with particular sentences. Up to this point, we have tacitly given the impression that the number might be one. It is now seen that this is incorrect. This realization is connected to the question of whether the rules which change trees into derived trees all apply *simultaneously* to some single remote tree or whether they apply *successively*. If they apply successively, each application produces a tree which is distinct both from the previous one and from the one to follow. This leads to a conception in which each sentence is associated with a multiplicity of remote trees. Given that the rules do apply successively, the question of the relative order in which they apply arises.

We are thus led to see each sentence as consisting of a sequence of trees. Such a sequence is defined as a *derivation*. Each derivation has an *initial tree*, which is the maximally remote tree for that sentence, and a *surface tree*, which is the minimally remote tree. The surface structure is the representation of the actual string of words. We then examine the relationship between the concepts of initial and surface tree and the fact that the set of sentences is infinite.

Our method up to now has been to focus attention on certain types of sentences and nonsentences of English and to extract from their grammatical behavior certain generalizations. Whatever success has been achieved has been due to a willingness to move away from the surface facts of presented examples to more abstract structures. Most of the grammatical regularities we have proposed have ended up applying to remote structures rather than to actual strings of words making up sentences. It then becomes obligatory to posit various rules, which we called transformations, to link remote structures to the actual strings of words through which sentences are superficially manifested.

For example, we dealt with sentences like:

(1) Why not devote ourselves to charitable works.

which have to be related to a remote structure of the form

(2) [Why we$_i$ not devote us$_i$ to charitable works]

by (i) a rule which determines reflexive form for one of two coreferent NPs which are clause mates and by (ii) a rule which deletes the subject NP (necessarily involving reference to second person) of certain "suggestion" clauses. The former is Rule 1G(a), the latter Why Not Deletion. The arguments given for relating sentences like (1) to remote structures like (2) are, to our minds, convincing. Thus the notions *remote structure* and *deletion rule* receive considerable initial support. The reader may have appropriately suspected, however, that the kind of discussions provided so far has only touched the tip of a substantial theoretical iceberg.

To provide a coherent account of the overall nature of grammatical structure, we must view the kinds of analyses we have been proposing as embedded within a particular overall theoretical context. They must be regarded in the light of a conception of grammatical structure which has so far only been hinted at. Our aim at this juncture is to take steps toward making this framework explicit. Then the reader can begin to see the initial analyses we have proposed as parts of an overall system which is, hopefully, a reasonable first approximation to that required for describing English and other natural languages.

A major gap in our treatment has been a failure to consider in any detail the relation between the entire body of information which is a person's knowledge of English and individual examples. A person's language is a whole of which, in some sense, individual sentences like (1) are parts. We need to consider the nature of the whole-part relation. So far, we have been concerned with showing that, in contrast to standard views, sentences are themselves highly complex objects, containing several levels of structure. While we have not finished with the development of this view, we know enough to ask how the individual complex objects called sentences are related to the larger whole of the system of language.

The simplest conception of the connection between an individual sentence and the whole language would take it to be nothing more than the relationship of set membership. This is the relationship which holds, for example, between one randomly chosen jelly bean and the totality of jelly beans in a bag, or between one planet and the totality of planets in some solar system, etc. From this point of view, English would merely be a set of highly structured, multi-faceted objects called sentences.

There is a sense in which a language can be regarded as the totality of its sentences. However, this sense does not get to the heart of characterizing the nature of linguistic systems. The reason has to do with the size of the set of sentences and the fact that linguistic systems must be partially[1] learned and entirely represented in human minds.

The number of sentences in English is unbounded, or infinite. Sentences can be made longer and longer and longer, just as this clause can be extended indefinitely by adding any number of *and longer* phrases to it. In Chapter 14 we examine in detail the mechanisms needed to account for this property of English. Here it is only important to stress the difference between infinite sets like English and finite sets like, for example, the states of the Union. The members of the latter can simply be listed (there are, in fact, 50 of them) but the former cannot (there is no limit to them).

The fact that the number of sentences in English is infinite means that what is mentally represented cannot be the sentences as such. There simply isn't space to store them nor time to learn them. Consequently, what each mature native speaker has represented in his mind cannot be the *infinite* set of sentences. Rather, it must be some *finite* system which has the ability to characterize or specify the infinite set of sentences. We refer to such a finite system as *a grammar*.

Therefore, when our earlier discussion postulated regularities like Rule 1G, I Deletion, etc., it referred to a few of the many elements of a large, complex, overall finite system: the grammar of English.

Implicit in our introduction of the concept of remote structure is a division of a grammar into two fundamentally distinct components. The basis of this division needs to be made explicit.

Possession of the finite system of grammar guarantees in principle knowledge of the infinite set of sentences of the language. Our inquiry has begun to lend more content to the notion 'knowing a sentence' by showing what kind of thing a sentence is. We have seen that each sentence has a superficial constituent structure. Therefore, a grammar of English must associate each string of words with a constituent structure, with what we have called a surface structure tree. We have also begun to see that, however complicated surface structures may seem, they represent only the visible shell of the full sentence. We have presented evidence that a wide range of sentences involve remote structures distinct from their surface structures. Two questions then arise.

First, is it true that every sentence involves levels of remote structure distinct from surface structure? Second, do sentences have only one remote structure? We have implied that the answer to the first question is positive and will now make this view explicit. We assume that every sentence involves remote structure distinct from its surface organization. We will not attempt to argue for this view directly. But it receives support from the rest of this manual in the sense that every sentence to be examined will involve levels of remote organization.

Consider the second question. It would be possible to assume from what has gone before that each sentence has only one remote structure. This would amount to the claim that in all cases the overall grammatical structure of a sentence consists of two and only two trees. But a closer look at the kind of descriptions we have been led to suggests that this cannot be so. Moreover, this is a conclusion which will be strengthened as we proceed. Recall sentences similar to:

(3) Promise me to dress yourself.

Earlier discussions showed that sentences like (3) involve the action of three distinct transformations. These are I Deletion, which accounts for the fact that the overall imperative main clause is subjectless; Equi, which accounts for the fact that the infinitive is subjectless; and Rule 1G(a), which accounts for the reflexive form of the object of *dress* in (3). If we "undo" the operations performed by these rules, we see that (3) involves a remote structure:

(4)

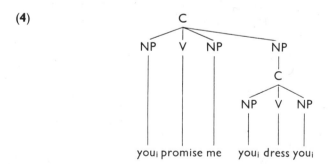

The claim that (4) is the *only* remote structure associated with (3) amounts to the claim that the three rules mentioned apply directly to (4), that is, that all three apply *simultaneously*.

If any one of the rules applied first, the others could not apply to (4) but only to some deformation of (4) produced by the first rule application. For instance, if Rule 1G(a)[2] marks the object of *dress* as reflexive before Equi or I Deletion apply, then these two rules apply not to (4) but to some structure containing a reflexive pronoun.

If the rules apply nonsimultaneously, that is, if some apply before others, there must be restrictions on their interaction. In particular, Rule 1G(a) marking the object of *dress* as reflexive must then apply before Equi. The reason is that a reflexive can only be determined by a coreferent clause mate. But when Equi applies, the coreferent clause mate triggering the reflexive marking is deleted. Similarly, Equi must apply before I Deletion. The reason is straightforward. Equi is a controlled deletion rule, requiring a coreferential controller to induce deletion of the subject of the subordinate clause. Therefore, if I Deletion applied first, there would be no such controller. And Equi would never apply. In other words, if Equi applied before Rule 1G(a) and also before I Deletion, the following incorrect result would be produced:

(5)   *Promise me to dress you.

And if Equi applied before Rule 1G(a) and I Deletion before Equi, the even worse (6) would result:

(6)   *Promise me you to dress you.

Finally, if Equi correctly applied after Rule 1G(a) but I Deletion applied before Equi, the incorrect (7) would result:

(7)   *Promise me you to dress yourself.

Therefore, *if* the three rules in question apply successively, there is only one correct order in which they may apply:

(8)   Rule 1G(a) *before* Equi *before* I Deletion.

Thus, a grammar where the rules do *not* apply simultaneously must contain, in addition to the rules themselves, some principles indicating the way these rules interact with each other, in particular, the order in which they apply.[3]

We conclude as follows. Either transformations like Equi, I Deletion, etc., apply simultaneously to remote structures or they apply one after the other. But, in the latter case, the choice of which precedes which is not in general free. Some additional principles must indicate the correct order. If the rules apply successively rather than simultaneously, any sentence whose description involves more than one rule will have more than one remote structure. In particular, if the three rules discussed with respect to sentence (3) apply successively, then (3) will have associated with it not only the remote structure (4), but also these intermediate structures:

(9) a

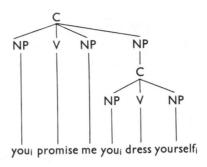

you$_i$ promise me you$_i$ dress yourself$_i$

b

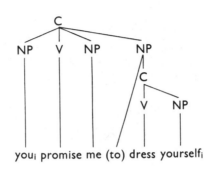

you$_i$ promise me (to) dress yourself$_i$

Structure (9a) would be derived from (4) by the operation of Rule 1G(a) and (9b) would be derived from (9a) by the operation of Equi. Only then would the surface form, (3), be derived from (9b) by operation of I Deletion, which removes *you$_i$* from (9b).

We see that if transformations-apply nonsimultaneously, sentences will in general have whole series of distinct remote structures associated with them, each derived from the one preceding by a single application of a single rule. The whole set of trees in such a case, including the maximally remote structure and the final tree, or surface structure, is called a *derivation*. If all rules applied simultaneously, derivations would in all cases consist of two trees, the maximally remote structure (which would be the only remote structure) and the surface tree.

The question arises whether rules apply simultaneously or successively. It would be logically possible for the answer to be mixed. That is, there might be some cases where application is simultaneous, others where it is successive, depending on types of rules, types of contexts, etc. There is nothing in the facts of examples like (3) which can serve as a basis for answering this question. The overall issue of how rules interact is a deep one, whose investigation continues. There is, however, no doubt that the view that *all* rules apply simultaneously is false. We begin to present evidence to show this in Chapter 22 and strengthen this conclusion immeasurably in Chapter 29. Thus, in many cases, it can be shown that rule applications are successive. Consequently, in general, sentences have more than one remote structure. For conceptual simplicity, we shall in this introductory work assume that *all* rule applications are successive, that is, that no two rules ever apply simultaneously. Therefore, every rule application involves the creation of a new derived structure. In general then, derivations will contain many trees, each derived from the one preceding it by the application of some rule.

The following partial picture emerges of the way a grammar containing a finite set of rules like Rule 1G, Equi, I Deletion, etc., describes particular sentences. Each sentence is regarded as involving a sequence of trees, the last being the surface structure. The surface structure will be derived from the minimally remote structure by application of some rule. This minimally remote structure will in turn be derived from the secondmost minimally remote structure by application of some rule. That tree will in turn be derived, etc. Clearly, this process must have a limit. There will be a maximally remote structure, the first tree in the derivation, whose origin must be distinct from that of all the other derived trees. What then is the source of these original trees, since they are not derived by transformations like all the other trees?

This question reveals a quite basic break in grammatical structures, a break which does *not* correspond to a simple division between surface structure and remote structure. This break groups together surface structures and all remote structures *except* the maximally remote ones and separates them from maximally remote structures. The basis of the division is that the former structures, including surface structures, are all derived from more remote structures by operations on trees called transformations. But maximally remote structures cannot have this origin. Let us refer to the maximally remote tree in any derivation as the *initial tree* (of that derivation). Hence from the point of view of this discussion, (4) is the initial tree of the derivation whose surface structure is (3).

We observed earlier that the number of sentences in English is unbounded or infinite. Since each sentence has a surface structure, the number of surface structures in English is also unbounded. But we are now assuming that each surface structure is simply the last tree in a sequence of trees called a derivation. If there are an infinite number of surface structures, there must be an infinite number of derivations. And, since each derivation has an initial tree, it follows simply that there must be an unbounded number of initial trees. This shows conclusively that the source of initial trees cannot be some finite list. Knowledge of English cannot consist in part of a complete inventory of initial trees, for the same reason that it cannot consist of a complete inventory of sentences. A finite apparatus like the brain cannot store an infinite set directly.

However, although the number of initial trees (as well as intermediate trees and surface trees) is unbounded, it does not follow that they do not have finite aspects. In particular, we can assume that the endless set of such structures is constructed out of a finite set of elements. Thus the question of the origin of initial trees within the grammar can be reduced to questions about the stocks of elements out of which such objects are constructed and the ways in which these are combined. These are matters to which we turn in the next chapter.

SUMMARY

The present chapter begins to fill in the general outlines of the overall framework of grammar. The system seems to be one in which initial trees, infinite in number, are constructed out of a finite stock of elements. It remains, however, to specify what these elements are and how they combine to yield the unlimited set of initial trees.

The system also contains transformational rules which operate successively to change initial trees into derived trees. Each one becomes more like the final, or surface tree. An initial tree, a series of increasingly less remote trees, and the surface tree constitute the *derivation* for any given sentence. Because there are an infinite number of surface trees, there must be an infinite number of initial trees, and hence also of intermediate remote trees. Consequently, a language must be a finite system which describes an infinite set of derivations. We have described how some deletion transformations can deform remote structures to yield surface trees. What needs to be considered more closely is the beginning points of derivations, that is, the source of those objects on which transformations operate. This leads to the question of the origin of initial trees.

NOTES

1. We say "partially" learned because we allow for the possibility that a certain amount of the substance of language is universal and innate, and thus need not be learned.

2. We are interpreting Rule 1G in this discussion along the lines sketched at the end of Chapter 6. See Chapter 17 for a further elaboration.

3. A priori, the nature of these principles is quite open. The worst possible case would be that the order among rules is entirely unpredictable. Hence individual grammars would have to contain particular statements indicating the order among rules. The best case would involve the existence of general principles of language predicting the order of application from the nature of individual rules. We suggest in Chapter 29 that at least some of the necessary ordering among rules is determined by general principles.

PROBLEMS

1. In this chapter it has been argued that transformational rules apply successively within derivations. In the example

(i) The camera freak bought a Bolex and made a movie about himself.

state in which order Rule 1G(a) and CCS Deletion must apply to give the appropriate surface structure. Give your reasons for assuming that order.

2. The number of sentences in English is infinite. Use this fact to argue that the number of initial trees is infinite as well.

CHAPTER 13   BASE RULES AND GRAMMATICAL RELATIONS

PREVIEW

In this chapter, the question of how the initial trees in derivations are to be characterized is confronted. The heart of the system for characterizing these trees is a set of rules specifying all of the "legal" combinations of grammatical categories such as C, NP, V, N, etc., and lexical elements such as *boy*, *hit*, *girl*, etc. These rules, called *base rules*, are of the general form:

$$A \longrightarrow B\ C$$

The letters stand for category labels like C, NP, V, N, etc. The arrow indicates that the category on the left side of the arrow immediately dominates the categories on the right side of the arrow. The order of categories on the right side of the arrow specifies the order in which these categories can appear in well-formed initial trees. The above rule, therefore, specifies that a configuration of the following form is a "legal" combination of categories:

In this structure, A immediately dominates B and C, and B is to the left of C.

Examples of real base rules used to form actual trees are examined. Given the notion of base rule, the question of expressing such traditional grammatical relations as subject, direct object, and indirect object is considered. These can be defined naturally in terms of base structures. However, certain apparent paradoxes arise. In particular, in a sentence like

I gave Melvin the book.

Melvin seems by different criteria to be both a direct and an indirect object. This conflict disappears, however, when one makes use of the multiple levels of structure provided by the theoretical framework adopted here. *Melvin* is an *indirect object* in the initial tree specified by the base rules developed in this chapter. It only becomes a *direct object* through the operation of a transformation that turns indirect objects into direct objects at a later stage.

At the conclusion of the preceding chapter, we asked how the class of initial trees in derivations is to be characterized. This reduced to the questions: What finite stock of elements underlies the endless set of initial trees? What modes of combination for these elements are possible? Under a particular assumption about the relation between initial trees and surface trees, we already know a great deal about the general character of initial trees. This assumption, implicit in our treatment so far, can be made explicit as follows:

(1) Initial trees are formally the same kinds of objects as surface trees.

This claim is implicit in the use of the term *tree* for both kinds and also suggests the condition:

(2) Remote structures which are neither initial trees nor surface structures are formally the same kinds of objects as surface trees.

Given (1) and (2), a general characterization of the kind of thing a surface tree is provides a basic account of remote trees as well. We have, however, devoted all of Chapter 4 to surface trees. In that chapter, trees were regarded as a combination of distinct kinds of elements, the lines, the points where the lines intersect, called nodes, the category labels affixed to the nodes, and the words and parts of words which occur at the ends of some lines. We also saw that these elements represented two basic linguistic relations, that of *precedence* (or immediate precedence), roughly left-to-right order, and that of *dominance* (or immediate dominance). The former is the relation between the NP and the V in:

(3)

The latter is the relation between, for example, the C and the NP, and between the V and *sing*.

We are now asking how a grammar characterizes the class of initial trees. The answer is that it will contain (i) a stock of the lexical and grammatical words and morphemes which make up the bottom lines of initial trees, (ii) a stock of the category types which label the nodes; and (iii) a set of principles indicating how these combine in terms of the basic relations of precedence and dominance. The first part of this answer implies that each language has a dictionary or *lexicon* of primitive elements. This is just common sense. We know that the vocabulary of English is different from that of Chinese, Turkish, etc. It follows that the overall linguistic systems of these languages must differ in the lists of vocabulary items they make available. Thus, the infinite set of initial structures can be factored into two conceptually separate finite portions, one of which is the lexicon. Although often quite huge, the set of primitive lexical elements is finite and listable. It contrasts with the set of sentences or the set of initial structures, which have neither of these properties. Put differently, while *memorization* is hopeless as an account of how the set of sentences (or initial trees) is internalized, it is a reasonable approximation of how the set of lexical elements is internalized. We return to the lexicon in Chapters 15 and 16.

We can also assume that English contains a stock of category types, C, NP, V, N, etc. One should not exclude the possibility that much of this stock is universal. But one should allow for the possibility of language-particular categories.

However, the heart of a system for characterizing the set of initial trees is neither the huge lexicon of lexical elements nor the (relatively quite small) stock of grammatical categories. Rather, it is a set of rules which indicate how these two types of element "legally" combine in terms of the relations of dominance and precedence to form allowable trees. To understand some of the problems here, consider the structure:

(4)

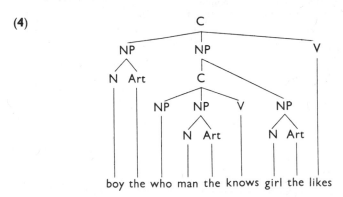

Structure (4) uses only English lexical and grammatical items, and only categories which are pertinent to the description of English. Yet it seems to specify a tree with no relevance to the description of English. In (4) articles (Art) follow nouns within NPs, restrictive relative clauses precede their heads[1] and verbs are final in transitive clauses. These properties are entirely foreign to English. Interestingly enough, there are many languages which have exactly these properties, for example, Japanese, Turkish, and Tibetan. Therefore, if one replaced the English words in (4) with the appropriate lexical elements in those languages, one would approximate reasonable remote structures for sentences which meant:

(5) 'The boy likes the girl who knows the man '

Evidently, the set of initial trees in English must be distinguished from structures like (4). The set of such trees must also be distinguished from entirely bizarre combinations of categories in which, for instance, articles dominate clauses, prepositions dominate NPs, etc.

What is needed is a finite system of rules, call them *base rules*, which can express the "legal" combinations of categories along the principal dimensions of tree structures, dominance and precedence. The general form of such rules is illustrated by:

(6) A $\longrightarrow$ B C

Such a rule uses letters to represent category labels. The symbol $\longrightarrow$ indicates that the category on the left side of it immediately dominates the categories on the right side. Finally, the order of categories on the right side indicates the proper precedence relations. Thus, a rule like (6) amounts to the statement that a configuration like

(7)

is a "legal" sub-tree, on the assumption that B and C dominate appropriate words.

Rule (6) has only two symbols on the righthand side. This is simply an accidental feature of one rule. In principle, one can allow one, three, four, or more symbols, as required. The suggestion is that a finite set of rules of the form (6) can in part at least properly characterize the "legal" combinations of constituents in initial trees, ruling out improper combinations.

To see what real English base rules look like, consider:

(8) a Promise me to come.
     b Jim promised me to come.

At the level of precision which concerns us here, previous discussions show that the initial structures for these will differ only marginally. Example (8a) will have a second person subject where (8b) has *Jim* as subject, and the tenses of their verbs will differ. I Deletion will ultimately remove the subject NP of (8a), so that this is subjectless in surface structure. In both cases, the rule Equi removes the subject of the subordinate clause. The general form of an initial structure for both (8a,b) would be:

(9)

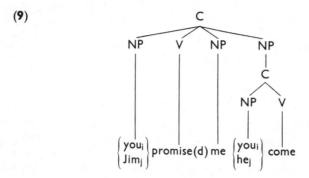

The initial structures of both (8a,b) involve an overall clause which contains an NP subject, a verb, and two NP objects. Moreover, one of the NP objects is itself clausal. To characterize structures like (9), we assume base rules like:[2]

(10) a C ⟶ NP V NP NP
   b NP ⟶ C

Rule (10a) says that a clause may contain the constituents NP V NP NP in that order. Rule (10b) specifies that an NP may exhaustively dominate a C, that is, that English NPs can consist of clauses. According to (10a), the following subtree is well-formed.

(11)

```
        C
      / | \
   NP  V  NP  NP
```

Such a rule is needed to permit the initial branchings in (9). Rule (10b) says that (11) can be further developed into:

(12)

```
        C
      / | \
   NP  V  NP  NP
              |
              C
```

Rule (10b) is needed to permit the unary branching of the NP into a C in structures like (9).

While the rules in (10) are necessary to specify trees like (9), they are not sufficient. In particular, although rule (10a) determines the proper branching for the top C node in (9), it does not characterize the subordinate clause. For this, one needs an additional rule:

(13)   C ⟶ NP V

Whereas (10a) characterizes clauses as containing a subject NP, a verb, and two object NPs, (13) specifies the existence of clauses containing only a subject NP, so-called *intransitive* clauses. However, there exist clauses like:

(14)   a   Melvin likes apples.
      b   The torpedo destroyed the ship.
      c   Jackson earned a large reward.

Therefore, it is also necessary to have a rule specifying clauses with one object:

(15)   C ⟶ NP V NP

This introduces simple *transitive* configurations.

Summing up, the following base rules have been introduced:

(16)   a   C ⟶ NP V NP NP
      b   C ⟶ NP V NP
      c   C ⟶ NP V

(17)   NP ⟶ C

The rules in (16) all specify crucial aspects of the structure of clauses in initial trees. Rule (17) specifies one possible structure for NP. The rules in (16) suggest that the various elements of clauses do not all have the same status. If (16) is representative, a clause may or may not have object NPs, but must have a subject NP and a verb. Thus a subject NP and a verb form the minimal skeleton of clause structure, *at the level of initial structure*. We are suggesting that the following regularities hold for initial trees in English:

(18)   Every clause in initial structure contains a verb (its main verb), that is, every C node in initial structure immediately dominates a V node.

(19)   Every clause in initial structure contains a subject NP, that is, every C node in initial structure immediately dominates a subject NP node.

These are generalizations which only recognition of remote structure permits us to formulate, for we have seen a variety of subjectless clauses at various derived levels of structure, and especially at the level of surface structure.

There are also surface clauses without verbs, such as those italicized in:

(20)   a   Harry buys beef and *Sheila pork.*
      b   Harry visits museums and *Sheila clothing stores.*

However, it is easy to argue that the surface clauses in such cases are truncated versions of initial clauses containing verbs identical to those in the preceding clauses. This would, among other things, account for the fact that, for example, *Sheila pork* means "Sheila buys pork" in (20a) but "Sheila eats pork" in:

(21) Harry eats beef and Sheila pork.

We can construct a notation which permits collapsing of rules like (16) in such a way that what is obligatory in all of them is distinguished from what is not obligatory. Such a notation is provided by placing optional elements in parentheses. This permits replacement of (16) by:

(22) C $\longrightarrow$ NP V (NP) (NP)

We can take this to be the base rule characterizing the fundamentals of all English clauses. Rule (22) introduces up to three distinct NPs into clause structures.

Since the beginning of this manual, we have been using traditional terms like *subject* and *object*. We can now consider in a more organized way how these terms relate to formal rules like (22). We assume that an NP introduced to the left of a V is the subject of the V and also the subject of the clause defined by the C node to which it is directly attached. This is entirely in accord with tradition, in several senses. In particular, note that it means that the one NP which occurs with an intransitive verb (see Chapter 16) is the subject of that verb. In other words, there are verbs without objects, but none without subjects (in initial structure). Transitive clauses have subjects and other structure as well. We shall see later (especially in Chapters 18, 20, 21, and 23) that NPs which are preverbal in initial structure can be displaced by other NPs which assume this position under the operation of certain transformations. Thus a fuller account of subject NPs does not limit them to preverbal positions *in initial structures alone*. That is, we will say that at any stage of remote structure, the NP which is in a position parallel to that introduced for the obligatory NP in (22) is the subject of the C at that stage. This allows for "change of subject" from one stage of derivation to another. We see later that such changes are typical of English grammar. That is, there are several rules which create new subjects and thereby displace old ones.

Next, we will call an NP generated immediately after a verb the *direct object* of that verb and an NP generated as the second NP after a verb the *indirect object* of that verb. This means that a verb with only one postverbal NP has a direct object but no indirect object. Indirect objects arise in the case of two postverbal NPs, that is, in so-called *bitransitive* or *ditransitive* clauses. It will also mean that, in a structure like (9) above, *me* is the direct object, the clausal NP the indirect object. This, however, conflicts with the traditional terminology, which would call *me* the indirect object in such a case. It might be thought that we are making arbitrary and confusing decisions which clash with tradition. The actual situation is, however, more complicated. This question is directly related to the fact that, unlike traditional accounts of English grammatical structure, the present account recognizes multiple levels of structure for each sentence. We just noted how this allows for the possibility that an NP might be a subject at one level and not a subject at a later derived level, or conversely. It also allows an NP to be a direct or indirect object at one level and not at a later level, or conversely. It turns out that (9) is not actually the initial structure most appropriate for the sentences in question. Rather, it is more representative of what we later see to be a derived structure. Thus, while (9) is relatively faithful to the order of words actually found in surface structure, and is thus natural as an introductory treatment, it is not faithful to the underlying relations which can ultimately be uncovered. Consider, for example, the sentences:

(23)   a   I gave Melvin the book.
        b   They bought us presents.

If we provide these with initial trees which follow the word order of the surface forms, we come up with:

(24)

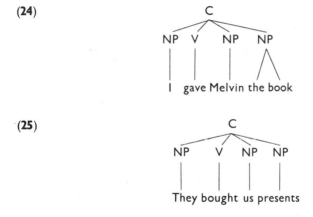

(25)

According to the terminology introduced above, *Melvin* would be the direct object in (24) and *us* would be the direct object in (25). Both of these assignments clash with tradition, which regards these elements as indirect objects. There are good reasons for analyses like those in (24) and (25), which render the NPs in question as direct objects. These reasons have to do with the possibilities of passivization, to be discussed in Chapters 18 and 23. However, there is also merit in the traditional treatment. From the point of view of passivization, the NP *Melvin* and *us* in (24) and (25) are direct objects. From other points of view, which tradition stresses, they are indirect objects.

    A framework which permits multiple levels of structure enables one to consistently adopt both points of view, to have one's cake and eat it too. It is only necessary to recognize that the apparently conflicting assignments of direct and indirect object status *pertain to different levels of remote structure.*

Consequently, we shall *not* assume that trees like (24) and (25) represent appropriate initial trees for sentences like (23). Rather, they represent remote structures derived by some transformation from initial trees in which the lineup of NPs is such that our terminology accords with tradition. In other words, in initial structure, sentences like (23) have representations in which the NPs *the book* and *presents* are immediately postverbal.

The validity of such an approach is strengthened by the existence of sentences closely related to those in (23). These manifest, even in surface structure, essentially that organization for postverbal NPs just posited as underlying sentences like (23):

(26) a I gave the book to Melvin.
    b They bought presents for us.

What is being claimed is both:

(27) a The initial structures of the paired sentences in (23) and (26) are the same.
    b These structures are more like the derived structures of (26) than of (23).

This says that there is a transformational rule, call it *Indirect Object Shift*, which is relevant for the derivation of sentences like (23) but not relevant for those like (26). This means that sentences like (26) more directly reflect the organization of their initial structures than do those of (23). Similarly, sentences which do not involve Equi more closely reflect their underlying structures than do parallel sentences which involve Equi, etc. Indirect Object Shift is the first transformation encountered which has the function of *rearranging* the position of elements. Hitherto, we have considered rules which changed the shape of elements, such as Rule 1G(a) for pronouns, and many rules which deleted elements, like I Deletion, Equi, etc.

We are taking structures like (26) to be more basic than those like (23). Consequently, we regard (24) and (25) as derived remote structures rather than initial structures. This raises an important question. Base rule (22) is capable of generating the needed configurations for both (24) and (25). It is not clear though that it can generate the needed configuration (26) if we take it to be basic. The examples in (26) involve what we are taking to be initial indirect objects marked with prepositions, *to* and *for*. And none of the base rules mentioned so far says anything about prepositions. This is not a limitation of the base rules. Instead, we claim that these prepositions are introduced by transformations. In particular, there must be a rule which introduces a preposition with indirect objects. This rule determines the particular shape of the preposition in terms of the main verb. An appropriate initial structure for (26a) is:

(28)

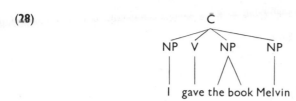

This will be connected to the surface structure of (26a) by the rule which marks the indirect object with *to*. If, however, the Indirect Object Shift rule applies, the original indirect object will become a direct object and cease to be an indirect object. If these rules are organized properly,[3] we can take this fact to provide an explanation of why the rule for adding prepositions to indirect objects does not function in examples like (23). The fact that indirect objects receive prepositions is a special case of a generalization about English, although one which has several large classes of exceptions:

(29) All NPs *except* subjects, direct objects,[4] and predicate nominals receive prepositions.

Within the context of (29), sentences derived by Indirect Object Shift, like (23), are exceptional in that the former direct objects, which have become nondirect objects, do not receive prepositions. However, there are a few cases where such NPs do receive prepositions. Compare:

(30) a I provided applesauce to the children. ⟹ I provided the children with applesauce.
   b They furnished arms to the rebels. ⟹ They furnished the rebels with arms.
   c They credited the victory to the prince. ⟹ They credited the prince with the victory.
   d They blamed the accident on him. ⟹ They blamed him for the accident.

In these cases, conversion of the original indirect object to direct object and concomitant conversion of the direct object to nondirect object does generate the prepositions which (29) predicts.

We conclude that the presence or absence of prepositions with NPs is partially a matter of derived structure. This amounts to the claim that some surface structure Prepositional Phrases (PP) are derived from initial structure NPs. In Chapter 16, however, we consider cases which appear to involve initial structure PPs.

In the terms just developed, a structure like (9) is not an initial tree but one derived by Indirect Object Shift.[5] More generally, all clauses based on *promise* with superficial postverbal NPs designating mind-possessing entities are derived by Indirect Object Shift. These include:

(31) a I promised Bob a new car.
      b I promised Bob to leave.
      c I promised Bob that I would leave.

Without the application of Indirect Object Shift, the initial structures of these would show up as:

(32) a   I promised a new car to Bob.
      b *I promised to leave to Bob.
      c *I promised that I would leave to Bob.

Evidently, there are further restrictions which have the effect of making Indirect Object Shift application obligatory when the direct objects in initial structure are complements.[6]

    Although indirect and direct objects occupy a limited domain of English grammar, our discussion of them illustrates an important general principle. The study of proper base rules cannot be separated from the study of transformational operations. Base rules generate initial structures. But if our knowledge of transformational operations is limited, we may take certain structures to be initial structures when they are in fact derived. Thus the discovery of transformations can effect, sometimes radically, the way one formulates base rules. It is a noteworthy fact about the grammatical sketch presented in this manual that it needs only very simple base rules because it recognizes transformational operations in a wide range of cases.

SUMMARY

The first base rules required to yield initial trees were presented in this chapter. These rules, when collapsed in terms of the parenthesis notation, are expressible as the single formula:

$$C \longrightarrow NP \ V \ (NP) \ (NP)$$

This expresses the generalization, stateable only at the initial tree level, that all clauses in English contain at least a subject NP and a V.

    The relational concepts of subject and indirect object were discussed in terms of the structures generated by the above rule. It was seen that some NPs (for example, initial structure indirect objects), acquire prepositions by rule just in case Indirect Object Shift does not convert these into derived direct objects. If Indirect Object Shift does apply, indirect objects are converted to direct objects and regularly fail to receive prepositions by virtue of principle (29). When initial indirect object NPs remain such and acquire prepositions by rule, the transformation which inserts the preposition also creates a new PP node that immediately dominates the preposition and the indirect object NP:

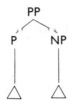

There are other PPs, however, which cannot be so derived. These are introduced via base rules and will be discussed in Chapter 16.

NOTES

1. The *head* of a relative clause, restrictive or not, is, in the simplest case, the noun which the relative clause modifies. So in

(i)   the *machine* which I invented
(ii) *Melvin*, whose mother is a singer

the heads are italicized. There can also be complex heads with structure beyond a simple noun, as in:

(iii) the *picture of Joan* which they burned
(iv)   a *friend of Melvin's*, who was arrested

2. We are again ignoring questions of the existence of a VP constituent dominating, among other things, the verb and its object, if any. We also ignore details of verb tense, leaving these to Chapters 26 and 27.

Many grammarians have assumed that a rule like (10a) would be replaced by:

(i)   C $\longrightarrow$ NP VP
(ii) VP $\longrightarrow$ V NP NP

This is meant to account, among other things, for the binary constituent break in the surface structures of such sentences as

(iii) Melvin [kidded Gladys]
(iv)   They [gave apples to the horses]

where the surface strings have bracketings as indicated (as first noted in note 1 of Chapter 5). In our view, bracketings like those in (iii) and (iv) can be accounted for without recognizing an initial structure VP constituent. See Chapter 27.

3. This is a question of the ordering of rules, as discussed in Chapter 12. Something must guarantee that application of the rule specifying a preposition on indirect objects is not permitted until after all applications of Indirect Object Shift. The former rule must not apply until after some initial indirect objects have been converted into direct objects, which regularly receive no prepositions (see (29) in the text).

4. Actually, as we see in note 5 below, the exception in (29) only holds systematically for the direct objects of pure verbs. We regard adjectives as also having direct objects, however. These regularly take prepositions.

5. Incidentally, the fact that the former direct object in such a case receives no preposition need not be regarded as exceptional. For it is a general fact about English that:

(i) Clausal NPs which have the form of *that* clauses or infinitival clauses never receive prepositions.

Observe such contrasts as:

(ii)   a   I am proud of that.
       b   I am proud of his being selected.
       c   I am proud (*of) to be here.
       d   I am proud (*of) that you won.

Proud, like almost every transitive adjective (*like* and *near* are exceptions), requires a preposition on its object NP. In other words, there is the regularity:

(iii)   A preposition is assigned to the direct object of an adjective.

However, the expected prepositions are regularly missing, as predicted by principle (i), when the object NP has the form of an infinitival or *that* clause. Note that gerundive or participial clauses, like that in (iib), permit such prepositions.

Note that deletion of the *that* marker of a *that* clause does not effect the applicability of principle (i):

(iv)   I am proud you won.
 (v)   *I am proud of you won.

Paradigms of related forms like (ii) play a role in supporting the claim that certain prepositions are not fundamental elements of grammatical structure. Many prepositions are late additions due to transformational insertion. These are subject to limitations which are in part exceptional and in part governed by subregularities banning insertions in certain contexts. The contrast in cases like (ii) should not obscure the fact that all these sentences have the same type of underlying structure (one in which the adjective *proud* occurs with following NPs). The presence or absence of prepositions is governed by the laws of the language, in particular, (i) and (iii).

6. The violations in (32b,c) are a function of a much more general constraint which blocks sentences containing "internal" *that* clauses and infinitives in English. That is, these kinds of clauses are not allowed when surrounded by certain other constituents. The exact nature of this "internality" has never been specified properly. But the same constraint can be seen at work in cases like:

  (i) a That is terrible.   a′ Is that terrible?
         b That he lost is terrible.   b′ *Is that he lost terrible?
  (ii) a I found out that.   a′ I found that out.
         b I found out that he was sick.   b′ *I found that he was sick out.
 (iii) a He told Jane that.   a′ He told that to Jane.
         b He told Jane to go.   b′ *He told to go to Jane.

For discussion of such questions of internality, see Kuno (1973).

PROBLEMS

1. What set of base rules are required to specify the following trees:

  (i)

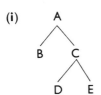

  (ii)

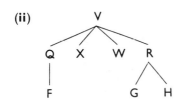

 (iii)

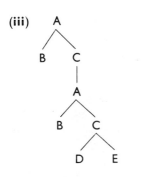

2. How can a single NP such as that italicized in

(i)   Melvin handed *Sally* the book.

be both a direct and an indirect object?

3. If examples like

 (i)   RCA stock went up in price.

are transformationally derived from the same initial structures as examples like

(ii)   The price of RCA stock went up.

what would you assume about the origin of the preposition *in*?

CHAPTER 14   **RECURSIVE RULES**

PREVIEW

In this chapter, the basic outline of the grammar is represented schematically as composed of a base component and a transformational component. The former is itself divided into a set of base rules and a lexicon.

Initially, two base rules are examined. They possess a crucial property. By allowing each to apply to the output of the other, an unlimited number of initial trees can be specified. The property of reapplication of rules without limit is called *recursion*, and rules which can apply to one another's (or to their own) output indefinitely many times are *recursive* rules.

In this chapter, three separate constructions in English are examined with respect to the question of their productivity. It is shown that NP complements, restrictive relative clauses, and conjoined NPs all involve recursive processes. It is indicated how each can be represented by sets of recursive base rules. Thus a crucial part of the answer is given to the question of how a finite grammatical system can characterize an infinite set of sentences. The answer is: by containing recursive rules.

In the preceding chapter we suggested that the unbounded class of initial trees, the beginning points of derivations, could be characterized by a finite system. This is divided into two portions, a lexicon and a set of base rules. We refer to these two jointly as the *base component* of a grammar. We have, in effect, reached the conclusion that the grammar of a language divides up into at least two components, a base component, and a transformational component. The former consists of a lexicon and base rules, the latter of transformations. The output of the base component is an infinite set of initial trees. These are converted into surface structures by the successive application of various transformations. Each application generates an intermediate remote structure. Schematically:

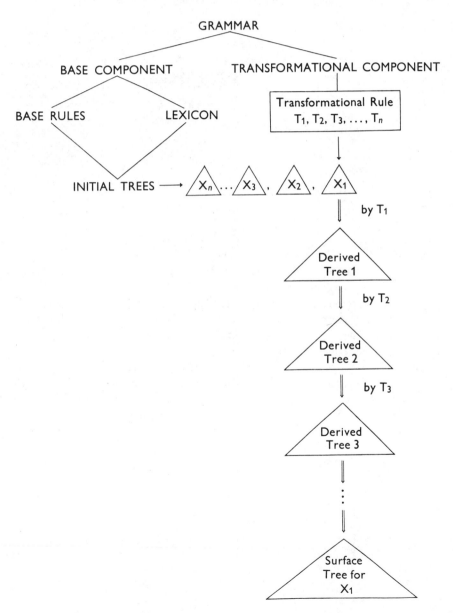

However, we have yet to consider in detail how the base rules and lexicon together specify the endless set of initial trees. In particular, we have not considered how the finite base component specifies an infinite set of base structures. And we have not considered the nature of the lexicon or how it interacts with the base rules. Turn to the first question.

We have introduced only two base rules:

(1) C ⟶ NP V (NP) (NP)

(2) NP ⟶ C

It was shown that (1) is a complex rule characterizing three fundamental types of clause. Interestingly enough, just these two rules are sufficient, if they interact properly, to specify an unbounded set of initial structures. Rule (1) permits an initial tree which begins as:

(3)

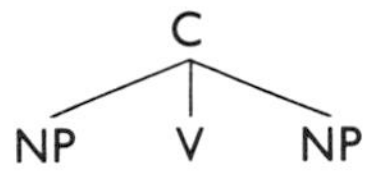

```
          C
        / | \
      NP  V  NP
```

Rule (2) permits (3) to be expanded into:

(4)

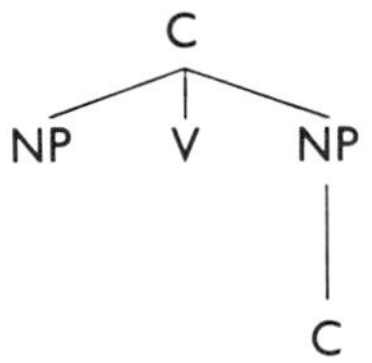

```
          C
        / | \
      NP  V  NP
              |
              C
```

That is, every configuration in (4) is permissable according to Rules (1) and (2). Moreover, rule (1) permits (4) to be continued as:

(5)

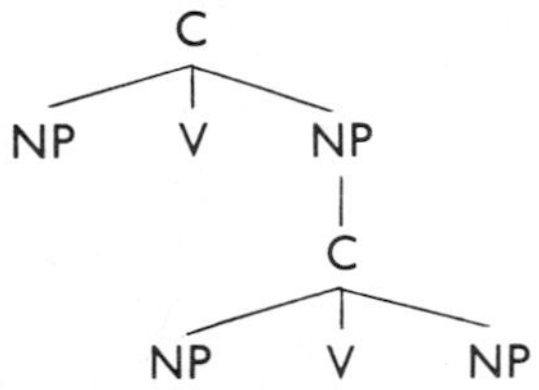

```
          C
        / | \
      NP  V  NP
              |
              C
            / | \
          NP  V  NP
```

And (2) applied again permits the development of (5) into:

(6)

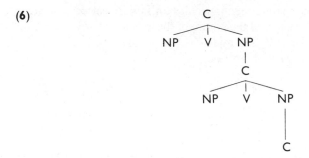

Reapplication of (1) permits this to develop into:

(7)

Structure (7) would be the proper top part of the initial tree for a sentence like:

(8)   Bob claimed he said Tom knew French.

This would have a representation like:

(9)

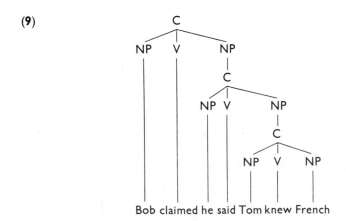

If we survey (5)–(7), we see that application of (1) permits the introduction of NPs as immediate constituents of Cs and that (2) permits the introduction of Cs as immediate constituents of NPs. Therefore, if (1) and (2) are allowed to reapply to the outputs produced by earlier applications of such rules, the size of the trees which are created, and hence the number of different trees, grows with each successive pair of reapplications. Thus, in (4), where (2) has applied once, there is a structure with one subordinate clauses. In (6), where (2) has applied twice, there is a structure with two subordinate clauses. If (2) applies again to (7), yielding

(10)

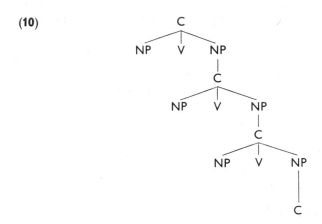

there will be a structure with three subordinate clauses. Thus, as the number of joint applications of rules like (1) and (2) increases, bigger and bigger structures result. These contain more and more subordinate clauses containing NPs which exhaustively dominate Cs. Let us refer to such clauses as *complements*. Thus the only limit on the number of trees which a pair of rules like (1) and (2) can specify is given by the limit on the number of times they can reapply. If we stipulate that there is no bound on the number of such applications, we account for the fact that there is no bound on the number of complements an English sentence may contain. Hence there will be no bound on the number of English sentences along this dimension.

Put differently, we can say that the reason an English speaker, whose storage space, memory, etc., are all finite, is able to internalize a language which consists of an infinite set of sentences is this: the language consists of precise rules like (1) and (2), which are finite and hence representable in the mind. In addition, it contains the precise instruction, also finite and hence equally representable, that the rules may be successively applied whenever their conditions of application are met. The condition of application for (2) is simply that there be some so far unexpanded NP symbol. The condition for (1) is simply that there be some unexpanded C symbol. Since (2) introduces a new C, it will always create the potential for further applications of (1). And since (1) introduces at least one and sometimes several NPs, it will always create the potential for further applications of (2). Application of one of these rules, therefore, always permits a further application of the other, without limit.

There is a minor problem implicit in this account. All of the NPs in initial trees are introduced by base rules, in fact, by (1) and (2). This is also true of most of the Cs. A survey of the initial trees given so far shows that in each (initial) tree there is one C which is not introduced by any base rule, namely, the highest C. This corresponds to the fact that every initial tree and every derived tree (including every surface structure) has a single root node, which is always labeled C. This is a result of the fact that trees are designed to characterize sentences. And sentences are maximal clauses, those not contained in any larger clauses.

These observations suggest that:

(11)   a   Every tree has a single root node, that is, a node which dominates other nodes but which is not dominated by any other nodes.

         b   The root node in every tree is labeled C.

Given (11), we can elaborate the conception of the base component as follows. The base component consists of a *base grammar* plus the lexicon. The base grammar in turn consists of the root symbol C^1 plus the set of base rules. The existence of an initial root symbol means that the rules expanding C have a fundamental status in the grammar. One such rule must always be the first base rule applied. Schematically:

(12)

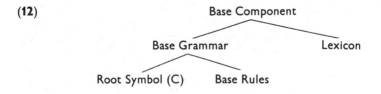

We have considered one set of rule interactions which makes the set of English sentences unbounded, namely, that involving complements. This is not, however, the only basis for our description of the unbounded or *recursive* nature of language. Another source of recursion is associated with restrictive relative clauses. These are illustrated by the italicized sequences in:

(13)   a   Bob wanted to call the nurse *who he had met.*

         b   The proposal *which was made by the attorney* was rejected.

         c   I will give you the money *that he promised you.*

To appreciate the relationship between such clauses and the infinite nature of English, it is necessary to understand the structures into which such clauses enter.

First of all, restrictive relatives are in fact clauses. Although they have special properties, particularly, the occurrence of so-called *relative pronouns* in initial position, they have otherwise the general form of clauses. More significantly, they interact with the phenomenon of reflexivization in ways which follow from the assumption that they are clauses:

(14) a Mary$_i$ got mad at the official who insulted $\begin{Bmatrix} \text{her}_i \\ \text{*herself}_i \end{Bmatrix}$

b The rock which fell on Johnson$_i$ injured $\begin{Bmatrix} \text{him}_i \\ \text{*himself}_i \end{Bmatrix}$.

c People who have watched those players$_i$ say $\begin{Bmatrix} \text{they}_i \\ \text{*them-} \\ \text{selves}_i \end{Bmatrix}$ are hopeless.

Such examples show that reflexives inside of a restrictive relative cannot have their antecedents outside of it, and that elements inside of such phrases cannot be antecedents for reflexives which are outside.[2] Given the clause mate constraint on reflexivization in Rule 1G, the facts in (14) are just what one would expect. We thus conclude that the italicized elements in (13) are clauses. Moreover, such clauses together with the elements in front of them form constituents, in fact, NP constituents. In (13a), *the nurse who he had met* is an NP; in (13b), *the proposal which was made by the attorney* is an NP; and in (13c), *the money that he promised you* is an NP. Observe the close parallelism in distribution and function between such complex sequences and simpler NPs:

(15) a The man is here.

a′ The man who you called is here.

b Is the man here?

b′ Is the man who you called here?

(16) a I gave the girl a ride.

a′ I gave the girl who you met a ride.

b I gave a ride to the girl.

b′ I gave a ride to the girl who you met.

(17) a I never met the girl.

a′ I never met the girl who he married.

b The girl, I never met.

b′ The girl who he married, I never met.

The complex phrases behave in various respects as NPs in the sense that they undergo rules which operate on NPs. For instance, there is a rule operating in (15) which shifts the order of subject NP and auxiliary verb in certain kinds of question clauses. This rule, called *Subject Auxiliary Inversion* (see Chapter 28), treats complex phrases containing restrictive relatives no different from simple ones. This indicates the NP-hood of the longer structures.

Thus, a phrase of the form *the box which exploded* has at least the structure:

(18)

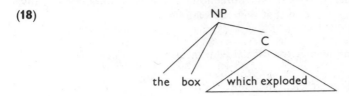

Moreover, the fact that the initial words in such phrases have themselves a form typical of independent NPs suggests that a more refined representation should be:

(19)

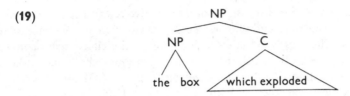

The validity of a representation like (19) is supported by the fact that not all NPs with restrictive relative clauses begin with definite articles. There are a variety of other possibilities:

(20) a *a box* which exploded
        b *some boxes* which exploded
        c *certain boxes* which exploded
        d *all boxes* which explode
        e *boxes* which explode
        f *those boxes* which explode
        g *that box* which exploded
        h *several* boxes which exploded
        i *three boxes* which exploded

All of the italicized sequences have the form of independent NPs. This supports the claim that all phrases like those in (20) have the structure:

(21)

At this point there are no means to characterize restrictive relative clauses with base rules because they involve a type of subordinate clause which is distinct from the complements which rule (2) introduces. However, given the assumption that such clauses enter into configurations like (21), this lack can easily be remedied by positing the rule:

(22) NP ⟶ NP C

Given (22), we can return to the question of how restrictive relative clauses permit the set of sentences to be unbounded along a dimension distinct from that created by complements. In fact, we will see that restrictive relative clauses make the set of sentences boundless along at least two different dimensions.

First, although the examples quickly become clumsy and difficult to understand because of the finiteness of our perceptual mechanisms, it is possible to have an unlimited number of such clauses successively modifying the same original "small" NP. These are sometimes referred to as *stacked* relative clauses. Examples include:

(23) a the shark which I caught
      b the shark which I caught which he wants to steal
      c the shark which I caught which he wants to steal which is in
         the boat

The possibility of such constructions[3] is a direct consequence of the form of rule (22). The interesting thing about this rule is that, unlike (1) and (2), it can generate an unbounded set of structures *without the help of any other rule*. It does so by successively reapplying to its own output. One application of (22) will yield a subtree of the form:

(24)

```
        NP
       /  \
     NP     C
```

This contains an unexpanded NP node to which (22) can reapply, giving:

(25)

```
          NP
         /  \
       NP     C
      /  \
    NP     C
```

And (25) contains an unexpanded NP node to which (22) can apply:

(26)

```
            NP
           /  \
         NP     C
        /  \
      NP     C
     /  \
   NP     C
```

Therefore, if (22) is allowed to reapply without limit, there will be in principle no bound on the complexity or length of stacked relative structures. According to (22), the structure of (23c) would be something like:

(27)

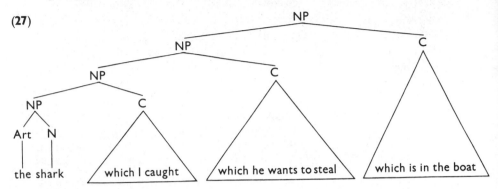

It follows that continued reapplication of (22) generates more and more complex NPs with restrictive relative clauses stacked up one after the other. Thus by itself, a rule like (22) permits English to have an infinite set of NPs and hence an infinite set of sentences.

Of course, technically, the base rules introduced so far will not produce trees like (27), since nothing has been provided to develop the small NP into words like *the* and *shark*. To remedy this we add a rule of the form:

(28) NP ⟶ Art N

Such a rule, in conjunction with a lexicon which specifies that *the, this, that, certain*, etc., are articles, and that *shark*, etc., are nouns, will permit the full development of NPs like (27). Observe that a rule like (28), in contrast to (22), has by itself no recursive properties. It can only produce a finite set of Art N combinations, on the assumption that the set of nouns is finite.[4]

We claimed that rule (22) provides English with an unbounded set of NPs and hence of sentences in two different ways. The first way, involving stacked relatives, has been illustrated. Now we illustrate how rule (22) interacts with rule (1) to yield an unbounded class of NPs in a fashion distinct from stacked relatives. In cases like (27), all of the restrictive clauses introduced ultimately modify the same minimal head (in (27), *the shark*). But sequential application of (22) and rule (1) permits other possibilities. Thus consider the following example of a type well-known from childhood:

(29) This is the cat that ate the rat that lived in the house that Jack built.

Although there are three restrictive relative clauses in such an example, namely,

(30) a that Jack built
  b that lived in the house that Jack built
  c that ate the rat that lived in the house that Jack built

they are organized in a fashion quite different from that manifested in (27). The most obvious difference is that some of the relative clauses in (30) occur inside of others. That is, (30a) is a part of (30b) and (30b) of (30c). None of the relative clauses in (27) is a part of any of the others. Correspondingly, where all of the relatives in (27) ultimately modify or identify the same head, those in (30) modify different heads. *That Jack built* modifies the head *the house, that lived in the house that Jack built* modifies the head *the rat*, etc. Example (29) has a structure something like:

(31)

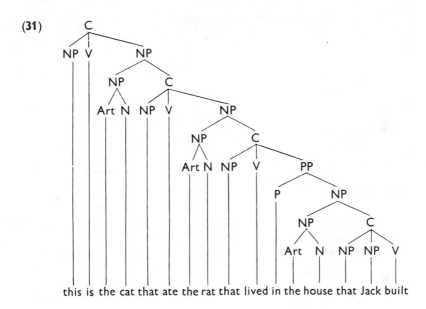

this is the cat that ate the rat that lived in the house that Jack built

In contrast to the situation in (27), structures like those in (31) are formed when applications of rule (22) are interspersed with applications of rule (1). Put differently, structures such as (31) are the result of using rule (22) to supply restrictive relative clauses to NPs that are inside of other restrictive relative clauses. Where the modifying clauses in (27) arise from the same stacked structure, those in (31) are really parts of distinct NPs. However, just as the mode of combination of NP nodes and C nodes illustrated in (27) can in principle be extended without limit, so can that in (31). Moreover, unlike such configurations as (27), those in (31) do not necessarily become incomprehensible as they get longer. As we recall from the nursery rhyme, extended combinations like (31) remain remarkably understandable.[5]

So far, we have illustrated three different ways in which the base rules of English guarantee that the set of sentences is unbounded, two involving restrictive relative clauses, one involving complement clauses. We shall consider one final type of recursion which is basic to sentence formation.

(32) a Melvin and Jim are Martians.
      b Melvin, Jim, and Tom are Martians.
      c Melvin, Jim, Tom, and that cop over there are Martians.
      d Melvin, Jim, Tom, that cop over there, and your uncle are Martians.
      e Melvin, Jim, Tom, that cop over there, your uncle, and the guy on
         the corner are Martians.

It is evident that the process of forming more and more complex subject NPs
illustrated in (32) is unbounded. This is the phenomenon traditionally known
as *coordination*. All of the NPs strung together in such examples are said to be
coordinated, which means that they all have equivalent status. There are two
modes of coordinating NPs in English, one involving the word *and*, the other
the word *or*:

(33) a Harry or Jack will do it.
      b Harry, Jack, or Tom will do it.

Formally, these two modes of coordination are entirely parallel. To understand what kind of base rule can introduce such structures, we must understand the nature of the bracketing they reveal. Consider an example like:

(34) Melvin, Jim, and Tom are Martians.

Clearly, the sequence *Melvin, Jim, and Tom* is a constituent and an NP, in fact
the subject of *are Martians*. And, in general, such sequences are NP constituents, and behave just like simpler NPs under various rules. Compare:

(35) a I like apples.   e Do I like apples?
      b Jim and I like apples.   f Do Jim and I like apples?
      c He called me.   g Me, he called.
      d He called me and Jack.   h Me and Jack, he called.

What then of the internal structure of the NP *Melvin, Jim, and Tom*? Clearly,
Melvin, *Jim*, and *Tom* are themselves individual NPs. In general, coordinated
constituents of a type A involve combinations of lesser constituents of the
same type A. If we could ignore the word *and*, it would then be natural to
represent the constituent in question as:

(36)

Such structures suggest an obvious account of what it means for constituents to be coordinated: two or more constituents of type A are coordinated if they are directly dominated by another constituent of type A, *which dominates nothing else*.

This leaves only the problem of the conjunction words *and* and *or*. A consideration of intonation and pausing,[6] plus our intuitive feel for bracketings, shows that such conjunctions are always bracketed with the element that follows them. That is, the superficial bracketings of

(37) a Mike and Tom
      b Mike, Tom, and Terry

are, respectively:

(38) a [Mike] [and Tom]
      b [Mike] [Tom] [and Terry]

This raises the question of what kind of constituent these constituents beginning with *and* (or *or*) are. The answer is not obvious. But it emerges if we wish to preserve the account of coordination mentioned above. Since *Mike* is an NP, if *Mike* and *and Tom* are coordinated, then *and Tom* must be an NP. And similarly in parallel cases.

In the coordinate NPs introduced so far, an *and* is found only on the rightmost conjunct. While this is perhaps the most natural and colloquial treatment, it is in principle possible to have conjunctions on the earlier conjuncts:

(39) a Pete and Mike and Louise are coming.
      b Pete and Mike and Louise and Fred are coming late.

The only thing that is totally blocked is a conjunction on the first conjunct:

(40) a *and Pete and Mike and Louise are coming.
      b *And Pete and Mike and Louise and Fred are coming late.

We are now ready to suggest a rule for introducing coordinated NPs. Recall configurations like (36) and the fact that a coordination can contain in principle an unlimited number of conjuncts What will be needed then is a rule which says that a particular NP node can be developed into 2, 3, 4, . . . , n other NP nodes. We can formulate such a rule initially as

(41) NP $\longrightarrow$ NP^n

This is interpreted to mean that a configuration of the form

(42)

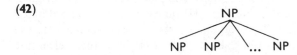

is well-formed as long as the dots are filled in by NPs directly attached to the top node.

However, (41) still does not account for the presence of the conjunction words (abbreviated conj) themselves. It will not do to add a further rule of the form

(43)   NP $\longrightarrow$ Conj NP

to develop the NPs which are introduced by (41). This would not account for the basic restriction on conjunctions, namely, that they occur only in constructions introduced by (41). Given (43), nothing would block application to an NP which is not coordinated yielding impossible structures like:

(44)   a   *And Bob is here.
          b   *I voted for and Melvin.

etc. Thus, we propose instead to replace (41) by:

(45)   NP $\longrightarrow$ Conj $(NP)^n$

(46)   Conj $\longrightarrow$ $\begin{Bmatrix} and \\ or \end{Bmatrix}$

We interpret (45) in the same way we did (41), that is, as allowing all configurations of the form:

(47)

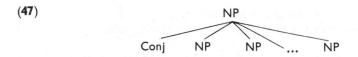

Thus, (45) generates combinations of a Conj node with 2, 3, 4, ..., n NPs. Of course, (45) does not describe the proper surface form of coordinate NPs. The reason is that it associates one conjunction with each coordinate NP as the initial element. Thus, (45) would yield such structures as:

(48)   a   [and Ted Tony are here]
          b   [or the man the woman was arrested]

These are obviously not proper combinations of morphemes if viewed from the point of view of surface structure. However, the difference between configurations like (47) and those actually occurring in sentences can be accounted for by transformational rules.

The first such rule, call it *Conjunction Copy*, will place a copy of the original initial conjunction in a configuration like (47) on each of the n coordinated NPs, simultaneously deleting the original. Moreover, we assume that the combinations of conjunctions and NPs so produced have themselves the structure of NPs. Thus, Conjunction Copy will function as follows:

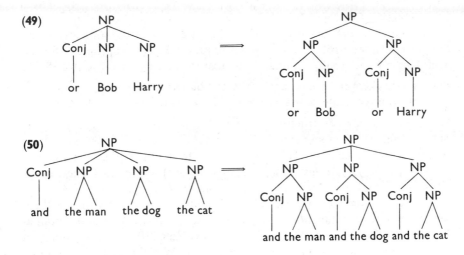

The outputs of Conjunction Copy, though still not perfect from the point of view of surface configurations, are far closer to adequacy than the inputs. In particular, the derived structures in (49) and (50) account for the grouping, observed in (38), which brackets a conjunction with the following conjunct.

The second transformational rule needed to convert structures produced by the base rules (45) and (46) into appropriate surface forms is one which will delete the conjunction from the first conjunct. This rule is absolutely obligatory. In no case can the first of *n* conjuncts contain a conjunction. We thus posit a further rule, call it *Initial Conjunct Erasure*, which removes the conjunction from the first of *n* conjuncts. Initial Conjunct Erasure will convert a structure like the righthand side of (49) to:

(51)

```
            NP
           /  \
         NP    NP
          |   /  \
         NP Conj NP
          |   |   |
         Bob  or Harry
```

By collapsing like nodes which do not branch, we get:[7]

(52)

```
            NP
           /  \
         NP    NP
          |   /  \
          | Conj NP
          |   |   |
         Bob  or Harry
```

This is an entirely appropriate surface structure for the overall NP in question.

Conjunction Copy and Initial Conjunct Erasure jointly suffice to convert coordinate configurations generated by the base rules into grammatical surface forms. They do not, however, suffice to produce all the appropriate forms. Thus, these rules permit configurations like (53a), but not those like (53b):

(53) a Rockets and bombs and shells and bullets were delivered.

   b Rockets, bombs, shells, and bullets were delivered.

While both types of structure are well-formed, those like (53b) are, as observed earlier, far more natural. While it is obligatory to delete the conjunction from the first conjunct, it is normal to delete all of the other conjunctions as well, *except for the last*. To perform this function, at least one further transformational rule is required, call it *Optional Erasure*.

We see how the pair of base rules (45) and (46), together with the three transformations Conjunction Copy, Initial Conjunct Erasure, and Optional Erasure can produce an unbounded set of coordinate NPs. Thus coordination is one of the principal mechanisms accounting for the fact that, though English is finitely representable, it involves an unbounded collection of sentences.

The base rules for describing coordinate NPs permit alternative bracketings for the same string of words. Consider:

(54) America and France and Germany and Italy signed agreements.

Restricting attention to the subject NPs, one derived structure would be:

(55)

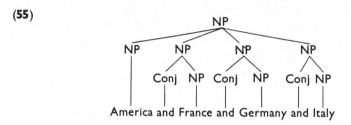

Such a structure would be derived by way of Conjunction Copy and Initial Conjunct Erasure from an application of rule (45) in which four NPs are directly attached to the top NP node. However, (54) also has a possible structure of the form:

(56)

Unlike structure (55), which depends on an initial use of rule (45) branching into four NPs, (56) depends on an initial use of rule (45) branching into only two NPs. The presence of four conjuncts then depends on the fact that each of the initial two NPs which are coordinated are themselves subjected to rule (45).[8] Clearly, this sort of process is unlimited in principle. As a consequence, as strings like (54) become longer and longer, they have more and more possible bracketings, that is, they are more and more ambiguous as to the grouping of their elements. This high degree of ambiguity is apparently tolerable because the semantic contrasts associated with the bracketing differences are, in general, minor.

It is also worth pointing out that the rule which optionally deletes conjunctions, except the last, serves to eliminate a certain amount of ambiguity. Thus an NP of the form

(57) America, France, Germany, and Italy

can only be interpreted as a reduced version of (55), that is, with all four NPs parallel conjuncts of the top NP. A structure of the form

(58)

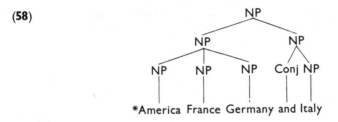

is excluded because there is no way in which all of the NPs conjoined under some node can lose all of their conjunctions, as a result of the condition on Optional Erasure that it not delete the conjunction of a final conjunct. This condition, which might initially seem arbitrary, actually plays a functional role in the language.

SUMMARY

In this chapter, two fundamental questions were raised, namely, how the finite base component specifies an infinite set of base structures and how the lexicon interacts with the base rules. The first has been answered. By taking advantage of the recursive property possessed by single rules of the form A ⟶ (B) A (C); or pairs of rules of the form A ⟶ (B) C (D); C ⟶ (E) A (F); or rules of the form A ⟶ (B) A^n, it is possible to construct an infinite set of base trees using only a finite set of rules. It was shown in some detail how rules of this type account for the productive properties of restrictive relative clauses (which turned out to be recursive in two different ways), complements, and conjoined NPs. The notion that a few finitely describable rules can specify an endless class of sentence structures thus becomes less mysterious.

However, the second question raised was not answered. We have not specified how the lexicon interacts with the base rules, nor said anything substantial about the nature of the lexicon itself. These topics are approached in the following two chapters.

NOTES

1. In line with the discussion of earlier chapters, in which clauses were represented with boundary symbols at their extremities, one might propose that rather than a single root symbol C the base grammar involves the string $\#C\#$. But to carry this out consistently, it would be necessary to introduce clause boundaries as well around any Cs introduced by other base rules.

2. Examples like

(i) Men who understand themselves are honest.

must not be regarded as counterexamples to the first part of this statement since in these the antecedent of the reflexive is *who*, not *men*. *Men* is in turn the antecedent of *who*, accounting for the coreference between *men* and *themselves*.

3. It is interesting that restrictive relatives contrast with nonrestrictive relatives here. Stacking is impossible for the latter:

(i) The man who I met who impressed me very much ... (restrictive)
(ii) *John, who I met, who impressed me very much ... (nonrestrictive)

This fact, as well as two other limitations on nonrestrictives, may be a function of the following principle:

(iii) A nonrestrictive clause must be the last element in the NP which it modifies.

Given (iii), examples like (ii) are ill-formed because, with more than one such clause, all but the last necessarily violate the requirement of final position. Principle (iii) also explains why, when an NP involves both a restrictive and a nonrestrictive relative, the nonrestrictive must be last:

(iv) a the man that I met, who Johnson hired ...
b *the man, who Johnson hired, that I met ...

Finally, (iii) can explain why nonrestrictive clauses cannot occur with the genitive morpheme, in contrast to restrictives:

(**v**)   a   the man who you met's wife ...
     b   *John, who you met, 's wife ...

4. We will see in Chapter 15 that this assumption is not in fact true of surface structures. But the unbounded character of the set of nouns in English will be attributed to transformational rules.

5. The comprehensibility of structures like (31) depends crucially on the fact that the restrictive relative clauses which are successively introduced are regularly to the right of the top C node. When this is not the case, intelligibility drops off precipitously. Consider the following structure, which is perfectly well-formed according to the rules we have given, and which is shorter than (31):

(i)

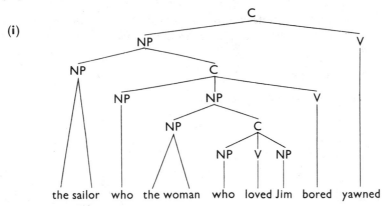

In spite of its relative brevity, (i) is harder to understand than (31). This emerges even more clearly when such embedded clause constructions are dealt with in terms of their verbal rather than written forms. Although a full understanding of this phenomenon has not been achieved, there is a formal property of (i) which distinguishes it from structures like (31), whose comprehensibility is resistant to increasing length and complexity. In (31), every restrictive relative clause is on the extreme right branch of an NP which is itself on the extreme right branch of another constituent. In (i), however, the NP *the woman who loved Jim* is not on a right branch but on a central branch. It turns out that embedded clauses which are on central branches or which are parts of constituents on central branches pose serious barriers to comprehensibility.

6. That a conjunction is more closely related to the constituent that follows it than to the constituent which precedes it is evident in part from the normal position of pauses in conjoined structures. Thus, a pause is more natural before the conjunction than after it:

(**i**)   John (*pause*) and Bill are coming.
(**ii**)   *John and (*pause*) Bill are coming.

A second indication that the conjunction goes with the following constituent is its behavior when reduced. In rapid or careless speech *and* is often pronounced as a simple *'n*, almost a nasal grunt. This reduced form belongs phonetically to the constituent which follows it:

(iii) Peten' Fred
(iv) *Peten' Fred

Both of these facts support the bracketing postulated in (38) .

7. The deletion of the *conj* node from the righthand side of (49) yields a tree (51) which contains an NP which immediately dominates another NP and nothing else. We assume that such subtrees immediately collapse as in (52). In general, whenever a transformation yields a subtree containing a node X that immediately dominates another identical node X and nothing else, the higher X node is eliminated.

8. The fact that rule (45) can itself apply to coordinated NPs which it generates provides the possibility of complex coordinate NPs combining both *and* and *or*:

(i) Melvin and John or Tom

This has two different possible structures:

(ii)   **(iii)**

PROBLEMS

1. Explain how appositive (nonrestrictive) relative clauses can yield an unbounded number of NPs.

2. The expression

(i) the sailor who visited the nurse who had rabies

is ambiguous. (Clue: Who has the rabies?) What is the source of the ambiguity?

3. Our rules introduce conjoined NPs. Find examples of at least two different types of constituents that can be conjoined. What does this suggest about the set of base rules we have given?

CHAPTER 15   **THE LEXICON AND PRODUCTIVE WORD FORMATION**

PREVIEW

In this chapter, attention is focused on the repository of words associated with English, on the nature of its *lexicon*. In particular, the question of the scope of the lexicon is raised. A reasonable first view might be that the lexicon contains all the words a speaker knows. Despite its superficial plausibility, this cannot be the case. Rather, the lexicon is seen to contain only a portion of the words used in the formation of sentences.

There are two main reasons for this conclusion. First, there is no upper bound on the length of possible words in English. This means that, like the number of sentences, the number of words is infinite. Therefore, the considerations which yield the conclusion that the set of sentences cannot be mentally represented in the form of a list justify the same inference in the case of words. The finite storage space and finite time for learning available to individuals offers at best the possibility of representing a finite list of words. Knowledge of the overall set of words must be represented in part in some fashion distinct from a mere list. This leaves open the possibility that there is a finite part of the lexicon in list form which represents a *subset* of the set of all words. Second, unless knowledge about some words is accounted for in terms of principles distinct from mere listing, certain obvious generalizations about the relations of some kinds of words to some kinds of syntactic phrases are missed. Finally, it is shown that while the lexicon does contain a great many words, it also contains nonword elements, that is, those which form subparts of words, so-called *morphemes*.

From time to time in the preceeding chapters, the role of *words* has been touched upon. It was noted that a grammar must contain as one of its major components a dictionary or lexicon. This lexicon is, as it were, the storehouse for the words which have appeared in the trees we have considered up to now. We want to explore more closely the proper content of a lexicon. Is a lexicon which is part of an explicit system for describing English anything like an ordinary dictionary, that is, simply a long list of words? Or is it something more?

Since the lexicons that are internalized by speakers represent the words that they know, it follows that lexicons will differ somewhat from speaker to speaker. Not everyone knows exactly the same words. For example, an engineer on a steamship will not only know the names of all of the machines in the engine room but also the names of their parts and subparts, words for referring to typical malfunctions, etc. His or her experience is unlike most people's and the words he or she needs to know will in part reflect this fact. But since everyone's experience is to some extent unique, it is unlikely that any two lexicons are identical. It seems necessary to suppose, rather, that lexicons, like fingerprints, vary from speaker to speaker. It is, however, plausible to assume that there is also a common core of words which every lexicon contains. It is because of this common core that English speakers can engage each other in at least a certain amount of mutually intelligible conversation. We thus do not expect to find mature speakers who cannot use and understand words like *is, love, want, me, that, trouble, eat, potato*, etc. On the contrary though, it would not be surprising to find hundreds or thousands of such speakers whose lexicons do not include such items as *peruse, mesmerize*, or *disparity*. While it is difficult to estimate the size of the core of vocabulary common to mature English speakers, this must certainly be on the order of several thousand words.

If mentally represented lexicons are anything like ordinary dictionaries, they will consist in part of lists of words, these lists varying in length from one speaker to another. One must also allow for variation at different stages of life for the same speaker. For it is a common activity to learn new words, and not uncommon to forget some as well. The question then arises whether it is possible for a particular speaker's lexicon at some point in time to exhaustively characterize all of the words which that speaker knows at that point in time.

The answer to this question must be negative. The reason is that speakers of English have the ability to make up new words in certain regular and productive ways. A mere list, no matter how large, cannot characterize such an ability. Consider, for instance, words such as:

(1)   a   ugly-looking
       b   evil-smelling
       c   sour-tasting
       d   harsh-sounding

These are all adjectives, as can be seen from the way they combine with nouns to form more complex NPs exactly like simple adjectives do:

(2) a   John is an $\left\{\begin{array}{l}\text{agile}\\\text{ugly-looking}\end{array}\right\}$ doorman.

  b   That is a $\left\{\begin{array}{l}\text{vile}\\\text{foul-smelling}\end{array}\right\}$ brew.

  c   Lemons are a $\left\{\begin{array}{l}\text{swell}\\\text{sour-tasting}\end{array}\right\}$ fruit.

Moreover, they can, like such primitive adjectives as *tall, hungry,* etc., be intensified with words like *very, quite,* etc.:

(3) a   very ugly-looking
  b   quite foul-smelling
  c   awfully sour-tasting

Thus it seems evident that the complex forms will have to be treated as members of the category Adj by a variety of grammatical rules.

This class of complex adjectives (of the form *Adj V ing*) is obviously related to sentences containing the so-called *sense* verbs *look, smell, taste,* and *sound,* which occur in sentences like:

(4) a   That looks ugly (to me).
  b   That smells bad (to me).
  c   That tastes sour (to me).
  d   That sounds harsh (to me).

In these, the sense verb is followed by the adjective which describes how the object referred to by the subject NP is sensed. The adjective is followed (optionally) by a phrase of the form *to* NP, which indicates the being(s) by whom the object is sensed in that particular way. Not all sense verbs can occur in constructions of this sort. While *perceive, see, hear,* etc., involve a senser or experiencer, this is not referred to by a postverbal NP preceded by *to,* but rather by the subject NP of the sense verb:

(5) a   John perceived that.
  b   Mary heard the bell toll.
  c   You can see the house from the window.

However, adjectives like those in (1) are only formed from those sense verbs which can occur in constructions in which the experiencer NP shows up in a *to* phrase. This property is possessed by *look, smell, taste, sound,* and *feel.* However, *feel* is exceptional:

(6) a   That feels soft (to me).
  b   *That is a soft-feeling pillow.
  c   That feels rough (to me)
  d   *That is a rough-feeling board.

Thus, only verbs of this sort form *Adj V ing* compounds, but not all of them do.

There are at least two possible approaches to the description of words like *nice-looking*, etc. One could assume that every such word is listed in the lexicon. Or, one could assume that at best only the component parts are listed in the lexicon and the compound forms derived by grammatical rules, derived in fact from constructions like those in (4). That is, constructions like (7b) would be derived by rule from those like (7a):

(7)   a   That soup smells delicious (to me).
       b   (To me)[1] that soup is delicious-smelling.

If we pick the second mode of description, we are immediately forced to conclude that not all words which a speaker knows are contained in his lexicon. Rather, we must assume that indefinitely many such words are derived productively from syntactic phrases.

The correctness of the syntactic-phrase description of compounds like those in (7b) becomes more apparent when one considers the very large number of elements like those in (7b) which mature speakers of English know. A tiny sample is:

(8)   **A**   **B**
        sour-tasting   pure
        good-tasting   bad
        foul-tasting   bland
        salty-tasting   dense
        bad-tasting   craven
        strange-tasting   rigid
        unfamiliar-tasting   cheap
        fishy-tasting   wild

The claim that the complex adjectives must be stored in the lexicon is the claim that those in column A do not differ essentially from primitive adjectives like those in column B. All of these must simply be remembered by a speaker. However, it would be absurd to suppose that the words listed in column A have the same status as those in B. This ignores the regularity of relationship in (7), whereby adjectives which can follow a sense verb may precede that sense verb's present participial (or-*ing*) form to yield a compound adjective word. Moreover, it ignores the fact that the grammatical and semantic relations in the compound adjectives are direct reflections of those in syntactic phrases like (4). This will be an automatic result of a derivation of the complex words from the relevant syntactic phrases. But it would be an accident if such words were listed in the lexicon.

One concludes that column B words and *the parts* of column A words must be listed in the lexicon, but that column A words themselves are not so listed. Rather, these are "manufactured" by grammatical rules from syntactic phrases. A further argument for this approach, as against mere listing, is provided by the productivity of the phenomenon in question. If all words like those in column A of (8) are simply listed in speakers' lexicons, there is no way of accounting for the fact that the introduction of a new adjective, characterizing the sensible properties of things, immediately permits the construction of new compound adjectives of the form in question. Thus adjectives like *far out*, *spaced out*, *stoned*, are relatively new coinages. But as soon as one learns to use these forms as simple adjectives, one can use compounds like:

(9) a far out-looking
      b spaced out-sounding
      c stoned-looking

Similarly, *wild* has only recently become an all-purpose adjective. But as soon as one learns to say things like (10a), one can immediately say and understand those like (10b):

(10) a This pizza tastes wild.
       b This is a wild-tasting pizza.

This instant extension from primitive adjective to compound is unaccounted for if every such compound has to be learned by rote. But it follows directly from a productive derivation of such compounds from independently existing phrases.

There are a variety of other examples of productive processes for forming words in English, processes which contribute to showing that it is impossible to regard the content of lexicons as coextensive with the set of all words. Consider, for example, *compound nouns*, nouns which are apparently made up of subparts which are themselves words:

(11) a Bóston flìght
      b New Yórk plàne
      c San Francísco shùttle
      d Wáshington tràin
      e Chárlotte tòur
      f Chicágo exprèss

In general, compound nouns in English are characterized by their *stress pattern*, the first element receiving greater stress than the second. In the examples in (11), primary stress is indicated by $'$ and secondary stress by $'^2$. Corresponding to the compound nouns in (11) are the syntactic phrases in (12), which seem to manifest essentially identical semantic and grammatical relations among the shared component parts:

(12) a flight$\begin{Bmatrix} \text{to} \\ \text{from} \end{Bmatrix}$Boston

b   plane $\begin{Bmatrix} \text{to} \\ \text{from} \end{Bmatrix}$ New York

c   shuttle $\begin{Bmatrix} \text{to} \\ \text{from} \end{Bmatrix}$ San Francisco

d   train $\begin{Bmatrix} \text{to} \\ \text{from} \end{Bmatrix}$ Washington

e   tour $\begin{Bmatrix} \text{to} \\ \text{of} \\ \text{from} \end{Bmatrix}$ Charlotte

f   express $\begin{Bmatrix} \text{to} \\ \text{from} \end{Bmatrix}$ Chicago

Obviously, all of the words which appear in the syntactic phrases in (12) must be entered in the lexicon. What of the compounds in (11)? They too are words. Should they also be entered in the lexicon?

To see the untenability of such a view, it is only necessary to note that the examples in (11) are only a miniscule fragment of the total number of analogous elements. There are literally thousands and thousands of *flight* compounds formed with a place name preceding *flight*, that is, there are thousands of nouns of the form ⎯⎯´ *flight*. But corresponding to each of these nouns there is a syntactic phrase or set of phrases like (12a). The grammar would miss a generalization if it were supposed that English has listed in its lexicon the enormous number of compound words which correspond to such phrases. In the face of the correlations between (11) and (12), the obvious move is to suppose that words of the (11a) variety are derived from syntactic phrases like (12a), etc.

There are, again, further supports for such a proposal. First, a phrasal derivation permits a natural explanation of the degree of ambiguity (if any) of the relevant compounds. Thus, *Boston flight* has two distinct meanings because it can be derived from either variant of (12a). *Charlotte tour* is ambiguous in at least three ways, because in addition to the two possibilities found with *flight*, *tour* also occurs with *of* phrases. Second, a derivation of compounds like *Boston flight* is productive in the same way that *Adj V ing* compounds are. Thus, most people will probably not have heard of a small city in India called *Dharamsala*. But immediately upon learning the existence of this place name, one can form a vast variety of compounds of the form:

(13) a Dharamsala flight
      b Dharamsala express

If all such compounds had to be learned by rote and stored in a fixed lexical list, it would be impossible to explain how the learning of a new place name immediately provides mature speakers with the ability to use the extensive set of compounds. We conclude that such compounds are not listed in the lexicon but are rather formed by rule from corresponding syntactic phrases. This again amounts to a rejection of the view that speakers' lexicons contain all of the words they use and understand.

Not very much has been said about the nature of the rules which derive compounds like *Boston flight* from phrases of the form *flight* $\left\{\begin{matrix} to \\ from \end{matrix}\right\}$ *Boston*. Many problems exist in the precise formulation of such rules. We shall not attempt to delve deeply into these processes here. Certain aspects of these operations deserve some attention, however. Consider an example of the form:

(14) I am waiting for the flight from Boston, which is where Greta lives.

In this sentence, the appositive relative clause, *which is where Greta lives*, modifies *Boston*. This argues that *Boston* is an NP constituent, since in general such modifying clauses are associated with NPs. Consider then:

(15) *I am waiting for the Boston, which is where Greta lives, flight.

The ungrammaticality of (15) argues that the element *Boston* in a compound like *Boston flight* is not an NP since, unlike its counterpart in (14), it cannot be modified by a nonrestrictive clause. That is, if we say *Boston* is not an NP in (15), then the impossibility of such modification will be an automatic consequence.

This seems to raise a problem for the claim that *Boston flight* is derived from *flight from/to Boston*, which does not seem to predict such a switch in categorization. However, this would be a real problem only if it were the case that such a loss of category membership were an idiosyncratic feature, typical of some compounds and not others. If, however, it is a universal fact (that is, at least universal for all compounds in English) that

(16) No compound noun dominates any NP nodes.

then it is possible to posit a general principle which erases the NP categorization of elements which are compressed into compounds. In that case, the rule which forms *Boston flight*, etc., would not itself have to carry out this NP erasing operation. We think that there is good support for principle (16) and thus that the loss of NP nodes is a general phenomenon independent of particular compounding rules. If so, the latter need only carry out the compounding. The loss of NP categorizations is an automatic result of the derivation of the compound structure.

There is another process, closely related to that illustrated in (11), which produces a class of compounds which also illustrate the loss of NP-hood phenomenon:

(17) a the Staten Island-to-Manhattan ferry

    b the Hongkong-to-Taiwan flight

    c the San Francisco-to-New York express

The stress patterns indicate that these forms, like *Boston flight*, etc., are compounds. They are related to fuller syntactic phrases like:

(18) a The ferry from Staten Island to Manhattan is slow.
    b I missed the flight from Hongkong to Taiwan.
    c Someday we should see the express from San Francisco to New York.

The place names in (18) are NPs, since they can be modified by nonrestrictive relative clauses:

(19) The ferry from Staten Island, which is where I live, to Manhattan, which is where she lives, is slow.

But the parallel modification in the corresponding compound is ill-formed:

(20) *The Staten Island, which is where I live, -to -Manhattan, which is where she lives, ferry is slow.

So again, the elements of the compound, though superficially similar to those in fuller phrases, do not function as NPs in the derived structure. This assumes that compounds like *the Staten Island-to-Manhattan ferry* are derived from syntactic phrases like *ferry from Staten Island to Manhattan*. The arguments favoring this view are parallel to those examined in the case of simpler compounds like *Boston flight*.

There are thousands of such compounds, each corresponding to a syntactic phrase expressing essentially the same meaning. Failure to derive the compounds from the phrases would mean that each of the compounds would have to be redundantly listed in the lexicon. Moreover, such a listing would fail to account for the instant productivity of the process. As soon as two new place names are learned, one can utilize compounds based on them as well as the syntactic phrases. Compounds like (17) thus furnish another example of a process in English whereby words are created by the syntactic part of the grammar rather than being drawn from a finite list.

We have been assuming without explicit discussion that the various compounds treated so far are in fact single words. There are various pieces of support for this view. First, words are primarily elements having an independent pronunciation and permitting pausing at their boundaries. Moreover, words are not made up of smaller elements *having these properties*. It is notable that the compounds in question do not naturally permit internal pauses, in contrast to the syntactic phrases with which they are associated. This indicates the wordlike character of the former. Thus compare:

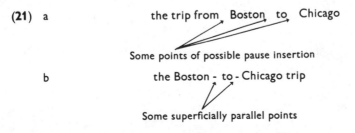

(21) a   the trip from Boston to Chicago

Some points of possible pause insertion

    b   the Boston - to - Chicago trip

Some superficially parallel points

In (21a), which is in our terms the presumed source for (21b), certain possible points of pausing are indicated. The insertion of pauses at these points is natural. In (21b), however, insertion of pauses at the marked points is unnatural and produces a certain effect, namely, that the speaker has forgotten what is to follow. The cohesion of structures like (21b) is similar to, though somewhat weaker than, the cohesion of multi-morpheme noncompound words like *international* or *superordinate*, in which pausing after the morphemes *inter* or *super* is out of the question. Correlated with the unnaturalness of pauses in (21b), as compared with (21a), is the impossibility of certain *parenthetical* expressions in the latter, expressions which occur quite happily in the former. This is a phenomenon somewhat analogous to the behavior of nonrestrictive clauses seen earlier:

(22) a   the trip from Boston to, I guess, Chicago
      b   the trip from, where was it, Boston, to Chicago

(23) a   *the Boston-to, I guess, Chicago trip
      b   *the, where was it, Boston-to-Chicago trip

Such facts involving pausing and parentheticals can be naturally expressed in a system which recognizes the single-word character of compounds by such simple principles as:

(24) a   Words cannot contain pauses.
      b   Words cannot contain parenthetical elements.

There is another peculiarity of compounds which argues for their single-word character. Consider such sentences as:

(25) a   The shuttle from here to New York takes six hours.
      b   The shuttle from Washington to there takes one hour.

These show that it is possible for such syntactic phrases to contain the coreferential pronouns *here* and *there*, which refer to locative NPs in certain kinds of contexts.[3] We would expect to find the same forms in compounds but, interestingly, this is impossible:

(26) a   *The here to New York shuttle takes six hours.
      b   *The New York to there shuttle takes one hour.

Given our assumption that forms like *Chicago-to-New York shuttle* are single-word nouns, while forms like *shuttle from Chicago to New York* are multi-word phrases, it is possible to explain the facts in (26) in terms of a very simple principle parallel to those in (24):

(27) Words cannot contain coreferential pronouns.

This principle predicts not only the distribution in cases like (26) but also those in simpler compounds:

(28) a   Harry likes gloves made out of leaves but I don't like gloves made
          out of them.

    b *Harry likes leaf gloves but I don't like themgloves.

    c Harry likes soup made out of bark, but I don't like soup made out of it.

    d *Harry likes bark soup but I don't like itsoup.

Thus, just as there are no compounds of the form *here-to-Chicago shuttle* or *Chicago-to-there flight*, there are none of the form *themgloves* or *itsoup*. Likewise, there is no compound analogous to *Boston flight* of the form *here flight* or *there flight*.

    Principle (27) supports the wordlike character of compounds because it is a generalization which holds of both compounds and simpler words. That is, just as there are no compounds in English containing *it*, *them*, *here*, *there*, etc., there are no words analogous to *international*, *superstar*, etc., containing them:

(29)

A (Phrases)	B (Single words)
person for {vivisectionists / them}	provivisectionist
	*prothemist
person against {abortions / them}	anti-abortionist
	*anti {them / it} ist
voyages across {oceans / them}	transoceanic (voyages)
	*transthemic (voyages)
play between {leagues / them}	interleague (play)
	*inter {them / it} (play)

    There is one further peculiarity of compounds in English which argues for their single-word character. A certain number of proper nouns in English, falling into various subtypes,[4] require that the definite article, *the*, precede them. Many place names have this property, and it is, for instance, general for all names based on the word *building*:

(30)

A

{ The Bronx / The Eiffel Tower / The Hague / The Empire State Building } is worth seeing.

B

{ *Bronx / *Eiffel Tower / *Hague / *Empire State Building } is worth seeing.

Significantly, none of the well-formed place names in column A of (30) can occur as the second element in compounds of the sort in (17):

(31) a   *the Queens-to-the Bronx ferry[5]
     b   *the Louvre-to-the Eiffel Tower tour
     c   *the Amsterdam-to-the Hague bus
     d   *the Rockefeller Center-to-the Empire State Building bus

If sequences like those in (17) are single words, facts like those in (31) can be treated in terms of a principle parallel to those in (24) and (27):

(32)   Words in English cannot contain the definite article (*the*).

Principle (32) is not only true of compounds like those in (17) but also of those analogous to *Boston flight*. Thus *moon* and *sun* are proper nouns[6] which require *the*:

(33) a   The sun sets at 10:00 today.
     b   *Sun sets at 10:00 today.
     c   The moon is lovely tonight.
     d   *Moon is lovely tonight.

Yet, when these form compounds, the definite article may not appear, as predicted by principle (32):

(34) a   *The best the sunlight is in the afternoon.
     b   The best sunlight is in the afternoon.

(35) a   *The first the moonflight was a great success.
     b   The first moonflight was a great success.

Compare:

(36) a   The best light from $\left\{\begin{array}{l}\text{*sun}\\ \text{the sun}\end{array}\right\}$ is in the afternoon.

     b   The first flight to $\left\{\begin{array}{l}\text{*moon}\\ \text{the moon}\end{array}\right\}$ was a great success.

We must then posit a rule to delete the definite article in compounds, with failure of this rule to operate blocking cases like (34a) and (35a) via principle (32)[7]. Principle (32) supports the wordlike character of compounds because it is true not only of compounds but of all simpler and simple words as well. No form which we have grounds to regard as a word contains the definite article.[8]

     We conclude that the variety of compounds like *moonflight*, *Boston flight*, and *Chicago-to-Boston flight* are single words formed productively from phrases. Because of their phrasal origin, they constitute examples of words which are not to be found in a proper lexicon.

     We have by no means exhausted the operations in English which productively supplement the finite stock of words in the lexicon with compositionally formed words. There are, for example, compound participles functioning as noun modifiers in cases like:

(37) a French-speaking doormen
       b English-speaking children
       c German-speaking workers

Obviously there is a direct relationship between such phrases and those like:

(38) a doormen who speak French
       b children who speak English
       c workers who speak German

Since the grammar of English gives rise to examples like (38) in any event, and since these have a form corresponding to a quite general construction in English (head noun and restrictive relative clause), it is natural to assume that forms like those in (37) derive from corresponding phrases like those in (38). Thus all words like *French-speaking*, etc., can be eliminated from the lexicon.

Again, considerations of productivity as well as simplicity impose such a solution. Compound participles like those in (37) can be formed from any language name. As soon as we learn there is a language Gwambamamba,[9] we can form the compound *Gwambamamba-speaking*.

Although the process in question is completely productive for the verb *speak* with language names, it is highly restricted otherwise, both with respect to the choice of verb and with respect to the choice of elements which will compound with the verb. Thus, even with language names, notice the impossibility of:

(39) a *French-reading children
       b *French-understanding doctors
       c *French-studying students
       d *French-learning diplomats

Therefore, the rules which form such compounds will have to be tightly constrained with respect to the choice of combinable elements. The proper way to impose such constraints remains far from clear.

The compound modifiers just discussed are based on the *-ing* or present participial forms of verbs. There is an analogous process based on the *-ed* or past participial forms of verbs:

(40) a Russian-made tanks
       b Turkish-built missiles
       c American-backed takeovers
       d Communist-instigated riots

The NPs in (40) are related to such superficially more complex NPs as:

(41) a tanks made by Russians
       b missiles built by Turks

c   takeovers backed by Americans
d   riots instigated by Communists

The variety of complex words discussed so far has been intended to show that not every word which is, in some sense, part of a speaker's vocabulary, finds its proper locus in that speaker's lexicon. Rather, as we have illustrated, the vocabulary appears to be divided into at least two separate segments. One segment consists of primitive words and parts of words which are basic in that they are not productively formed from the results of some other segment of the grammar. The other portion consists of words which are formed from independently derived structures. In the former lie words like *apple, love, sad*; in the latter those like *apple turnover, love-hungry, sad-looking*.

There is, it should be stressed, an even stronger argument than any of those given so far, showing that not all words can be represented lexically. Recall the discussion in Chapter 14 about sentence recursion. There, several different syntactic constructions were shown to have the property of infinite or unlimited extendability, as a consequence of which the sets of sentences they yield are infinite in number. We concluded from this that sentences cannot be listed in the mind. Rather, they must be formed in productive ways out of a finite stock of rules and primitive sentence elements. Significantly, along certain parameters, the set of words in English is unbounded. This gives the strongest argument of all that words cannot all be in the lexicon, since by definition a lexicon is finite.

Recall the possibility of making compound nouns. From the forms

(42)   a   elephant
      b   hide

one can form the compound:

(43)   elephant hide

Moreover, this process can continue, using already formed compounds as components of still larger compounds:

(44)   a   elephant hide wallet
      b   elephant hide wallet buckle
      c   elephant hide wallet buckle snap
      d   elephant hide wallet buckle snap store
      e   elephant hide wallet buckle snap store manager
      f   elephant hide wallet buckle snap store manager training
      g   elephant hide wallet buckle snap store manager training school

It seems that such compounds can be made longer and longer without limit. In opposition to such a claim, however, it might be argued that each increment in length requires use of at least one additional morpheme, and since there are only a finite number of morphemes, the process must ultimately terminate. This would mean there is some set of maximally long compounds.

However, the assumption that each increase of length requires use of a new morpheme is incorrect, since they may repeat. Thus from (44g) we may form:

(45) elephant hide wallet buckle snap store manager training school manager

And from (45):

(46) elephant hide wallet buckle snap store manager training school manager
     training

We could then add *school* again to the end of (46), giving a still longer compound. Since there is no bound on the number of times a particular element can appear in a compound,[10] there is truly no bound on the length of compounds, hence no bound on the number of compounds. There is thus, as a matter of logic, no possibility of listing all the compound words of English in some lexicon. Productive rules for forming compounds are an absolute necessity. This recursive property of compounds forms the strongest argument for the view that the set of all words in English is not coextensive even with the combination of the sets of words in all the lexicons of all the speakers of English. While speakers' lexicons may contain many of the words they know, there will be infinitely many words known which will not be lexically stored. To this extent, the contents of the lexicon and the set of words are by no means coextensive.

This is true for another reason. It is not the case that the lexicon contains only words. Recall from Chapter 4 that words are composed out of subparts we now call *morphemes*. We earlier displayed the word *anti-integrationist*, which is constructed out of the following list of morphemes:

(47) a anti-
     b -ion
     c -ist
     d integrat

It is possible that *integrat(e)* ought to be regarded as composed of a stem *integr*, appearing in such related words as *integral*, *integer*, and *integrity* and a further verbalizing affix *-at(e)*. If we survey the vocabulary of English, the number of subword elements like those in (47) is seen to be quite large. As noted in Chapter 6, there is a traditional typology of morphemes associated with such terms as *stem* or *root*, *derivational affix*, and *inflection*. The number of inflections, tense endings, plural and genitive markers, etc. is tiny. The number of derivational affixes, *-ion*, *-ist*, *anti-*, etc., is larger but still relatively restricted. Furthermore, like the inflections, affixes are largely fixed over periods of time. However, the stems or roots are vast in number and subject to constant accretions. This is the core of the language's lexical resources. In English, it is traditional to distinguish among noun stems (*dog, apple, god*, etc.), verb stems (*like, hate, try*, etc.), and adjective stems (*sad, nice, wild*, etc.).[11] In many cases in English, a language with limited inflection, stems can occur in sentences as words. Many languages do not permit this, but only allow words containing various types of inflectional affixes.

In any event, an overall account of the set of possible English words will require a lexicon which lists not only those forms capable of occurring as full words but also the various morphemes which make them up. It would, for instance, make no sense to list in the lexicon every complex adjective based on the derivational element *un-* found in such words as:

(48) a unhappy
b unwilling
c unable
d unreal
e unexciting

Rather, what is desired is some way[12] of saying that *un-* combines with adjective stems, that is, *some* adjective stems, to yield derived adjectives. It is only the stems that should be listed directly in the lexicon. The validity of this conclusion is supported by arguments analogous to those given earlier for deriving various compounds. In particular, *un-* combines with various subsets of adjective bases which are themselves productively formed:

(49) a uncrushable
b unbreakable
c undrinkable

Clearly there is some kind of process forming adjectives from a subset of transitive verbs (*crush*, *break*, *drink*, etc.) plus the affix-*able*.[13] But these derived adjectives are themselves capable of further expansion with *un-*. Obviously though, one should not list forms like *breakable* in the lexicon, since this seems productively formed from *break*. It follows that *unbreakable*, formed from *breakable*, should not be listed.

A proper lexicon will contain a variety of morphemes—stems, affixes, and inflections—some of which are coextensive with words and some of which are not. In general, a lexicon is smaller than the set of all words, in that many words are productively derived and not listed, and bigger than the set of primitive words, in that lexicons must also contain the full set of subword-sized elements like *un-*, *anti-*, etc.

SUMMARY

In this chapter, we examined certain crucial features of the content of the lexicon. It has been shown that, despite its superficial reasonableness, one cannot suppose that all the words known by speakers are contained in their lexicons. Rather, infinitely many words are formed by various productive rules from independently characterized constructions. Unless this fact is recognized, a variety of generalizations about English word formation will be overlooked.

It was also pointed out that words are constructed not only out of other word-sized elements, but also from subparts which are smaller than words. That is, there are morphemes, falling into various subtypes: derivational affixes (*anti-*,*-ist*, *un-*), inflections (genitive, past tense) and most importantly stems or roots, of which there are thousands. All of these morphemes must also be assumed to be in the lexicon. Thus, the lexicon is the repository of all of the morphemes but of only some of the words. Morphemes, not words, are the truly primitive lexical elements.

In passing, several important laws governing the possible internal structures of words in English were noted, laws which govern simple words as well as those compounds and complex forms derived by productive rule. These were:

- **(i)** Words cannot contain pauses.
- **(ii)** Words cannot contain parenthetical elements.
- **(iii)** Words cannot contain coreferential pronouns.
- **(iv)** Words cannot contain the definite article.

It is worth stressing that although we claimed the existence of a variety of productive operations for forming complex words, we did not attempt to formulate any of these explicitly. This is a task which would carry us far beyond the bounds of an introductory study.

Finally, although we have explored the limits on the classes of items which must stored in lexicons, we have not yet specified how the lexicon functions in combination with base rules to form initial trees. This topic is addressed in the following chapter.

NOTES

1. The occurrence of these *to* phrases in examples like (7) is a further indication of their relation to those like (6), which also can contain these. However, for many speakers at least, such phrases are well-formed with the complex adjectives only when they are preposed:

- **(i)** a   That soup smells delicious to me.
  -    b   To me, that soup smell delicious.
- **(ii)** a   *That soup is delicious-smelling to me.
  -      To me, that soup is delicious-smelling.

We have no explanation for this peculiarity.

2. In English there is one syllable in each word which is more prominent than any of the others. This prominence is called *accent* or *stress*, and part of a speaker's competence involves the knowledge of which syllable in a word receives the greatest prominence. For example, in the word *alphabet*, the first syllable is the most prominent, roughly, the loudest. This prominence can be indicated by placing a slash over the vowel of the syllable. Hence: *álphabet*. The most prominent syllable is not always the initial syllable: *Berlín, veránda, América, désert, associátion*.

The most prominent syllable in a word is said to receive *primary stress*, the stress indicated by ´. However, many words have more than one stress. That syllable which receives less than primary stress but which is still stressed is said to receive *secondary stress*. This can be marked by a slash going in the opposite direction ` : *cómpensàte, ànticipatòry, tỳphóon, rèferée*. Syllables with no marking over them are effectively stressless.

It is a general property of compound nouns, like those in (11) in the text, that the first element of the compound receives primary stress and the second secondary stress. This is true for all types of compounds. Some further examples: *fóuntain pèn, mánagement tràining, negòtiátion posìtion*.

The facts mentioned here are in accordance with certain specific and well worked out rules for the placement of stress in English words. Based upon these rules, it is possible, given proper phonological representations for morphemes, to predict which syllables in words, simple or complex, and even in larger phrases composed of words, receive primary, secondary, or no stress. This constitutes a significant result of recent theoretical work on English phonology. However, this lies outside of the scope of the present manual, in which we have decided to utilize the traditional orthography, rather than more adequate phonological representations.

3. Only some locative NPs can be so referred to:

(i)   Jack lives in Boston$_i$ but I don't live there$_i$.
(ii)   *John doesn't want to live in Boston$_i$ because there$_i$ is having a lot of riots.

Locative NPs occurring in subject positions cannot have the form *there*, which is restricted to adverbial contexts (a notion which has never been characterized adequately).

4. For instance, names of people do not generally take *the*. But they do when pluralized or when modified by a restrictive relative clause (which is rare):

(i)   Jenkins is here.
(ii)   *The Jenkins is here.
(iii) *Jenkins $\begin{Bmatrix} who \\ that \end{Bmatrix}$ I met yesterday is here.

(iv) The Jenkins $\begin{Bmatrix} \text{who} \\ \text{that} \end{Bmatrix}$ I met yesterday is here.

(v) *Jenkins are here.

(vi) The Jenkins are here.

Similarly, names of island groups (*The Azores*) and mountain ranges (*The Himalayas*) regularly require *the*, as do ocean names (*The Pacific*) but not lakes ((*The*) *Lake George*).

5. When *the Bronx* appears as the first element of such compounds, as in

(i) the Bronx-to-Queens ferry

the result is well-formed. This contrast between first and second positions seems to be general for the set of all proper nouns which must occur independently with *the*:

(ii) a the Louvre-to-Notre Dame tour
  b the Eiffel Tower-to-Versailles excursion
  c the Hague-to-Amsterdam express

It might be thought that this is due to the presence of an immediately preceding *the* in such cases. However, the *the* occurrences in (ii) are not associated with the following proper nouns but with the entire NP and are, moreover, unnecessary for well-formedness. Good NPs result from replacing these by indefinite articles like *a*, *certain* (with pluralization of the final morphemes to *tours*, etc.) or with the demonstratives *this*, *that*, *these* (again with pluralization):

(iii) An Eiffel-Tower-to-Versailles excursion would be exhausting.

It seems then that one must simply say that the rule which deletes the definite article from proper nouns when they become word-internal by compounding can only operate on those *the* which are word-initial. That is, representing word boundaries for the moment by #, it can only work in the context:

(iv) X, #the _____ #

Such deletion will not be able to operate in a case like (31a), which has the structure

(v) the # Queens-to-the Bronx ferry #

in which the relevant *the* is word-internal. It must thus remain in the structure which is then ruled out by principle (32) in the text.

6. That is, they can be. They also function as common nouns in cases like:

(i) That planet has no moons.

(ii) Some solar systems are blessed with two suns.

As proper nouns, these designate the particular celestial bodies of our solar system. As common nouns, they refer to any bodies meeting the conditions of satellitehood and starhood.

7. As discussed in note 5. Actually, the rule deleting *the* may only be restricted to word-initial occurrences in compounds, but not in other types of words. See note 8.

8. There are other cases in which expected definite articles do not show up. Thus, it is natural to derive forms like

(i) underground
(ii) Papal

from phrases involving

(iii) under the ground
(iv) The Pope

in which *the* is obligatory. Thus, there might be derivations like:

(v) explosions under the ground $\Longrightarrow$ explosions #under the ground#

In order to derive (i) then, it is also necessary that *the* disappear since it is not present in the result (if it were, it would violate principle (32)). However, according to the discussion leading to example (iv) in note 5, the environment for deletion is not met in this case. Perhaps the environment in (iv) should be slightly extended to permit deletion not only of word-initial *the* but also of those *the* preceded by a small number of affixes like *under*. This is a matter we have not explored in depth.

9. In fact, there is no such language. This makes the point even clearer.

10. In many cases, it even appears relatively natural to form compounds in which occurrences of the same element are contiguous:

(i) lion hunters
(ii) lion hunter hunters
(iii) lion hunter hunter hunters
(iv) lion hunter hunter hunter hunters

Example (iv) seems a relatively acceptable way of referring to people whose task is to hunt people who hunt people who hunt people who hunt lions.

11. Of course, many stems will fall into two or more such sets. Thus, *clean* is both a verb stem and an adjective stem, *pickle* both a verb stem and a noun stem, etc.

12. It is natural to attempt to derive complex words with *un-* from phrases involving the negative *not*:

(i) Joe is not willing to go $\Longrightarrow$ Joe is unwilling to go.

Although attractive for some cases, such an approach quickly runs into unsolved problems. In many cases, the meanings are not properly correlated. An unhappy man is not necessarily the same thing as a man who is not happy, since the latter allows for a neutral state between the two extremes. Moreover, many adjectives do not combine with *un-*:

(ii) a *ungood
     b *undead
     c *unsick
     d *undirty

Thus, while it is natural to attempt to derive *un- Adj* words from phrases involving negative words, no successful treatment of this sort has yet been worked out.

13. It is natural to attempt to relate the *-able* element which occurs in these words to the adjective *able* of such clauses as:

(i) John is able to walk now.

This also combines with *un-*:

(ii) John is unable to walk now.

One might try to derive elements like *crushable* by getting the *crush* from the complement of *-able*. Derivations might be something like

(iii) [NP is able to crush that] $\Longrightarrow$ That is crushable.

or perhaps:

(iv) [that is able to be crushed] $\Longrightarrow$ That is crushable.

Such derivations involve many problems, somewhat analogous to those in note 12. In particular, the meanings and combinatorial possibilities of the two *able*'s are not identical. Although (v) is fine, (vi) is anomalous and (vii) attributes the ability to *one* while (v) attributes it to *that*:

(v)   That is (un)knowable.
(vi) *That is (un)able to be known.
(vii) ?One is (un)able to know that.

PROBLEMS

1. Formulate arguments justifying the view that the complex past participles in (40) in the text derive from the corresponding multi-word phrases in (41) in the text.

2. Are there any reasons why the following words should not be listed in the English lexicon:

  (i)   builder
  (ii) home-builder
 (iii) sharpener
  (iv) knife-sharpener

3. The following pairs of English words

  (i)   possible—impossible
  (ii) regular—irregular
 (iii) complete—incomplete

reveal an important property of morphemes. Can you say what it is? In formulating your answer, it will be necessary to determine a common feature of the three words on the right.

CHAPTER 16 **THE LEXICON AND LEXICAL INSERTION**

PREVIEW

Every tree appearing in this manual has contained particular English words. However, the base rules postulated up to this point do not in general give rise to particular words. This raises the question of how words find their way from the lexicon into particular initial trees. The present chapter sketches an answer to this question.

A principle of lexical insertion is established which bridges the gap between the lexicon and the tree fragments produced by the base rules. For this principle to function, the information associated with lexical elements must include an indication of grammatical category membership, for example, that *sleep* is a V, that *nut* is an N, etc. Further, more refined distinctions must be made; for example, there must be a way to mark the difference between Vs like *sleep*, which cannot occur with direct objects; Vs like *hit*, which can occur with direct objects but not indirect objects; and Vs like *write*, which can occur with both direct and indirect objects. This leads to the recognition of the labeling of the syntactic properties Intransitive, Transitive, and Ditransitive, which are associated, respectively, with *sleep*, *hit*, and *write*. Such information plays a crucial role in making sure that a V like *sleep* is not inserted in such a way as to give rise to ill-formed results like *The girl sleeps the hotel*.

However, the principle of lexical insertion, together which such markings as V, Transitive, etc., will not be able to prevent the generation of examples like *The apple called Betty*. To deal with these, semantic considerations

must be appealed to. Sentences with main verbs like *call* require
subjects which refer to mind-possessing entities. The bizarre example just
given violates this semantic condition on *call*.

In the preceding chapter, we examined some aspects of the content of the
lexicon. However, the interaction of the lexicon with the base rules has
not really been dealt with. Recall that the base component was represented
schematically as:

(12)

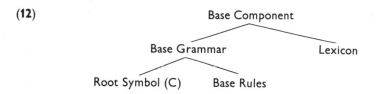

Base Component

Base Grammar   Lexicon

Root Symbol (C)   Base Rules

The base rules elaborated so far are:

(2) a   C $\longrightarrow$ NP V (NP) (NP)
    b   NP $\longrightarrow$ NP C
    c   NP $\longrightarrow$ C
    d   NP $\longrightarrow$ Conj (NP)^n
    e   Conj $\longrightarrow$ $\begin{Bmatrix} and \\ or \end{Bmatrix}$
    f   NP $\longrightarrow$ Art N

A glance at these reveals a glaring limitation. Although every tree necessarily
contains particular lexical morphemes, which are the *terminal* elements of
the structures, the base rules given do not, with the exception of (2e), introduce any lexical elements. But we know that the lexicon is a repository
containing all of the lexical elements. What is needed is some way for particular entries from the lexicon to be inserted as the labels of the ultimate nodes
in trees, those from which no structure emanates downward. These are the
terminal nodes of the trees. Put differently, what is required is a way for the
category labels Art, N, V, etc., to come to dominate particular lexical morphemes and words. At the moment, the rules in (2) cannot really generate
complete initial trees nor can they make use of the lexicon to carry out this
function. All they can do is produce incomplete trees (or tree fragments)
like:

(3)

C

NP   V   NP

Art N   Art N

Let us call Art, N, V, etc., *lexical categories*. This term will be applied to any category which immediately dominates whole words. It corresponds rather closely to the traditional *part of speech* (see the discussion in Chapter 4). Lexical categories are thus contrasted with nonlexical categories like C, NP, etc. To provide for the insertion of words under lexical categories in initial trees, we shall introduce a special mechanism, namely, a base rule which expands *every lexical category* (and no other) as follows:

(4)
$$\left\{\begin{matrix} \text{Art} \\ \text{N} \\ \text{V} \\ \vdots \end{matrix}\right\} \longrightarrow \ \diamondsuit$$

Adding this base rule to (2), the tree fragment in (3) can be further developed into:

(5)

The symbol $\diamondsuit$ is a dummy symbol, a blank or arbitrary label, as it were. It labels the terminal nodes of all the configurations generated by the base rules alone. It is to be interpreted as a place holder for lexical elements from the lexicon.

Given this new mechanism, it is now possible to introduce a general principle of lexical insertion. This will characterize the way that entries from the lexicon can be added to the output of the base rules to give genuine initial trees in place of placeholder-containing structures like (5);

(6) Lexical Insertion Principle
    a   Every occurrence of $\diamondsuit$ must be replaced by an item from the lexicon.
    b   An occurrence of the symbol $\diamondsuit$ may be replaced by a lexical item only if the lexical item is marked as a member of the lexical category which immediately dominates that particular occurrence of $\diamondsuit$.
    c   Otherwise, replacement of $\diamondsuit$ by lexical elements from the lexicon is *syntactically* constrained only by contextual restrictions built into particular entries (see principles (15), (19) and (32) below).

Principle (6a) is needed since every instance of $\diamondsuit$ must be replaced by a word or morpheme in order for a well-formed tree to result. Principle (6b) is needed in order to insure that a lexical item such as *write* does not end up dominated by Art, or that *John* does not end up dominated by V, etc. Trees in which such mismatches occur will obviously be ill-formed. They make incorrect claims about items, that is, that *write* is an Art (and hence similar to *the*, etc.), that *John* is a V, etc.

To insure that lexical items can replace ◇ only in proper ways, it will be necessary to associate with each item in the lexicon a formal marker indicating the lexical category to which it belongs. For example, there will have to be entries in the English lexicon along the lines of:[1]

(7) [*write*, V, ...]   [*eagle*, N, ...]   [*letter*, N, ...]
    [*John*, N, ...]   [*girl*, N, ...]   [*electron*, N, ...]
    [*the*, Art, ...]   [*boy*, N, ...]   [*note*, N, ...]

Returning to the tree in (5), the Lexical Insertion Principle will allow the various instances of ◇ to be replaced by items from (7) in several satisfactory ways:

(8) a

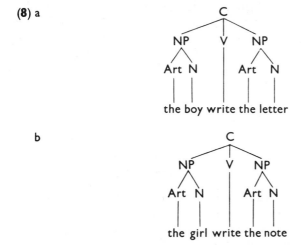

   b

The Lexical Insertion Principle provides the means for bridging the gap between the lexicon and the structures derived by the base rules. The joint functioning of this principle and rule (4) permit complete initial trees to be formed.

While the Lexical Insertion Principle will allow words to enter base trees at those ◇ nodes immediately dominated by the appropriate categories, there are other relationships between words and categories in base trees which (6) alone does not account for. For example, (6) will properly permit the insertion of lexical items as in (8a), but is unable to prevent:

(9)

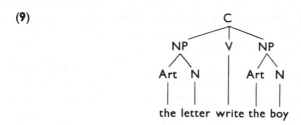

This initial tree would ultimately give rise to surface forms like:

(10) The letter wrote the boy.

Such examples violate some kind of constraint on the formation of proper clauses. Which kind? What is wrong with (10) is that the verb *write* carries with it certain assumptions contradicted by the nature of the NP subject in (10), *the letter*. The verb *write* requires a subject NP which refers to a mind-possessing individual. Since letters do not have this property, (10) manifests a clash between the meaning of its subject NP and the meaning which *write* demands that its subject NP have. This clash accounts for the bizarreness of (10). Example (10) is, in other words, not syntactically ill-formed, but rather semantically odd or anomalous.

It follows that a complete account of violations like those in (10) would require a treatment of the representation of the meanings of sentences and their parts, a treatment which lies beyond the scope of the present work. Such a treatment would have to expand the information associated with lexical entries to include an account of their meanings, an account which would contain specifications such as one requiring *write* to have certain kinds of subjects, etc.

Because sentences can be semantically bizarre as a result of assumptions associated with the meanings of forms, if these assumptions are modified, so too will the possibilities of bizarreness. Consider:

(11) a The little red engine felt sorry for the little boy.
b The little boy felt sorry for the little red engine.

There is nothing odd about (11b). *Feel* requires subject NPs referring to mind-possessing entities, and *the little boy* in (11b) fits this requirement. Example (11a), on the other hand, may well strike a reader as semantically anomalous, because engines are not normally deemed to be in possession of minds. However, in many contexts (11a) is not bizarre. This is not because it is wrong to say of *feel* that it requires a subject NP that refers to a mind-possessor. Rather, to understand a sentence like (11a), one must alter one's assumption about a particular *little red engine*. Specifically, one may suppose that the object in question is, surprisingly, endowed with intelligence. Sentences like (11a) are characteristic of children's stories. It is a common property of such stories that they alter normal assumptions about inanimate objects or about creatures not normally supposed to possess minds. *The Three Little Pigs* or *The Little Engine that Could* are cases in point. Such stories contain many sentences free of the bizarreness manifested by (10) because the reader alters his normal assumptions about the world for the duration of the story. This mental process even has a traditional name, personification. It is familiar to readers of poetry.

We claim, therefore, that the bizarreness of (10) and the bizarreness or lack thereof of (11a) are not the function of grammatical violations. Consequently, we do not regard it as an inadequacy of the base component that

It does not prevent the generation of examples like (10) and (11a). Such examples can be regarded as syntactically well-formed. They strike us as bizarre in certain contexts only when they clash with assumptions about the world which we hold in those contexts.

Returning to lexical insertion proper, there are certain problems which principle (6) does not deal with. For example, beginning with a tree like (5), the Lexical Insertion Principle has no way of preventing a verb like

(12) [*sleep*, V, . . .]

from being inserted to yield the ill-formed initial tree:

(13)

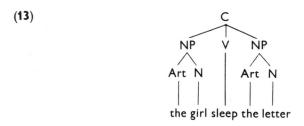

Example (13) is ill-formed because *sleep* is an intransitive verb. Recall Chapter 13, where verbs were classified as transitive and intransitive. Transitive verbs take direct objects, which were defined as NPs immediately to the right of verbs in the same clause. The difficulty in (13) is that *sleep* cannot appear in an initial tree clause containing a direct object. Lexical insertion of *sleep* in a configuration like (13) produces a violation of the intransitive character of *sleep*.

This raises the question of how information about such conditions on lexical items is to be represented. We assume these conditions are stated as special instructions in lexical entries:

(14) [*sleep*, V, Intransitive, . . .]

The syntactic property Intransitive will be taken to represent the following condition:

(15) Intransitivity Condition: Vs marked Intransitive can undergo lexical insertion only into the V nodes of clauses *lacking* direct objects.

Given the Lexical Insertion Principle and the Intransitivity Condition, (14) cannot be inserted in (13). However, consider:

(16) The girl slept in a hotel.

The discussion in Chapter 13 suggested that some Prepositional Phrases (PP) were introduced transformationally while others might be introduced by base rules. The sentence in (16) contains the PP *in a hotel* and the problem is whether its origin lies in the base or in the functioning of certain transformational rules. Considerations of the earlier part of this chapter suggest an answer. Suppose the base tree for (16), prior to lexical insertion, were to contain a NP to the right of the V:

(17)

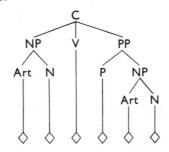

That is, suppose the PP *in a hotel* were viewed as an initial structure NP with the preposition *in* inserted by a later rule.

This alternative involves the difficulty that, beside the intransitivity condition (15), the grammar of English also needs an analogous condition for verbs like *hit*, which *require* direct objects. This is needed to allow sentences like (18a) and rule out those like (18b–c):

(18) a   The girl hit the boy.
       b   *The girl hit.
       c   *The girl hit in a hotel.

The relevant condition can be stated as:

(19)   Transitivity Condition: Vs marked Transitive in the lexicon can undergo lexical insertion only into the V nodes of clauses *containing* direct objects.

The Transitivity Condition will allow *hit* to be inserted into a tree like (17). But if (17) can be a remote structure not only of (18a) but also of sentences like (16), that is, if (16) is regarded as a transitive clause, it would also be possible to insert *hit* into (17). This would then be further modified by a rule which inserted a preposition *in*, resulting in the ungrammatical:

(20)   *The girl hit in a hotel.

This failure can be avoided by supposing that the *in* phrase in (16) arises from a node PP introduced in the base. Thus, while (17) is a remote tree for (18a), it is not a possible remote tree for (16). Example (16) will have a remote tree of the form:

(21)

The tree in (21) will permit the insertion of *sleep* since the tree does not contain a direct object. Why not? A direct object is an NP *immediately* to the right of a V. There is no such NP in (21). Therefore, lexical insertion of *sleep* is possible in (21). Moreover, lexical insertion of *hit* is impossible in (21), thereby ruling out (20). This follows since *hit* requires a direct object in any clause into which it is inserted. Since (21) does not contain a direct object, principle (19) prevents it from being lexically inserted.

The present base rules do not allow structures like (21). This is easily rectified by adding two new base rules:

(22) C $\longrightarrow$ NP V PP
     PP $\longrightarrow$ P NP

These rules, coupled with those which appear in (2), are sufficient to generate trees like (21). They are not, however, sufficient to produce initial trees for sentences such as:

(23) The girl hit the boy in a hotel.

This sentence contains a direct object, *the boy*, and the PP, *in a hotel*, as well. An appropriate initial tree for this sentence is:

(24)

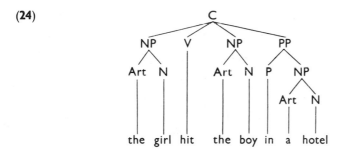

An additional rule is needed to permit direct objects and PPs to co-occur in initial trees:

(25) C $\longrightarrow$ NP V NP PP

At this point let us consolidate some of the proposed base rules:

(26) a C $\longrightarrow$ NP V NP PP
    b C $\longrightarrow$ NP V PP
    c C $\longrightarrow$ NP V

There is again an obvious relationship among them. Rule (26b) is contained in (26a) and (26c) is contained in (26b). We represent this relationship by making use of parentheses as in earlier chapters, replacing the three rules in (26) by the single formula:

(27) C $\longrightarrow$ NP V (NP) (PP)

As before, placing category labels in parentheses means that the elements so parenthesized may or may not be chosen in forming particular trees. Thus, when none of the options represented by the parentheses are chosen, the kind of tree that results is the primitive intransitive configuration:

(28)

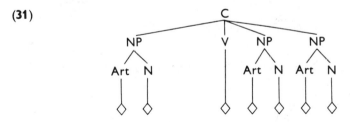

This is a remote tree for sentences such as *John slept* or *The girl is sleeping* (ignoring questions of tense and aspect, of course).

In addition to intransitive and transitive verbs, Chapter 13 also mentioned ditransitive verbs. These can occur in initial trees containing both an indirect object and a direct object. *Give* is such a verb:

(29) The boy gave the girl a present.

It was noted that the NP immediately to the right of the V was superficially a direct object but more remotely—and in line with traditional discussions of grammar—an indirect object. Thus, in

(30) The boy gave a present to the girl.

the underlying indirect object remains one. Prior to lexical insertion, a sentence like (30) has the structure:

(31)

A verb which can undergo insertion into such a tree must be marked Ditransitive. An additional condition is thus required:

(32) Ditransitivity Condition: Vs marked Ditransitive in the lexicon can undergo lexical insertion only into the V nodes of clauses containing both direct and indirect objects.

An indirect object is, of course, an NP which is both immediately to the right of a direct object and which is itself immediately dominated by the same C. Thus in (31) the first NP to the right of V is the direct object and the second NP is the indirect object.[2]

The lexical entry for *give* is:

(33) [*give*, V, Ditransitive, ...]

This will allow *give* to be lexically inserted under the V in (31). However, the Intransitivity, Transitivity, and Ditransitivity Conditions as now stated do not prevent a verb like *hit* from being (incorrectly) inserted into a base tree like (31). That is, they do not prevent the generation of sentences like:

(34) a *The girl hit a present to the boy.
   b The girl hit the boy a present.

It is, therefore, necessary to modify Transitivity Condition (17) so that it admits only simple transitive verbs into trees not containing indirect objects. Thus, (19) is replaced by:

(35) Transitivity Condition (modified): Vs marked Transitive in the lexicon can undergo lexical insertion only into the V nodes of clauses containing direct but not indirect objects.

The base rules given so far can specify base trees which underly sentences like:

(36) The boy wrote a novel in the park.

However, they cannot account for:

(37) The boy wrote a letter to the girl in the park.

To do this a further base rule must be added:

(38) C $\longrightarrow$ NP V NP NP PP

This allows trees like:

(39)

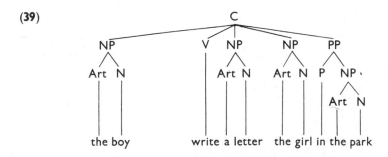

At this point, all of the base rules given for expanding C, including (2a) and the new (38) above, can be represented by the single formula:

(40) C $\longrightarrow$ NP V (NP) (NP) (PP)

We have examined each of the expansions of (40) and have found an example of each. Moreover, we have shown that in each case the Lexical Insertion

Principle coupled with the Intransitivity, Transitivity, and Ditransitivity Conditions can bridge the gap between the base rules and the lexicon.

Further points should be made about PP nodes. The first is that several such nodes can occur together:

(41)   a   The boy wrote a letter to the girl in the park on Sunday.
       b   The boy wrote a letter to the girl in the park on Sunday at 5 o'clock.

It is apparent that (40) must be extended to account for these as well. An appropriate modification of (40) might be:

(42)   C $\longrightarrow$ NP V (NP) (NP) (PP) (PP) (PP)

No attempt will be made to provide an exhaustive account of the number or type of PPs than can occur to the right of V. Rule (42) indicates that at least three such PP nodes may appear. We shall content ourselves with this degree of complexity.

Consider the initial tree for sentence (16):

(43)

Such a tree can give rise to:

(44)   The girl slept in a hotel.

The Lexical Insertion Principle will permit the intransitive verb *sleep* to be inserted into (43). What has not been illustrated is how the principle functions for prepositions. For example, in (44) the preposition *in* has been inserted. The Lexical Insertion Principle will allow for this if it is assumed that the lexical entry for *in* indicates the grammatical information that it is a member of the category P (for Preposition):

(45)   [*in*, P, ...]

There are a great many other prepositions as well:

(46)

A	**B**
[*beside*, P, ...]	[*to*, P, ...]
[*behind*, P, ...]	[*for*, P, ...]
[*over*, P, ...]	[*from*, P, ...]
[*under*, P, ...]	[*through*, P, ...]
[*at*, P, ...]	[*after*, P, ...]

The prepositions in column A will all produce good sentences when inserted into a tree like (43):

(47) The girl slept $\begin{Bmatrix} \text{beside} \\ \text{behind} \\ \text{over} \\ \text{under} \\ \text{at} \end{Bmatrix}$ a hotel.

Those in column B, on the other hand, when inserted into the same environment, yield bizarre results:

(48) The girl slept $\begin{Bmatrix} \text{for} \\ \text{to} \\ \text{from} \\ \text{through} \\ \text{after} \end{Bmatrix}$ a hotel.

Earlier in this chapter we were confronted with a similar problem when comparing sentences like:

(49)   a   The boy wrote the letter.
      b   The letter wrote the boy.

We claimed that semantic considerations rendered (49b) bizarre, since *write* is a verb requiring a subject that refers to an entity that possesses a mind. A similar tack will be taken with respect to the bizarre examples in (48). It is claimed that lexical insertion operates freely to introduce any and all prepositions into positions dominated by nodes labeled P. To say this another way, we are claiming that examples like (48) are generated by the grammar. The unacceptability of such sentences is to be attributed to roughly the same kind of semantic clashes which account for the bizarreness of examples like:

(50) The thermometer hates Frederick.

Thus, the preposition *through* requires its object NP to designate a portion of space serving as the "container" of the movement described by the main verb of its clause. Since *sleep*, for example, does not characterize a movement, the semantic condition on *through* cannot be met in examples like:

(51) The girl slept through a hotel.

On the other hand, in acceptable examples like:

(52) The girl ran through a hotel.

ran does characterize a movement through space and no semantic clash results.

SUMMARY

To characterize the interaction between the lexicon and the trees produced by the base rules, a new base rule introducing the symbol ◇ was postulated. A Lexical Insertion Principle was introduced requiring that a ◇ be replaced by a word belonging to the grammatical category immediately dominating that ◇ in the tree. This device provides a way for words to ultimately be inserted as terminal symbols in the trees produced by the base grammar. In addition, the Intransitivity, Transitivity, and Ditransitivity Conditions were formulated. These are necessary to ensure that intransitive verbs are only inserted into trees not containing direct objects, that transitive verbs are only inserted into trees containing direct objects, and that ditransitive verbs are only inserted into trees containing both direct and indirect objects.

NOTES

1. Given principle (6), it is now possible to provide a treatment of the conjunctions *and* and *or* which is consistent with the introduction of other morphemes. We eliminate base rule (2e) and add Conj to the list of categories in (4). Then *or* and *and* are listed in the lexicon as $\left[\left\{ \begin{matrix} and \\ or \end{matrix} \right\}, \text{Conj}, \ldots \right]$. In this way no morphemes are introduced by the base rules.

2. Indirect objects are, of course, ultimately assigned a preposition by transformation unless they undergo Indirect Object Shift and become direct objects. The insertion of a preposition creates a PP node which dominates both the preposition and the indirect object NP.

PROBLEMS

1. What is the source of the ungrammaticality of the example:

(i) *Koufax sighed the ball to the pitcher.

2. Construct lexical entries at the level of detail given in this chapter for the following verbs:

  (i)   cauterize
 (ii) hand
(iii) faint

3. Construct a sentence to illustrate each of the possibilities permitted by rule (42).

CHAPTER 17 **TRANSFORMATIONAL RULES**

PREVIEW

Throughout this manual, we have spoken of the need for remote structures to account for generalizations governing knowledge of English. The postulation of remote structures required postulation of a separate theoretical device: a set of rules which change remote structures into sur-face structures. These are called transformational rules. This chapter outlines how such rules operate.

A derivation was defined as a sequence of trees, beginning with an initial tree and ending in a surface tree. A change from one stage to a subsequent stage must be accomplished by a transformational rule. Each transformation must be stated in sufficiently general terms so that it can apply to an infinite set of trees. For example, there are an infinite number of trees which can potentially undergo reflexive marking. Obviously, such trees must be operated on by the same rule since, in each case, the same process is involved: a reflexive pronoun is distributed according to certain conditions on coreferentiality and clause mates, as seen in earlier chapters.

Thus transformational rules are like *templates* which are used to inspect particular trees to see if they are suitable for modification. Transformations then specify what changes particular trees must undergo. These two functions of transformational rules are referred to frequently enough to be given names. That part of a rule which determines whether or not specific trees are suitable for modification by that rule is called the *structural condition* or *structural description*. That part of the rule which specifies how the tree is to be modified is called the *structural change*. The two parts of a transformational rule are separated by a double arrow, written as ⟹, with the structural description or the template portion of the rule appearing on the left side of the arrow, and the structural change appearing on the right side:

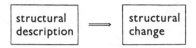

This chapter will characterize the contents of these boxes.

We are attempting to sketch the overall framework of a theory of grammar in which each sentence has a derivation involving the successive construction of a surface structure from an initial tree by way of intermediate remote-structure stages. We have so far given fairly detailed accounts of the functioning of base rules, the form of the lexicon, and the way in which lexical insertion characterizes the interaction of the lexicon with the structures provided by the base rules. We have not, however, directed much attention to the nature of transformations per se, or the way they apply to remote structures.

All that has been stated is that transformations change trees into trees by making some sort of formal changes and that in general transformations operate successively rather than simultaneously. Moreover, we have seen that there are various kinds of transformations. Most attention has been directed at deletion rules, in particular, rules which delete NPs, and in fact pronouns. We have seen that there are two fundamental types of such rules, uncontrolled deletions, like I Deletion, and controlled deletions, like Equi and CCS Deletion. In the latter, a pronoun is deleted subject to its coreference to some other NP in the input tree, called the controller or trigger. There are other types of deletion which do not involve the erasure of NPs as such, for instance, Gapping, which is the rule responsible for the deletions in (20) and (21) of Chapter 13.[1]

Several other types of transformation in addition to deletions must be recognized. One, briefly alluded to in Chapter 13, involves the rearrangement or movement of constituents from one point in a tree to another. Important examples of this sort of transformation will be considered in later chapters. There are also transformations, like Conjunction Copy of Chapter 14, which insert new elements into trees. Rules which introduce prepositions are also of this type.

Questions of how to formulate transformations and how these apply to structures are highly technical and complicated. A great deal about this remains to be understood. It would not be appropriate to deal with this question in depth in a work of this type, whose major goals are to indicate the need for remote structures and hence for transformational rules, and to illustrate these in the description of a range of English constructions. However, we can give a general sketch of the way such rules function and there are certain points about their operation that can be treated seriously. One of these, the question of the cyclic ordering of such rules, is dealt with substantially in Chapter 29. In general though, our practice will be, in what follows, largely what it has been up to this point, to argue for the existence of various transformations, to name them, but to describe them only in sketchy terms.

One can think of a transformation as having two parts. The first can be called its *structural condition* or *structural description*. This must be a statement which picks out the class of trees which can undergo the rule. For instance, some NPs must undergo Conjunction Copy, and others must not. The structural condition of Conjunction Copy must be formulated in such a way as to properly divide up NPs.

Second, a transformation must contain a formulation of the particular operation it is supposed to perform on the trees which meet its structural condition and which are thus proper *inputs*. This can be called the *structural change* of the transformation. Earlier discussion shows that structural changes fall into various types: deletions, movements, insertions, etc., and sometimes certain combinations of these.

When occasions arise where reasonable precision in the formulation of transformations is both possible and appropriate, such rules can be described in the following general format. The structural condition can be given in the form of a schema describing the possible form of inputs. This schema occurs on the left side of a double arrow. On the right side will be a schema describing the form of the *output*. These schemas will, representationally, look essentially like (parts of) incomplete constituent structure trees, *with certain exceptions*. To show this in greater detail, let us take for illustration the rule Conjunction Copy, mentioned in Chapter 14.

This can be formulated as follows in the terms just indicated:

(1a) Conjunction Copy

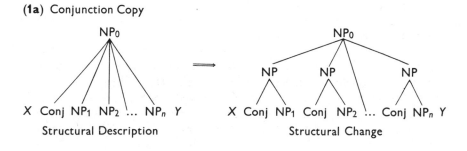

| Structural Description | Structural Change |

The *structural description* determines whether a given tree is modifiable by the rule. In order for the rule to make such a determination, it must have an input tree to work on. Let us take the input tree fragment discussed in Chapter 14 in connection with this rule:

(1b)

The structural description of Conjunction Copy in (1a) includes different sorts of symbols. Some, like Conj., NP,[2] etc., correspond to actual node labels in the input trees.

To the left and right of the labeled structure there are capital letters X and Y. These are called *variables*. They stand for *any arbitrary portion of structure at all*. To understand how the labeled structure and the variables of the structural description of Conjunction Copy operate, imagine that (1b) is actually part of a complete tree:

(1c)

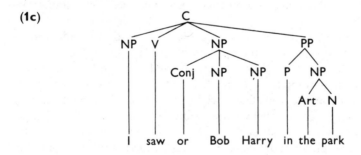

To determine whether the structural description of (1a) will apply to (1c), imagine that (1a) is printed on a piece of transparent plastic rather than on an opaque page. Imagine also that the piece of transparent plastic is moveable. Then imagine superimposing the transparent plastic over (1c) until it completely overlaps the input tree. If the structural description does completely overlap the input tree, then the rule is applicable.

It is actually impossible for the structural description of (1a) to overlap (1c) completely since the latter contains structure both to the left and right of the subtree in (1c) which is identical to that in (1b). Here the variables X and Y come into play. A variable is a symbol that stands for any structure at all, including no structure. If the structural description of (1a) is superimposed over (1c), then the X and the Y must stand for the parts of the tree as indicated in (1d):

(1d)

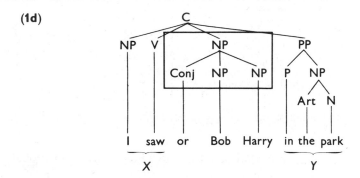

X   Y

Since X and Y can stand for any structure, they can stand for the particular portions embraced by the brackets. The portion enclosed in the box, on the other hand, cannot be just any structure. It must be the structure indicated in the structural description in (1a). Structure (1a)—excluding the variables X and Y—is a schema specifying an NP_0 which dominates a Conj node and any number of NP nodes from two up.

Since the phrase "any number of NP nodes" means, according to this convention, at least *two* NP nodes, the schema in (1a) includes this specific structure as well:

(1e)

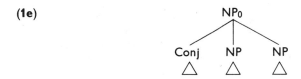

A glance at the boxed structure in (1d) shows that it is identical to that in (1e). Thus (1a), including the variables, completely overlaps (1d). Therefore, Conjunction Copy is applicable to the tree in (1d). This means that (1d) must be modified in accordance with the structural change indicated in (1a), that is, in accordance with the tree structure which appears on the righthand side of that rule.

In particular, the *structural change* of (1a) indicates how any tree which meets the condition of the left side must be reorganized. Namely, for each NP node attached to NP_0 on the left, a new NP node is created which dominates one of the conjuncts plus a copy on the left of whatever conjunction is in the input. The resulting order is parallel to that in the input. Moreover, the original occurrence of Conj is deleted.[3] So the resulting coordinate NP dominates only NPs. Thus, (1c) would be modified by the structural change of (1a) as follows:

(1f)

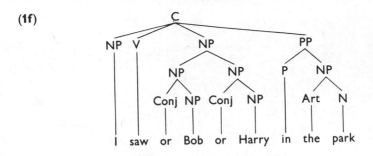

We have gone into a great deal of detail to show how a transformational rule reorganizes input trees. Conceptually, the structural description of a transformation has been viewed as a template designed to fit over specific input trees. If the fit is a perfect one, then the tree which the template fits is reorganized in accordance with the changes indicated to the right of the arrow, in the structural change. However, the fit must be perfect. If there is the slightest failure of overlap, the structural description is not met and the rule does not apply. In what follows, we shall not go into this kind of detail with respect to how structural descriptions fit trees and how the trees are reorganized. We shall simply state the rules and assume that the proper fit has been made and the proper reorganization affected.

In the preceding terms, the proper formulation of the structural description and change for CCS Deletion is as follows:

(2)   CCS Deletion

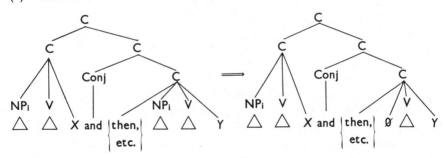

Here again X and Y are variables. The subscripts indicate coreference, just as in earlier sentence representations, and the symbol $\emptyset$ is the null symbol. The rule says that the subject NP node in the second conjunct and everything it dominates is replaced by null, that is, deleted.

Structure (2) illustrates for the first time that formulations of transformations can, on occasion, mention *particular morphemes* as well as category types. Thus, CCS Deletion contrasts with Conjunction Copy. The latter mentioned the node Conj but not the morphemes this dominated. This was due to the fact that Conjunction Copy applies regardless of whether Conj dominates *and* or *or*. But CCS Deletion only involves the conjunction *and*.

Observe that none of the base rules we gave will actually generate trees which could be input to CCS Deletion. That is, our highly restricted set of rules provided for coordinate NPs, but not for coordinated categories of other types. In particular, they do not introduce coordinate clauses, although these evidently exist. One can, however, make use of analogous base rules, with other categories taking the role of NP in the base rules we provided for co-ordinate NPs. Derivations involving other coordinated categories will also require analogues of Conjunction Copy and the rules to delete some con-junctions. For the patterns of conjoined nonNPs are, in these respects, essen-tially identical to those for conjoined NPs. Thus our treatment of NP co-ordination deals with only one facet of the range of coordination in English. But space does not permit either a deeper or more extensive exploration of this domain.

In a parallel fashion, one can offer the following as a first approximation[4] to a statement of Equi:

(3) Equi

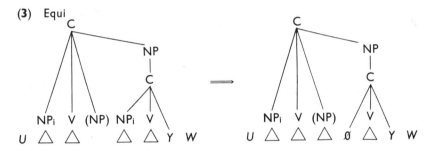

The variables permit the rule to apply to cases in which the relevant clause is itself a part of a larger structure, as in:

(4) I think John promised (Bill) to drink the tequila.

Here U represents *I think*. The variable Y represents everything in the clause whose subject is deleted, that is, *the tequila* in (4). The variable W represents everything which follows the object complement. Thus in

(5) I promised Bill to go because I felt sorry for him.

W would represent *because I felt sorry for him*. Since such a main clause can itself be followed by something

(6) I promised Bill to go because I felt sorry for him and then it snowed.

W can also represent *because I felt sorry for him and then it snowed*, etc. In some cases, variables stand for sequences which are constituents. But this is the exception. Thus W in (6) encompasses a nonconstituent.

The variables U and W in a rule like (3) are called *end variables*. As just shown, these are required to permit rules to apply even when the domain of the rule is embedded in a larger structure. End variables thus represent ir-relevant portions of the trees on either side of that structure which is actually involved in the operation of the rule. Although end variables are necessary, they complicate the task of reading rule statements. For convenience in what follows, we surpress end variables. Thus, we would write Equi without the *U* and the *W* on either side of the arrow in (3). Similarly, we would formulate (1a) without the *X* and the *Y* on both sides of the arrow.

Another notable feature of (3) is the presence of a parenthesized constituent, which indicates that it may or may not be present. This is to permit Equi to apply equally well in both:

(7)   a I promised to come.
      b I promised Sally to come.

We have thus sketched the way in which controlled deletion rules can be formulated. The formulation of uncontrolled NP deletion rules, like I Deletion and Why Not Deletion, which we posited earlier, involve a number of difficult and unresolved problems. Consider first I Deletion. This rule must delete second person subjects and only these. But it is not clear how a grammar formally represents such properties of grammatical elements as person (also number, gender, etc.). That is, how are second person pronouns formally marked in such a way that the rule of deletion can mechanically determine that these pronouns are second person, but that *he*, *I*, *one*, etc., are not, and even more fundamentally that *Bob*, *apples*, and *those proofs* are not?

It might be thought that the problem can be handled simply by listing in the deletion rule the pronouns which can be deleted, namely, *you* (singular) and *you* (plural). But because these two have identical shapes, this would at best reduce one unsolved problem, that of marking person, to another, of exactly the same sort, namely, that of marking number. Moreover, even ignoring this difficulty, the discussion of General Deletion showed that not all occurrences of singular *you*, *yourself*, etc., are second person pronouns. Some are variants of general pronouns. It follows that a grammar must, in general, have a way of marking such abstract properties of forms which goes beyond the mere (often homonymous) morphological form. One approach to this is to assume that there is a set of further grammatical categories—singular, plural, second person, etc.—and that these categories are associated appropriately with the entries of the relevant words in the lexicon.

For instance, one might argue that there is a category Pronoun, and that in the lexicon, *you*, *he*, *I*, *it*, etc., are associated with a marker indicating membership in this category, while *pickle*, *theory*, *deity*, etc., are not. In the same way, *you* could be associated in the lexicon with a marker for the category Second Person, which would not be assigned to *he*, *I*, *it*, etc. Initially an approach recognizing extra categories and markers to assign forms to them in the lexicon is not unattractive. However, it quickly runs into a variety of difficulties. And it is safe to say that no generally adequate approach to this realm of descriptive problems has been worked out. One general difficulty is that the categories which need to be recognized seem to overlap to differing degrees with *semantic* categories. Hence the positing of extra grammatical types seems redundant.

In part, what seems necessary is some way of letting grammatical rules refer to semantic information. But this is not too helpful practically at the moment, because there are not well-worked out systems for representing semantic information precisely.

In an introductory manual of this type, it would be a mistake to adopt some particular mechanisms for dealing with such descriptive problems. Rather, our strategy will be to recognize that the problem exists and to point out in particular cases what subcategorization of forms is necessary. In general we will not offer any formal means for imposing the needed subcategorization. Thus, in the case of I Deletion, we will say that:

(8) I deletion deletes the subject NPs of certain main clauses, subject to the condition that these subject NPs are exclusively second person.

By "exclusively," we mean that inclusive first person plurals cannot be deleted, nor can conjoined NPs of the form *you and Harry*, etc. Thus we state informally the subcategorization of NPs needed, leaving it an open matter for future research to determine the best methods of specifying such conditions precisely. In the same way, we would specify General Deletion by saying that the NP subjects it deletes must be general pronouns, and we would specify Why Not Deletion by saying that the NP subjects it deletes must be pronouns which include second person. We do not, however, commit ourselves to any representational technique for imposing subcategorizations like "general pronoun" or "pronoun involving second person ".[5] This is just one of very many points where the attempt to specify something interesting about grammatical structure runs into an area where crucial things are not known.

The same point is illustrated by another feature of constructions involving the uncontrolled deletion rules we have recognized. Consider Why Not Deletion, which yields such sentences as:

(9) Why not visit Majorca.

These involve the deletion of subjects whose reference includes second person. Hence the existence of such subjects in remote structure must be postulated. However, the key fact is that there are no sentences of the general form in (9), that is, with preverbal *not* and no auxiliary, which have not undergone Why Not Deletion. This appears to mean that somehow the base rules which form the remote structures for such sentences must limit the class of *why not* suggestion clauses to just those containing subjects of the form which Why Not Deletion can erase.

Actually, however, this is not necessarily true in the case of examples like (9), because of the existence of semantically similar sentences like:

(10) a Why doesn't Bob visit Majorca.
      b Why don't they visit Majorca.
      c Why don't you visit Majorca.

These show that *why not* suggestion clauses occur freely with all types of subjects *in the presence of an auxiliary do*. Therefore, the possibility exists of claiming that the more reduced suggestion clauses like those in (9) are derived from the fuller versions in (10), in which no special restrictions on subjects in remote structures are needed. Following this tack then, the subject restriction can be built into Why Not Deletion. Why Not Deletion will operate on a subset of remote structures of the type which underlie (10), removing just subjects which include reference to second person. A later obligatory rule will delete the auxiliary in such cases. Schematically, the situation is:

(11)   [why doesn't Bob visit Majorca] ⟹ Why doesn't Bob visit Majorca.

(12)

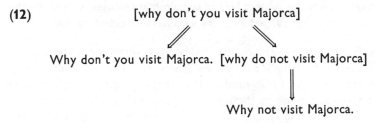

Within these terms then, there are no special restrictions on subjects occurring in the remote structures of *why not* suggestion clauses.

Unfortunately, such a solution to parallel restrictions is not always available. Consider I Deletion, which is restricted to removing second person subject NPs and only these, from imperative clauses. Unlike the case of *why not* suggestions, in which there are clauses showing a variety of subject types, there are no imperative clauses not containing second person subjects. Therefore, there is no approach to specifying the class of imperative clauses analogous to that just sketched for Why Not Deletion. Imperative clauses cannot be generated in the base with a free choice of subjects. The only imperative clauses which exist are those with second person subjects in remote structure, either ultimately deleted, as in (13a), or retained, as in (13b):

(13)   a   Open the door.
       b   You open that door.

Therefore, the base rules must limit imperative clauses to second person subjects, since this is not a job which can be accomplished by I Deletion. However, it is not clear what is the proper way to impose such conditions. Possibly this is a problem analogous to the question of subcategorizing NPs, pronouns, etc., into subtypes involving person, gender, number, etc. Perhaps one should take the position that clauses must also be so categorized, into imperative clauses, suggestion clauses, question clauses, declarative clauses, etc. In part, such a categorization is, of course, traditional. What would be needed among other things, is some way of formally assigning C nodes to such categories and equally importantly, a way of constraining the expansion of C nodes by base rules in terms of the category type of the clause (see Chapter 28). In particular, a mechanism would be needed to guarantee that the subject NPs of imperative clauses are restricted to second person. However, there exist at the moment no satisfactory solutions for this kind of descriptive difficulty. We content ourselves in this work with informal descriptions of the constraints needed.

Rule 1G of Chapter 6, which specifies the conditions determining the choice between reflexive pronouns, object pronouns, and subject pronouns, is one of the basic aspects of English grammar dealt with in this manual. It is natural to ask, therefore, how it can be formulated in terms of explicit transformational rules relating remote structures to each other and ultimately to surface structures. First of all, it seems clear now that Rule 1G is a combination of several rules which determine proper forms for pronouns. It is significant then that pronouns are a subcategory of NP. Therefore the attempt to formulate these rules runs up against the problem of subcategorizations discussed just above. The base rules for expanding NPs given so far say nothing about pronouns. The only relevant base rules given have expanded NP into a Conj plus any number of coordinated NPs, into NP C, or into Art N. One might hazard than that there is a further expansion of NP, as follows:

(14) NP $\longrightarrow$ Pronoun.

Pronoun would then be added to the list of lexical categories expanded by rule (4) of Chapter 16 into the symbol $\diamond$. Then the various pronouns could be listed in the lexicon with a marker for the category Pronoun, just as *dirt*, *proof*, etc., are listed with N.

But the difficulty is apparent. Take the trio of singular masculine pronouns *he, him, himself*. Suppose these are listed in the lexicon and inserted freely in Pronoun slots generated in trees by rule (14). Then the grammar will not be imposing the regularities on the distribution of these forms formulated in Rule 1G. That is, nothing would block inserting *himself* as a subject, *he* as an object, etc. What this approach seems to miss is that, as indicated in Rule 1G, *he, him, himself* (and analogously for the other parallel groups of pronouns) are not so much three *separate forms*, as three variants of a *single* masculine singular pronoun. In other words, what should be listed in the lexicon is that there is a single masculine singular pronoun. The choice as to whether this is represented in some context by *he, him*, or *himself* is then a function of Rule 1G. But the question arises: what form should be listed in the lexicon to represent this element. The choice seems *arbitrary*, just as it is for most of the other triples.

One might therefore come to the conclusion that a lexical approach to pronouns is incorrect. Rather, the symbol *Pronoun* in (14) might be further expanded by base rules into various abstract symbols which represent the various triples. We again face the question of subcategorization. Although no satisfactory approach to this exists, it is perhaps worthwhile attempting to sketch the outlines of a *possible* solution in this case, one which illustrates certain general dimensions of the problem.

Consider the four pronouns *he, it, him, them.* We find that, although each is grammatically different from all of the others, certain subsets share certain properties. For example, the first three are *singular* as against the last, which is *plural. He* and *him* are *masculine,* while *it* is neuter, and *them* can be used for collections regardless of gender, and is hence not marked along this dimension (or, alternatively, is ambiguous).

We have seen so far how grammatical categories like C, NP, V, etc., can be regarded formally as the labels of nodes in constituent structure trees. In the previous chapter, we saw how morphemes can be regarded in the same way, as a special class of node labels, namely, those associated exclusively with terminal nodes. A grammar turns out then to be based in significant part on a vocabulary of node labels—C, NP, *pig, run, fat,* etc.—which fall into two sets. One type labels nonterminal nodes and defines grammatical categories. The other labels terminal nodes. These are morphemes, most drawn from the lexicon.

If we examine the node labels dealt with so far, we can see that, terminal or nonterminal, they share a formal property. Namely, the labels are *atomic.* Any two labels are either identical or distinct. From the point of view of grammar,[6] the labels introduced so far have no internal structure. One possible approach to the kind of subcategorization problems raised by pronouns is to abandon this implicit view and to allow labels which are *complex symbols.* Such symbols are *partially* similar to other labels in ways which can be taken account of by grammatical rules.

Let us illustrate how this might work with the pronouns dealt with by Rule 1G. Suppose one represents complex node labels inside of paired brackets, with their component elements separated by commas. And suppose the following categories are recognized as relevant to the English pronominal system:

(15)

Category	Abbreviation
Pronoun	Pro
Third Person	III
Second Person	II
First Person	I
Animate	An
Neuter	Neu
Masculine	Masc
Feminine	Fem
Plural	Pl
Singular	Sing

Given such categories, it is possible to analyze the existing pronouns into overlapping types, recognizing that some of them are ambiguous. Some illustrative analyses are:

(16) *he* [Pro, III, An, Masc, Sing]

(17) *I* [Pro, I, An, Sing]

(18) *us*   a   [Pro, I, II, An, Pl]
            b   [Pro, I, III, An, Pl]
            c   [Pro, I, II, III, An, Pl]

(19) *her*   [Pro, III, An, Fem, Sing]

Here *us* is recognized as ambiguous, the ambiguity lying in whether in addition to the speaker, *us* designates just the hearer or hearers (18a), just individuals distinct from the hearer(s) (18b), or both hearer(s) and other individual(s) (18c).

An important fact about the set of categories recognized in (15), which is not necessarily complete, is that not all combinations of them will correspond to actual or even possible pronouns. For instance, there will be nothing corresponding to

(20) *[Pro, I, Neu, Sing]

or to:

(21) *[Pro, II, Neu, Pl]

One way of representing this kind of fact is to asume that there is a set of rules specifying the possible combinations of categories, rules which operate by filling in the categories of initially unspecified complex symbols.

Suppose now, having assumed that Pro is a category which exists as part of complex symbols, we replace (14) above by:

(22)   NP $\longrightarrow$ [Pro, ...]

We can then posit further base rules like the following, which limit the combinations of categories to those actually found:

(23)   Pro $\rightsquigarrow$ a $\left\{ \begin{array}{c} I \\ II \end{array} \right\}$ An Sing

             $\rightsquigarrow$ b   I $\left\{ \begin{array}{c} II \ (III) \\ III \end{array} \right\}$ An Pl

             $\rightsquigarrow$ c   II III An Pl

             $\rightsquigarrow$ d   III Neu $\left\{ \begin{array}{c} Sing \\ Pl \end{array} \right\}$

             $\rightsquigarrow$ e   III An Pl

             $\rightsquigarrow$ f   III An $\left\{ \begin{array}{c} Masc \\ Fem \end{array} \right\}$ Sing

In rules like (23), a wavy arrow is used to distinguish rules which assign complex labels from branching rules and transformational rules. Parenthesized elements are, as usual, optional, and curly brackets enclose sets of elements which are possible in the same position, thus in effect abbreviating as many rules as there are members. Rule (23a) thus abbreviates the two rules:

(24) Pro ⟾ I An Sing

(25) Pro ⟾ II An Sing

Rule (23) defines the legitimate combinations of the recognized pronoun categories, eleven in all. Each of these is now regarded as a complex terminal symbol. In order to relate these to the actually pronounceable morphemes, *I*, *they*, etc., it is necessary to have a set of *spelling rules*. These produce pairings like those in (16)–(19). However, we immediately see an important limitation of (23).

It does not account for any difference between reflexive and nonreflexive forms, or between subject forms and object forms. Thus, in terms of (23), *she*, *her*, and *herself* receive identical analyses; hence, no spelling rule would be able to apply to the output of (23) to properly introduce the correct morphemes.

This difficulty brings us back, appropriately enough, to where we began this discussion of pronouns: to the question of formulating Rule 1G. It now becomes possible to think of Rule 1G as imposing a further categorization on the output of rule (23). Suppose, that is, we recognize three further categories of pronouns:

(26) Reflexive—Ref
Subjective—Sub
Objective—Ob

It now is feasible to regard the reflexivization rule, Rule 1G(a), as one which assigns the syntactic property Ref to a subset of elements marked Pro, to regard the rule for subject pronouns, Rule 1G(bi), as one which assigns the marker Sub to a subset of pronouns, and to regard the one for object pronouns, Rule 1G(bii), as one which assigns the marker Ob. What is necessary is to combine these assumptions with a statement of the environments in Rule 1G.

For the case of reflexive marking, a reasonable approximation would be:

(27) Reflexivization

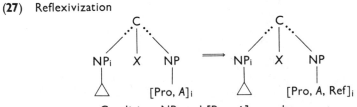

Condition: NP_i and $[Pro, A]_i$ are clause mates.

Here *A* is a new kind of variable, one which stands for arbitrary sets of category markers in a complex terminal symbol. We are now also introducing a new type of structural change which transformations can carry out, namely, the insertion of further category markers into complex symbols. Rule (27) is thus a reformulation of Rule 1G(a) of Chapter 6 and will from this point on be referred to as Reflexivization.

Analogously, one can formulate Rule 1G(bi) as follows:

(28) Subject Pronoun Marking

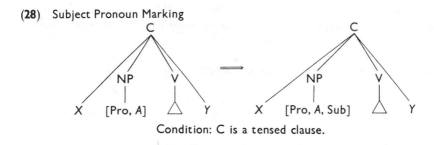

Condition: C is a tensed clause.

Of course, (28) remains only partially formalized, since we have given no precise account of what it means for a clause to be a tensed clause. That is, we have not provided a mode of representation in trees for this aspect of sentences.

Finally, Rule 1G(bii) can be formulated as follows:

(29) Object Pronoun Marking

$$\begin{array}{ccc} \text{NP} & & \text{NP} \\ | & & | \\ [\text{Pro, A}] & \Longrightarrow & [\text{Pro, A, Ob}] \end{array}$$

Condition: A does not include Sub or Ref.

Object Pronoun Marking can be formulated this simply only on the assumption that (28) is applied to trees before (29) is. If so, and if Reflexivization also applies to trees before (29), the only pronouns which will be able to be input to (29) are those which should have object pronoun form (we are ignoring genitives like *his*, *my*, etc.).

After Reflexivization, Subject Pronoun Marking, and Object Pronoun Marking apply, every pronoun generated by (23) is further marked with either Ref, Sub, or Ob. It is relatively straightforward to formulate a set of spelling rules to associate these more complex terminal symbols with the appropriate phonological shapes. For instance, two such rules would be:

(30) [Pro, III, An, Masc, Sing, Sub] $\longrightarrow$ *he*

(31) [Pro, III, An, Masc, Sing, Ob] $\longrightarrow$ *him*

Rules like (30) and (31) could be interpreted as the instruction to *replace* the complex symbol on the left with the phonological information[7] on the right. Or, they could be regarded as the instruction to add the information on the right to that already present, giving even more complex terminal symbols of, for example, the form:

(32) [Pro, III, An, Masc, Sing, Sub, *he*]

Arbitrarily, we assume the first interpretation.

The spelling rules for reflexives involve certain extra complexities beyond those of rules like (30) and (31). One problem is that every reflexive pronoun, that is, in the terms just elaborated, every pronoun with the marker Ref, will end up with the morpheme *self/selve* in it. It would clearly be missing a generalization to list this same morpheme in every spelling rule for reflexives. Rather, it would seem that there is an insertion rule of the form:

(33)

$$\begin{array}{ccc} \text{NP} & & \text{NP} \\ | & & \diagup\diagdown \\ [\text{Pro, A, Ref}] & \Longrightarrow & [\text{Pro, A, Ref}] \;\; self/selve \end{array}$$

Rule (33) can then be supplemented by spelling rules of the same form as (30) and (31):

(34) [Pro, III, An, Masc. Sing, Ref] $\longrightarrow$ *him*

Given the similarity of (31) and (34), it is possible to combine them:

(35) $\left[\text{Pro, III, An, Masc, Sing} \left\{ {\text{Ref} \atop \text{Ob}} \right\} \right]$ $\longrightarrow$ *him*

In the same way the rules for object *them* and reflexive *themselves* could be combined, as could those for object *her* and reflexive *herself*, object *it* and reflexive *itself*, and object *one* and reflexive *oneself*. That is, in all exclusively third person pronouns,[8] the shape of the element before *self/selve* is identical to the object pronoun shape. However, in the other reflexives, the shape of this element contrasts, in standard English,[9] with the object pronoun form and is, rather, identical to the genitive form:

(36) a   me, myself, my (book)
      b   you, yourself, your (book)
      c   you, yourselves, your (books)
      d   us, ourselves, our (books)

Thus, ultimately the rules for these reflexives should be combined with those for the genitive shapes. However, we are not dealing with genitives in this work.

This completes our sketchy treatment of the assumptions which might be proposed as a (partial) basis for permitting a more precise formulation of the set of rules earlier abbreviated as Rule 1G. This complex-symbol analysis has only been offered as an illustration of a possible approach to the subcategorization issues involved. Many difficulties exist in such an account and a variety of questions are raised whose treatment lies outside the bounds of a work of this nature.

We have now finished our description of the formulation of transformations. One major type of transformation, that involving movement of constituents, has not been illustrated here. However, many following chapters deal with this type of operation. It will be more convenient to discuss such rules in the immediate context of the facts which motivate them.

SUMMARY

In this chapter, two separate but related topics were dealt with. First we presented an account of how transformations apply to trees; the structural description of a transformation was conceptualized as a template to be superimposed on a candidate tree. If the template fits perfectly, the tree is a candidate for reorganization. The requisite reorganization is specified by the structural change, the part which appears on the right side of the double arrow.

Second, a review of the various kinds of rules showed that certain types, notably I Deletion, require reference to a specific grammatical category (in this case, second person). However, specification of such a category is not a straightforward matter. A considerable amount of abstract apparatus is necessary even to approach a workable account. One was given, based upon the introduction of a category label Pronoun and the new notion of *complex symbol*. The complex-symbol notation not only enabled the various kinds of pronouns in uncontrolled deletion rules to be specified, but provided a way to deal with one of the central rules of this manual, Reflexivization.

NOTES

1. Gapping relates underlying structures similar to the surface forms of (i) to surface structures like (ii):

(i)   Mary dates soldiers and Betty dates marines.
(ii) Mary dates soldiers and Betty marines.

Gapping always deletes at least one V in the second conjunct, but may also delete other material, including NPs.

2. (1a) also illustrates the use of subscript numbers to keep track of constituents. These subscripts must also be regarded as a type of symbol capable of occurring in the description of transformations.

3. Conjunction Copy is thus a complex combination of the operations of insertion and deletion, with the insertions triggering certain new bracketings and labelings. This kind of insertion has sometimes been called *Chomsky-adjunction*, after the person who first suggested it. Chomsky-adjunction involves an operation on subtrees of the form:

(i)

That is, an element B is added as a *sister* constituent of a constituent A under a newly created node of the category type A. The added element can either be a left sister, as in Conjunction Copy or a right sister, as in (i).

4. Structure (3) leaves many aspects of Equi unaccounted for. In particular, it does not impose the necessary condition that the truncated clause generated by Equi must never have the form of a tensed clause. Thus:

(i) a   Jack$_i$ insisted that he$_i$ be allowed to go.
    b *Jack insisted (that) be allowed to go.
    c   Jack insisted on being allowed to go.

Moreover, it is not possible to handle all such facts by specifying that the output of Equi must be converted to either infinitival or gerundive form. For whole sets of complement clauses simply do not permit Equi:

(ii) a   Jack$_i$ believed he$_i$ was innocent.
     b *Jack believed to be innocent.
     c *Jack believed being innocent.

Even though (iia) meets the conditions of Equi, as stated in (3), it must be prevented from undergoing it; similarly so must sentences with many other verbs of this sort. We will not deal with the problem of subcategorizing verbs (or complement clauses) with respect to their susceptibility to Equi operation. A full grammar of English will have to involve such a division.

5. However, toward the end of this chapter, we shall consider in some detail a potential approach to this problem.

6. Of course, from a phonological point of view, the labels of morphemes are not atomic. Morphemes like *pickle, pin, police*, etc., share an initial element, [p]. But the syntax treats morphemes as single items. There is no syntactic rule referring to all morphemes beginning with *p*.

7. Since this work is concerned exclusively with grammar, we are not making use of a serious phonological representation of forms. Instead we use the standard orthography. This can be regarded as a rather outdated, very crude, and inaccurate system of phonological representation. For more serious systems see Chomsky and Halle (1968).

8. An "exclusively" third person pronoun is one whose complex symbol contains the marker III, but not I or II. Such pronouns have references which exclude both the speaker and all hearers.

9. There are dialects of English, usually regarded as substandard, having reflexive forms like *hisself*. These seem to involve an extension of the rule for nonthird person forms, illustrated in (36), to the exclusively third person domain.

PROBLEMS

1. Explain why the rule in (i) does or does not apply to the tree in (ii):

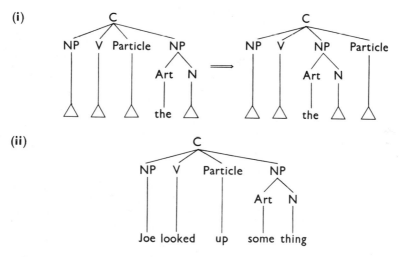

2. What problem for grammatical description is raised by the fact that all imperative clauses have second person subjects?

3. Make an analysis similar to those in (16)–(19) in the text for various genitive pronouns *my, his, her*, etc. Assume that all these pronouns are characterized by the feature Gen.

PART III SOME FUNDAMENTAL GRAMMATICAL OPERATIONS

CHAPTER 18 **PASSIVIZATION**

PREVIEW

In this chapter we discuss the relation between active and passive clauses like:

(i) Captain Marvel tasted the seaweed.
(ii) The seaweed was tasted by Captain Marvel.

The existence of such paired clauses is a general feature of English in the case of transitive verbs like *taste*. Several types of similarity between such paired clauses are pointed out—similarities in truth conditions, semantic relations, and selectional restrictions. These lead to the conclusion that such pairs have a common underlying structure. Weak arguments are given for assuming that this structure is more like active than passive clauses. Finally, a more detailed look at selectional restrictions is used to justify the view of a common remote structure for active and passive.

In Chapter 16 we discussed the need to distinguish at least three subtypes of verbs, intransitives, transitives, and ditransitives. These correspond to the traditional distinction between *transitive* and *intransitive* verbs, with the former taking, and the latter not taking, direct objects. We further subdivided transitive verbs:

(1)

```
                          Verbs
          ┌─────────────────┴────────────┐
   Intransitive                     Transitive
                              ┌──────────┴──────────┐
                      (simple) Transitive      Ditransitive
```

All transitive verbs take direct objects, but the ditransitives also take indirect objects. So, what we called transitive verbs in Chapter 16 should more precisely be called *simple* transitive verbs, since ditransitives are also transitive. We will generally adhere to the simpler terminology. Some examples are:

(2) Transitive
- a Harry ate the whale.
- b Harry combed Joan's hair.
- c Harry studied oceanography.

(3) Ditransitive
- a Harry gave things to Sally.
- b Harry bought things for Joan.
- c Harry told that to the police.

(4) Intransitive
- a Harry slept soundly.
- b The balloon rose.
- c The price of meatballs fell.

At a still more detailed level of analysis, one can distinguish between *pure intransitive verbs*, which can never take objects, and *mixed intransitives*, which can:

(5) Pure Intransitive
- a *Harry slept the banana.
- b *The balloon rose the box (off the ground).
- c *The price of meatballs fell the price of tomatoes.

(6) Mixed Intransitive

a	The door opened.	b	Harry opened the door.
c	The water froze.	d	Harry froze the water.
e	The ball slid.	f	Harry slid the ball.

Similarly, one can distinguish between *pure transitive verbs*, which must take objects, and *mixed transitives*, which have intransitive uses:[1]

(7) Pure Transitive

a	They issued a proclamation.	b	*They issued.
c	Tom resolved the problem.	d	*Tom resolved.

(8) Mixed Transitive

    a   Melvin ate dinner.   b   Melvin ate.

    c   Tom reads novels.   d   Tom reads.

These distinctions will obviously have to be made somewhere in the grammar. But it is not necessary that they all involve categorizations of the kind discussed in Chapter 16. It can be argued that the mixed transitive verbs are, in initial structures, really transitive. The cases where no objects show up are due to deletion. Other cases are more problematical, and we will not consider them here.[2]

    A fundamental feature of English is the existence, for the bulk of transitive verbs, both simple and ditransitive, of a pair of related sentence patterns, the traditional *active* and *passive*.[3] Thus, taking a transitive verb such as *pickle*, we find both:

(9) a   Active   Harry pickled the vampire.

      b   Passive   The vampire was pickled by Harry.

An active transitive sentence consists minimally of a subject NP, a transitive verb, and an object NP. The passive consists typically of a subject NP, a form of the verb *be* (*was* in (9b)), a transitive verb with the past participle ending,[4] and a prepositional phrase of the form *by* NP. In most cases, however, the *by* phrase is omissable, so that a minimal passive sentence from the surface structure point of view can be as bare as (10a). Not all verbs which occur in passive clauses permit this, however, as illustrated by (10b,c):

(10) a   The vampire was pickled.

       b   Harry was adored by his students.

       c   *Harry was adored.

    The existence of pairs like (9a,b) raises questions. What is the relation between such linked active-passive clauses? How can one describe the intuitively close relation between them? Before trying to answer the latter question, let us consider the nature of this relationship.

    First, despite the striking grammatical differences, the meanings of pairs like (9a,b) are very much the same. While it is no doubt true that there is a difference, this is quite subtle. In particular, in declarative clauses, active and passive in general[5] *have the same truth conditions*—whatever assertion is made by (11a) is made by (11b), and conversely. Hence the conditions which guarantee the truth of one must do so for the other:

(11) a   Melvin robbed the bank.

       b   The bank was robbed by Melvin.

Thus for a particular individual named Melvin and for a particular bank, if it is true that that individual robbed that bank, then it must also be true that

that bank was robbed by that individual. Moreover, in the case of sentence pairs like (11a,b), the subject NP of the active clause is understood as agent of the transitive verb (as the NP designating the doer) and the post subject *by* phrase NP of the passive clause is understood as the agent. More generally, whatever the semantic relations may be between the set of NPs and the transitive verb in the active clause, the same relations are manifested by the set of NPs in the passive clause. But in a sense they are "reversed." The subject NP of the active bears the same semantic relation as the post-*by* NP in the corresponding passive, and the object NP of the active bears the same semantic relation as the subject NP of the corresponding passive:

(12) a Melvin understands Swahili.
 b Swahili is understood by Melvin.

Here the subject NP of the active is not understood as an agent but rather as the possessor of the mind having the property described by the verb. The subject is a so-called "experiencer." Just so then, the NP in the corresponding passive is understood as an experiencer. Similarly, the object NP of (12a) designates the thing understood, and the subject of the passive has the same feature.

The existence of paired clauses with this sort of relation between them is relatively unique. One must face the question of how the grammar of English characterizes such pairs. Within the framework we have been developing, there is the basis for a somewhat unusual answer. Suppose it is argued that the similarities between corresponding active-passive clauses are to be represented in the grammar by generating them from substantially similar initial structures. Therefore, some transformational rule (or rules) would be responsible for the palpable surface structure differences. This would mean, for instance, that (11a,b) and (12a,b) would have initial structures which were substantially, if not entirely, the same. In particular, they would share all of that structure which defines the relations between the various NPs and the central transitive verb.

Since corresponding active and passive clauses differ particularly in the order of NPs, the assumption just hazarded would mean that the rules relating remote to surface structures would have to include a type encountered only in passing before (see the discussion of Indirect Object Shift in Chapter 13), namely, rules which rearrange the positions of constituents. It turns out that such rules are one of the most important types that English manifests. Much of the rest of this manual will be taken up with a consideration of several different rules of this type.

Before considering the nature of the common remote structure which will be attributed to active-passive pairs, it is worth restressing an easily overlooked property of remote structures, illustrated by those so far suggested. While remote structures are distinct from surface structures, they are the same kind of thing. They are formed from the same sorts of elements, in the same sorts of relationships. That is, they are trees, with terminal and nonterminal elements, node labels, etc. This is not an accidental feature of the limited class of remote structures so far considered, but a reflection of a basic feature of language.

With this in mind, consider again the problem of active-passive pairs. There would seem to be, *a priori*, three possible assumptions consistent with the view that such pairs share a common core of structure at earlier levels of derivations:

(13) The common remote-structure configuration is:
    a More like the surface structure of active clauses;
    b More like the surface structure of passive clauses; or
    c Neither a nor b.

We shall assume that (13a) is correct. In particular, we shall assume that in the remote structures of both active and passive clauses (based on transitive verbs taking agents), the agent NP is subject. Thus, we can provide the following provisional common remote structure for the pair in (11):

(14)

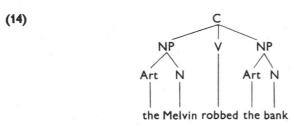

Such a remote structure is related rather directly to the surface form of the active clause. But in the case of the passive, the relations between a structure like (14) and a form like (11b) are relatively complex. At least the following processes are involved:

(15) a The presence of a form of *be* must be guaranteed.
    b The presence of the past participle ending on the verb must be specified.
    c The subject NP in the remote structure must be displaced to the right of the verb and marked with the preposition *by*.
    d The object NP in the remote structure must move into subject position.

No argument has been given for choosing alternative (13a). Alternative (13b) would also require a complex set of operations for the active case, roughly the reverse of (15). And it is impossible to say what any of the endless number of solutions consistent with (13c) would require.

Although it will not be possible to provide strong arguments for the choice of active-like remote structures for passive sentences at this point (see Chapter

23), certain things can be said. If one takes intransitive verbs which occur with agents, the agent NP shows up as subject:

(16) Louise $\begin{cases} \text{wept} \\ \text{giggled} \\ \text{laughed} \\ \text{ran} \end{cases}$.

One could imagine a situation where, instead of (16), one found:

(17) * $\begin{cases} \text{Wept} \\ \text{Giggled} \\ \text{Laughed} \\ \text{Ran} \end{cases}$ by Louise.

But, of course, this is impossible in English. These facts then suggest the following principle:

(18) Agent NPs are subjects in all initial structures containing them.

This principle is consistent with an active-like initial structure for passive sentences, but not with a passive-like one. It follows that the only sentences in which agents will not be subjects are those which undergo some special rule, like that responsible for passive sentences, that is, the rule sketched in (15c).

A second weak argument in favor of active-like underlying structures for active-passive pairs is also derivable from the properties of intransitive clauses. These do not normally involve verbs with the past participle ending. Thus, verbs generally do not occur with this marker, which is only provided by special statements in limited contexts. Again though, such an approach requires taking passive clauses as derivable from the normal case.

A third argument for active-like structures involves passive sentences based on idiomatic sequences like *keep tabs on*, *take heed of*, etc.:

(19) a Tabs were kept on leftists by the FBI.
   b Little heed was taken of that suggestion by the doctors.

These passive clauses correspond to actives like:

(20) a The FBI kept tabs on leftists.
   b The doctors took little heed of that suggestion.

The point is that, in active-like structures, the idiomatic sequences are contiguous, but not so in the passives. If one thinks that lexical items (idioms in particular) are inserted into remote structures as units, active-like remote structures are preferable to passive-like ones at the point of lexical insertion. This follows under the assumption, implicit even in traditional dictionaries, that forms like *keep tabs on* are to be listed as units in the lexicon of the language.

These are weak arguments for preferring active-like to passive-like remote structures for active-passive clause pairs. In Chapter 23 we present strong arguments, which show that there is no indeterminacy on this point.

While we have now given some grounds to prefer active-like to passive-like underlying structures, we have given only rather tenuous reasons for assuming that such pairs share a common structure in the first place. At this point, it will be of use to give some sturdier reasons for this view.

In describing the sentences of a language it is necessary for the overall description to impose a set of restrictions on the types of NPs which can occur in a clause with particular verbal elements. These restrictions are now typically called *selectional restrictions*. They were briefly alluded to in Chapter 16. Sentences violating such restrictions are marked in this chapter with an initial exclamation point. For example, consider such contrasts as:

(21)   a   That argument is inconsistent.
       b   !That pickle is inconsistent.

(22)   a   Hurricanes occur periodically.
       b   !Your mother-in-law occurs periodically.

The trouble with (21b) is that pickles are not the sorts of things which can be inconsistent. The problem with (22b) is that mothers-in-law are not the sorts of things which can occur, still less periodically. A full account of English clauses must provide restrictions as to the kinds of subject NPs that can occur with elements like *inconsistent* and *occur*. These restrictions are based on the semantic assumptions inherent in the meanings of particular lexical items.

Similar contrasts exist for objects:

(23)   a   Max betrayed his comrade.
       b   !Max betrayed the chicken soup.

(24)   a   They prohibited public kissing.
       b   !They prohibited the sun.

Chicken soup is not the kind of thing that can be betrayed, nor the sun the kind of thing that can be prohibited. Grammars must thus impose selectional restrictions between particular verbal elements and the types of NPs they cooccur with in clauses.

We argued earlier that this kind of restriction is essentially semantic. In claiming that a grammar must impose such restrictions, we are not deviating from this view. In an example like (23b), the deviance is a function of the meanings of the verb and the object NP. However, what is grammatical is the determination of the particular pairs which must meet particular conditions. For instance, contrast:

(25)   a   !Max amazed the car wax.
       b   !The car wax interrogated Max.

Both examples are deviant. But to change them into nondeviant examples, different revisions are necessary. In (25a), one must change the object NP, say to *the car salesman*, while in (25b), one must change the subject, say to *the policeman*. More generally then, *amaze* must have objects which designate things with minds while *interrogate* must not only meet this condition but must also have the same sort of subject. Thus the conditions themselves are semantic and not part of the syntax proper. But the determination of which NPs must bear which relations to which NPs involves notions of syntax like subject and object.

Let us consider the selectional restrictions in some active-passive pairs:

(26) a Martha criticized Tony.
      b Tony was criticized by Martha.

(27) a !The wonton soup criticized Tony.
      b !Tony was criticized by the wonton soup.

(28) a Martin threatened the doctor.
      b The doctor was threatened by Martin.

(29) a !Martin threatened the liver.
      b !The liver was threatened by Martin.

These examples reveal an invariant property of such pairs. The selectional restrictions involving "corresponding" NPs in the pairs are identical. For example, those NPs which can be the subjects of *criticize* in active clauses, like *Martha*, can be the post-*by* NP in passive clauses based on *criticize*. And those NPs which cannot be the subject of *criticize* in active clauses, like *the wonton soup*, cannot be the post-*by* NP in passive clauses with this verb. Just so, those NPs, like *the doctor*, which can be the objects of *threaten* in active clauses, can be the subjects of passive clauses based on this verb. Concomitantly, those NPs, like *the liver*, which cannot be the objects of *threaten* in active clauses, cannot be the subjects of the corresponding passive clauses. One can represent this typical situation graphically:

(30) a Active [subject NP] Verb$_x$ [object NP]

      b Passive [subject NP] *be* Verb$_x$ *by* [NP]

The general principle is:

(31) The selectional restrictions for corresponding NPs in active-passive pairs are identical.[6]

Principle (31) provides in itself considerable support for the claim that corresponding active-passive pairs should have a common remote structure.

Under this assumption, it will be possible to determine the relevant pairs for these restrictions just once for both types taking account of the generalization in (31). This can be done by specifying those elements (subject-verb, object-verb, etc.) which involve some selectional restriction at a level where the superficially different structures still have a common representation.

Under the assumption that active-like structures are more basic, this means stating the restrictions on both the subject NPs of active clauses and the ultimately post-*by* NPs of passive clauses at a point where the latter, like the former, are in subject position. For example, the post-*by* NP in clauses headed by the verb *criticize* must designate a mind-possessing entity. This will be stated as a restriction on the subject NPs of *criticize* at the level of initial structure. Generalizing, the linkage of restrictions in active-passive pairs will be accounted for by stating the relevant pairs and the constraint that links them only once, for the active-like structures.[7] Thus the grammar will say that the verb *criticize* requires subjects which designate mind-possessing entities, blocking (27a). Then the view that active-like structures underlie passives automatically projects this restriction to (27b) with no further statement. That is, it is projected to the post-*by* NP.

The linkage of selectional restrictions in corresponding active-passive pairs is a correlative of the fact, noted earlier, that such pairs manifest the same semantic relations between NP and verb (with, however, the positions of the terms of these relations inverted).[8] That is, the semantic relation borne by the subject of the active is borne by the post-*by* NP in the passive; the relation borne by the object of the active is borne by the subject of the passive. Thus, in

(32) a Harry moved the melon.
     b The melon was moved by Harry.

Harry is the agent of *move* in both cases, the NP designating the mind-possessing entity which wills the action. Similarly, *the melon* refers to the thing which moves, which is affected by the action in both cases. Hence, in two senses, the difference between active and passive clauses is superficial. The selectional restrictions are essentially unaffected, and the semantic relations holding between NP-verb pairs are unaffected. In one sense, passivization simply rearranges the subject and object NPs in a clause, making the other correlative changes outlined in (15) above. Statement (15) mentions four different operations as necessary to convert active-like remote structures into passive clauses. However, there is no reason to regard these as all being on a par. Rather, it is natural to think of (15c,d) as fundamental, with the others being dependent revisions, triggered by these operations. That is, fundamentally, passivization says:

(33) Make the object NP of a transitive clause into the subject of that clause, displacing the original subject to the right and marking it with the preposition *by*.

Rule (33) explains why passivization is inapplicable to intransitive clauses. This is not an *a priori* necessary fact. It could have been the case that English had related sets of sentences like (34a,b) or (34a,c) or (34a,d):

(34) a   Henrietta giggled.
    b   *Was giggled by Henrietta.
    c   *(by) Henrietta was giggled.
    d   *Was by Henrietta giggled.

But this is predictably impossible if passivization is fundamentally an operation which makes an object into a subject, thereby displacing a prior subject, since neither (34a) nor its initial structure contains any object NPs.

We close this chapter with a statement of the passivization rule:

(35) Passive

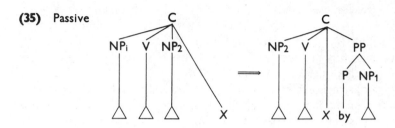

Several observations should be made about this formulation.[9,10] The rule does not account for the form *be* in passive clauses. This question is discussed in Chapters 26 and 27. There it is shown that the auxiliary *be* found in passives has the same sort of origin as other occurrences of *be*, such as those found with adjectives as in:

(36) Melvin is tired.

The origin of *be* is independent of the origin of the passive proper.

Second, the rule does not account for the presence of the past participle ending on passive verbs. A lexical approach to this matter is discussed in Chapter 27.

SUMMARY

In the preceding discussion, it has been argued that in general transitive verbs permit the formation of two distinct clause types, active and passive. The extensive commonalities between these types suggest, in spite of the obvious surface differences, the existence of a common underlying structure for them. Selectional restrictions contribute substantially to this conclusion.

We assumed on the basis of certain evidence, to be strengthened in Chapter 23, that the common underlying structure is like the surface structure of active clauses. This leads to the necessity for positing the rule Passive to derive passive from active structures. We claimed that tde key process in these rules is the transformation of the active object NP to subject position, simultaneously displacing the original subject NP to the right and marking it with the preposition *by*.

NOTES

1. Arguments are needed to justify these classifications. One might simply take the mixed transitives and mixed intransitives to be the same set. Among reasons for distinguishing them are their interpretations. Mixed transitives are treated semantically as if they had missing, unspecified objects. Example (8b) means Melvin ate a meal. Mixed intransitives, however, have no such interpretation. Example (6a) does not mean the door opened something. Thus we regard the intransitive uses of mixed intransitives as basic, while the transitive uses of these are in fact related to them causatively. Thus (6b) means roughly that Harry *caused* the door's opening. On the other hand, we take the transitive uses of mixed transitives to be basic, with the intransitive uses derived by object deletion.

2. Mixed transitives involve no causative relation. Compare (6a,b) with:

(i) Tom sings.
(ii) Tom sings songs.

Two contrasts are visible. First, (ii) is not the causative of (i). Second, (i) and (ii) have subjects in the same relation to the verb, while in (6a) and (6b) the relation borne by the subject in the former is borne by the object in the latter. These differences confirm the contrast between mixed intransitive verbs and mixed transitive verbs.

3. The traditional terminology often speaks of *active voice* and *passive voice*, voice being one of the major interacting dimensions along which clauses (also verbs) may be categorized. Thus, voice in this sense is independent of *mood*, which distinguishes clauses according to whether they are interrogative, declarative, imperative, exclamatory, etc. We shall have little occasion to utilize these traditional terms in what follows.

4. This ending is sometimes of the shape *-en*, sometimes of the shape *-ed*. Compare:

(i) a The gorilla was seized by the giant.
     b The gorilla was eaten by the giant.

The *-ed* form is the *productive* shape, in the sense that new verbs added to the language take this one. If we invent a new verb *speet* meaning "to show something/someone was lying" we would expect that paired with the active (iia) would be the passive (iib) and not (iic):

(ii) a   Harry speeted the government.
     b   The government was speeted by Harry.
     c   *The government was speeten by Harry.

In general then, the past participle ending is identical with the regular and productive form of the past tense ending, although there are some verbs whose forms for the latter are irregular:

(iii) a   I ate the melon.
      b   *I eated the melon.
      c   I saw that film.
      d   *I seed that film.

5. There are special conditions under which they do not or at least need not. Thus, when quantifier words like *every* and *some* occur on the NP in question, the meaning is in part determined by which comes first. Hence (i) and (ii) are rather different:

(i)   Every captain commands some ship.
(ii)   Some ship is commanded by every captain.

Example (i) is a normal assertion which says that for every captain there is at least one ship which he commands. It makes no claim that all captains command the same ship. Example (ii), however, is most naturally read as saying, oddly, that there is some one particular ship which *all* captains command. Thus special principles are needed in a full grammar for cases involving quantifiers.

6. The claim in (31) is *not* the same as the claim that any NP which can occur in one position in (30) can occur in the corresponding position in the other type of clause. The latter is false, because there are a variety of other types of constraints, *distinct from selectional restrictions*, which come into play. Most obviously, the distribution of pronouns is different:

(i) a   I visited the museum.
     b   *The museum was visited by I.

(ii) a   Jack visited me.
      b   *Me was visited by Jack.

Of course, these facts are an automatic consequence of the rules for the distribution of subject and object pronoun forms worked out earlier. These only permit subject forms like *I* in the subject positions of tensed clauses, and they do not permit object forms like *me* there.

Similarly, active clauses containing reflexive objects have no natural passive counterparts:

(iii)   a   Jackson criticized himself.
        b   *Himself was criticized by Jackson.

Sentences like

(iv)   Jackson was criticized by himself.

are only well-formed if the reflexive word has contrastive stress. But such sentences have no active counterpart:

 (v)   *Himself criticized Jackson.

Many other restrictions distinct from questions of selections prevent the kind of direct identity which would otherwise exist.

7. We are not dealing here with the question of how these aspects of the language will be precisely stated.

8. The reason why selectional restrictions correlate with semantic relations is that, as stated before, the former are essentially semantic. This is connected to the point noted earlier that selectional restrictions correlate with assumptions about the real world. Hence in contexts where ordinary assumptions are suspended, selectional restrictions may vanish, as in fairy tales, etc. So, out of context, the following manifests a selectional violation

(i)   !The meatball complained about the gravy.

since *complain* requires a subject designating a mindful entity. But in the context of a story in which the meatball is personified, (i) is fine, as it is in the report of a dream. Personification seems to consist, in fact, of attributing minds to things which are ordinarily regarded as being without them.

9. In Chapters 13 and 16 we distinguished between prepositions generated in the base and those later inserted by transformations. Our assumption that passive clauses are derived from initial active structures leads to the conclusion that the preposition *by* is inserted transformationally. This follows since the NPs following *by* start as initial structure subjects and these, of course, are not associated with prepositions by the base rules (see the formulation of (35) in the text).

10. The position of the variable X in the structural change of (35) represents the fact that that the *by* phrase is normally ordered to the right of post direct object material in the input:

  (i)   Melvin handed the banana to Greta.
 (ii)   The banana was handed to Greta by Melvin.
(iii)   *The banana was handed by Melvin to Greta.

PROBLEMS

1. How would you account for the unacceptability of the following examples?

(i) ! The sum of 3 and 3 was tasted by Bob.
(ii) ! The rolls were impeached by the butter.

2. Consider:

(i) Bob entered the room and was seized by FBI agents.
(ii) He was seized by FBI agents.

What do these examples tell us about the order of application of Passive and CCS Deletion (see Chapter 10)?

3. Explain the nonexistence of passives corresponding to the active forms of intransitive clauses.

CHAPTER 19 **EXTRAPOSITION**

PREVIEW

In this chapter we examine a variety of complex clauses such as:

(i) a It is likely *that he will quit.*
   b It worries me *that he hasn't yet arrived.*

An explanation is sought for where the italicized clauses in such examples
come from; why sentences containing such clauses exhibit the subject
it and no other; and certain peculiarities of the superficial bracketing in
such cases. If it is assumed that the italicized clauses originate in initial
structure as subjects, then the questions above are answered, plus
a few more. This assumption requires the postulation of a rule that
moves such clauses to final position. Such a rule, called *Extraposition*, is
described, and its relation to other phenomena, like passivization, is
considered.

In earlier chapters, we considered a variety of data which led to the postulation of remote structures related to surface structures chiefly through various
processes of deletion. In Chapter 18, however, the discussion of passivization
led to a treatment of remote structures connected to surface forms by processes of rearrangement or movement. Here we treat a further case of this
type.

Consider a verb like *frighten* in:

(1) That frightens me.

Frighten here is obviously a transitive verb. One of its notable features is that the class of subject NPs it takes is extremely free. Most types of subject NPs can occur as subjects of *frighten*.[1] A few examples:

(2)
$$\left\{\begin{array}{l} \text{Harry} \\ \text{The way you talk} \\ \text{Aspirin} \\ \text{Most dentists} \\ \text{Hindus} \\ \text{Sarcasm} \\ \text{The fact that Dolly is drunk again} \\ \text{Cold months} \end{array}\right\} \text{frighten me.}$$

In particular, the subject NPs of *frighten* can consist of isolated clauses of any of the three major declarative[2] types:

(3) a Joan's screaming frightened me.
  b For Joan to scream would frighten me.
  c That Joan screamed frightened me.

The occurrence of sentences like (3), with clauses in subject position, is, of course, one of the reasons for regarding such clauses as being NPs. Others will be mentioned as we progress. Thus, as noted earlier, one of the base rules of English grammar is:

(4) NP $\longrightarrow$ C

This says that an NP node may consist exclusively of a single C node.

The grammar has to characterize the class of clauses which can exist with *frighten* as main verb. The relevant rules should say that such clauses must consist minimally of a subject NP, an occurrence of *frighten*, and an object NP, in that order. Given the base rule

(5) C $\longrightarrow$ NP V NP

much of this is accomplished by listing *frighten* in the lexicon as transitive (see Chapter 16).

Now, note sentences like:

(6) a That you bought two guns and a knife frightens me.
  b It frightens me that you bought two guns and a knife.

The problematical cases are those like (6b), which consist of a subject NP, the main verb *frighten*, an object NP, and a following clause. One thing is immediately evident. A rule like (5) might be adequate for generating sentences like (2) and (6a). But it does not suffice, in combination with the lexicon, to yield those like (6b).

Must a new base rule be added to account for cases like (6b)?

(7)   C ⟶   NP V NP C

A rule such as (7) would claim that pairs like (6a,b) do *not* have common remote structures. There are, however, good reasons for rejecting a base rule like (7) as a basis for examples like (6b). First, the semantic relations between pairs like (6a,b) are of the same order as those earlier seen to link paired active-passive clauses. Namely, (6a,b) seem to be essentially identical in meaning. The relation between the *that* clause and the verb in one is the same as in the other. Hence, what frightens " me " in (6a) is the same as what frightens " me " in (6b). These are the sorts of facts which we sought to represent in the case of passivization by postulating a common remote structure. And it is natural to follow a parallel course here.

Second, it was noted that the class of subjects occurring with *frighten* in clauses like (2) is quite free. But in sentences like (6b), not only is this not the case, the possible subjects are maximally restricted. That is, only the word *it* can occur as subject in such clauses:

(8)   *   ⎧ That
⎜ Those
⎜ Most apples
⎨ Nuclear refrigerators   ⎱ frightens me that you are
⎜ Your uncle   ⎰ quitting.
⎜ John's slapping several cheerleaders
⎩ The fact that you like wonton soup ⎭

Thus, where a rule like (5) can correctly describe *frighten* clauses for a wide range of developments of the subject⁻NP, a rule like (7) would have to be supplemented with special restrictions of the subject NP to the single form *it*.[3] Rule (7) thus involves two sorts of deficiency, a failure to relate intuitively similar structures like (6a,b) and a failure to account for the strict limitation on the subject NP in cases like (6b). These suggest that one should look for an alternative to rule (7).

From many points of view, pairs like (6a,b) seem like trivial variants of each other, differing chiefly by an optional repositioning of the subordinate clause. Within the framework we have been developing, this recognition of similarity can be easily formalized. One need only say that (i) such pairs have common remote structures, and (ii) these remote structures are similar to the more superficial forms of examples like (6a). That is, we assume that, in initial structure, the clause which occurs in extraposed (i.e., clause-final) position in surface structure is actually part of the subject NP constituent. The price of such moves is obvious. It is necessary to postulate a rule to move such clauses from their original position to extraposed position. Let us refer to this rule as *Extraposition*.

Extraposition moves a clause contained in an NP to extraposed position and leaves a marker *it* in its original position. With such a rule in the grammar, pairs like (6a,b) can have the same remote structure. And there is no need to supplement the base rules with (7). Moreover, no special restrictions are needed to limit the subject NP of *frighten* to *it* when there is a clause in extraposed position.

There is a further benefit of an Extraposition analysis of sentences like (6b). To reveal this, one must examine such sentences carefully with respect to their constituent bracketing. Let us examine:

(9) a It frightens me that he loves guns.
     b I believe that he loves guns.

We have been regarding sentences like (9b) as having the bracketing:

(10)

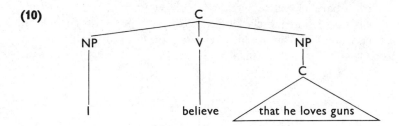

Occasionally, however, we have pointed out that a transitive verb and its object NP (plus other things that follow) form a constituent in surface structure. Thus, in (9b) *believe that he loves guns* is a superficial constituent. Hence the superficial structure of (9b) must really be:

(11)

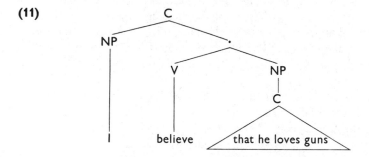

(We return in Chapter 27 to the origin of this structure and to the labeling of the node marked by a dot here.) Now consider (9a). Although the main constituent break in (9b) is between the subject and the verb, this is not the locus of the major division in (9a). Intuitively, the bracketing of (9a) is such that *that he loves guns* is one of the two major constituents of the whole clause. Hence, in contrast to (11), (9a) has the superficial bracketing:

(12)

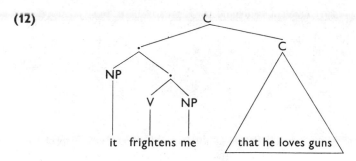

It might be thought that the bracketing difference between (11) and (12) is related to the fact that the latter involves the sequence V NP C, the former only the sequence V C. This is not really relevant, though. Consider:

(13) It happens that he loves guns.

This, although lacking a postverbal NP, is otherwise bracketed like (9a), not like (9b):

(14)

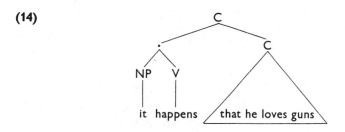

Clauses in extraposed position are generally bracketed as in (12) and (14) and not like the sentence in (11). This typical bracketing of clauses in extraposed position is unaccounted for by any rule along the lines of (7). It can, however, be regarded as the direct result of the operation of the rearrangement carried out by Extraposition. That is, Extraposition takes the subject clause, detaches it from its original clause and reattaches it as one major constituent of a new C node which it creates. The other constituent of this is the original clause-defining node. Therefore, the rule is:[4]

(15) Extraposition

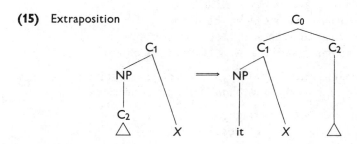

In order to exemplify how this rule operates let us return to (6a). It has a constituent structure of the form:

(16)

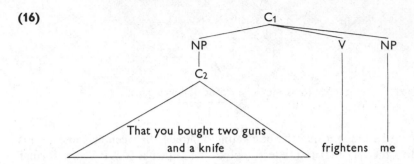

Extraposition as it appears in (15) will clearly apply to the tree in (16). The higher C corresponds to C_1 of the structural description of the rule, the lower C corresponds to C_2. The X of the rule can correspond to any sequence of subtrees. In (16) it corresponds to the sequence *frightens me*. The tree which results from the operation of Extraposition to (16) is:

(17)

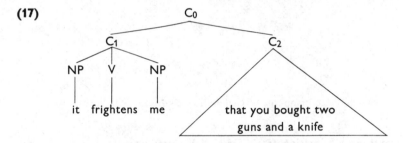

Extraposition has been largely discussed so far in terms of the verb *frighten*. However, this general rule functions for a very large class of predicational elements, including pure verbs, adjectives, and other elements:

(18) a That you are right is obvious.
     b It is obvious that you are right.
     c That we have no money worries me.
     d It worries me that we have no money.
     e That she owes you money is disturbing.
     f It is disturbing that she owes you money.
     g That they rejected the offer is of no importance.
     h It is of no importance that they rejected the offer.

Extraposition is illustrated in (18) only for *that* clauses. But it functions also for infinitival clauses, both those with and without surface subjects:

(19) a For us to lose would be tragic.
     b It would be tragic for us to lose.

    c For them to fire you would be out of character.
    d It would be out of character for them to fire you.
    e To do that would be considered impolite of you.
    f It would be considered impolite of you to do that.

The reader should verify for himself that, like *that* clauses, infinitival clauses in extraposed position are bracketed as one major constituent of the whole, consistent with the rule in (15).

Curiously, and for reasons which, if they exist, no one has so far discovered, Extraposition does *not* apply to gerundive clauses:

(20) a   John's mistreating his wife disgusted us.
      b   *It disgusted us John's mistreating his wife.
      c   (Their) Continually being late is offensive.
      d   *It is offensive (their) continually being late.

This must then apparently be regarded as an ad hoc restriction on Extraposition.[5]

We have now proposed an analysis of passive clauses and a more precise analysis of extraposed clauses. It will be useful to consider the way these distinct phenomena interact. For if our treatments of the separate components are correct, the interactions should have natural descriptions with no necessary special restrictions. Let us then examine:

(21) a   The authorities discovered that Bob was a foreigner.
      b That Bob was a foreigner was discovered by the authorities.
      c It was discovered by the authorities that Bob was a foreigner.

Compare (21a,b) with:

(22) a   The authorities discovered that.
      b That was discovered by the authorities.

It is evident that (21a,b) must be regarded as corresponding active and passive, just like (22a,b). The simple object NP in (22a), *that*, undergoes Passive and becomes the subject of the passive sentence. Just so, the complex object NP in (21a), *that Bob was a foreigner*, undergoes Passive and becomes the subject of the passive sentence.

Now examine (21c), with the extraposed *that* clause. This has the bracketing predicted by rule (15). An Extraposition analysis of clauses in extraposed position correctly predicts the existence of sentences like (21c) and their binary bracketing. Moreover, the Extraposition analysis permits one to say that both (21b,c) are passives corresponding to (21a). This, in turn, permits us to maintain the independently desirable assumption that (21c), like (21b), shares a common remote structure with (21a). Hence, by having Extraposition operate on a remote structure itself derived by Passive, in this case (21b), nothing special need be said in the grammar to derive sentences with both passivization and extraposed clauses like (21c).

It is not easy to imagine a treatment of sentences like (21c) along the lines of a rule like (7) which would allow such a general treatment. That is, suppose sentences like (21c) were not derived from structures like (21b) by Extraposition, but were the direct reflex of an initial structure. How would it be possible to provide (21c) and (21a) a common remote structure? By claiming the *that* clause originates as the NP object of *discover* in such cases, sentences like (21b) are automatically described by the same rule, Passive, needed for simpler examples like (22b). And (21c) follows directly from a subsequent application of Extraposition.

Hence, the treatments of passivized and extraposed clauses offered here do interact naturally without special statements needed to describe sentences like (21c), which involve both passivization and extraposed position.

SUMMARY

In this chapter we have postulated a rule, Extraposition, which reorders the clause of a complement NP to clause-final position within the clause which contains it. We saw that this rule is restricted to infinitival and *that* clauses and that it contrasts with another rule, Right Dislocation.

We showed how an Extraposition treatment of the relevant constructions naturally describes the selectional restrictions, semantic relations, and bracketing features of such pairs as:

(i)   It proves nothing that he was caught in there.
(ii) That he was caught in there proves nothing.

An important virtue of the analysis suggested is that it combines with the independently proposed treatment of passivization in Chapter 18 to correctly describe the facts in sentences involving both passivized and extraposed clauses.

NOTES

1. Objects of *frighten*, on the other hand, are restricted selectionally to NPs designating entities with minds:

(i)   ! That frightened { the banana / the national debt / all of the plastic / such rhetoric / an amazing degree of sincerity / nonsense }.

2. Interrogative clauses also occur as NPs, as in:

(i)   a   Where he lives is unknown.
      b   When he left is not obvious.
      c   Why he smokes crushed alfalfa seeds eludes me.

But these do not occur with *frighten*:

(ii)   *When he left frightened me.

3. Moreover, there is no natural way to build this kind of restriction into rules like (7), so that the representation of this restriction in the base component would require an extension of theoretical devices in a new direction.

4. We describe Extraposition here as operating on clausal subjects, but it turns out that it is more general, as illustrated by:

(i)   a   I took that for granted.
      b   I took it for granted that you were finished.

Example (ia) shows that *take for granted* allows an NP postverbally. Example (ib) shows an *it* in this slot with a clause in extraposed position, one bracketed in just the way Extraposition brackets the trees it derives. It is natural to extend the rule ultimately by eliminating the particular reference to subject position.

5. There are examples like:

(i)   It is terrible, Melvin's divorcing Sally.

These are well-formed and *look* like cases of Extraposition applied to gerundive clauses. Some speakers may, in fact, find (20b,d) in the text well-formed. If so, they are further instances of the same type as (i). However, there are reasons to deny that such sentences are a function of Extraposition. Rather, they should be attributed to the action of another rule, called *Right Dislocation*, which also operates on nonclausal NPs, as in:

(ii)   a   That restaurant is terrible.
      b   It is terrible, that restaurant.

Right Dislocation moves NPs to the right of clauses, leaving behind pronouns which agree with the originals in person, gender, and number:

(iii)   a   They are coming tonight, Jack and Fred.
       b   She won't agree to that, your mother.

Thus, in this respect, Right Dislocation contrasts with Extraposition, which always leaves behind the unique NP *it*.

Among the reasons for arguing that sentences like (i) are a function of Right Dislocation rather than Extraposition is that the intonation contours in such sentences are like those in (iii). They have a rather sharp break at the point indicated by the comma. Sentences derived by Extraposition do not require such a sharp hiatus. Moreover, NPs which have been thrown to the right by Right Dislocation preclude questioning and relative clause formation:

(iv)   a   I bought a picture of Fred yesterday.
         b   the person who I bought a picture of yesterday . . .
         c   Who did you buy a picture of yesterday?

(v)   a   I bought it yesterday, a picture of Fred.
        b   *the person who I bought it yesterday, a picture of . . .
        c   *Who did you buy it yesterday, a picture of?

Thus, examples like (iva) permit formation of relatives and questions but those like (va) do not. *Right Dislocation seems incompatible with these processes.* Extraposition, however, is perfectly compatible with them:

(vi)   a   It is obvious that Tony called Sally.
        b   the person who it is obvious that Tony called . . .
        c   Who is it obvious that Tony called?

Therefore, by determining how sentences like (i) behave along this dimension, we have a good test of whether they are derived by Extraposition or Right Dislocation. And they behave like Right Dislocation examples:

(vii)   a   It is terrible, Melvin's divorcing Sally.
         b   *the person who it is terrible, Melvin's divorcing . . .
         c   *Who is it terrible, Melvin's divorcing?

We conclude then that sentences like (i), etc., do *not* conflict with the view that Extraposition does not operate on gerundive clauses.

PROBLEMS

1. What kind of restriction on Extraposition is suggested by the following facts?

   (i)   That Bill has two heads proves that he is a Martian.
  (ii)   *It proves that he is a Martian that Bill has two heads.
 (iii)   For it to snow would show that it was below freezing.
 (iv)   *It would show that it was below freezing for it to snow.

2. What do the following examples suggest about the order of application of the rules Extraposition and Passive in the derivation of (ii)?

 (i)   That Edward was a Martian was argued by the director.
 (ii)   It was argued by the director that Edward was a Martian.

3. Given the examples

(i)   To help the poor is nice.
(ii)   It is nice to help the poor.
(iii) *This is nice to help the poor.

what accounts for the ill-formedness of (iii)?

CHAPTER 20 **A FIRST LOOK AT RAISING**

PREVIEW

In the present chapter, we undertake the analysis of a new range of clauses containing infinitives, those with such main verbs as *seem* and *appear*, as in:

  (i) Irving seems to be happy.

There is an initial similarity between examples like (i) and:

  (ii) Irving wants to be dappy.

  We have previously taken examples like (ii) to involve application of the rule Equi (see Chapter 11). They manifest erasure of the complement subject under coreference with the main clause subject. However, examples like (i) do *not* have derivations involving Equi. Rather, the underlying form of (i) is essentially that of examples like:

(iii) It seems that Irving is happy.

What is involved in the formation of the surface structure of (i) is a rearrangement rule which, among other things, makes the subject of the complement clause into the main clause subject. This rule is called *Raising*. A variety of arguments based on various NPs of highly restricted distribution, including chunks of idioms, are given to justify the application of such a rule in the derivations of sentences like (i).

Consider sentences like:

(1) a Johnny seems to be $\begin{Bmatrix} \text{sad} \\ \text{mean} \end{Bmatrix}$.
      b Larry appears to know Turkish.

In surface structure, these are reminiscent of:

(2) a Larry wants to know Turkish.
      b Johnny promised not to be mean.

These were described in Chapter 11 as involving application of the rule Equi. The latter deletes the subject NP of the infinitival complements. This accounts for the fact that the main clause subject is understood as a coreferent of the intuitive, but unexpressed, subject of the complement.

    The sentences in (1) are similar to those in (2) in that the main clause subjects again seem to be understood as the intuitive subjects of the complement clauses, although in surface structure these are subjectless. Thus, in (1b), for example, it is the person designated by the main clause subject, *Larry*, who knows Turkish. It would be natural to try to regard sentences like (1) as further examples of Equi application. However, this is not possible. Rather, sentences like (1) are the first illustration of a different process relevant to complements, one which we shall call *Raising*.

    What reasons are there to doubt that Equi plays a role in cases like (1)? There are several different sorts. The first involves idioms which undergo passivization, briefly touched on in Chapter 18. So, there is an idiom *make headway* (*on NP*) which can undergo Passive:

(3) a The Russians are making some headway (on this problem).
      b Some headway is being made (on this problem) by the Russians.

Except for this construction involving *make*, *headway* does not in general occur in English sentences:[1]

(4) a *We discussed some headway (on that problem).
      b *A lot of headway (on that problem) bothered Joan.
      c *We are studying a great deal of headway (on that problem).
      d *He insisted on a great deal of headway (on that problem).

It thus seems that one must say that [make $_{NP}$[_____ headway]$_{NP}$ (on NP)] is an idiom and that *headway* is not introduced as an ordinary noun head of NPs, like *progress, results, beer, faith, banana*, etc. Sentences like (3b) can then be generated by Passive from structures containing this complex idiom.

However, strangely enough, *headway* NPs also occur as the subjects of sentences with the same verbs as in (1):

(5) a Little headway seems to have been made on this problem (by those students).

 b A great deal of headway appears to have been made by the Russians on the problem of thermonuclear cigarette lighters.

An attempt to account for sentences like (5) by way of Equi would mean positing remote structures for (5a) of the form:

(6)

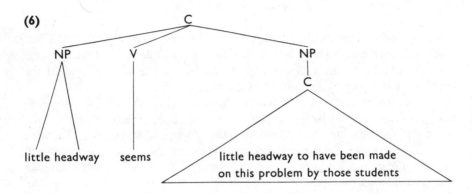

Now, the embedded or subordinate clause in (6) appears to cause no problem (but see below). It can be regarded as a passive clause, produced with no special statement, just as (3b) is. That is, this clause can be derived from the idiom [make $_{NP}$[——— headway]$_{NP}$ (on NP)]. But, in (6), *headway* also occur as the head noun of the subject NP of *seems*, although normally *headway* only occurs in the idiomatic sequence with *make*. Hence, an Equi analysis of *seem* sentences like (5a) forces one to make special ad hoc provisions for *headway* with respect to *seem*.

Moreover, *headway* NPs can only occur as subjects of *seem* if the complement is of the type in which *make* has undergone Passive:

(7) *Little headway seems to have $\left\{\begin{array}{l}\text{existed}\\\text{bothered him}\\\text{been expected}\\\text{been nice}\end{array}\right\}$.

This argument is not restricted to *headway*. It can be based on any similarly idiomatically restricted NP. *Tabs* in the idiom *keep tabs on* is of the relevant type. In general *tabs* only occurs in active clauses with the main verb *keep* or in the passives of these:

(8) a The police kept tabs on the pushers.

 b Tabs were kept on the pushers by the police.

 c *Harry discussed tabs on the pushers.

    d *Tabs bothered Joan on the pushers.
    e *Jim advocated tabs on the pushers.

However, *tabs* occurs as the subject of *seem, appear,* when the complements of these verbs are *keep* passives:

(9) a Tabs seem to have been kept on the pushers by the police.
       b Close tabs appear to have been kept on you by several spies.

Again, therefore, an Equi analysis of sentences like (9) requires remote structures in which *tabs* occurs not only in the idiom *keep tabs on* but as an independent subject of main verbs.

    These factors already indicate that sentences like (5a) and (9a,b) are not Equi-derived. A further argument for this negative conclusion is immediately available. Recall that Equi depends on a coreference linkage between two NPs. And there are grounds for insisting that the deleted NP always be a pronoun.[2] But it is impossible to derive sentences like (5a) and (9a,b) from structures of the general form in (6) while meeting this condition. In (6) the subject of the complement clause which would be deleted must be an NP containing the idiom noun itself, and not a pronoun. Moreover, it seems impossible in many cases to have any clause similar in form to that in (6) in which there is a pronominal element. Thus, in the case of *tabs*, it is impossible to justify a structure for (9a) of the form

(10)

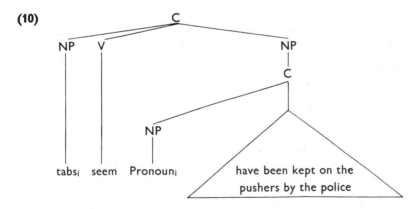

since there are no actual clauses in English containing a pronoun coreferential to an NP like *tabs*:

(11) *Harry kept tabs$_i$ on the chickens but they$_i$ were not close enough.

In fact, it is probably the case that (11) is necessarily ungrammatical since the possibility of coreference requires that the NP in question be capable of having reference. But it is doubtful whether it makes any sense to speak of an NP like *tabs* as meeting this condition. Thus, on independent grounds, it seems impossible to claim that (10) or anything like it could serve as a proper input to Equi, which depends on coreference. It is then doubly impossible to maintain an Equi analysis for *seem* or *appear* sentences whose surface subjects are chunks of idioms.

Verbs like *promise*, *want*, and *expect*, which were seen earlier to serve as the main verbs of constructions in which Equi *does* function, do not permit idiom chunks as their subjects:[3]

(12) ⎧ *Tabs promised to be kept on the spies ⎫
      ⎨ *Tabs expected to be kept on the spies ⎬ (by the FBI).
      ⎩ *Tabs wanted to be kept on the spies ⎭

This further supports a contrast in construction types between cases involving *want*, etc., and those involving *seem*.

The arguments just given depend on idiomatic NPs. But they are based on features of these which are more generally manifested. Certain kinds of NPs are quite tightly restricted with respect to the kinds of simple clauses they occur in. An example of this independent of idioms is the word *now*. This is generally called an adverb in occurrences like:

(13) a John is now dead.
      b I will leave now.
      c Now tell me how to wiggle my ears.

However, there are contexts in which *now* must be regarded as an NP:

(14) a Now is the time for us to call Arthur.
      b Now is the moment to push the button.
      c Is now the time for us to call Arthur?

However, *now* can occur as the subject NP in no other *simple* clauses except those of the declarative form:

(15) [$_{NP}$[now]$_{NP}$ be NP]

Thus:

(16) a *Now worries me.
      b *Now is disgusting.
      c *Now is a pain in the neck.
      d *Now makes you wonder about tomorrow.

Strikingly, however, *now* can also occur as subject of *seem* and *appear*:

(17) a Now seems to be a good time to invest in coffins.
      b Now appears to be a poor time to visit Syria.
      c Doesn't now appear to be a poor time to visit Syria?

Note, though, that *now* can appear in these positions only when the complement clause is of the form in (15):

(18) a *Now seems to be nice.
      b *Now appears to bug you.
      c *Now appears peculiar to many authorities.

An Equi analysis of sentences like (17) would require one to state as an ad hoc fact that *now* can occur as the subject of *seem* and *appear*, etc., as well as in contexts like (15). The objection to such an analysis is thus parallel to that for the idiom chunks.

One might try to overcome these objections to an Equi analysis of sentences involving *seem* and *appear* with infinitival complements if there were no alternative. But there is. Observe that verbs such as *seem* and *appear* occur not only in constructions with infinitival complements, but also with *that* clauses:

(19) a It seems that Bob is unhappy.
     b It appears that they will lose.
     c It seems that tabs were kept on their movements by the police.
     d It appears that now is a poor time to invest in horseshoe manufactur-
        ing.

Sentences like (19) are familiar from the preceding chapter. They reveal clauses in extraposed positions, with fixed subjects of the form *it*. By substituting any other NP for *it* in (19a–d), it is easy to see that no other subject is permissible in such contexts. It would appear that sentences like (19) are derived by the rule Extraposition from underlying structures in which the subjects consist of *that* clauses. This is what we assume.

However, there is one peculiarity of Extraposition-derived sentences like (19), in comparison to those considered earlier. The *that* clauses in (19) cannot occur in subject position:

(20) a *That Bob is unhappy seems.
     b *That they will lose appears.
     c *That tabs were kept on their movements by the police seems.
     d *That now is a poor time to invest in horseshoe manufacturing
        appears.

Therefore, if one claims that sentences like (19) are derived by Extraposition from remote structures like (20), one must say that the operation of Extraposition in these contexts is obligatory. We assume this also. An apparent problem, revealing the complexity of the conditions on obligatoriness, arises from examples like:

(21) a It seems obvious that Melvin is drunk.
     b That Melvin is drunk seems obvious.
     c It appears to be possible that they have nuclear missiles.
     d That they have nuclear missiles appears to be possible.

Examples like (21b,d) are unexpectedly good, showing that when elements like *obvious, to be possible*, etc., follow *seem* or *appear*, Extraposition is not obligatory. We shall return to this matter in the following chapter, providing a statement which predicts the contrasts between (20) and (21).

At this point, we return to sentences like (19), which can now be taken to have remote structures like (20), with clausal subjects. Consider then:

(22) a Bob seems to be clever.
      b It seems that Bob is clever.

It has been shown that there are severe problems with an Equi analysis for *seem* and *appear* sentences with infinitival complements. Now one notices that pairs like (22a,b) seem to be paraphrases and apparently share all relevant semantic relations. This is the kind of situation encountered before with sets of related sentences. We sought to deal with it by positing common remote structures. Let us consider this course here.

Evidently, the kind of remote structure which an Equi analysis of (22a) would require would not be feasible for sentences like (22b), in which there is no subjectless clause. Suppose one were to assume something of the opposite: that it is the remote structure of (22b) which provides the clue as to the remote structure of (22a). One can see that under an Extraposition analysis of sentences like (22b), the remote structure of such a sentence appears to involve an intransitive verb with a clausal (that is, complement) subject. Assume this also for the remote structure of (22a). Both examples of (22) would then have a remote structure along the lines of:

(23)

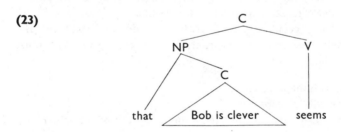

Given this,[4] one must ask what rules derive the relevant surface structures in (22).

For (22b) the answer, implicit in previous discussion, is that the sentence is derived by Extraposition. Application of this rule is subject to the constraint that, in a specified class of cases, the rule is obligatory with a verb like *seem*. The real problem involves (22a).

To determine the outline of a derivation of (22a) from a structure like (23), it is useful to contrast them directly. Taking just the strings of words, one finds:

(24) a [That Bob is clever seems] (= (23))
      b [Bob seems to be clever] (= (22a))

Superficially, these are very different indeed. One difference involves the contrast between infinitival complement and *that* clause complement. But the more striking differences are in constituent order. In (24a) *seems* has a clausal subject, while in (24b) the original subject of the subordinate clause subject has become the subject of *seems*. We regard this as the funda-mental process in the derivation of sentences like (24b). That is, such sen-tences are derived by a rule which takes the subject of a complement clause and makes it the main clause subject. We call this rule *Subject Raising*, but shall refer to it simply as *Raising* from this point on.

The rationale for this nomenclature should be clear. The rule in question takes a subject constituent of a subordinate clause and makes it the subject constituent of the immediately containing main clause. Although this process itself seems simple enough, an explicit statement of the mapping from (24a) to (24b) is more complex. It involves not only further differences of comple-ment type, but also repositioning of the rest of the original subject clause to the right of the main verb. The operations just described may be represented schematically as:

(25)

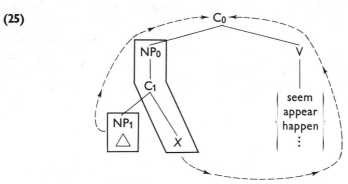

The result of these operations is that the original complement clause (C_1) is in effect split into two, one part, its subject, appearing before the main verb as its new subject. All the rest appears in infinitival form after the main verb. We state the required rule as:

(26) Raising

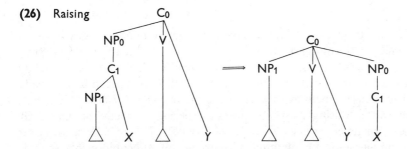

At this point, we will concentrate on whether sentences like (24b) are indeed derived by a rule which lifts the subject of a complement clause into main clause subject position. Among other things, such an analysis is an alternative to an Equi analysis of sentences like (24b).

The most obvious advantages of a Raising treatment of *seem* and *appear* sentences with infinitival complements are (i) it permits pairs like (24a,b) to have common remote structures, in accord with their common semantic relations; and (ii) it permits one to describe clauses in which *seem, appear* have as subjects idiom chunks, restricted NPs like *now*, etc., with no further special statements. Since (i) is obvious, let us consider (ii).

Because of sentences like

(27)   a   Little headway seems to have been made by the Bengalis.
      b   Close tabs appear to have been kept on them by the FBI.
      c   Now seems to be a poor time to move.

an Equi treatment of infinitival clauses with *seem* and *appear* was forced to claim that otherwise almost totally restricted NPs could occur as subjects of *seem, appear*. In such terms, main clauses with these verbs were, in cases like (27), exceptions to otherwise valid regularities about restricted NPs. Under a Raising analysis of the relevant sentences, the exceptions disappear. Sentences like (27) are now derived from remote structures in which the restricted NP appears only once, and *in the complement*. Take (27a) as a typical illustration. It would have, in a Raising grammar (i.e., one with a Raising rule), a remote structure of the form:

(28)

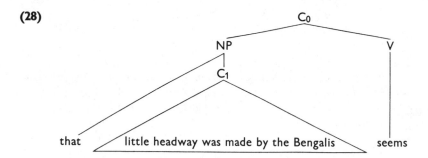

Moreover, the C_1 clause in (28) will have a still more remote structure in which *little headway* is the object of *made*. This structure is related to that in (28) by Passive, as already discussed. Thus, in a grammar in which (27a) is derived by Raising from a structure of the form in (28), *little headway* can be originally inserted in clause structures as part of the idiom *make headway*. Unlike an Equi analysis, a Raising analysis requires no special statement about *headway* to account for its occurrence in sentences like (27). This remark carries over to other similar idioms containing passivizable NP subcomponents such as *keep tabs on, take heed of*, etc. Moreover, it also carries over to restricted NPs like *now*. All of the apparently special restrictions on these forms violated in *seem* sentences remain unviolated under a Raising treatment. This follows if they are stated to hold at some level of remote structure prior to the level at which Raising applies.

Put differently, a Raising treatment of the sentences in question is a way of saying that a verb like *seems* is selectionally "transparent." This means that any time there is a well-formed clause of the form

(29) [NP$_a$ X]

there will automatically be a well-formed *seem* clause of the form:[5]

(30) [NP$_a$ seem Infinitival form of X]

Thus, *seem* is transparent because NP$_a$ relates to the infinitival form of X just as if *seem* were not present in the string.

A Raising analysis of infinitival cases with *seem, appear* automatically predicts the whole range of highly restricted subject cases, each of which would require a special ad hoc statement under an Equi analysis (or any other analysis distinct from a Raising treatment). This leaves little doubt of the essential validity of a Raising treatment of the relevant sentences.

To see the power of a Raising grammar in this regard, it is perhaps worth considering other cases not dealt with so far. The word *there* normally functions as a locative adverb. But there are examples where it is the subject of a clause:

(31) a There is no reason to believe that.
  b There are yaks in that zoo.
  c There exists no other alternative.

The key factor is that subject *there* can only occur in those clauses whose main verbal element is a form of *be, exist,* or a few other verbs having "exist" as part of their meaning (*arise* = "come to exist", etc.). Moreover, these verbs must be followed by an NP or a prepositional phrase:

(32) a *There is sad.
  b *There eats a gorilla in that cage.
  c *There exists.
  d *There giggles (in France).
  e *There proves something.

However, just as a Raising analysis predicts, this kind of *there* (call it *existential there*) occurs as the subject of *seem* or *appear* just in case the infinitival complement is of the sort containing *be, exist,* etc.

(33) a There seem to be gorillas in that cage.
  b There seems to exist no other alternative.
  c *There seems to eat a gorilla in that cage.
  d *There seems to giggle (in France).

Within a Raising framework, the independently necessary restrictions distinguishing simpler clauses like (31) from those like (32) automatically yield the contrasts in (33). On the other hand, an Equi analysis would require special statements to permit *there* to occur as a remote subject of *seem*, *appear*.

Moreover, although existential *there* functions as an NP in the grammar, it is impossible to assign it any potential reference. Therefore, there is no way in which a rule like Equi, which is stated in terms of coreference, could apply to delete a hypothetical *there* controlled by an antecedent *there*. On these independent grounds, similar to those for many idiom chunks, an Equi analysis of *seem*, *appear* infinitival sentences with *there* is not only burdened with ad hoc restrictions but in fact is impossible. It is worth noting that in those cases originally taken to involve Equi in their derivations, that is, main clauses with *promise*, *want*, etc., *now*, existential *there*, and idiom chunks, are impossible in surface subject position:

(34) a *There promised Bob to be a riot.[6]
      b *There wanted to exist other solutions.
      c *Now expects to be a good time for overseas investment.
      d *Now wants to become then.

This further supports the contrast between Equi-derived and Raising-derived structures.

As a final indication of the validity of a Raising analysis of infinitival cases with verbs like *seem*, one can consider so-called *clausal idioms*:

(35) The cat is out of the bag.

While (35) has, of course, a literal reading, on which it asserts something about the successful exit of some feline from a bag, it also has a special, unpredictable meaning. Namely, it states that something hitherto secret has become public. English must contain some kind of principle to associate this meaning with clauses of the sort in (35). Just as a Raising grammar predicts, this special meaning is found in:

(36) That cat seems to be out of the bag.

A Raising grammar can predict this with no special statements, if it is claimed that the special principle responsible for the idiomatic meaning of clauses like (35) applies to remote structures (in particular, to remote structures of a level no less abstract than those upon which Raising operates). Once more the "transparency" of *seem*, *appear*, etc., determined by Raising, is of paramount importance in explaining otherwise mysterious facts.

Important questions about Raising and the derivations it determines as well-formed (or fails to determine as well-formed) have not even been raised. Nonetheless, the considerations of this chapter leave little doubt that *seem* clauses with infinitival complements are derived by Raising. We shall consider further properties of Raising in following chapters, expanding the domain for which it is taken to be relevant, further refining the mode of its operation, and considering its interaction with other grammatical phenomena, like Reflexivization.

SUMMARY

A variety of evidence indicates the existence of a rearrangement rule called Raising. This rule makes the subject of a subordinate clause the subject of the main clause containing that subordinate clause. It operates on a class of cases determined by a set of main verbs, including *seem* and *appear*, which, we argued, take their complements as underlying clausal subjects.

The chief arguments for Raising so far are based on the "transparency" of the italicized elements in contexts like:

(i) $[\text{NP-}\begin{Bmatrix} seem(s) \\ appear(s) \end{Bmatrix}\text{-infinitive}]$

Roughly, a structure of the form (i) is well-formed just in case the NP and infinitive are of the sort which would make a proper independent clause. This condition is an automatic consequence of a Raising analysis, which derives the NP from a remote structure in which it is in fact the subject of the infinitive.

The most telling arguments of this sort involve cases where the NP in question is a part of an idiom or an NP occurring normally only with a very restricted class of predicates, like existential *there* or *now*. Several such arguments were gone over in detail. Taken together they provide impressive support for the postulation of Raising.

On a more general level, the arguments leading to recognition of Raising provide a new kind of evidence for the view of grammatical structure being argued for in this manual. In this theory, remote structure is a crucial element of the overall description of sentences, and in particular cases, remote structures and surface structures differ in relatively extreme, though formally specifiable, ways.

NOTES

1. There is one strange exception to this regularity, the fact that *headway* can occur as the head of a restrictive relative clause:

  (i) The headway which they have made on this problem is amazing.
  (ii) The headway which has been made on this problem is amazing.

However, this is restricted, and is only possible when, as in (i) and (ii), the main verb of the relative clause is *make*, in either its active or passive forms:

  (iii) a *The headway is amazing.
         b *The headway which they discussed is amazing.
         c *The headway which was discussed by the committee is amazing.

2. More generally, it can be claimed that in every case where an NP is deleted subject to coreference to an antecedent NP, the *deleted* NP is a pronoun. This is to say that an example like

(i)   Harry got in the car and then _____ fainted.

involving CCS Deletion derives from a remote structure of the form

(ii)   Harry$_i$ got in the car and then he$_i$ fainted.

not from one in which a full NP *Harry* is the subject of *fainted*. Similarly, it means that

(iii)   All of the men expect to quit.

involving Equi, derives from

(iv)   All of the men$_i$ expect that they$_i$ will quit.

and not from anything like:

(v)   All of the men$_i$ expect that all of the men$_i$ will quit.

As one argument for this, (iii) and (iv) are essentially equivalent in meaning, while both contrast sharply with (v).

3. An apparent exception to this involves *expect* clauses which have been passivized:

(i)   Tabs were expected by most observers to be kept on all of the spies by the FBI.

Here Passive has applied to both the main and the subordinate clauses. The existence of (i) is automatic given Passive, once it is noted that there exist sources like:

(ii)   Most observers expected tabs to be kept on all of the spies by the FBI.

Thus the constraint that *tabs* does not occur in the subject position of verbs like *expect* is true, but at the level of remote structure prior to application of Passive, not at the level of surface structure.

4. In (23), and following structures, we adopt for the first time an analysis of the clause marker *that* which treats it as attached to the NP directly above the C node with which *that* is associated.

5. Actually, this statement is too strong, since there are general restrictions of various sorts blocking many kinds of infinitival clauses. For instance, no modal (verb)—*will, can, may, shall, should, would, might, could, ought*—can occur in an infinitive (more generally in an untensed clause), so that pairs involving these in *that* clauses have ill-formed correspondents under Raising:

(i)   a   It seems that Harry can afford steak.
   b   *Harry seems to can afford steak.

(ii)   a   It appears that Joan will escape.

        b   *Joan appears to will escape.

However, this need not be regarded as a constraint on Raising. Rather it is a function of a general ban on modals in untensed surface clauses. Hence, Raising can be allowed to generate potential sentence forms like (ib) and (iib) freely. These will be marked as syntactically deviant by independently needed principles. This independence is shown by such examples as the following, which have nothing to do with Raising:

(iii)   a   I will arrange for Harry to (*will) go.

        b   I planned that he should arrive late.

        c   *I planned for him to (*should) arrive late.

Other constraints similar to those on modals also block some expected Raising sentences. For instance, the element *supposed* of sentences like

(iv)   He is supposed to brush his teeth.

can only occur directly below a tensed form. This constraint eliminates potential clauses like those in:

(v)   a   He is supposed to go.

       b   *if he were to be supposed to go, . . .

       c   *His being supposed to go is disgusting.

It also predictably eliminates potential Raising examples like (vib)

(vi)   a   It seems that he is supposed to go.

        b   *He seems to be supposed to go.

with no requirement of any special restriction on Raising.

6. The reader might note that sentences like (34a) sometimes become well-formed if the indirect object NP, in (34a), *Bob*, is removed:

(i)   There promised to be a riot.

We would argue that this type of clause involves a different verb from more standard *promise* clauses like that in:

(ii)   I promised to go.

The meaning difference is obvious. We assume that sentences like (i) involve a verb which behaves essentially like *seem*, that is, (i) is derived by Raising.

PROBLEMS

1. Why does the figurative meaning of an example like

(i)   The cat seems to have your tongue.

bear on the analysis of *seem* complements?

2. Explain the contrast between:

(i) Now seems to be a good time for wheat.

(ii) *Now appears to produce a lot of wheat.

3. Given the following contrast in simple clauses

(i) The important thing to him is money.

(ii) *The important thing to him bothers me.

what does a grammar containing Raising predict about *seem* sentences?

CHAPTER 21 **MORE ON RAISING**

PREVIEW

In what follows we provide further evidence in favor of the Raising rule. The discussion of Raising with verbs like *seem* is expanded to include cases where prepositional phrases based on *to* are present. This permits one to consider the interaction of Raising with the Reflexivization rule. The remote structures previously assumed for Infinitival cases with *seem* and *appear* would be independently needed in order to correctly handle the distribution of reflexive and nonreflexive pronouns as well as other phenomena behaving in a parallel way (*own*, etc.).

It turns out that the main verbs of clauses taking complements are the chief determinants of whether Raising can apply or not. It is convenient to have a term for those verbal elements which permit this. The name R(*aising*)-*trigger* is introduced for this purpose. The class of R-triggers extends well beyond *seem* and *appear* to include a group of perhaps fifty elements.

Finally, the interaction of Raising with several other grammatical features encountered earlier is treated. It is shown how the postulation of this rule explains certain facts and provides the basis for natural description of others.

In Chapter 20 we presented various grounds for the view that infinitival complement constructions with the main verbs *seem* and *appear* involve a rearrangement rule called Raising. Our arguments involved the lack of feasibility of an Equi analysis of such constructions, especially the behavior of various highly restricted types of NPs, idiom chunks, *now*, and existential *there*, etc.

Let us return to such constructions. Although not previously noted, verbs like *seem* and *appear* can occur with another NP preceded by the preposition *to*:

(1) a It seems to me that he is dishonest.
     b Didn't that seem strange to you?
     c It must have appeared to them that we were incompetent.
     d That must have appeared to them to have been deliberate.

Naturally, these complement clauses can contain reflexives:

(2) a It seems to me that Jim underestimates himself.
     b Jim seems to me to underestimate himself.

In sentences like (2a), the presence of reflexives is unproblematical. The clause mate condition, which was seen to be crucial for this process, is apparently met, even in surface structure. That is, *Jim* and *himself* in (2a) appear to be surface clause mates. There is no reason to posit any remote structure for (2a) in which the relevant elements are not clause mates. But (2b) is a different story.

One might try to argue that the reflexive in

(3) Jim seems to underestimate himself.

is due to the fact that *Jim* and *himself* are clause mates *even in surface structure*. It has already been shown that Reflexivization cannot properly be described in terms of surface structure (on the basis of a variety of NP deletion rules). One might still struggle to maintain a surface structure account for other cases. However, this will not do for infinitival constructions with *seem* and *appear*. For consider a typical example like (2b), which we repeat here along with a nonreflexivized version:

(4) a *Jim$_i$ seems to me to underestimate him$_i$.
     b Jim seems to me to underestimate himself.

The contrast shows that reflexive marking in this context is not only possible, but required, as in the other cases dealt with earlier.

If application of Reflexivization in (4b) is due to the fact that *Jim* and *himself* are superficial clause mates, it follows that *me* and *himself* are clause mates at that level. Therefore, if the element *himself* is replaced by a pronoun coreferential to the *me* occurring after *to*, this sort of account would predict that Reflexivization operation with *me* as antecedent would be obligatory. But it is impossible:

(5) a   Jim seems to me to underestimate me.[1]
      b   *Jim seems to me to underestimate myself.

The sharp contrast between pairs like (4) and (5) shows that it is impossible to apply the clause mate rule for reflexivization to the relevant sentences in such a way as to predict the facts. As in many earlier cases, the attempt to restrict rules to surface structures yields anomalies.

    Throughout this manual, we have adopted a standard tactic in the face of such anomalies. Namely, we search for appropriate remote structures for which the relevant regularities will hold without anomaly. We have already proposed certain remote structures for infinitival constructions with *seem* in the preceding chapter. This proposal was based on facts *entirely distinct from* the interaction of such constructions with Reflexivization. And while it is true that the *seem* and *appear* sentences considered in Chapter 20 lacked phrases of the form *to* NP, there is no reason to think that this makes a crucial difference. We should, unless forced to conclude otherwise, assume that the remote structures of *seem* and *appear* constructions with and without *to* NP phrases differ in no other respect than the presence or absence of such phrases.[2] Consequently, on the basis of the evidence in Chapter 20, both of the sentences in

(6) a   Joan seems to me to understand herself.
      b   It seems to me that Joan understands herself.

have the same initial structure:[3]

(7)

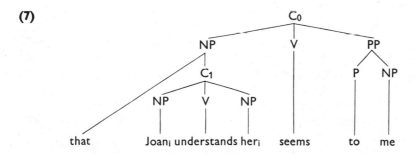

Since the pair of coreferential NPs are clause mates in C_1 in (7), Reflexivization will apply, and a subsequent operation of Extraposition will yield (6b) with no problems.

    The interesting case is (6a), which also derives from (7). Again, Reflexivization is determined by (7). But then, instead of Extraposition, Raising will apply. This will separate the subject of C_1 and make it the new subject of *seems*, with the rest of C_1 moving to the right of the verb. It then assumes, in some way so far unspecified, infinitival form. Hence application of Raising does automatically yield (6a) from (7), just as Extraposition yields (6b). Moreover, such a derivation automatically blocks a sentence like:

(8) *Joan$_i$ seems to me to understand her$_i$.

Why? Such a sentence would also have to derive from (7). But it does not reveal the application of Reflexivization. However, such an application is obligatory in a clause like C_1 of (7). Hence (8) can only be derived by violating conditions requiring Reflexivization.

So far, the Raising analysis arrived at in Chapter 20 on the basis of entirely different considerations automatically interacts with Reflexivization to predict the facts in (4) and (6). What then of (5), which shows that a post-*to* NP in such constructions does *not* trigger Reflexivization of a coreferent NP inside of the infinitival complement? To see why it does not, consider the relevant remote structure:

(9)

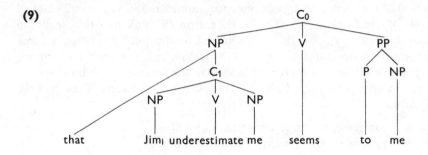

Here, no single minimal clause, in particular not C_1, contains a pair of coreferent NPs. Hence Reflexivization cannot apply. In (9), the two coreferential occurrences of *me* are not clause mates, since they are separated by the clause boundary after the clausal subject of *seems*. A principle stating that Reflexivization applies at this stage of the derivation then correctly predicts that no reflexive marking should take place in (9). Moreover, even if Reflexivization could operate on the *output* of Raising as applied to (9), no application of this rule is predicted. In the tree describing the output of Raising, the clause mate condition is still not met between the two *me*'s:[4]

(10)

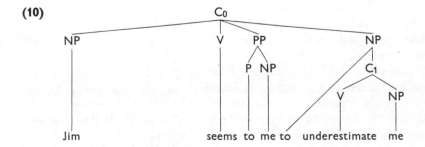

Here also a clause boundary intervenes between the two coreferents.

Contrasts like those between (4) and (5) are impossible to account for in terms of regularities of surface structure. They *seem* to be anomalous with respect to the clause mate account of Reflexivization. They are nonetheless automatic consequences of the Raising analysis of *seem* constructions worked out in the previous chapter on entirely different grounds. Thus another case has been found to support the central role in grammar of remote structure and the transformational derivation of surface structures.

Note too that the analysis of *seem* and *appear* infinitival constructions worked out in Chapter 20 and the clause mate analysis of Reflexivization dovetail perfectly. Jointly, they predict the proper distribution of reflexive versus nonreflexive pronouns in the infinitival complements of main verbs like *seem*. This provides considerable additional support for both the posited account of Reflexivization and the Raising analysis of the constructions in question.

In previous chapters dealing with NP deletions, it was shown that a variety of other phenomena behaved similarly to Reflexivization. They were also used to support analyses justified by the distribution of reflexives. These phenomena should behave in a fashion parallel to reflexives in the infinitival complements of verbs like *seem*. We will briefly show that this is true with respect to *own*, "agreeing" idioms like *crane X's neck*, predicate nominals, and adverbs of the form *by* plus reflexive. We shall see that the form in question behaves, when in the infinitive of *seem* (like ordinary reflexives), as if it were really in a clause with the superficial subject of *seems*, as it is in remote structure under a Raising analysis:[5]

(11)   a   Jim$_i$ seems to me to hate his$_i$ own mother.
      b   *Jim seems to me to hate my own mother.

(12)   a   Jim seems to me to have craned his neck too much.
      b   *Jim seems to me to have craned my neck too much.

(13)   a   *Jim$_i$ seems to me to be the one who shot him$_i$.
      b   Jim seems to me to be the one who shot me.

(14)   a   Jim seems to me to have gone there by himself.
      b   *Jim seems to me to have gone there by myself.

These facts also dovetail perfectly with a Raising analysis of the constructions in question and further justify the accounts given so far. Again the relevant facts cannot be described generally in terms of surface structure alone.

We have shown how the Raising analysis introduced in the last chapter properly interacts with the range of phenomenon utilized in earlier chapters to first justify the notion of remote structure. All the analyses suggested are thus further supported. Let us now turn to some other ramifications of the existence of Raising within the grammar of English.

We need a term to refer to verbs like *seem* and *appear*, which serve as the main verbs of clauses derived by Raising. For these are the major determinants of Raising application. We refer to such forms as *R(aising)-triggers*. So far, the only R-triggers explicitly recognized as such, have been *seem* and *appear*. But the number of R-triggers is on the order of fifty or sixty. (See Chapters 26 and 27 for further discussion of the scope of Raising.) A few others include:

(15)	Pure Verbs	Adjectives
	happen	likely
	continue	certain
	turn out	bound

While we will not take the space to justify this listing in detail, it is worth providing some grounds for one member of each type. Take first *turn out*:

(16) a It turns out that close tabs were kept on him by the FBI.
  b Close tabs turn out to have been kept on him by the FBI.

One sees that *turn out*, like *seem* and *appear*, occurs in both infinitival and *that* clause contexts. In the former, it takes idiom chunks as subjects, supporting a Raising analysis. Moreover, pairs like (16) are paraphrases of each other and share the same semantic relations. *Turn out* differs from *seem* and *appear* in that it takes no *to* phrase. However, it is similar to the earlier R-triggers in that Extraposition is apparently obligatory under the same circumstances:

(17) a *That he is insane turns out.
  b That he is insane turns out not to be obvious.

Consider the adjective *likely*. This also occurs with both types of complements:

(18) a It is likely that he will lose.
  b He is likely to lose.

Again the key fact is the possibility of highly restricted NPs as subjects:

(19) a Tabs are likely to be kept on all of his movements.
  b Now is likely to be a poor time to eat swordfish.

Like all adjectives, *likely* normally requires a form of *be* as an auxiliary verb. We shall discuss this phenomena further starting in Chapter 26. There we will raise the question of how such elements as *be* and adjectives enter trees and what the proper relations are between the categories Adj and V and between both of these and the categories of auxiliary and modal verb.

All of the elements in (15) are intransitive. And it is from the clausal subjects of these that Raising extracts the subject NP, making it into a new derived subject. Once it is seen that there are a variety of R-triggers, an interesting set of questions arises. Namely, what happens when the main verb of a clausal subject of an R-trigger is itself an R-trigger? Can this happen? If so, can Raising apply more than once? And so on. The answer to these questions is yes. Consider a sentence like:

(20)   There are likely to turn out to be germs in this soup.

Here the subject of *likely* (or of *are likely*[6]) is existential *there*, a highly restricted NP. Moreover, both *likely* and *turn out* are R-triggers and both occur with infinitival complements. These are only found with these forms when Raising has applied. One concludes that *there* has become the subject of *are likely* through application of Raising. This means that underlying (20) is the remote structure:

(21)

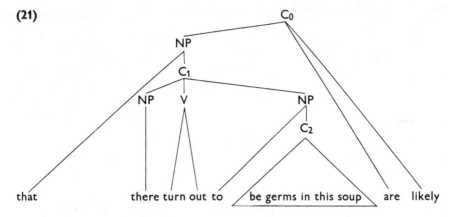

However, the substructure C_1 in (21) is the kind of structure which is itself derived by Raising. *There* has become the subject of *turn out* in (21) through a previous application of Raising. Hence, underlying (21) must be the still more remote structure (22):

(22)

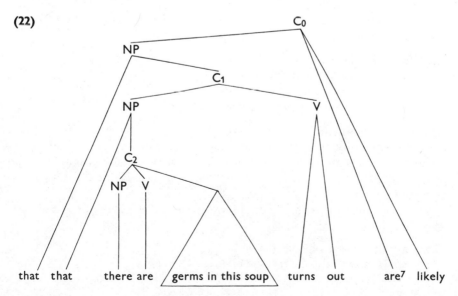

Thus (20) is derived by successive applications of Raising, first within C_1 to make *there*, which starts out[8] as a subject of *are germs* . . ., into the subject of *turns out*, and then within C_0 to make *there* the subject of *are likely*. Given the appropriate structures containing R-triggers "stacked" up one below the other, Raising can operate in a successive or iterative fashion. In principle, there is no bound on such "stacking." It is thus possible for an NP which starts out deeply embedded to successively move leftward up a complex tree away from its original co-constituents. It ends up minimally separated from them by all of the R-triggers which determine its movement. Hence, in (20), the word *there* has become separated from *are germs* . . . by both *likely* and *turn out*. We shall consider this iterative application of rules like Raising further (see especially Chapter 29).

The explanatory power of Raising is further revealed by cases like (20), in which there are multiple applications of this rule. In ordinary, purely superficial terms, it would be even more difficult to describe sentences like (20) and the restrictions they manifest than it is to describe simpler examples. In such examples, the highly restricted NP *there* occurs, but only subject to strict constraints on the character of the rightmost complement. Thus the entire sequence *are likely to turn out* is "transparent" in such cases:

(23)　a　Now is likely to turn out to be a poor time to buy a windmill.
　　　b　*Now is likely to turn out to annoy you.

Such facts are, however, automatic consequences of the Raising analysis, given the restrictions needed for simpler clauses, that is, in the case of (23), the restrictions needed to distinguish:

(24)　a　Now is a poor time to buy a windmill.
　　　b　*Now annoys you.

Next, one can make use of the knowledge gained about Raising to shed some light on the peculiar contrast in Extraposition behavior noted for R-triggers like *seem*, that is, such contrasts as:

(25)　a　*That he is sick seems (to me).
　　　b　It seems (to me) that he is sick.
　　　c　That he is sick seems obvious (to me)
　　　d　It seems obvious (to me) that he is sick.

The question is why (25a) contrasts with (25c). We will be unable to provide any *explanation* for this fact. We are not able to show that this distinction follows from any independently motivated principle of the grammar. But, given Raising, one is at least able to provide a *description* of the difference, as follows.

First, we will surely wish to regard sentences like (26a) as minor variants of those like (26b):

(26)　a　That seems obvious (to me).
　　　b　That seems (to me) to be obvious.

They will have the same initial structure, the former being derived by a rule which deletes *to be*. The deletion has the concomitant effect, whether or not this is accomplished by an independent rule, of altering the possible positions of *to* NP:

(27) a   That seems quite obvious to me.
       b   *That seems to me quite obvious.
       c   That seems to me to be quite obvious.

The advantages of deriving such pairs from a common remote structure are (i) that it explains the identical selectional and semantic properties of the pairs and (ii) that it integrates the description of sentences like (26a) into a Raising grammar. As we have seen, applications of this rule regularly yield infinitival form for the original underlying complement.

Let us reconsider such contrasts as:

(28) a   *That Harriet is lonely seems (to me).
       b   That Harriet is lonely seems obvious (to me).

In (28a), the *that* clause which remains, "illegally," in subject position is the underlying subject of *seems* at the deepest level of analysis so far contemplated. Thus the *that* clause in (28) is both the surface and initial subject of *seems*. However, the structure of (28b) is somewhat different and rather more complex. It has been argued that (28b) derives from:

(29)   That Harriet is lonely seems (to me) to be obvious.

In such a structure, *seems* has an infinitival complement. This is a pattern which we know to be a function of Raising. Hence, the *that* clause in superficial subject position in (29) (and hence (28b)) is not the underlying subject of *seems*, but rather the underlying subject *of its complement* clause. This becomes the surface subject of the higher verb only because of Raising. Thus, underlying both (28b) and (29) is:

(30)

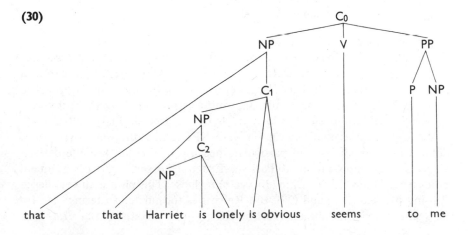

The *that* clause which "illegally" ends up in subject position of the main clause in (28a) starts out as the subject of that main clause. However, the *that* clause which occurs in the subject position of *seem* in (28b) and (29) starts out as the subject of *is obvious*. It becomes subject of *seems* only because Raising applies. Given this difference in the origin of the *that* clauses, one might try to describe contrasts like (28) as follows:

(31)   Extraposition, normally optional, is obligatory with the clausal subjects of a certain set of main verbal elements including *seem*, *appear*, etc., just when these clausal subjects are also the initial structure subjects of *seem*, *appear*, etc.

Alternatively, and, we think, preferably, one can replace (31) by a rather different sort of rule. In sentences like (28a), *seems* follows its underlying clausal subject, while, if Extraposition applies, it precedes it. One can then account for ill-formedness like (28a) by saying:

(32)   A certain class of main verbal elements including *seem*, *appear*, etc., cannot occur in well-formed structures in which they *follow* their initial structure complement subjects.

Statement (32), unlike (31), attributes the irregularity in (28a) entirely to the class of verbs in question, leaving Extraposition without special restrictions. Neither account of course *explains* the facts in (28). In each case, the limitation on clause positioning remains a brute fact about the verbs in question, a brute fact which distinguishes them from freer verbal elements like *disturb*, *worry*, etc.

Next, one should say something about surface structure bracketing. It was observed earlier that Extraposition produces a binary pattern, with the extraposed clause one of the constituents, everything else the other. Consider then:

(33)   a   [It seems to me][that Joe is loyal].
          b   Joe seems to me to be loyal.

Example (33a), derived by Extraposition, has the binary pattern to be expected. But what of (33b)? In such cases, there is no reason to suggest that *Joe seems to me* is a surface constituent. Rather, *seems to me to be loyal* appears to be a constituent at that level. This also is consistent with the analysis proposed here. Although (33a,b) have the same initial structure, only (33a) involves application of Extraposition, which yields the superficial binary pattern.

We argued earlier that *that* clauses were NPs because they underwent rules defined in terms of NPs, in particular, because they could become derived subjects under application of Passive. Exactly the same sort of argument holds here. The subject of C_1 in (30) is a *that* clause. This phrase must undergo Raising to yield (28b) and (29). But Raising is formulated in terms of NPs. So again the relevant phrases must be NPs. Thus the status of *that Harriet is lonely* in (30) is the same as that of the simpler phrase *that truth*, which, if substituted for the subject of C_1 would yield:

(34) a That truth seems to me to be obvious.
      b That truth seems obvious to me.

Example (34b) is derived by parallel applications of Raising, the rule which deletes *to be*, and the principles which determine the proper positioning of *to* NP.

SUMMARY

A Raising analysis of *seem*, *appear*, and similar verbs with infinitival complements was originally motivated on grounds having nothing to do with reflexives. The chief result of this chapter is that such an analysis is independently necessary to account for such reflexivization paradigms as:

(i) $Mary_i$ appeared to understand $\begin{Bmatrix} herself_i \\ *her_i \end{Bmatrix}$.

(ii) $Mary_i$ appeared to us to understand $\begin{Bmatrix} *ourselves \\ us \end{Bmatrix}$.

This provides striking exemplification of the principle that grammatical regularities cannot in general be stated on surface structures. Sets like (i) and (ii), though anomalous and irregular from a superficial point of view, are automatic consequences of the kind of grammar advocated here. In a system based on the notions of remote structure and transformational derivation, Raising can be recognized. Then, Reflexivization will operate on complement clauses like those underlying (i) and (ii) *before* Raising dismembers the complements.

Phenomena parallel to reflexive marking support the conclusions just drawn by behaving in an entirely parallel way. The interaction of Raising and these phenomena reinforces the conclusions of earlier chapters of this manual. These underscored the need to recognize that surface structure provides only the shell of sentence structure as a whole.

NOTES

1. As throughout our discussions, the final pronoun in (5a) must be read as weakly stressed, that is, without contrastive stress. Moreover, for some speakers, examples like (5a) are not perfectly well-formed. This is irrelevant here. Even for these speakers, (5a) is far superior to (5b), showing that Reflexivization cannot apply in such cases.

2. Conceivably, the initial structures do not even differ in this way. It is possible that all of the relevant sentences contain *to* NP structures, these being deleted in certain cases to yield the simpler forms.

3. In (7) we again ignore the grammatical insight that, at superficial levels of structure, English clauses without auxiliaries tend to have a binary structure separating the subject from the rest. We shall continue to ignore this until Chapter 27.

4. It has sometimes been suggested (Ross (1969)) that certain operations on clause structures lead to the *pruning* or elimination of C nodes. In particular, Ross argued that *subject loss* under rules like Equi and Raising has this effect. If this were so, the C_1 node in (10) would be eliminated in the course of the derivation from (9). However, we reject this view. It is claimed here that such pruning takes place in subordinate clauses *only* when these lose their main verbs. Thus we would recognize the pruning of the subordinate C node in a derivation like:

(i)   the man $_c$[who has a knife]$_c$ $\Longrightarrow$ the man [with a knife]

Hence, in derived structure, we would not regard the bracketed sequence on the right of the arrow as a clause. This pruning is determined not by subject loss, but by the elimination of the main verb, *has*.

5. In order to appreciate the following examples, it may be necessary for the reader to refer back to earlier chapters in which the regularities governing the particular forms have been described.

6. The relations between *are* and *likely* or, more generally, between an adjective and the form of *be* which precedes it, will be considered in detail in Chapter 26. Here we shall *artificially* treat them more or less as if they were a unit.

7. The plural form of the verb here (*are*, instead of the singular *is*) raises many questions which we have so far ignored. There is a restriction between the *number* of a subject NP and the inflection of the verb of which it is the subject. As it is traditionally put, *a (finite) verb agrees in number with its subject NP*. Moreover, as (22) suggests, this agreement is in part dependent on derived subjects determined by the application of rules like Raising. Hence, as it stands, the highest NP in (22) would determine singular agreement. The ultimate sentence has plural agreement because of the functional plurality of *there*, which is promoted to main clause subject by successive applications of Raising.

8. Ultimately, it can be shown that *there* does not start out as the subject but is made into a subject by the rule which introduces it into existential contexts. This has no relevance for the present discussion.

PROBLEMS

1. Try to provide some evidence showing that the adjective *apt* is an *R*-trigger.

2. Produce the initial structure of

(i) John is apt to turn out to be likely to go.

3. In the example

(i) Melvin is apt to contradict himself.

state the order in which the rules Raising and Reflexivization must apply. Give the reason for this order.

CHAPTER 22 ANOTHER KIND OF RAISING OPERATION

PREVIEW

In the present chapter we investigate contrasts between pairs of examples like:

(i) They proved (that) *Melvin* was guilty.
(ii) They proved *Melvin* to be guilty.

By considering the way the italicized NPs (called *pivots* for convenience) interact with passivization, it is shown that the pivot is a constituent of the subordinate clause in (i) but a constituent of the main clauses in (ii). On the other hand, a variety of considerations involving highly restricted NPs (*there*, chunks of idioms, etc.) considered in earlier chapters indicate that the pivot in examples like (ii) has the properties of a subordinate clause subject. The solution to this paradox is to posit a new Raising operation, analogous to that discussed in the previous two chapters. The new operation creates derived objects instead of derived subjects. This rule is called o-Raising, in contrast to that introduced in Chapter 20, which is renamed s-Raising.

The preceding two chapters dealt with a rule called Raising, which turns the subjects of certain complement clauses into main clause subjects. We now turn our attention toward a distinct but similar process. Consider:

(1) a The count proved (that) there are vampires in Bulgaria.
   b The count believed (that) tabs were kept on his movements.
   c The count expected (that) considerable headway would be made on
      the guillotine.

Such sentences provide no great problems for the description of English. They
can naturally be taken to be made up of subject NPs, verbs, and object NPs
in the form of tensed clauses, optionally marked by the element *that*. The
complement clauses themselves are of the sort previously encountered. Each
contains one of those highly restricted types of NP which were appealed to
earlier as a basis for arguments in favor of Raising. Example (1a) involves
there, restricted to existential type sentences; (1b) involves *tabs*, restricted to
the verb *keep* and occurring in examples like (1b) only because the complement has undergone Passive. Finally, (1c) involves *headway*, restricted to
make and also occurring as a complement subject only because the subordinate clause has undergone Passive.

Now consider:

(2) a The count proved there to be vampires in Bulgaria.
   b The count believed tabs to have been kept on his movements.
   c The count expected considerable headway to be made on the
      guillotine.

These sentences seem to be essentially identical to the corresponding forms
in (1), differing only superficially in the choice of complement-marking
devices. The former contain tensed (inflected) verbs with the possibility of an
initial *that*; the latter have infinitival forms. The feeling of essential identity
between the corresponding examples is reinforced by the synonymity of such
pairs.

It would be natural then to describe sentences like (2) as also consisting of
subject NPs, main verbs and object NPs but differing from (1) in that the
clausal objects are infinitival. This would account for the possibility of the
various highly restricted NPs in the sentences of (2) on exactly the same
grounds as those in (1). No special statements or principles would be required.
Such an analysis is attractive. However, it runs into unexpected difficulties.

There are good grounds for taking sentences like (1) to have the structure
NP V NP, that is, for taking *that* clause complements to be NPs. For instance,
sentences like (1) have passive analogues, somewhat unnatural ones without
the application of Extraposition, as in (3), but entirely acceptable ones with it,
as in (4):

(3) a That there are vampires in Bulgaria was proved by the count.
   b ? That tabs were kept on his movements was believed by the count.
   c ? That considerable headway would be made on the guillotine was
      expected by the count.

(4) a It was proved by the count that there are vampires in Bulgaria.
b It was believed by the count that tabs were kept on his movements.
c It was expected by the count that considerable headway would be made on the guillotine.

But, since only NPs can undergo Passive, the postverbal sentences in (1) must be NPs. Independently, main verbs like *prove*, *believe*, and *expect* occur with directly following NPs, because of sentences such as:

$$\textbf{(5)} \quad \text{The count} \begin{Bmatrix} \text{proved} \\ \text{believed} \\ \text{expected} \end{Bmatrix} \begin{Bmatrix} \text{that} \\ \text{something terrible} \\ \text{nothing} \\ \text{that sort of thing} \end{Bmatrix}.$$

In these, the NP character of the postverbal material is obvious. Hence the NP status of the *that* clauses is part of a wider pattern permitting such main verbs to occur with object NPs.

If sentences like (2) were fully parallel to those like (1) (except for markers of complementation), one would expect to find passives parallel to (3) and (4) in which the complement is infinitival, as in (2). This is impossible, however:

(6) a *(For) There to be vampires in Bulgaria was proved by the count.
b *(For) Tabs to have been kept on his movements was believed by the count.
c *(For) Considerable headway to be made on the guillotine was expected by the count.

d *It was proved by the count (for) there to be vampires in Bulgaria.
e *It was believed by the count (for) tabs to have been kept on his movements.
f *It was expected by the count (for) considerable headway to be made on the guillotine.

A parallel treatment of infinitival and *that* clause complements after *prove*, *believe*, etc., with respect to Passive application in the main clause would be desirable. However, *that* clauses behave like NPs, but infinitival sequences do not.

There is an important correlate of the unexpected contrast between (3) and (4) versus (5a-c) and (5d-f). This also involves main clause application of Passive. Since all of the verbs *prove*, *believe*, *expect* work the same, we can for ease of exposition restrict ourselves to the first with no loss in generality:

(7) a The count proved (that) the bat was harmless.
b The count proved the bat to be harmless.

(8) a *The bat was proved (that) was harmless by the count.
b The bat was proved to be harmless by the count.

That is, the intuitive subject of the complement clause in (7) can passivize within the main clause when the complement is infinitival, but not when the complement is finite.

The passivization contrasts just revealed show that at certain stages of derivation apparently quite similar sentences like (7a,b) differ in structure in a significant way. This inference is so far based exclusively on differences in passivization behavior. Moreover, we know only that there is a difference, not what the difference is. It would be desirable to show that there was a structural contrast between the relevant infinitival and tensed clause cases with the following properties: (i) it has a natural origin in the grammar; (ii) it automatically predicts the differences in passivization behavior; (iii) it is supported by the way it interacts with a variety of other structural aspects of English; and (iv) it is not inconsistent with a description of the close similarities between pairs like (7a,b), in particular, not incompatible with a treatment of the highly restricted NPs in cases like (1) and (2).

Suppose we now argue that, at the stage of main clause passivization, sentences like (7a,b) differ in the clause memberships of NPs like *the bat* (henceforth, for convenience, we shall refer to NPs in these positions as *pivots*). In particular, suppose it is claimed that in examples like (7a), the pivot is at that stage a constituent of the subordinate clause, while in (7b) the pivot is a constituent of the main clause. This would assign tree structures at that stage of the following forms (pivots italicized):

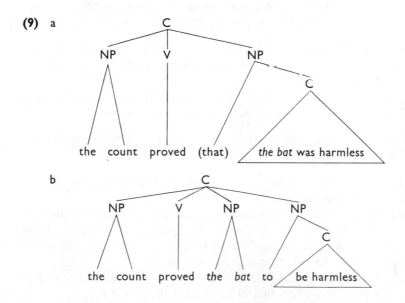

Such a structural contrast between the pivot NPs suggests a natural basis for the passivization differences which have been documented. Suppose it is claimed that Passive can only operate on an NP which is *a sister of*[1] the main verb of the clause being passivized. As a consequence, the NP which Passive turns into a new derived subject must always be a clause mate of the relevant verb in the input. This is a condition met by the pivot NP, *the bat*, in (9b) but not in (9a). Moreover, there is a natural statement, based on structures like (9), to account for why the clausal NP passivizes in (9a) but not (9b). Only in the former is this NP immediately postverbal.[2] In (9b), there is an intervening NP.

The description of Passive in Chapter 18 already requires that the NP to be passivized both (i) be a sister of the main verb of the clause and (ii) not be separated from it by any intervening NP constituents. These specifications on Passive combine with structures like (9) to account completely for the passivization contrasts noted at the beginning of this chapter.

The claim that Passive requires that the postverbal NPs be sisters of the verb is supported by the failure of any of the following italicized NPs to passivize:

(10) a Jack resented *there* being no more beer.
      b They resented *your* lying to them.
      c They favor *addicts* being treated in hospitals.
      d The troops dislike *Mike*'s criticizing our emperor.

(11) a *There was resented being no more beer by Jack.
      b *You(r) were resented lying to them by them.
      c *Addicts were favored being treated in hospitals by them.
      d *Mike('s) was disliked criticizing our emperor by the troops.

Such facts will follow naturally from the clause mate condition on Passive, under the otherwise valid assumption that there are clause boundaries before the italicized NPs in all of (10a–d).[3] There are no known cases where Passive has the power to "reach down" into a lower clause for the NP which it makes into a derived subject.[4] Thus the following principle is valid:

(12) If an NP undergoes Passive with a main verb, V, that NP is a clause mate of V in the tree which is input to Passive.

Given (12), the fact that one finds sentences like (8b) shows that the pivot NP in (7b) is a main clause constituent, as in the tree in (9b).

So far it has been argued on the basis of facts relating to passivization that sentences like (7a,b) differ as in (9). That is, they differ with respect to whether the pivot NP is a main clause or subordinate clause constituent. Let us consider other evidence for the structural contrast in (9).

Significant evidence for this derives from a rule of English which we shall call *Complex NP Shift*. The action of this rule is illustrated in:

(13) a I consider him intelligent.
      b *I consider intelligent him.
      c I consider intelligent — anyone who voted for our candidate.

(14) a   Joan gave that to Betty.

      b   *Joan gave to Betty that.

      c   Joan gave to Betty — the Italian meatball which had been prepared by her grandmother.

(15) a   They elected Arthur dogcatcher.

      b   *They elected dogcatcher Arthur.

      c   They elected dogcatcher — the oldest son of the mayor's second wife.

Such examples indicate that there is a rule which displaces certain NP constituents from their standard positions to the right of their containing clauses. The most basic constraint on this operation is that the NP to be moved must be *complex* (in some difficult-to-specify sense). Among the factors involved in this complexity are sheer length and whether or not the moved NP dominates a clause.

As the boldfaced dashes in (13)–(15) schematically indicate, Complex NP Shift produces a derived constituent structure in which the moved constituent and everything else are the two constituents of some new constituent. Hence we can represent the rule as:

(16)   Complex NP Shift

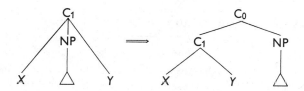

Stated as in (16), Complex NP Shift is a completely general rule which should be able to operate on any NP in a clause, given only the requirement of complexity. This is far from the truth and there are many special conditions. Only one class of these is of relevance here, illustrated by:

(17) a   People who put Pernod in their oatmeal don't know any better.

      b   *Don't know any better — people who put Pernod in their oatmeal.

(18) a   Everyone who knows either French or Turkish is eligible for immediate induction.

      b   *Is eligible for immediate induction — everyone who knows either French or Turkish.

(19) a   Tony believes that most of the girls living in this dorm are from Uranus.

      b   *Tony believes that are from Uranus — most of the girls living in this dorm.

(20)   a   For someone who is as uncouth and gross as you to win would be disgusting.

        b   *For to win — someone who is as uncouth and gross as you would be disgusting.

All the (b) examples in (17–20) are terrible. Some principle must thus block Complex NP Shift in these cases. The relevant condition cannot involve complexity, since the displaced NPs are quite complex. There is, however, an obvious generalization governing these examples. In each bad example, the displaced NP was a subject at the point of Complex NP Shift application. This suggests the existence of a general constraint:

(21)   Complex NP Shift does *not* apply to *subject* NPs.

There are no known exceptions to (21), which makes a significant contribution toward restricting the *excessive* generality of (16).

Given the knowledge that Complex NP Shift is further governed by principle (21), let us return to clauses based on verbs like *prove*:

(22)   a   Bob proved (that) most girls who had dyed hair were insecure.

        b   Bob proved most girls who had dyed hair to be insecure.

(23)   a   *Bob proved (that) were insecure — most girls who had dyed hair.

        b   Bob proved to be insecure — most girls who had dyed hair.

Strikingly, pivot NPs are subject to Complex NP Shift in the infinitival cases but not in the tensed clause cases. Although illustrated only for *prove*, the same generalizations hold for other verbs like *believe*, etc. Significantly, just this distinction is predicted, given condition (21) and structures like those in (9). For, if the pivot NP in the tensed clause cases is a constituent of the subordinate clause, it is in fact a subject. Hence, it is not susceptible to Complex NP Shift, according to (21). In the infinitival case, however, the pivot NP is not a subordinate clause constituent, but a main clause one. Therefore, it cannot be the subject, since the preverbal NP is the subject. So it is not covered by the restriction in (21). It follows that the tree representations in (9) correctly interact with condition (21) on Complex NP Shift to predict otherwise bizarre differences in behavior with respect to this displacement rule.

What has just been illustrated is a correlation between Passive behavior and Complex NP Shift behavior. Those pivot NPs which are subject to Passive in the main clause are subject to Complex NP Shift, and those which are not are not. This follows directly from the assumptions made about Passive and Complex NP shift, given structural differences like those in (9). These structural differences are then further supported. Recall that, in contrast to verbs like *prove*, there are verbs like *resent*, which do not permit passivization of following NPs:

(24)   a   Tom resented there being no more beer.

        b   Tom believed there to be no more beer.

(25) a *There was resented being no more beer by Tom.
b *There was resented by Tom being no more beer.
c There was believed by Tom to be no more beer.

If, as argued earlier, the failure of passivization in (25a,b) is due to the fact that the post-*resented* NP in (24a) is a subordinate clause constituent (and hence a subject), then principle (21) predicts that Complex NP Shift is inapplicable to post-*resent* NPs (even when these are complex). And this is the case:

(26) a *Tom resented being shot — nine of the spies who he had be-friended in the fort.
b *Tom resented quitting — most of the people who he had hired while he was manager.

This strengthens the claim that the difference between pairs like (24a,b) involves the clause memberships of the pivot NPs.

At this point, there seems to be solid evidence that pairs like

(27) a I believe (that) Jack is weird.
b I believe Jack to be weird.

differ in the clause membership of their pivot NPs. However, although these contrasts explain the differences in behavior with respect to Passive and Complex NP Shift, they themselves provide a paradox. For this means that sentences like (27), despite their great similarity and synomymity, have different structures. In particular, the claim that pivot NPs in infinitival constructions are main clause constituents raises difficulties in the case of highly restricted NPs like *there*, *headway*, etc. For, of course, these can occur as pivot NPs in such cases. The question is how this is to be predicted by the grammar.

Take a typical pair:

(28) a I believe (that) tabs were kept on Harry's movements.
b I believe tabs to have been kept on Harry's movements.

In the case of (28a), where the pivot NP is a subordinate clause constituent, there is no problem. *Tabs* will become the subject through the action of Passive applying to the subordinate clause (and hence by operations entirely independent of the main clause). That is, the facts in (28) follow just as do those in the independent sentence:

(29) Tabs were kept on Harry's movements.

It was pointed out earlier that it would be desirable to account for the facts for pairs like (28) in the same way. And yet this now *seems* impossible. For we have provided evidence that the pivot NP in sentences like (28b) is in the main clause.

The solution to this problem is suggested by the discussions in Chapters 20 and 21. There also we encountered constituents, in particular those italicized in (30), which behaved *selectionally* as if they were subordinate clause constituents, but which were in other ways (obviously) main clause constituents:

(30) a *Tabs* seems to have been kept on Tom's movements.
b *Little headway* appears to have been made on that problem.
c *There* turned out to be gorillas in his attic.

The solution was to posit that the italicized NPs were constituents of the subordinate clauses in underlying trees, but were moved up into main clause positions later, through action of a rule called Raising. A similar approach would handle the facts in cases like (28). We can posit that the initial structure of (28b) is essentially like that of (28a), with the pivot NP the subject constituent of the subordinate clause. This will account for the selectional facts, that is, the occurrence of the restricted NP, on the same grounds as in (28a). No special statements will be required. We then posit the existence of a further raising operation. It extracts the subject NP from the complement and makes it a derived constituent of the main clause, turning the remnant of the complement infinitival. In this way, the grammar expresses all of the generalizations of relevance, both those which link pairs like (28a,b) and those which show that the pivot NP is a main clause constituent in (28b). For, in the kind of system underlying our description, it is possible to say that the same NP is a subordinate clause constituent at one stage, and a main clause constituent at a later stage, these stages being mediated by a raising operation. And this is, of course, just what we want to say about the pivot NP in infinitival cases like (28b).

There is already a rule raising complement clause subject NPs into main clause *subject* position with certain main verbal elements like *seem*, *appear*, *turn out*, etc. We now postulate that English also has a rule raising complement clause subject NPs into main clause *object* position with a different class of main verb elements, including *prove*, *believe*, and *expect*. We have thus recognized two different raising rules. Since one produces derived subjects and the other derived objects, let us henceforth refer to them respectively as *s-Raising* (working with *seem*, etc.) and *o-Raising* (working with *prove*, etc.).

The operation of o-Raising can be sketched as follows:

(31)

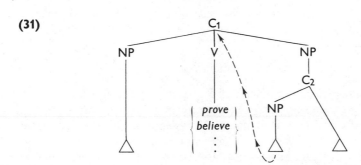

We can formulate the needed rule in our familiar notation as:

(32) o-Raising

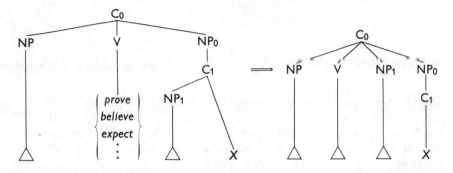

It was shown earlier that Reflexivization application is dependent on a clause mate condition linking antecedent and reflexive forms. Since o-Raising has the property of altering clause mate relations, one might expect its operation to be reflected in differences of reflexive possibilities. Compare then:

(33) a   Bob$_i$ proved (that) $\begin{Bmatrix} \text{he}_i \\ \text{*himself}_i \end{Bmatrix}$ was innocent.

   b   Bob$_i$ proved $\begin{Bmatrix} \text{himself}_i \\ \text{*him}_i \end{Bmatrix}$ to be innocent.

That is, given what has previously been ascertained about Reflexivization, the pivot NP in the infinitival cases behaves like a clause mate of the subject of the main verb, while the pivot NP in the finite complement cases does not. This is predicted by an analysis of sentences like (33b) in terms of o-Raising, since the latter rule lifts the pivot NP up into the main clause. Thus, after o-Raising has applied, the pivot and the subject of *proved* are clause mates. But in (33a), the pivot and the subject of *proved* do not start out as clause mates, and, since o-Raising never applies, they never become clause mates. Hence nonapplication of Reflexivization is also correctly predicted. Thus the analysis of infinitival complements like those in (33b) in terms of o-Raising, which has been proposed in this chapter, dovetails properly with our treatment of Reflexivization. We shall have more to say about the interaction of o-Raising and Reflexivization in Chapter 29.

It was noted in Chapters 20 and 21 that application of s-Raising is typically correlated with infinitival form for the complement from which a subject NP is extracted. We can now see that this is also true for complements from which an NP is extracted by o-Raising. Hence there appears to be a generalization linking these two processes:[5]

(34) Raising the subject of a complement into the immediately higher main clause determines infinitival form for that complement.

This regularity argues further for treating in parallel fashion the various kinds of infinitival constructions.

SUMMARY

This chapter argued for a new raising rule, o-Raising. It operates on the subjects of the complements of a restricted class of verbs, *prove, believe,* etc. It generates new, derived objects for these verbs. The chief evidence for this operation was based on independently needed generalizations about Passive and Complex NP Shift. The former *only* operates on sisters of the main verb being passivized; the latter *cannot* operate on subjects. These restrictions correctly predict the contrastive behavior of the pivot NPs in the relevant constructions. But this requires the assumption that the pivots in the case of infinitival complements have undergone o-Raising and become nonsubjects and sisters of the main clause verb.

The o-Raising analysis interacted perfectly with the clause mate account of Reflexivization worked out in earlier parts of this work. Finally, o-Raising, like s-Raising, "de-finitizes" complements whose subjects it extracts, turning these normally into infinitives, but occasionally into gerundive structures.

NOTES

1. Two constituents A and B are said to be *sisters* if they are both directly dominated by some third constituent. Put differently, they are sisters if they are both immediate constituents of a third constituent. Thus in

(i)

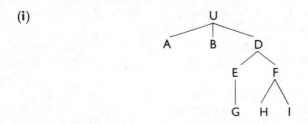

The following pairs, and only these, are sisters:

(ii)

a	A B
b	B D

```
c     A D
d     E F
e     H I
```

Sister of is a stronger relation than *clause mate of* since, if A and B are sisters, they are clause mates. But two constituents can be clause mates without being sisters. For example, in a tree like

(iii)

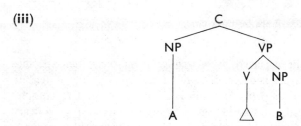

A and B are clause mates but not sisters. Thus if, as in the text, we impose a condition that two elements be sisters, we are saying they must be clause mates (and more).

2. Ultimately, the formulation of Passive will have to allow for certain minor elements to intervene between V and NP, in particular, some prepositions, as in:

(i) a That was decided *on* by the officers.
     b Jones will be dealt *with* by the court.

3. That is, constituents like *your lying to them* are gerundive complement clauses. Notice that such sequences behave like NP constituents with respect to passivization in the main clause:

  (i) a Jack believes you to be healthy.
       b Jack resents your being healthy.

 (ii) a *(For) you to be healthy is believed by Jack.
       b Your being healthy is resented by Jack.

Concomitantly, the pivot NP is passivizable in (ia) but not in (ib):

(iii) a You are believed to be healthy by Jack.
       b *You are resented being healthy by Jack.

4. It is the same principle that blocks passives like those which might otherwise be expected in cases like:

  (i) a The guards insisted he be manacled.
       b *He was insisted be manacled by the guards.

 (ii) a Jack learned what to eat.
       b *What was learned to eat by Jack.

5. Actually, (34) is not correct. There are certain cases in which both s-Raising and o-Raising yield gerundive complements rather than infinitival ones:

(i) s-Raising

a (if) there $\begin{Bmatrix} \text{starts} \\ \text{continues} \end{Bmatrix}$ being a shortage of rice flour, . . .

b Tabs ended up being kept on her movements.

(ii) o-Raising

a Jack stopped there from being a riot.

b Jack prevented tabs from being kept on her movements.

Ultimately, (34) should be replaced by a weaker principle which specifies only that the complement verb is determined to be *nonfinite*, that is, untensed, (uninflected). The distinction between infinitival versus gerundive complements is due either to regularities so far undiscovered or to simply arbitrary distinctions associated with particular main verbs. Some verbs, like *continue*, permit both types.

PROBLEMS

1. How does a sentence like

(i) Now is believed to be a poor time to invest in gold.

support the existence of o-Raising?

2. Give as complete a characterization as you can of the grammatical structure of:

(i) Joe was believed to be proud of himself by most of the guests who saw him perform in the colliseum.

3. Why is

(i) *I believe (that) are dishonest — most of the people charged with governing this great nation.

ill-formed?

CHAPTER 23 **MORE ON PASSIVIZATION**

PREVIEW

In Chapter 18, the rule Passive was introduced. We argued briefly for the conclusion that in active-passive pairs like

(i) a Melvin robbed the bank.
    b The bank was robbed by Melvin.

the active form is more basic. That is, we argued for the view that English really has a process of passivization rather than, as is logically possible, a process of activization. The latter would treat structures like (ib) as more fundamental. In the present chapter, we pursue this argument, providing crucial evidence for its correctness.

    This evidence is of two sorts. It involves first the way Passive interacts with o-Raising and second the way Passive interacts with the process of Indirect Object Shift, which makes indirect objects into direct objects.

L et us examine the following sentences:

(1) a The director proved that Sylvia was a Martian.
  b The director proved Sylvia to be a Martian.
  c That Sylvia was a Martian was proved by the director.
  d It was proved by the director that Sylvia was a Martian.
  e Sylvia was proved by the director to be a Martian.
  f Sylvia was proved to be a Martian by the director.

Example (1a) is a relatively straightforward sentence with a sentential object. Examples (1c,d) can then be regarded as passives of (1a), differing only in whether the optional rule Extraposition has applied (subsequent to Passive) or not. The significant examples are (1b,e,f). We are not really concerned with the difference between (1e,f) here, since we regard this difference of word order as irrelevant to the issues we are presently[1] dealing with. We can then regard (1e,f) as essentially the same sentence. From this point of view, (1b) and (1e,f) form an active-passive pair not fundamentally different than an elementary set like:

(2) a Bill dropped the glass.
  b The glass was dropped by Bill.

Thus the NP that is the object of the verb in the active sentence (2a), *the glass*, is the subject of the passive sentence (2b). Just so, the NP which is the subject of the active sentence shows up in the passive preceded by the preposition *by*. In (1), the facts are the same. *Sylvia* is the object of *prove* in (1b), but the derived subject in the passive sentences (1e,f). Similarly, the original subject of *prove*, *the director*, shows up in (1e,f) preceded by the preposition *by* and in postverbal position. It is evident that the processes which connect (1b) to (1e,f) are the same as those which connect (2a) and (2b).

We are interested in showing that in *all* cases active structures are closer to initial structures than passive ones. To do this it suffices to show that *some* kinds of active-passive pairs are such that the active form must be basic. Having shown this for certain cases, the simplest and most general grammar must assume it to be so, barring clear counterevidence, for all cases. The alternative would require two different treatments of passivization.

Examples (1b) and (1e,f) form just such a pair. We have already shown in Chapter 22 that a sentence like (1b) is derived by o-Raising from an underlying structure like (1a). Thus *Sylvia* in (1b) becomes the derived object of *proved* only because of the operation of o-Raising. Originally, such objects were the subjects of the complement clauses, as shown in Chapter 22 by the occurrence of the various highly restricted NPs in that position, NPs like

there, tabs, etc. An o-Raising analysis of sentences like (1b) is compatible
with a rule Passive which derives structures like (1e,f) from those like (1b).
In these terms, the derivation of (1e,f) would proceed as follows. The
maximally remote structure of relevance would be that underlying (1a):

(3)

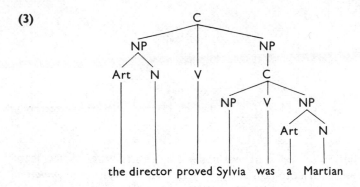

To this structure, o-Raising would apply, making the original complement
subject, *Sylvia,* the derived object of *prove.* The result, including a marking of
the complement as an infinitive, would be:

(4)

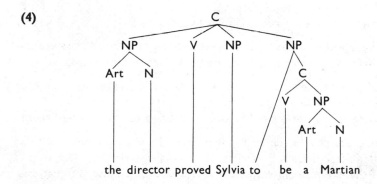

At this point, Passive would be applicable in the main clause. It would make
the object of *prove,* now simply *Sylvia,* into its new subject, triggering the
marking of the old subject with the element *by.* Independent operations
involving *be*[2] and the participial character of *prove* as well as the word order
of postverbal elements would then complete the derivation.

Consider though the alternative description required for such sentences if,
instead of Passive, English had a rule *Active* deriving sentences like (2a)
from remote structures like those underlying (2b). In that case, the remote
structure of both (1b) and (1e,f) would have to be like that of (1e,f) rather
than like (1b). That is, underlying both would be a structure:[3]

(5)

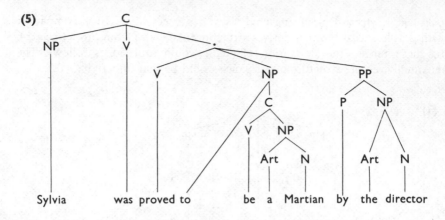

This is to say that, in the relevant maximally remote structures, *Sylvia* is the subject of the clause for both (1b) and (1e,f). But this analysis *is incompatible with* the o-Raising treatment of sentences like (1b). In a grammar containing Active instead of Passive, sentences like (1b) cannot be related by o-Raising to those like (1a). They must instead derive from remote structures like those underlying (1e,f) (that is, (5)), in which *Sylvia* is the subject of the main clause. Given the strong evidence for o-Raising analyses of forms like (1b), a treatment involving Active has to be rejected.

This is particularly clear from examples like:

(6) a   There were proved by the director to be no germs in the soup.

       b   *There were proved by the director to love meatballs.

(7) a   Close tabs were shown by the director to have been kept on the witnesses.

       b   *Close tabs were proved by the director to have interested them.

That is, the relevant passive sentences can contain as subjects highly restricted NPs. These manifest tight and peculiar selectional restrictions with respect to the rest of the complement clauses. Such restrictions follow automatically under an o-Raising and Passive analysis, because the main clause subjects then start out as complement subjects. But in a grammar with Active instead of Passive, the subjects of sentences like (6) are generated directly as main clause subjects. Moreover, in such a grammar, passive main verbs like *proved* occur with complements which are not full clauses (that is, they have no subjects), and these must be specially described. They will not be related in any definite way to the complements in sentences like (1a,c,d).

For these reasons, the relation between active-passive pairs like (1b) and (1e,f) is properly described by taking active forms as more basic and assuming a Passive rule. For only this is compatible with the proper description of sentences like (1e,f) and (1b), which involve o-Raising. The interaction between Passive and o-Raising does then provide a clear argument picking a grammar of English based on Passive over a logically possible alternative of one with a rule Active.

The same choice of a grammar with a rule Passive is dictated by constructions involving indirect objects, discussed briefly in Chapter 13:

(8) a Irma gave the bomb to the police.
   b Irma gave the police the bomb.
   c The bomb was given to the police by Irma.
   d The police were given the bomb by Irma.

In a grammar with Passive, such related forms can be described along the following lines. Examples (8a,b) have the same remote structure and examples like (8b) are derived by the rule called *Indirect Object Shift* in Chapter 13. This will move the indirect object into direct object position. Passive will then operate on structures like (8b) to yield those like (8d) (as well as on those like (8a) to yield those like (8c)). In each case, the NP which Passive moves into subject position must be in direct object position at the point when Passive applies. There will be derivations like:

(9) a Irma gave the bomb the police[4] $\xrightarrow{\text{Passive and } \textit{To} \text{ Insertion}}$ (8c)

   b Irma gave the bomb the police $\xrightarrow{\text{Indirect Object Shift}}$ (8b) (= (9c))

   c Irma gave the police the bomb $\xrightarrow{\text{Passive}}$ (8d)

Hence Indirect Object Shift accounts for the existence of two distinct passive sentences like (8c,d) as well as two different active structures like (8a,b). Together, Passive and Indirect Object Shift permit sets like (8) to have a single initial structure, correctly representing the semantic and selectional unity of such sets.

Moreover, the Passive and Indirect Object Shift analysis of such sets is compatible with a single lexical analysis for the verb *give*. It is specified as taking a subject NP, a direct object NP, and an indirect object NP. In terms of Chapter 16, *give* is uniformly a *ditransitive* verb. This permits one to say that both the subject and indirect object NPs have selectional restrictions. They must both designate persons or personlike[5] objects. Other verbs which form paradigms like (8) include *offer*, *loan/lend*, *hand*, *send*, *issue*, and *assign*:

(10) a The captain assigned that room to Jack.
   b The captain assigned Jack that room.
   c That room was assigned to Jack by the captain.
   d Jack was assigned that room by the captain.

Consider, however, a grammar which tries to take active structures as derivative rather than basic and which hence has Active instead of Passive. In such a system, examples like (8c,d) and (10c,d) must be taken as basic. Those like (8a,b) and (10a,b) must be derived from them by Active.

In contrast to active structures like (10a,b), the possible base structures with the passive verb *assigned* taken as basic are not readily describable. It must be said that *assigned* (*given*, etc.) takes a subject and indirect object and a *by* phrase *or* that it takes a subject, a direct object, and a *by* phrase. The former description characterizes (10c), the latter (10d).[6] Moreover, in the latter case, the subject must be personlike, but not so in the former:

(11) a   The $\begin{Bmatrix} \text{gold} \\ \text{slave} \end{Bmatrix}$ was given to the emperor by the people.

b   The $\begin{Bmatrix} *\text{gold} \\ \text{slave} \end{Bmatrix}$ was given the knife by the emperor.

(12) a   The $\begin{Bmatrix} \text{gold} \\ \text{slave} \end{Bmatrix}$ was assigned to the captain by the general.

b   *The $\begin{Bmatrix} *\text{banana} \\ \text{slave} \end{Bmatrix}$ was assigned the room by the general.

Thus, if passive structures are taken as basic, one cannot characterize generally the kinds of postverbal elements which occur in the relevant clauses. These must be described with lists. Nor can one characterize uniformly the kinds of subjects which such verbals take. One must relate the different subject types to the choice of postverbal elements. No such complications arise if actives are taken as basic. In a grammar with Passive, the two different types of subjects found in passives, with their different restrictions, are automatically accounted for. One type will derive from underlying direct objects, the other from underlying indirect objects which have been transformed into direct objects by Indirect Object Shift. Indirect object constructions, then, corroborate the conclusion based on the interaction of passive facts with raising phenomena: Passive, not Active, is a rule of English grammar.

The two arguments of this chapter are consistent with the conclusions to the same effect already reached in Chapter 18. There we justified a choice of Passive on the basis of two different sorts of preliminary considerations. First, intransitive structures like:

(13) Harry smiled.

have the active morphology. It would be hard to account for this if the active morphology in transitive sentences was a function of Active rather than the standard form assigned to any verb in a finite clause. That is, in a grammar containing Active, active verbal morphology would have to have two distinct origins.

Second, it was noted that the existence of passives based on chunks of idioms like

(14) Tabs were kept on their movements by the government agents.

would be difficult to describe if passives were regarded as basic. Altogether then, there are at least four independent reasons for taking passives to be a derived clause type. The choice of a grammar of English containing Passive is therefore supported.

SUMMARY

We provided two different arguments for the view that active clauses are more basic than passive clauses, that is, for the claim that English contains Passive rather than Active.

One was based on the interaction of Passive with o-Raising. This argument depends crucially on the fact that a grammar incorporating Active is incompatible with an o-Raising analysis of passive clauses like:

(i) There was proved by the director to be no basis for that rumor.

In an Active grammar, *there* must be generated directly as the main clause subject. However, independent considerations show that it originates as the complement subject and only enters the main clause through the operation of o-Raising.

A second argument was based on sets of related constructions involving indirect objects with verbs like *give*. It involved the fact that an Active grammar requires different base configurations with several special restrictions, all unnecessary if active structures are basic.

These two arguments are consistent with the two given in Chapter 18 (on active morphology in intransitive clauses and the passivization of chunks of idioms). The combination of these four arguments leaves little doubt that passive clauses are derivative.

NOTES

1. One general principle here seems to be that an infinitive and a *by* phrase in such cases are ordered so that the "heavier" or more complex phrase is final. But other factors enter as well. For instance, if the infinitive itself ends in a *by* phrase, then the main clause *by* phrase will have to be preinfinitival:

(i)   Joan was proved by the police to have been beaten by the killer.
(ii) *Joan was proved to have been beaten by the killer by the police.

2. These were discussed informally in Chapter 18. The key point is that a passive clause ends up with an extra verb, namely, *be*, with the original verb in past participle form. See note 3 below.

3. In (5) for the first time we take the verb *be* of passive clauses (appearing in (5) as *was*) to be a main verb taking a complement much like other intransitive verbs such as *seem* or *happen*. This relationship is further sharpened in Chapter 26.

4. Recall from Chapter 13 that indirect objects are introduced without prepositions in base structures. These prepositions are later added by a separate rule in case Indirect Object Shift does *not* apply.

5. In certain cases, nonpersons, in particular, institutions, are treated as persons for the purpose of such restrictions.

(i)   He gave the money to $\left\{\begin{array}{l}\text{the library} \\ \text{the United Fund} \\ \text{United Cerebral Palsy}\end{array}\right\}$.

6. Actually, the situation is even worse than so far indicated. In Chapter 13 we defined an indirect object as the NP following a direct object after a verb. But in (10c) this definition will fail, and there is no formal basis for distinguishing *Jack* in (10c) from *that room* in (10d), although semantically and selectionally they are very different. Only the former has a preposition. Thus the kind of base structures required if we were to take passive clauses as basic would necessitate a different account of what an indirect object is.

PROBLEMS

1. Consider the following example:

(i)   Now is believed by most authorities to be a poor time to invest in gold.

How does this sentence help support Passive over a potential rule Active?

2. Take the sentence:

(i)   Mary was believed by most authorities to have been assigned the room by the colonel.

How does *Mary* get to be the subject of the main clause? In answering, specify the position of *Mary* in initial structure.

PART IV SOME ASPECTS OF THE VERBAL SYSTEM

CHAPTER 24   **FLOATING QUANTIFIERS**

PREVIEW

In this chapter, we consider words like *all*, *both*, and *each*, members of the larger set of *universal quantifiers*. In particular, we deal with the relations between quantifiers in cases like

  (i)   All of *the men* (now) agree.

where the quantifiers are part of the NP, and those like

(ii)   *The men* (now) all agree.

in which they are not. In the latter contexts they are called *floating* quantifiers. We introduce a term, *binding*, to describe the semantic relation which holds between the quantifier and the italicized NP in cases like (i) and (ii).

    The thrust of this chapter is that floating quantifiers are derived syntactically from remote structures common to examples like (i), that is, from quantifiers internal to NPs. This requires postulation of a rule to detach quantifiers from their initial positions and to move them to their ultimate loci. A rule to accomplish this is proposed and designated *Quantifier Floating*. We consider how this rule relates to the difference between subject NPs and nonsubject NPs, and, in particular, how it interacts with rules which create new subjects, like s-Raising and o-Raising.

Certain sorts of English NPs can contain one or another of the elements *all, both, each.* Let us refer to these words as (*Universal*) *Quantifiers* (Q):[1]

(1)   a   All of his wounds were bleeding.
       b   I called both of the columnists....
       c   He sent tickets to each of the nurses.

Here the phrases *all of his wounds, both of the columnists,* and *each of the nurses* are NPs, functioning respectively as subject, direct object, and indirect object.

Qs can also occur in English sentences in positions where they cannot be regarded as parts of the NP:

(2)   a   His wounds were *all* bleeding.
       b   They seem to have *both* resigned.
       c   We must appear to have *each* told a different story.

None of those structures normally regarded as NPs can occur in positions like those in (2):

(3)   a   *His wounds were three doctors bleeding.
       b   *They seem to have their friends resigned.
       c   *We must appear to have most couples told a different story.

Let us refer to those Qs which occur in nonNP positions like (2) as *floating Q.*

A striking fact about floating Qs is that semantically they are understood as related to particular NPs. For instance, in

(4)   Those doctors seemed to us to all know Turkish.

all is understood to be related to *those doctors* and not, for instance, to *us.* Example (4) involves a statement about all of the doctors, not about all of us. We shall say that in (4) the word *all binds* the NP *those doctors.* In the case of nonfloating Qs like those in (1), the Q always binds the NP which follows it. So *all* binds *his wounds* in (1a). But, because this relationship is directly indicated by the superficial grammatical organization, it is trivial to specify in the case of nonfloating Qs which NP a quantifier binds.

It is, however, not trivial to specify the "binding" relations for floating Q. Some of the problems involved are highlighted by such examples as:

(5)   a   The bats all seemed to us to have been rabid.
       b   The bats seemed to us to all have been rabid.
       c   The bats seemed to us to have all been rabid.
       d   The bats seemed to us to have been really[2] all rabid.

Despite the variation in positions, the occurrences of *all* in (5) bind the NP *the bats*, just as in:

(6) All of the bats seemed to us to have been rabid.

An adequate grammar of English will have to generate examples like (5). It will also have to characterize them so that the proper binding relations are established. There are at least two different approaches to this problem. First, one could formulate special rules, operating on superficial structures like those in (5), rules whose function is simply to establish binding relations. This would involve generating floating Q in initial structures in their surface positions, or at least in positions external to the NPs they bind. Or, second, one could posit rules which derive floating Qs from nonfloating structures like those in (6). In this case, no special rules establishing binding relations for floating Qs would be needed. Under this second approach, the binding in cases like (5) would be established by the same principles operative for (6). These would apply before structures like (6) are converted into any of those like (5). In these terms, rules *to separate Qs from the NPs they bind* are needed. These will determine the various positions in which such separated Qs can occur. We adopt the second approach, consider evidence in its favor, and explore the generalizations involved.

First, we must characterize the structure of phrases like $\left\{ \begin{matrix} all \\ both \\ each \end{matrix} \right\}$ *of the bats*, since it is upon such structures that the separation rules for Qs operate. Here, unfortunately, we run into serious problems. At the present time no adequate account of this structure is available.

Initially, such phrases appear to have a simple analysis, which can be given as follows, once a constituent type Q is recognized:

(7)

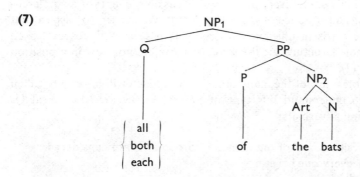

This is a reasonable first approximation to an account of the *surface* representation of such constituents. But it does not do justice to more subtle properties of the phrases in question.

The most obvious problems arise from the fact that those elements preceding the preposition, which are in (7) simply characterized as Q, have certain properties which lead to the view that they are NPs. For instance, *each* can occur with a following pronoun:

(8) a Each of the planes is equipped with radar.
     b Each one of the planes is equipped with radar.

Morover, at least in the presence of the pronoun *one*, the preprepositional sequence can serve as the head for a relative clause, a head distinct from the NP following *of*. This is shown by contrasts in verb agreement:

(9) a *Each one of the men who were selected* had to be interviewed.
     b *Each one of the men who was selected* had to be interviewed.

The italicized sequences have different structures. In (9a) *the men who were selected* is a complex NP containing a head NP and a restrictive relative clause. But in (9b) *the men who was selected* is not even a constituent, and it is *each one of the men* which functions as the singular antecedent of the relative clause[3].

Congruent with these observations is the fact that the pre-*of* sequence in such phrases can serve as the antecedent for coreferential pronouns, an antecedent distinct from the post-*of* NP:

(10) a Each one$_i$ of the nurses who thought she$_i$ had a right to be promoted said so.
      b Each one of the nurses$_j$ who thought they$_j$ had a right to be promoted said so.

However, up to this point, every phrase serving as antecedent for a coreferential pronoun was an instance of the category NP. We are led to suspect that a structure like (7) is insufficiently articulated, at least with respect to an account of remote structure. At the same time, we are not now in a position to improve on (7).

We simply note a few of the many other factors which will have to be taken into account to understand this type of phrase. First, some Universal Qs permit modifying adverbials:

(11) Almost $\left\{ \begin{array}{l} \text{all} \\ \text{every one} \\ \text{*both} \\ \text{*each} \end{array} \right\}$ of the monetary proposals were considered.

Ultimately, the constituent characterizing words like *every*, *each*, etc., will have to permit the presence of certain modifiers, subject to special restrictions.

Second, the pattern illustrated in (7) is a special case of a more general structure in English in which other, nonuniversal quantifiers and quantifierlike elements occur instead of Universal Qs. A quite incomplete list would include:

(12)
$$\left\{\begin{array}{l}\text{Some}\\\text{Few}\\\text{Not all}\\\text{Many}\\\text{Lots}\\\text{None}\\\text{Not one}\\\text{Two}\\\text{Three}\\\text{Seven hundred}\\\text{Which (one)}\\\text{How many}\end{array}\right\} \text{ of the bats} \left\{\begin{array}{l}\text{were}\\\text{was}\end{array}\right\} \text{sighted.}$$

With these, too, there is sometimes the possibility of a preceding modifier (*almost none, nearly seven hundred, *almost many*). It follows that the proper treatment of complex NPs containing Universal Qs cannot be separated from the treatment of a wider body of forms. Unfortunately, the analysis of this range of phenomena remains very limited.

We assume for purposes of discussion that rules that separate Universal Qs from their containing NPs operate on structures like (7). As we have seen, this is a simplifying assumption, which ultimately cannot stand. This discussion is another illustration of how areas of understanding of grammatical structure shade off at this point into areas of nonunderstanding. Summing up, however, the points about (7) which do not appear to be controversial are that the whole structure in an NP and that the post-*of* sequence is an NP.

Consider now:

(13) a All of the bats died.
      b The bats all died.

According to what we have said, (13a) contains a subject NP of the general form of (7). Example (13b) then contains a subject NP of the form of NP_2 in (7). We have decided to derive sentences like (13b) from structures like (13a). The facts in (13) suggest that NP_2 takes on the position and function of NP_1 (of which it was originally a part). As a consequence, both the preposition (and the node which dominated it) and NP_1 must be eliminated. The position which the Q takes on remains to be described.

In (13), the Q moves to a position immediately in front of the verb. Taking this situation to be typical, one could formulate the relevant rule along the following lines:

(14) Quantifier Floating

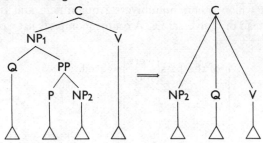

In this formulation, the Q^4 becomes a clausal constituent.[5]

Given a formulation like (14), a number of consequences follow. First, since floating Qs originate under NP nodes, it should be impossible for those NPs in which Qs originate to also possess other Qs in the presence of a floating Q. This is correct:

(15) a   *Each of the girls all left.
      b   *All of the girls each left.
      c   *Both of the girls all left.
      d   *Both of the girls both left.

Facts like (15) form an important argument for deriving floating Qs by detaching them from complex NPs with incorporated Qs. Second, rule (14) requires that floating Qs only cooccur with NPs of the sort that can contain incorporated Qs. This is also true:

(16) a   *Each of the rice tasted bitter.
      b   *The rice each tasted bitter.

(17) a   *All of some people left.
      b   *Some people all left.

(18) a   *Both of few girls drink beer.
      b   *Few girls both drink beer.

However, the most interesting consequence of rule (14) has still not been made explicit. Rule (14) is formulated in such a way that a detachable Q must be part of an NP *in subject position*. This is in effect a claim that floating Qs in English can only come from, and hence only bind, subject NPs. And this is true.[6]

Every example given so far meets this condition. Moreover, all other examples in which Qs float away from nonsubjects are ill-formed.[7]

(19) a   *I both kissed the girls.
      b   *He each gave apples to the girls.
      c   *She all struck the door with the clubs.
      d   *I both talked about them.
      e   *Shirley all has worked for them.

So far rule (14) seems a plausible candidate for an account of the process of Q floating. However, nothing said yet seems to offer any way of accounting for examples like those in (5), where the floating Q has a variety of possible loci. For rule (14) assigns only a single locus to the Q that floats.

There is a solution to this problem requiring no alteration or extension of rule (14). There is a way to derive all of the existing sentences using analyses of the relevant csases already in significant part implicit in earlier discussions:

(20)   a   We all seem to like snails.
        b   We seem to all like snails.

The floating Q can obviously occur as a (left) sister of[8] the main verb *seem* or as a sister of the complement verb *like*. We already understand a good deal about sentences with *seem* from discussions of s-Raising. In particular, we know that *seem* sentences with infinitival complements are the result of the application of s-Raising. Consequently, we know that the superficial subject of *seem* in (20) was originally the complement subject. An example like

(21)   Jack seems to know Finnish.

has the remote structure

(22)

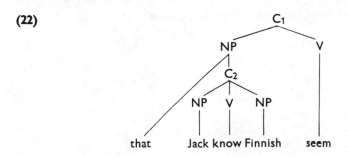

It follows that in examples like (20) the main clause subject, *we*, was originally (part of) the complement subject. That is, underlying both (20a,b) would be

(23)

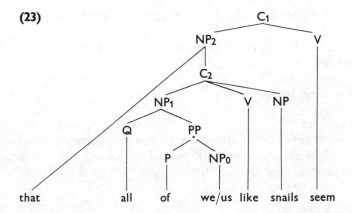

In this structure, NP_1, which starts out as subject of *like*, will by s-Raising end up as the subject of *seem*, unless Quantifier Floating applies to destroy it.

If Quantifier Floating operates on C_2 in (23), which its structural condition says it can, the result will be the following derived C_2:

(24)

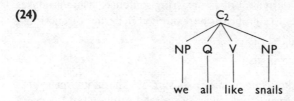

In (24), the NP *we* is the subject of the complement clause. Therefore, if s-Raising applies at that point, it will raise *we*, leaving the *all* behind. The result is (20b).

However, Quantifier Floating is an *optional* rule. It does not have to apply when its conditions are met. Therefore, instead of applying Quantifier Floating to (23), it is possible to apply s-Raising directly. In (23), NP_1 is the subject of the complement, and it will be raised and made the derived subject of *seem* by the direct application of s-Raising:

(25)

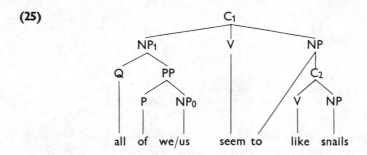

At this stage, Quantifier Floating is again applicable. If applied, the result will be (20a).

On the other hand, if the option of Quantifier Floating is taken at *neither* stage, the result will be:

(26)   All of us seem to like snails.

This is also a fine sentence.

We see how an unchanged rule of Quantifier Floating can generate alternative loci for Qs by its interaction with s-Raising. For Quantifier Floating expresses the generalization that Qs float from subject NPs to the verbs of which these NP are subjects. But in a grammar with s-Raising, some NPs are at different points in derivations subjects of different verbs. It is therefore expected that through application of Quantifier Floating at different stages of derivation, floating Qs can be assigned different positions.

Accordingly, it ought to be possible for floating Qs to occur in more than one position in a sentence just in case each of those positions corresponds to a subject-verb pairing at some stage in the derivation. This says in effect that the distribution of floating Qs *can be a partial test for the occurrence of s-Raising*. For instance, the verb *happen* must trigger s-Raising because of such distributions as:

(27) a All of us happen to own boats.
     b We all happen to own boats.
     c We happen to all own boats.

Example (27c) shows that the underlying NP, *all of us*, was once subject of *own*. It was the subject at a stage before Quantifier Floating turned *us* into the subject of *own*. The rule s-Raising then made this pronoun the subject of the main verb, *happen*.

Consequently, in cases where elements triggering s-Raising are embedded one below the other, more distinct positions for floating Qs should be possible. This is so:

(28) a All of them tend to seem to be honest.
     b They all tend to seem to be honest.
     c They tend to all seem to be honest.
     d They tend to seem to all be honest.

This distribution follows from our analysis, given that both *tend* and *seem* are s-Raising triggers.

The combination of o-Raising and Passive can also generate multiple loci for floating Qs:

(29) a Jack proved all of those girls to be Martians.
     b Jack proved those girls to all be Martians.
     c All of those girls were proved to be Martians by Jack.
     d Those girls were proved to all be Martians by Jack.
     e Those girls all were proved to be Martians by Jack.

These examples all involve the application of o-Raising. The final three manifest the operation of Passive as well. Thus, all would have a common initial structure like:

(30)

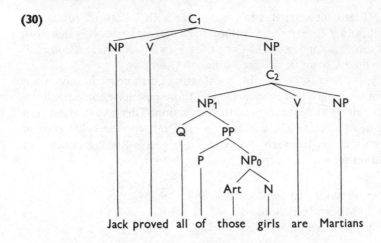

Jack proved all of those girls are Martians

In these terms, (29a) involves application of o-Raising alone. NP_1 is the complement subject which is raised into main clause object position. Example (29b) involves application of Quantifier Floating within the subordinate clause previous to the application of o-Raising. Hence it is NP_0 which becomes the new subject of *are* and which is raised into object position, leaving the floated Q behind next to the subordinate verb. Example (29c) involves application to the structure underlying (29a) of o-Raising and Passive, in that order, with no application of Quantifier Floating. Example (29d) involves application to the structure underlying (29b) of Quantifier Floating, o-Raising, and Passive, in that order. Finally,[9] example (29e) is formed from (30) by application of o-Raising followed by Passive, which yields (29c). This is followed by application of Quantifier Floating in the main clause.

Thus any process, or combination of processes, which derive new subjects can derive new environments in which Quantifier Floating can apply.

SUMMARY

In this chapter, we argued for a derivation of floating Qs from Qs embedded in subject NPs. We postulated a new rule, Quantifier Floating, which optionally moves any of the Qs *all*, *both*, *each* out of certain kinds of subject NPs into the rest of the clause.

We considered the interaction of Quantifier Floating with certain rules and rule combinations which create new subjects. Together, they account for alternative positions of floating Qs in what otherwise appear to be identical sentence structures. In particular, we treated the Interaction of Quantifier Floating with s-Raising and with the combination of o-Raising and Passive.

The phenomenon of floating Qs is dependent upon the existence of a prior subject-verb relation. Therefore, the distribution of detached Qs can serve as a test showing that certain NPs were the subjects of certain Vs at earlier levels of structure, even if they do not maintain this status at the level of surface structure. This property will be utilized in the following chapter to draw and support some possibly surprising conclusions about the English verbal system.

NOTES

1. There are other Universal Qs, in particular, *every* and *any*:

(i) Every one of the columnists was criticized.
(ii) Any(one) of the columnists can be criticized.

These differ from the three mentioned in the text in never appearing as what will be called floating Qs.

2. The word *really* is inserted here because, without it, the sentence is ill-formed for many speakers. This involves a restriction on floating Qs and adjacent untensed forms of *be*. This restriction is briefly described in Chapter 25.

3. In Chapter 14 it was claimed that complex NPs containing restrictive relative clauses have the structure:

(i)

In these terms, the structure of the overall NP in (9b) would have to be:

(ii)

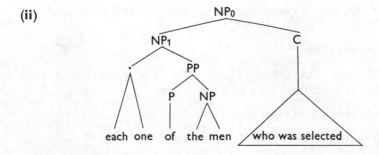

In (ii), NP₁, the head of the relative clause structure, is singular. If the unlabeled node is also a (singular) NP, the singularity of NP_1 can be made a function of a general principle determining the number of containing NPs in terms of the NPs they immediately dominate. Hence in

(iii)

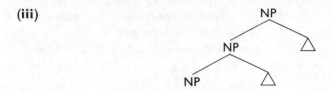

the number of the highest NP will be successively determined by the number of the immediately lower NP. Or, in more picturesque terms, number will flow up the tree. This is an argument for the NP-hood of unlabeled constituents like those in (ii), because the principle in question is needed independently for simpler relative clause phrases:

(iv)   a   *The man who won* is here.
      b   *The men who won* are here.

The italicized NPs must be, respectively, singular and plural, in order to determine singular and plural verb forms (*is* versus *are*). But the overall NPs receive their number from their heads (*the man*, *the men*) which are, respectively, singular and plural.

4. Rule (14) allows only for the possibility of moving an isolated Q. But in some cases, it appears possible for a modifier to accompany the Q, so that a more adequate treatment would have to allow this as well:

(i)   We now almost all agree on that.

Here the *almost* originates in a structure like

(ii)   Almost all of us now agree on that.

and not in one like:

(iii)   All of us now almost agree on that.

5. That the Q becomes a constituent of the clause is at least debatable in simple cases like:

(i)   The pilots all rebelled.

Here one might argue that Q is the last constituent of the subject. But this proposal collapses when there is an adverb present:

(ii)   The pilots certainly all rebelled.

In (ii) there is no real choice about the constituency of the Q.

Examples with adverbs raise a further difficulty with the formulation of Quantifier Floating. Rule (14) says nothing about adverbs and would only work on contiguous subject NPs and verbs. On different grounds then, (14) is only a first approximation.

6. Languages such as French, German, and Japanese have freer rules analogous to Quantifier Floating, permitting detachment not only from subjects but also from direct objects and, in certain cases, indirect objects as well.

7. Apparent counterexamples to this claim include:

(i) Jack gave *them* five dollars each.
(ii) To *those voters*, I sent three circulars each.

Here, the occurrences of *each* bind the italicized NPs, which are certainly not subjects. However, rather than being an exception to the subject regularity about Quantifier Floating, these cases illustrate *a distinct rule*. This is similar to Quantifier Floating in that it extracts Qs from NPs, but it contrasts with Quantifier Floating in many ways. One contrast is that the rule illustrated in (i) and (ii) only works with *each*. Ill-formedness results from substituting *all* or *both* for *each* in these cases. Second, instead of making Qs clause constituents, this rule seems to move them to the end of indefinite, numerically quantified NPs, like *five dollars*.

8. For an account of the notion of sister, see note 1 of Chapter 22.

9. There seems to be a further example derivable from (30):

(i) Those girls were all proved to be Martians by Jack.

The origin of this type of example is closely tied to questions of the origin and status of the verb *be* which shows up in passive clauses and, more generally, with the status of auxiliary verbs. This topic is treated in the following two chapters.

PROBLEMS

1. CCS Deletion (see Chapter 10) is the rule responsible for converting structures like

(i) The robbers$_i$ backed out of the bank, and then they$_i$ ran away.

into:

(ii) The robbers backed out of the bank and then ran away.

How do sentences like the following support the postulation of CCS Deletion:

(iii) The robbers ran out of the bank and then all ran away.

2. Explain how the quantifier and the NP it binds achieve their positions in:

(i) The candidates tend to turn out to all be incompetent.

3. What is the basis for the contrast between:

   (i)   I believe all of the men.
  (ii)   *I believe the men all.
 (iii)   I believe all of the men to be incompetent.
  (iv)   I believe the men to all be incompetent.

CHAPTER 25 FLOATING QUANTIFIERS AND THE VERBAL SYSTEM

PREVIEW

In the preceding chapter, we found a basic regularity underlying the distribution of floating Qs. A particular Q could be extracted from an NP and made a constituent of a clause just in case the NP in question was at some stage a subject of the main verb of that clause.

This assumption leads to unsuspected and perhaps surprising analyses of constructions involving adjectives, progressive, perfective and passive participles, and auxiliary verbs. All of these are analyzed in this chapter as members of the category V. Further, we conclude that the auxiliary verbs *be*, *have*, *do* and the various modals *can*, *must*, *will*, etc., are fundamentally like *seem*, *appear*, *turn out*, etc., previously seen to trigger s-Raising. As a consequence, we take the structure of (i) and (ii) to be parallel to that of (iii):

(i) Jack [is] *tired of Sally*.
(ii) Jack [has] *tired Sally*.
(iii) Jack [seems] *to tire Sally*.

In each case, the italicized phrase is viewed as the remnant of the underlying clausal subject of the bracketed main verb. This remnant was separated from its original subject, which became the main clause subject, by the operation of s-Raising. We thus treat (i)–(iii) as involving embedded (complement subject) clauses in initial structure.

t was argued in Chapter 24 that the distribution of floating Qs offers a basis for determining crucial aspects of certain derivations. If a particular Q is found in a position next to a verbal element, it has to have come from a subject of that element. This generalization led to new evidence for analyzing some constructions in terms of s-Raising.

The same assumption about floating Qs shows that some *apparently* similar constructions must be analyzed in contrasting ways.

(1) a   The witnesses are likely to eat.
  b   The witnesses are difficult to eat.

These seem to differ only in the choice of adjective. However, a consideration of floating Qs yields contrasts:

(2) a   The witnesses are likely to all eat.
  b   *The witnesses are difficult to all eat.

In view of previous knowledge about floating Qs, (2) suggests that *the witnesses* is a (part of a) onetime subject of *eat* in (2a) but not in (2b). This is consistent with our intuitions. *The witnesses* is understood as the object of *eat* in (1b), but the subject of *eat* in (1a). The possibility of adding superficial object NPs to sentences like (1) is consistent with these intuitions and the facts of Q distribution:

(3) a   The witnesses are likely to eat cheese.
  b   *The witnesses are difficult to eat cheese.

The facts of Q distribution are also consistent, but in the opposite way, with the possibilities for adding superficial subjects:

(4) a   *The witnesses are likely for the cannibals to eat.
  b   The witnesses are difficult for the cannibals to eat.

Thus, the original conclusion suggested by floating Qs is supported: (1a,b) are different kinds of constructions. In (1a), the main clause subject acts as a former subject of *eat*. In (1b), it acts like a former object.[1] Our conception of the floating Q phenomenon is consistent with our observations about (1)–(4). This adds to our confidence in the argument that the distribution of floating Qs can help discover underlying subject-verb relationships.

Let us turn to examples like:

(5) a   All of those officials are surly.
  b   Those officials all are surly.
  c   Those officials are all surly.

Example (5a) is an elementary clause type containing a form of *be* and an adjective. This is the standard pattern for adjectival clauses. Previous base rules have not made any provision for the generation of this kind of clause. Nor has anything explicit been said about the status of the verb *be* which occurs here. *Be* along with *have* and the modals *will, can,* etc., are usually called *auxiliary verbs* or just *auxiliaries.* These have many special properties, some of which will be noted in this and the following chapters.

The auxiliary *are* in (5b) behaves, with respect to Quantifier Floating, exactly like nonauxiliary verbs such as *eat, like, vanish, push, give,* etc. Therefore, we regard the various forms of *be* which cooccur with adjectives as members of the category V. The occurrences of *be* in passives, with progressive verbs, etc., behave like those in (5). Therefore, we regard all occurrences of *be* as instances of V. Further, Q positioning depends on *subject-verb* relations. Thus, in (5a), *all of those officials* must be the subject of *are. Are* must then be the main verb of the clause. This conclusion is consistent with the general position of *are* and with the fact that it *agrees with* the subject in number, as other tensed (finite) verbs do.

What then of (5c)? Here, in contrast to (5b), the Q is between the auxiliary verb *be* and the adjective *surly.* How can one account for this locus? One answer is to add a special rule to derive the Q position in examples like (5c) from positions like those in (5b). The latter are previously produced by applications of Quantifier Floating. Postulating such a rule would claim that the word order in (5c) is an accident, a combination of forms which does not follow from independent features of the grammar. So far, it has not been necessary to appeal to any such ad hoc statements. We have been able to show that the distribution of floating Qs follows from the general principle embodied in our formulation of Quantifier Floating. They are detached from subject NPs and placed in front of the verbs of which those NPs are subjects. Alternative Q positions follow from the interaction of this principle with other rules of the grammar which make particular NPs the subjects of different verbs at different stages. It would be significant to show that the distribution of Qs like those in (5c) follows automatically from Quantifier Floating.

There is a way to accomplish this. Qs float in front of elements which are (i) verbs and (ii) verbs of which the NPs containing these Qs are (sometime) subjects. (This is made more precise in Chapter 29.) Thus, to describe examples like (5c) in terms of Quantifier Floating alone, adjectives must be members of the category V. Moreover, main clause subjects in cases like (5c) must have been at one point subjects of the adjective.

These two claims combine in an analysis of adjectival constructions which makes maximum use of independently needed rules and structures. The analysis assumes that the auxiliary *be,* which occurs with adjectives, is an intransitive verb, taking a complement clause subject. The main verb of the complement clause is an adjective. Underlying a sentence like (5c), then, will be the remote structure:

(6)

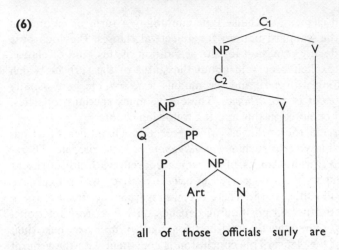

How are structures like (6) related to surface structures? Quantifier Floating accounts for the Q distribution. Since *surly* in C_2 is represented as a V, no impediment exists to the normal functioning of this rule. However, something must turn the remaining complement clause subject, *those officials*, into the main clause subject. But a rule which can accomplish just this already exists, namely, s-Raising. For the latter promotes the subject NP of the complement in an intransitive clause into the new subject of that clause.[2] Therefore, after Quantifier Floating applies to (6), the result must undergo s-Raising.

The above analysis of sentences like (5) parallels the s-Raising treatment of:

(7) a All of those officials seem to lie.
  b Those officials all seem to lie.
  c Those officials seem to all lie.

Recall that the difference between (5b,c), which are similar to (7b,c), was simply whether Quantifier Floating applied before s-Raising, yielding (5c), or after it, yielding (5b). More generally, then, the class of adjectives is a subset of the category V.

The construction *be* adjective, as analyzed here, involves several restrictions. *First*, adjectives, unlike most other verbs, do not occur *freely* as the main verbs of clauses. They can only be the main verbs of those clauses embedded directly below *be*.[3] As a consequence, adjectives never occur with any of the inflections typical of other verbs. That is, they do not occur with the tense inflections present and past or with the aspectual inflections for progressive and perfective:

(8) a *Harry bigs.
  b *Harry intelligented.
  c *Harry is obstreperousing.
  d *Harry has sicked.

(We will consider the inflectional defectiveness of adjectives below.) *Second*, although adjectives are the main verbs of infinitival clauses induced by application of s-Raising, they do not cooccur with the infinitive marker *to*:

(9)   a   *Those men are to (all) surly.
     b   *Joan is to obstinate.

Third, the analogy between triples like (7) and those like (5) based on an identical s-Raising analysis only holds given a further claim that *be* is an obligatory s-Raising trigger. Recall that *seem* only optionally involved the operation of this rule. If s-Raising does not apply with *seem*, then Extraposition must. Consequently, corresponding to (7a,b,c), one finds:

(10)   a   It seems that all of those men sing.
      b   It seems that those men all sing.
      c   It seems that those men all sing.[4]

If *be* were *fully* parallel to *seem*, one would then expect to find as well:

(11)   a   *It is that all of those officials surly.
      b   *It is that those officials all surly.

These are, of course, totally impossible. We can block all such examples[5] by insisting that s-Raising is obligatory in configurations like (6). This will force the complement subject to be raised, converting the complement clause to infinitival form. A subsidiary rule, not limited to adjectives,[6] will then delete the expected infinitive marker, to account for facts like (9).

     Examples of the type

(12)   Joe is fond of Mary.

have hitherto been treated as simple clauses, that is, as containing no embedded clauses as parts. We now claim that they have essentially the same complex structure as:

(13)   Joe seems to like Mary.

That is, they involve a main verb, *is*, which triggers s-Raising out of its underlying subject complement clause. The special feature of the subject complement clause in cases like (12) is that its main verb is an adjective, a type of V which can only occur in such complements. This analysis makes use of types of remote structure, such as (6), which are independently required, and of rules, like s-Raising, which are independently part of the grammar of English. Our analysis requires, however, certain restrictions on the cooccurrence of adjectival Vs with other elements of the verbal system. We return to these below.

     We have applied assumptions about the regularities underlying Quantifier Floating to the construction *be* Adjective. Other cases of *be* yield almost identical results. Consider the distribution of Qs with the *be* of passive clauses and the *be* associated with progressive aspect:

(14) Passive *be*
    a   All of the fighters were destroyed by the defenders.
    b   The fighters all were destroyed by the defenders.
    c   The fighters were all destroyed by the defenders.

(15) Progressive *be*
    a   All of the fighters are diving.
    b   The fighters all are diving.
    c   The fighters are all diving.

We can see from such examples that the NP from which the Q is extracted acts like a subject *both* of the form of *be and* of the passive participle and the progressive participle. This can be accounted for automatically by a treatment parallel to that for the *be* Adjective construction. In both cases a main verb takes a subject complement. The main verb of the complement clause is the passive verb in the first case and the progressive verb in the second. Underlying (14) and (15) will be, respectively:

(16)

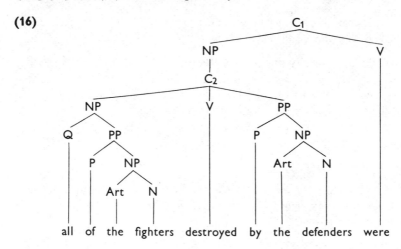

(17)

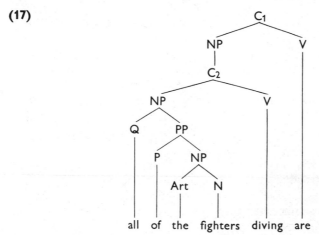

We know from Chapters 18 and 23 that the structure of C_2 within (16) is derived from a more remote active structure by Passive.[7]

We now claim that passive and progressive clauses are, like adjectival clauses, complex in remote structure. All involve a main clause with *be* as its main verb (we revise this slightly in Chapter 27 for passive clauses). The restrictions for adjectives with respect to structures like (6) also hold for progressive and passive participles in (16) and (17). The participles must only occur in configurations embedded directly below a form of *be*. Moreover, they must occur without the infinitive marker. Finally, s-Raising is also obligatory with these occurrences of *be*:

(18) a *It was that all of the fighters destroyed by the defenders.
     b *It is that all of the fighters diving.

Thus a cluster of restrictions hold equally for the three constructions: *be* $\begin{Bmatrix} \text{Adjective} \\ \text{Progressive participle} \\ \text{Passive participle} \end{Bmatrix}$. We consider below how to express these restrictions.

Progressive and passive participles can combine in a single complex structure:

(19) The fighters are being destroyed by the defenders.

Here are two forms of *be*, one inflected for tense (in this case, present), the other for progressive. Before analyzing such sentences, it is crucial to consider the distribution of floating Qs. All speakers seem to accept:

(20) a All of the fighters are being destroyed by the defenders.
     b The fighters all are being destroyed by the defenders.
     c The fighters are all being destroyed by the defenders.

These examples show that both *are* and *being* act as verbs of which the NP *all of the fighters* was a onetime subject. However, speakers divide as to whether they accept:

(21) ? The fighters are being all destroyed by the defenders.

This appears to involve the restriction, previously touched on in Chapter 24, which blocks a sequence of the form *be* $\left(\begin{Bmatrix} \text{-ing} \\ \text{-ed} \end{Bmatrix} \right)$ Q in surface structure. That is, untensed *be* followed by a Q is unacceptable for many speakers. A suitable choice of intervening adverb should, and does, improve examples like (21) for such speakers:

(22) The fighters are now being systematically all destroyed by the defenders.

The unacceptability of (21) does not therefore argue that *all of the fighters* was not a onetime subject of *destroyed*.

The proper representation of examples combining Passive and progressive aspect involves *multiple embeddings* under occurrences of *be*, and hence multiple applications of s-Raising. Thus, underlying (19) will be, at one stage, the remote structure:

(23)

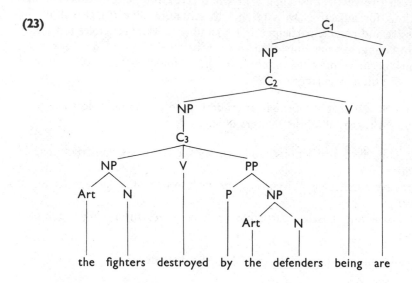

The structure of C_3 would itself be derived from a more remote structure by Passive. In (23), the subject of C_3 must first undergo s-Raising and become the subject of C_2. This postposes the rest of C_3 to the end of C_2 and makes it an infinitive. Then, the *newly derived* subject of C_2 must be made the subject of C_1, postposing the rest of C_2 to the end of C_1 and making it an infinitive. The restrictions noted earlier apply at both levels. The rule s-Raising is obligatory in both cases. The infinitive marker shows up in neither. A construction like (19) thus involves at least two embedded clauses.

We have been led to regard the auxiliary *be* as a main verb obligatorily triggering s-Raising, and adjectives, progressive and passive participles as verbs obligatorily embedded under *be*.[8] The distribution of floating Qs has been a major motivation for this analysis.

Parallel conclusions are reached for the construction type with *have* and perfective participles:

(24) a   Melvin has died.
       b   She has eaten the roast.

Triples like

(25) a   All of the gluttons have tasted the venison.
       b   The gluttons all have tasted the venison.
       c   The gluttons have all tasted the venison.

show that *All of the gluttons* is a onetime subject not only of *have* but also of the participle *tasted*. We can account for this by recognizing these as complex clauses having a subject complement with a main verb *have*. Underlying (25) would be the remote structure:

(26)

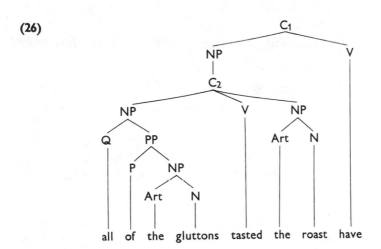

The same restrictions noted for *be* cases are found here. *Have* also obligatorily triggers s-Raising, the complement participle only occurs directly below *have*, and the infinitive marker does not show up. Examples (25b,c) differ only in whether Quantifier Floating applies before or after s-Raising, as in (5), (7), (14), (15) and (20).

As in the case of examples like (19), perfective participles can occur in complex constructions with other verbal forms for which we have provided an s-Raising analysis.

(27) Perfective and Passive
He has been indicted by the grand jury.

(28) Perfective and *be* Adjective
He has been sick.

(29) Perfective and Progressive and Passive
? He has been being tortured by the guards for hours.[9]

These provide no special problems. They simply involve multiple layers of embedding, as illustrated by the structure of (28):

(30)

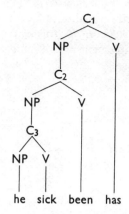

As before, the subject of C_3 must undergo s-Raising twice, becoming in stages the subject of C_2 and C_1. The remnants of C_3 and C_2 are postposed along the way.

We have so far concluded that the auxiliaries *be* and *have*, passive, perfective and progressive participles, and adjectives are all the main verbs of clauses in initial structure. One class of auxiliary verb has not yet been investigated. These are the so-called *modals*, principally *can, could, may, might, must, shall, should, will, would*.[10] All of these behave the same with respect to the relevant properties here. We illustrate with selected examples:

(31) a   All of the nurses can leave.
     b   The nurses all can leave.
     c   The nurses can all leave.

This is a type of distribution we have seen before. Given our assumptions, it suggests that the modal and the following nonmodal are instances of V. Each heads a separate clause in initial structure. Thus we posit as a remote structure for such triples:

(32)

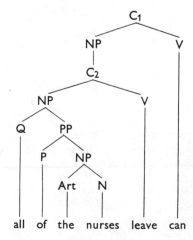

The only difference between (31b,c) is whether Quantifier Floating applies before or after s-Raising. As with the auxiliaries *be* and *have*, s-Raising is obligatory for the modal *can*, in fact, for all modals.

The following appears to be the case:

(33) Auxiliary verbs in English are Intransitive V:

   a Requiring *complement* subjects,[11]

   b Obligatorily triggering s-Raising, and

   c Requiring the *nonappearance* of *to* on the infinitive produced by s-Raising.

If (33) is valid, then the restrictions for *be, have, can*, etc., can be stated once and for all in the grammar as a set of properties of auxiliary verbs. However, *some formal way of marking certain verbs as auxiliaries* will be required, just as it will be necessary to mark some as adjectives, etc. This is a special case of the problem of *subcategorization* touched on in another connection in Chapter 17. We will consider it further in the following chapter.

As in previous cases, modals can combine with other forms to yield complex constructions involving multiple obligatory applications of s-Raising:

(34) a Jack will have eaten by then.

     b Jack must be intelligent.

     c Judy may have been bitten by the snake.

     d They must be eating.

We find a modal and the perfective construction, a modal and the *be* Adjective construction, a modal and the perfective and passive construction, and a modal and the progressive construction. They all involve multiple embeddings. We illustrate with the remote structure of the most complex, (34c):

(35)

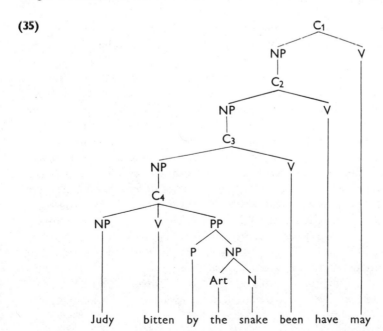

Here, the subject of C_4, *Judy*, must undergo s-Raising obligatorily three times in succession, with the concomitant shifting of the remainder at each level. Ultimately then, the underlying order of verbs is successively reversed, and the subject of the most deeply embedded clause becomes the subject of the main clause.

Our study of floating Qs has led to the conclusion that auxiliary verbs, like *seem*, trigger s-Raising. They differ in obligatorily requiring this operation. An auxiliary verb we have not yet treated is *do*:

(36) a Does Ted understand biodynamics?
  b They don't like me.
  c We do plan to leave.

If (33) is valid, these *do*'s must be intransitive verbs with subject complements undergoing s-Raising, like *be*, *have*, and the modals. The distribution of Qs supports such an analysis:

(37) a All of them do vote.
  b They all do vote.
  c They do all vote.

Consequently, it seems that *do* fits into the treatment of auxiliaries in this chapter. However, we shall see in Chapter 26 that there are special problems associated with this form.

Before concluding this chapter, we should say a word about the sentences in (1) of the Introduction. Recall the contrast in (1d) of that chapter:

(38) They are $\left\{ \begin{matrix} \text{*difficult} \\ \text{likely} \end{matrix} \right\}$ to all understand.

We are now in a position to understand this difference. The example with *likely* is well-formed because the NP *all of them* was the subject of the verb *understand* in remote structure. Thus this NP could undergo Quantifier Floating, making the Q a sister of *understand*. Then *they* was lifted into the main clause by s-Raising, which operates on the subjects of complements.

In the example with *difficult*, *all of them* is the object of *understand* in remote structure. It becomes the main clause subject through the action of the rule mentioned in note 1 of this chapter. This rule applies only to nonsubjects. At no stage is *all of them* the subject of *understand*. Therefore, the ill-formedness of the example with *difficult* is in accord with the basic regularity governing the distribution of floating Qs. In both cases *all of them* has a remote structure locus distinct from the main clause subject position possessed by *they* in the surface structure. But the contrast between these loci accounts for the contrast in floating Q behavior, given our account of the rule Quantifier Floating. Evidently, it is difficult to imagine any account of the original contrast which does not appeal to remote structure.

We said, in commenting on this contrast in the Introduction, that a satisfactory account of the phenomenon had to await the development of a highly articulated theory of grammar. We are now in a position to appreciate what was meant by this. The explanation of the contrast depends on the notions of remote structure, complement clause, the existence of a transformational rule Quantifier Floating, the existence of a transformational rule s-Raising, the existence of the rule mentioned in note 1, and on the subject condition on Quantifier Floating.

Obviously, an account of this contrast which limited itself to superficial grammatical structure would have been doomed to failure. Moreover, Q floating has even deeper aspects which remain to be uncovered. These require an even more articulated theory. Some of what is required is dealt with in Chapter 29.

SUMMARY

Standard discussions of the English verbal system assume a variety of distinct categories including finite verbs, participles, auxiliaries, and adjectives. This chapter claims that:

(i)   All of these are instances of the category V.
(ii) Auxiliaries are intransitive verbs taking subject complements.
(iii) Auxiliaries require the operation of s-Raising.
(iv) Adjectives and progressive, passive and perfective participles must be embedded directly below be.
(v)   The infinitives produced by s-Raising with auxiliary main verbs lack the marker to.

In this discussion we have proposed that the range of s-Raising is greater than at first appears. If s-Raising really functions systematically for auxiliaries, then it is the basic operation involved in forming most English clauses. This includes even those normally taken to be elementary clauses. If what we are claiming is correct, of course, none of the relevant cases with auxiliaries are elementary. Rather, all auxiliary-containing clauses involve one or more levels of subject complement embedding.

A novel feature of this discussion is the way that the generalization underlying floating Q distribution reveals the role of s-Raising in auxiliary constructions.

A variety of issues are raised by these new analyses, particularly problems about subcategorization and combinatorial restrictions. There is the problem of how to represent formally that a particular V is an auxiliary or an adjective, etc. These matters will be dealt with in the following chapter.

NOTES

1. It is possible to formalize these observations by taking *likely* to be an s-Raising trigger as in Chapter 21. Hence, ignoring the form *be* (see below and Chapter 26), underlying a sentence like (3a) would be the structure:

(i)

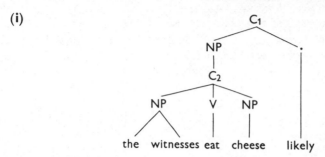

The observations about *difficult* can be formalized by positing a new rule similar to s-Raising. This will also raise NPs out of *subject complements*. But, instead of raising the subjects of these complements, it raises nonsubjects. Ignoring the auxiliary *are*, a sentence like (4b) would have the configuration:

(ii)

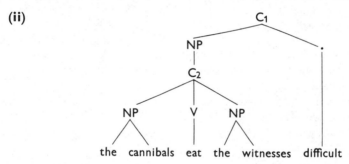

The new raising rule promotes the object NP, *the witnesses*, to main clause subject, postposing everything else and turning the remnant to an infinitive, just as s-Raising does. If the new rule does not operate on (ii), another possible output is:

(iii) For the cannibals to eat the witnesses is difficult.

Or, if Extraposition applies to (iii):

(iv) It is difficult for the cannibals to eat the witnesses.

We will not discuss the nonsubject raising rule in this manual. But such an operation obviously fits into the overall framework we have developed.

2. It simultaneously postposes the rest of the clause in question, normally turning it into an infinitive.

3. There are sentences in which adjectives occur below other verbs, as already noted for *seem*:

  (i) Melvin seems sick.
 (ii) Melvin seems to be sick.

But we argue that (i) derives from (ii), so that at a more remote level the generalization about adjectives requiring *be* holds. And we expect that the same is true in other cases, including some in which no versions containing *be* are possible:

(iii) Melvin $\begin{Bmatrix} \text{became} \\ \text{got} \\ \text{stayed} \end{Bmatrix}$ sick.

(iv) The weather $\begin{Bmatrix} \text{turned} \\ \text{remained} \end{Bmatrix}$ cold.

(v) Melvin $\begin{Bmatrix} \text{looks} \\ \text{sounds} \\ \text{feels} \\ \text{smells} \end{Bmatrix}$ dead.

4. Since s-Raising has never applied here, Quantifier Floating can only operate in the subordinate clause. Thus there is no real analogue to (7c).

5. This includes those which undergo Extraposition and those which do not. The following are no better than (11a,b):

  (i) *That all of those officials surly is.

 (ii) *That those officials all surly is.

These are ruled out by the principle operative for (11), since s-Raising has operated in neither.

6. We see below in (33) that this is a regularity governing infinitives directly below auxiliary verbs.

7. Underlying clause C_2 in (16) is a remote structure for:

(i) The defenders destroyed all of the fighters.

We have now decided that the *be* which occurs in passive clauses is not introduced by Passive, but is rather a main verb taking as clausal subject the clause which undergoes Passive. Thus, the process described in (15a) of Chapter 18 is independent of the rule Passive proper. This is consistent with the formulation of Passive in (35) of Chapter 18, which does not mention *be*.

8. The *be* which occurs with so-called predicate nominals has not been treated:

  (i) Melvin is a surgeon.

This construction reveals an apparent embarassment for our account of floating Q distribution:

(ii) a Those doctors all are surgeons.
  b Those doctors are all surgeons.

Example (iia) causes no difficulties, but how can (iib) be derived, since *surgeons* is an NP and there is no visible V for the *all* to have floated to? Our suspicion is that such constructions involve a *deleted adjective*. If so, the so-called predicate nominal is the object NP of an adjective which does not have a surface form. Underlying (iib) would be a structure of the form:

(iii) Those doctors are all Adj surgeons.

And since this adjective, like all adjectives, is an instance of V, the distribution of floating Qs is perfectly regular. This means that we take the real anomaly in (iib) to involve deletion of an adjective rather than something about the placement of Q.

9. Such examples involving all three types of participles are stilted at best and rejected by a wide range of speakers. Attempts to study the interaction of floating Qs with such cases run afoul of their marginality and of the restriction discussed earlier, which blocks Qs directly after untensed forms of *be*. This excludes *all* directly after *been* and *being* and permits at best only examples with adverbs:

(i) ?They have been recently all being tortured by the guards for hours.

(ii) ?They have been being recently all tortured by the guards for hours.

These are also marginal, but not significantly worse than examples like (29).

10. Other more marginal examples of modals include *need*, *ought*, and *dare*.

11. This follows from the fact that they must trigger s-Raising, since the latter can only operate on complement subjects. As a consequence, there are no *full* sentences like:

(i) Apples have.

(ii) Those guys must.

Such examples are well-formed only when understood as *elliptical* shortenings of structures of the sort which involve complement subjects. Thus (i) is appropriate in a context like

(iii) a What has a lot of vitamin W?
  b Apples have.

where it is understood as elliptical for:

(iv) Apples have a lot of vitamin W.

We would assume that (i) derives from structures like (iv). It is thus not a counterexample to (33).

PROBLEMS

1 Explain the locus of the floating Q in:

(i) My friends will all have seen the detective.

2 What kind of subject NP does the auxiliary verb *have* require in initial structure?

3 What is the source of the difference in position of the floating Qs in:

(i) The problems must all have worried him.

(ii) The problems must have all worried him.

CHAPTER 26 VERBAL SUBCATEGORIES: ADJECTIVES AND AUXILIARIES

PREVIEW

In the preceding chapter, we argued that adjectives, participles, and auxiliary verbs are all instances of the category V. In this chapter we consider the representation of needed subcategories of V, in particular, adjective (Adj) and auxiliary (Aux).

We consider the status of adjectives as Vs, and treat the fact that they do not take tense and aspectual inflections. We argue that this is a function of the requirement that adjectives be embedded below the auxiliary *be*.

We then turn to a range of distributional facts which distinguish auxiliary verbs from all others. These are the major motivation for recognizing the subcategory Aux.

Finally, we encounter some special properties of the auxiliary *do* and consider some constructions in which it appears.

Through a consideration of floating Qs we have come to novel conclusions about certain aspects of the English verbal system. This system is too vast and complicated to consider in real depth. We do, however, need to clarify the kind of analyses introduced in the previous chapter. We are claiming that the auxiliaries *be*, *have*, *do*, and the modals, adjectives, and participles, as well as inflectable verbs, are all introduced into initial trees in the same way. They are inserted by the Lexical Insertion Principle (see

Chapter 16) under V nodes generated by the basic expansion rule for clause structure (ignoring prepositional phrases):

(1) C ———→ NP V (NP) (NP)

Therefore a pair of examples like (2a,b) will share the clause component described in subtree (2c):

(2) a Joan considers him.
    b Joan is considerate of him.

    c

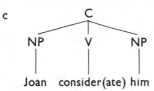

One class of problems raised by such common structures for partially different verbal types (auxiliaries, adjectives, inflectable verbs, etc.) concerns subcategorization. Although we are taking all of these elements to be instances of V, we have already seen that certain rules must distinguish different subtypes. That is why these sets are traditionally regarded as distinct categories. For example, as noted in Chapter 13, rules that assign prepositions to object NPs distinguish objects of adjectives from objects of inflectable verbs or participles:

(3) a   He is proud of his son.
    b   *He is proud his son.
    c   *He likes of his son.
    d   He likes his son.
    e   *He is visiting of his son.
    f   He is visiting his son.
    g   *He has visited of his son.
    h   He has visited his son.

We will see below how auxiliaries are distinguished from nonauxiliaries and, within the class of auxiliaries, how modals must be distinguished from nonmodals. Other distinctions exist as well. How can these differences be represented in a system in which all of the relevant elements are members of the category V? There is nothing about this problem which is uniquely attributable to our particular assignments of grammatical categories. The same questions arise with respect to proper nouns, human nouns, animate nouns, abstract nouns, etc. All of these are distinct from other classes in terms of some type of grammatical behavior. Yet everyone agrees that they all are members of the category N. There is simply a general problem of subcategorization in grammar.

One approach, briefly mentioned earlier, is to adopt a system in which single nodes are labeled by more than one category symbol. In this way, elements can be members of overlapping, partially similar but partially different categories. The rudiments of such a system for pronouns were sketched in Chapter 17. An analogous treatment is possible for the different types of verbals.

Let us consider what may have seemed the most surprising, even offensive claim of the previous chapter: that adjectives fall under the same category as traditional verbs. With respect to a particular pair of items, say *die* and *dead*, this means that such forms will be listed in the lexicon as:

(4) a [*die*, V, ...]
    b [*dead*, V, ...]

Neither of these takes direct objects. Therefore, their representations must include the feature Intransitive. This contrasts with a pair such as *desire*, *desirous*, which would be marked Transitive.

Adjectives and verbs are, however, distinctly categorizable with respect to certain grammatical processes. For instance, the choice of tense-bearing auxiliary (*be* for adjectives, but *do* (as we see below) for nonadjectives) and the choice of preposition or not on direct objects (standard for transitive adjectives) depend on a distinction of the two classes. However, all that is necessary to account for the differences is to recognize some property, call it *Adjective* (Adj). It will be associated with just those Vs which are adjectives. Given such a syntactic feature, the representations in (4) expand to:

(5) a [*die*, V, Intransitive, ...]
    b [*dead*, V, Adj, Intransitive, ...]

There is now a formal way to pick out those Vs which are adjectives, without giving up the equally formal representation of their similarity to inflectable verbs. That is, the feature Adj defines the subcategory of adjectival Vs.

However, the real difference between *die* and *dead* is not the trivial formal contrast in (5). Rather, it lies in the consequences this contrast has for those grammatical rules and constraints which are sensitive to it. For instance, we saw earlier that adjectives are linked to an immediately higher occurrence of the auxiliary *be*. Since this is not true of inflectable verbs, the constraint expressing this linkage is sensitive to the contrast in (5). Second, we saw that, unlike inflectable Vs, adjectives are inflectionally defective. Those parts of the grammar which account for this distinction must also be sensitive to the difference in (5). Let us look at the notion of inflectional defectiveness more closely.

A typical nonadjectival verb, say *sing*, can occur in a variety of different morphological variants:

(6) a As the main verb of a tensed clause, hence with two subvariants:
    (i) Present tense: Jackie *sings*.
    (ii) Past tense: Jackie *sang*.

b As the main verb of an infinitive: I want Jackie to *sing*.
c As the main verb of a gerundive clause: (His) *singing* amused Jackie.
d As a past participle in a perfective construction: Jackie has *sung*.
e As a present participle in a progressive construction: Jackie is *singing*.

Moreover, if a verb is transitive, it can typically also occur:

(7) As a past participle in a passive construction: The song was *sung* by Jackie.

The double peculiarity of adjectives as described in this manual is that (i) they occur only as in (6b), and (ii) then only with the infinitive marker *to*, missing. Thus, adjectives enter none of the other combinations in (6). Consequently, they occur with none of the standard verbal inflections.

The major inflectional contrast between adjectives and verbs like *sing* seems to cast doubt on the combination of these into a single category. This conclusion is not warranted, however. It turns out that the defectiveness of adjectives follows from a single basic restriction on these Vs, given certain assumptions about the origin of the inflections. The restriction is:

(8) Adjectives must be embedded as the main verbs of subject complements of *be*.

In other words, adjectives must occur in the initial structure configuration:

(9)

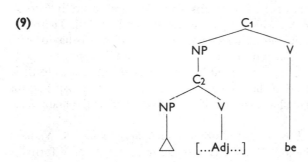

Be obligatorily triggers s-Raising. Therefore, adjectives will typically end up as the main verb of an infinitive, subordinate to the main verb *be*.[1] It is not easy to show how this restriction explains the inflectional defectiveness since we are not, in this manual considering seriously the origin of the tenses and aspects. Note, however, that even for inflectable verbs like *sing*, *chew*, etc., the tense inflections cannot occur when such elements are the main verbs of infinitives (more generally, of untensed clauses). Thus the restriction in (8) explains the failure of adjectives to occur with tense inflections by guaranteeing that they occur as the main verbs of untensed clauses. An analogous, but more complicated, explanation of the impossibility of aspect inflections is possible under certain assumptions (see note 10 of Chapter 27).[2] But we will not be able to elaborate this.

In Chapter 27, we argue that the possibility for verbs like *eat*, etc., which are nonauxiliaries, to inflect for tense or aspect depends ultimately on the deletion of the auxiliary *do*, under which they must be initially embedded in a configuration otherwise like (9). When *do* is preserved, it is *do* which inflects. In these terms, adjectives cannot inflect because *be*, unlike *do*, does not delete. Thus *be* persists and bears the inflections which might otherwise go on adjectives. The restriction in (8) thus means, we claim, that the inflections which one might otherwise expect to show up on adjectival Vs show up on the *be* associated with them. Where without (8) we would say

(10) *John fats.

we actually say

(11) John is fat.

with the present tense inflection on *be*. Where without (8) we would say

(12) *John has fatted for a long time.

with the perfective inflection on *fat*, we say

(13) John has been fat for a long time.

with that inflection on *be*.

We conclude that there is no reason to deny verbhood to adjectives because of their inflectional defectiveness, which is explainable in terms of condition (8). This condition makes reference to the marker Adj distinguishing adjectives from inflectable (nonauxiliary) verbs like *sing* and from inflectable auxiliaries like *have* and *be*, which will also not be marked Adj. There are, though, a variety of reasons for taking adjectives to be Vs; their behavior with respect to floating Qs (considered in Chapter 25), the fact that they take subjects and objects like ordinary verbs (and bear selectional restrictions to these in the same way), the fact that they function semantically like verbs,[3] and the fact that they are distributed as expected if they functioned as the main verbs of (infinitival) clauses.

We have said that *be*, *have*, *will*, and other modals are auxiliaries. We have also said they are members of V. To characterize this subtype of V formally we recognize a further grammatical marker, call it Auxiliary (Aux). We distinguish such pairs as *will* and *happen* $\left(He\ happens\ to \left\{ \begin{array}{l} be\ dead \\ own\ a\ horse \end{array} \right\} \right)$ as follows:

(14) a [*happen*, V. Intransitive, ...]
     b [*will*, V, Aux, Intransitive, ...]

The real difference between auxiliaries and nonauxiliaries is not given simply by the formal distinction in (14). It lies in the consequences this distinction has for those principles of English grammar which are sensitive to the categories Aux and nonAux. Let us turn to the distributional behavior of auxiliary verbs. It is most noteworthy with respect to (i) negative clauses; (ii) interrogative clauses; (iii) tag questions; and (iv) truncated clauses.

To each positive declarative clause there typically corresponds a negative clause, containing the form *not* or its contracted variant, *n't* (see Chapter 28):

(15) a Melvin will resign.   a′ Melvin will not resign.
      a Tom is sick.   b′ Tom is not sick.
      c Mary has resigned.   c′ Mary has not resigned.

Will, is, and *has* are auxiliaries. Even from the small sample in (15) one sees that when the positive sentence contains an auxiliary, the negative sentence is formed by placing *not* immediately after the auxiliary. For positive clauses without auxiliaries, however, the analogous move is impossible:

(16) a Melvin resigned.   a′ *Melvin resigned not.
      b Those men caught the crook.   b′ *Those men caught not the
                                           crook.

We return below to how well-formed negatives of clauses like those in (16) are formed. But we can conclude for now that an auxiliary verb permits the addition of a following negative.

Let us turn to interrogatives which are answered by *yes* or *no*. We find that to each declarative main clause there in general corresponds an interrogative clause:

(17) a Melvin will resign.   a′ Will Melvin resign?
      b Tom is sick.   b′ Is Tom sick?
      c Mary has resigned.   c′ Has Mary resigned?

We see that in main clauses with *auxiliary* main verbs, the yes-no question clause is formed by *inverting the order of the auxiliary and the subject NP*.[4] However, in main clauses with nonauxiliary main-verbs, this is impossible:

(18) a Melvin resigned.   a′ *Resigned Melvin?
      b Those men caught the crook.   b′ *Caught those men the
                                           crook?

We return below to the question of how well-formed yes-no question analogues of clauses like those in (18) are constructed. At this point, we conclude that the same set of verbs which form negatives with postposed *not* form yes-no questions by inverting with their subject NPs.

Main clauses in English can typically form an expanded *tag clause question* by adding a tag contrasting along the positive-negative dimension. The tag has special word order properties. From the clauses in (15a,b,c) one can form (tags italicized):

(19) a Melvin will resign, *won't he?*
      b Tom is sick, *isn't he?*
      c Mary has resigned, *hasn't she?*

From those in (15a',b',c') one can form:

(20) a   Melvin will not resign, *will he?*
     b   Tom is not sick, *is he?*
     c   Mary has not resigned, *has she?*

Already the generalization emerges. The tag part of such clauses consists essentially[5] of an occurrence of the same auxiliary verb in the main clause plus a pronoun agreeing with the main clause subject. However, the analogous principle of formation does not work for nonauxiliary verbs:

(21) a   *Melvin resigned, resignedn't he?
     b   *Those men caught the crook, caught not they?

Again there is a systematic difference between auxiliaries and nonauxiliaries.
    Finally, there are truncated clauses formed with *so* like those italicized in:

(22) a   Melvin will resign and *so will Tom.*
     b   Tom is sick and *so is Jim.*
     c   Mary has resigned and *so has Betty.*

The italicized clauses are understood respectively, to involve resigning, sickness, and resigning, as in the antecedent clause, and they have the word order [*so*—V—subject NP]. But in all cases the V is an auxiliary. Significantly, there is no analogue for nonauxiliary verbs:

(23) a   *Melvin wants to resign and so wants Bob.
     b   *Melvin intends to catch the crook and so intends Ted.

    Overall then, we have illustrated four major ways in which auxiliaries are different from other verbs but similar to each other. These are the chief basis for the distinction between Vs marked Aux and those which are not so marked.
    However, Vs marked Aux do not form a completely homogeneous group. A major distinction separates the modals (*can, could, may, might, must, shall, should, will, would*) from *be* and *have*. Modals can never occur in gerundive or infinitival clauses. They can only be the main verbs of so-called tensed clauses, while *be* and *have* are not so limited:

(24) a   Jack believes that he is innocent.
     a'   Jack believes himself to be innocent.
     b   Jack believes that he can survive.
     b'   *Jack believes himself to can survive.

(25) a   The fact that John has never visited Paris is irrelevant.
     a'   John's never having visited Paris is irrelevant.
     b   The fact that John can never visit Paris is irrelevant.
     b'   *John's never caning visit Paris is irrelevant.

Note the contrast between modals and adjectives. While the latter must always occur in (unmarked) infinitives, modals never occur in infinitives (marked with *to* or not) nor in gerundive clauses. Modals are thus also quite defective inflectionally. They take neither the aspect inflections nor the gerundive clause inflection,[6, 7]

Let us return to the contrast between auxiliaries and nonauxiliaries. Four general types of behavior, involving negatives, interrogatives, etc., distinguish these two classes. In each case, we saw that there was a process of clause formation which did not seem to function with nonauxiliaries. For instance, the process of forming negatives seemed to be blocked in cases like:

(26)   a   Melvin understands calculus.
       b   *Melvin understands not calculus.

However, there is, of course, a way to form the negative of (26a):

(27)   Melvin does not (doesn't) understand calculus.

In such a clause, the verb *do* is inflected for tense, while the main verb in the positive clause occurs as a *bare stem* (see note 2 of Chapter 6). The relation between pairs like (26a) and (27), and, more generally, the status and origin of the verb *do* in such cases is one of the more complicated and initially confusing problems in the study of English grammar.

One can state first that the *do* in (27) is behaving like an auxiliary. It stands directly before the negation marker. Moreover, with respect to the other major processes characterizing auxiliary behavior, *do* also behaves like an auxiliary:

(28)   a   Bill likes Joan.
       b   Does Bill like Joan?

(29)   Bill likes Joan, doesn't he?

(30)   Bill likes Joan and so does Jack.

In all of the constructions cited earlier, where nonauxiliaries could not adopt the special behavior of auxiliaries, *do* is used to form the required structures.[8]

It follows that *do* is an auxiliary. This means in our terms that *do* is an intransitive verb in initial structure. It takes subject complement clauses and obligatorily triggers s-Raising. From this point of view, the relation between *do* and *attract* in (31a) is the same as that between *be* and *attractive* in (31b):

(31)   a   Does Melvin attract girls?
       b   Is Melvin attractive to girls?

That is, *attractive* is the main verb of an unmarked infinitive and so is *attract*. Example (31a) derives from an initial structure in which the clause [Melvin attract girls] is the subject of *do*, with *Melvin* subsequently raised to subject of *do* by s-Raising. This analysis is consistent with the conclusions about *do* reached at the end of Chapter 25, on the basis of the interaction of *do* with floating Qs.

A problem arises at this juncture. The distributional similarity between *be* and *do* in (31) is only partial. Thus, corresponding to (31) are the active forms:

(32)   a   Melvin attracts girls.
         b   Melvin is attractive to girls.

If *do* and *be* were *fully* parallel, one would expect either to find (33) well-formed:

(33)   *Melvin attractives to girls.

or to find that the active correspondent of (31a) was

(34)   *Melvin does attract girls.

Neither of these is the case.

Readers may object that we have mistakenly starred (34), which they may feel is well-formed. Here the standard orthography obscures a fundamental distinction. As usual, the orthographic representation in (34) is an ambiguous account of more than one sentence. In this case, one is ill-formed and one well-formed. The property of importance is the *stress* on the word *does*. In the interrogative (31a), *does* may be either weakly stressed or contrastively (very strongly) stressed. But the string of words in (34) is well-formed only when *does* has very strong stress. Thus, the star on (34) is a representation of the fact that (34) is not the declarative correspondent of the weak-stressed *does* sentence in (31a). For the rest of this discussion, let us indicate strongly stressed verbs by capitalization wherever this is of relevance. Ordinarily stressed ones will be written normally. In these terms then, (31a) should be replaced by:

(35)   a   DOES Melvin attract girls?
         b   Does Melvin attract girls?

And (34) should be replaced by:

(36)   a   Melvin DOES attract girls.
         b   *Melvin does attract girls.

There is a *gap* but only in the set of *positive* declarative clauses with unstressed *do*:

(37)   a   Melvin DOES'nt attract girls.[9]
         b   Melvin doesn't attract girls.

Simple clauses like (32a) fill the gap left by the impossibility of cases like (36b). In other words, the proper declarative correspondent of (35b) is (32a).

We have just encountered a situation which recurs frequently in grammar. There is a paradigm of examples differing regularly along certain dimensions. However, the paradigm contains a gap. A combination does not occur which the pattern would lead one to expect should occur. There also exists a morphologically irregular form or combination of forms which fills the gap functionally. The natural description in such cases is to let the general rules generate the nonoccurring combination and to add special rules to change the nonoccurring forms into the morphologically irregular forms which do occur. We shall apply this strategy to the present case. This means deriving clauses like (38a) (the morphologically irregular combination of forms) from structures like those underlying the ill-formed (38b) (the regular but nonoccurring combination which the pattern leads one to expect should occur):

(38)   a   Audrey sings.
      b   *Audrey does sing.

English grammar must then contain rules which, in certain contexts, (i) delete unstressed *do* and (ii) switch the tense inflection which would *otherwise* go on this *do* to the verb of its complement. In other words, we now suggest that all clauses like those italicized in

(39)   a   *Jim fired them.*
      b   *Jim didn't fire them.*
      c   *Did Jim fire them.*
      d   *Jim didn't fire them,* did he?
      e   *Jim fired them,* didn't he?

have parallel initial structures containing a main verb *do*, which is an auxiliary, and a subject complement clause whose main verb is *fire*. The derivations differ in that the rule which removes *do*, let us call it *Do Erasure*, operates only in (39a,e).

It remains to consider the formulation of *Do Erasure* and to characterize the environments which permit it, and thus which distinguish examples like (39b–c) from (39a). This is dealt with in Chapter 27.

SUMMARY

The chief result of this chapter is that the grammatical differences among the different elements we have combined into a single category V do not preclude this combination. The mechanism of subcategorization permits us to simultaneously describe their similarities (recall the facts of floating Qs) in terms of the category V and to represent their differences in terms of differential markers like Adj and Aux.

The logic of this treatment is identical to the (traditional) account of intransitive, transitive, and ditransitive verbs. That is, the similarities between these three groups are represented by assigning them to the same category (V). The differences are marked by the syntactic features Intransitive, Transitive, and Ditransitive.

It was shown that the inflectional defectiveness of adjectives does not provide a basis for rejecting their assignment to the category V. This defectiveness follows from a restriction limiting adjectives to the complements of *be* in initial structure.

Finally, we argued for the existence of a rule, *Do Erasure*, deleting auxiliary *do* under certain, as yet to be determined, conditions.

NOTES

1. That is, adjectives will normally end up in the derived configuration:

(i)

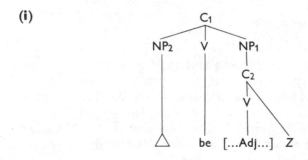

Our account of adjectives in this chapter does not appear compatible with the traditional characterization of adjectives as modifiers of nouns. This usage is based on occurrences of adjectives internal to NPs, as in:

(ii)   enormous mountains
(iii) grotesque analyses
(iv)   intelligent grammarians

However, it is easy to account for these usages within the framework of our description. One need only assume that structures like (ii)–(iv) are derived from clauses in (i) functioning as relative clauses. Thus (iii), for example, would derive from:

(v) [analyses *which are grotesque*]

And in this structure, the italicized portion has the structure in (i). The same general analysis will account for NP-internal modifiers of a participial character such as

(vi) the sleeping princess
(vii) the smashed bottle

which will derive, respectively, from

(viii) [the princess who is sleeping]
(ix) [the bottle which is smashed]

2. The basic idea is that the aspect and tense suffixes originate in trees in positions superordinate to the clauses where they end up. They reach their ultimate loci through the action of affixation rules. These turn what would otherwise end up as independent verbal words into endings by Chomsky-adjoining them (see note 3 of Chapter 17) onto the *immediately lower* verbal element. Schematically:

(i)

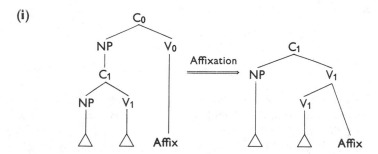

In these terms, any verbal element which must, like adjectives, occur below *be* (or some other fixed auxiliary) is blocked from receiving affixes because the auxiliary intervenes between the particular element and the still higher affix. Thus, the affix will be placed on the auxiliary. And, as illustrated in the text, this is just what happens in the case of adjectives. The situation is, ultimately, more complicated, since various combinations of aspects and auxiliaries are possible. This yields structures containing multiple occurrences of auxiliaries:

(ii) Marianne has been arrested by the FBI.
(iii) Marianne has been thin for a long time.
(iv) Marianne is being difficult.

In each of these, there are two auxiliaries, one bearing a tense affix, the other an aspect affix. These can ultimately be fitted into the framework in (i) by assuming that, like adjectives, the aspects themselves must be embedded directly below certain auxiliaries. That is, Progressive must be embedded directly below *be*, Perfective directly below *have*. Therefore, for example, the complex initial tree for (iii) would be:

(v)

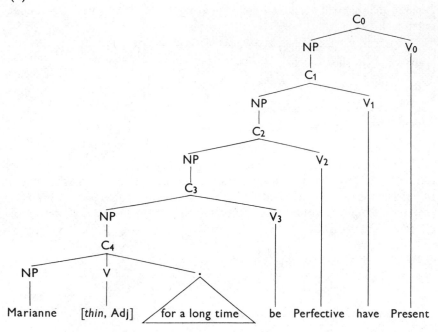

The Adjective and Perfective both meet the conditions specified. When Affixation functions for the affixal elements Present and Perfective, these will be lowered onto the immediately subordinate Vs, as specified in (i). Thus the required presence of *be* blocks the attachment of Perfective to the adjective *thin*. Notice that if some rule existed to delete this *be* before Affixation applied, it would be possible for inflected adjectives to exist. We claim in Chapter 27 that just such an operation is the source of inflected nonauxiliaries. There it is the deletion of the auxiliary *do* which is relevant.

3. That is, adjectives, like ordinary verbs, act as predicates from a logical point of view. Thus, the semantic function of the italicized verb in (i) is exactly the same as the function of the italicized adjective in (ii):

(i) 2 and 2 *equals* 4.
(ii) 2 and 2 is *equal* to 4.

And similarly in:

(iii) Tarantulas *disgust* me.
(iv) Tarantulas are *disgusting* to me.

Moreover, note that adjectives enter into selectional restrictions (see Chapter 16) with their subjects and objects exactly like other verbs. So, there is the same kind of violation in (v) as in (vi):

(v) !The meatball was fond of the gravy.
(vi) !The meatball liked the gravy.

That is, *fond* requires its subject to designate a mind-possessing entity, just as *like* does.

4. Correlated with this is a difference in *intonation*. The question clause typically has a rising contour instead of the falling pattern of declaratives. We shall not attempt to describe this in the present work.

5. There is also a negative if the main clause is positive, a lack of negative if the main clause is negative.

6. There is a tradition of *pairing* at least some of the modals as follows

   (i)   will—would
   (ii) shall—should
   (iii) can—could
   (iv) may—might

and, moreover, of regarding these as being marked for present and past tenses, respectively. This does not make any sense in clauses like

   (v)   He will leave.
   (vi) He would leave.

where clearly the difference has nothing to do with reference to time.
However, the traditional account does seem correct in cases where the tense of verbs is not determined freely by semantic considerations but is controlled by the tense of other verbs, in other words, where there is *tense agreement*. This is the case in a context like:

(vii) That he $\left\{\begin{array}{c} \text{was} \\ \text{*is} \end{array}\right\}$ ill didn't bother Ted yesterday.

Here the past tense form of *be* in the complement is required by the past tense in the main clause. When modals occur in such contexts, it is the so-called past tense form which is required:

(viii) That he $\left\{\begin{array}{c} \text{could} \\ \text{*can} \end{array}\right\}$ be fired didn't bother Ted yesterday.

Thus it seems that the grammar should say that *would* is the past tense agreement form of *will*, *could* of *can*, etc. But this does not tell us how to regard the relation of *will—would*, etc. in cases like (v,vi), where there is no question of tense agreement.

There is a systematic manifestation of the pairings in (i–iv) in counterfactual versus noncounterfactual contexts in conditional clauses, with those on the left in (i–iv) occurring in clauses referring to the real world, those on the right occurring in clauses referring to hypothetical worlds. So, compare:

   (ix) If he can fly, he will be a hit at the circus.
   (x)   If he could fly, he would be a hit at the circus.

Example (ix) is a sentence referring to the actual reality of this world, and hence uses *can* and *will*. Example (x) deals with a hypothetical situation and so uses *could* and *would*. It seems, then, that *could* is also the hypothetical variant of *can*, *would* of *will*, etc. Why the hypothetical use and the past tense agreement use should correspond morphologically is a mystery, as is the way these uses relate to those in contexts like (v) and (vi).

The investigation of pairings like those in (i–iv) involves the study of conditional clauses, tense agreement, etc., topics far beyond the province of an introductory work like this. We ignore relations like those between *will* and *would*, etc. We make the simplifying assumption that the modals are all independent verbs with no interesting grammatical links between them. In a fuller treatment this assumption cannot stand.

7. In any grammar, it must be noted that the modals are unable to show agreement. Thus, even if *can* is regarded as a present tense analogue of past *could*, one must specify that it cannot show person or number agreement:

(i) a He sings.
   b I sing.
   c They sing.

(ii) a He$\left\{\begin{array}{l}\text{can}\\ \text{*cans}\end{array}\right\}$sing.
   b I can sing.
   c They can sing.

8. The auxiliary *do* must be distinguished from a morphologically identical *do*, which is an ordinary verb. By morphologically identical, we mean that it involves the same inflectional set (*do*, *does*, *did*, *doing*, *did*). But nonauxiliary *do* has the same distribution as a standard V. It is found in such sentences as the following, where it combines with auxiliary *do* under the same conditions as any other verb:

(i) a He$\left\{\begin{array}{l}\text{did}\\ \text{ate}\end{array}\right\}$something.

   b What did he$\left\{\begin{array}{l}\text{do}\\ \text{eat}\end{array}\right\}$?

   c He didn't$\left\{\begin{array}{l}\text{do}\\ \text{eat}\end{array}\right\}$anything.

   d He is$\left\{\begin{array}{l}\text{doing}\\ \text{eating}\end{array}\right\}$terrible things.

Therefore, claims about auxiliary *do* must not be rejected on the basis of facts about nonauxiliary *do*. This is one among many cases where a single morphological verb functions syntactically as two or more distinct elements.

9. There is, apparently, a special restriction on stressed DO with negation, namely, that contraction is obligatory:

(i) a   I DO'nt like mayonnaise.
    b   *I DO not like mayonnaise.

However, the restriction is probably more general and covers all auxiliaries:

(ii) a   *He IS not sick.
     b   *He WILL not go.

PROBLEMS

1. In note 1 of this chapter it was mentioned that NPs like

  (i)   grotesque analyses

are derived from NPs containing relative clauses like:

  (ii)   analyses which are grotesque

The same process which derives (i) from (ii) will also derive (iii) and (iv) from (v) and (vi), respectively:

(iii)   the sleeping princess
 (iv)   the smashed bottle
  (v)   the princess who is sleeping
 (vi)   the bottle which is smashed

Make use of these facts to construct an argument that adjectives and participles should be assigned to the same category.

2. What does the fact that adjectives are lexically inserted under V nodes generated by the base rule

  (i)   C $\longrightarrow$ NP V (NP) (NP)

tell us about transitive adjective constructions like:

(ii)   Max is fond of antipasto.

3. Present some sentences to show that *dare* can occur as an auxiliary.

CHAPTER 27 DO ERASURE, SURFACE BRACKETING, AND SO-CALLED VERB PHRASES

PREVIEW

In the preceding chapter, we encountered evidence suggesting that unstressed *do* in negatives, interrogatives, tag questions, and truncated clauses behaves like the other auxiliary Vs (*have, be, will*, etc.). In apparently simple declarative sentences, however, *do* behaves differently when unstressed. Whereas the other auxiliaries appear adjacent to a V, for example, *John will go*, *do* cannot appear adjacent to a V, for example, **John does go*. To account for this, it is proposed that a rule be postulated which deletes unstressed *do* in certain environments. In this chapter, we explore in detail the rule Do Erasure and attempt to specify the environments in which *do* deletes. The major factor is that unstressed *do* does not occur tenseless. Declaratives like *John goes* are in initial structure composed of two clauses, one whose main verb is *do* and whose subject is the complement clause [John go]. Tense is associated with the auxiliary *do* in remote structure but appears on *go* in surface structure. That is, one finds *John goes* and not **John does go*. A rule called *Tense Extraction*, which removes tense from *do* and places it on main verbs like *go*, is postulated. When Tense Extraction operates, *do* is left tenseless. Do Erasure is shown to delete occurrences of tenseless, unstressed *do*. The surface appearance of unstressed *do* in negatives, interrogatives, tag questions, and truncated clauses results from the failure of Tense Extraction to apply in these cases. The conditions under which Tense Extraction is blocked are specified.

It is shown that the analysis of *do* requires minor modifications in previous descriptions of passivization.

Finally, we consider the relation between *do* and the surface bracketing of English clauses. The question of the existence of a primitive verb phrase category (VP) is discussed. We conclude that this constituent is unnecessary since it can be defined in terms of the more primitive categories NP and C.

A t the end of Chapter 26, we came to certain conclusions about the derivation of English clauses containing inflected nonauxiliary verbs. We concluded that they were derived from remote structures containing the auxiliary verb *do* by processes which included a rule Do Erasure. This accounts for the absence of *do* in such surface forms as:

(1) a Audrey sings well.
     b Bob called Tony.

Thus, our conclusion was that the initial structures of sets of examples like

(2) a Jim fired them.
     b Jim did not fire them.
     c Jim DID fire them.
     d Did Jim fire them?
     e DID Jim fire them?

are essentially the same. All involve the presence of a remote structure *do*. Clauses like (2a), which lack *do* in surface structure, were claimed to be the reflexes of the expected but nonexistent:

(3) *Jim did fire them.

This led us to postulate the existence of Do Erasure, which will relate structures like (2a) to remote structures which would otherwise surface as (3). We did not, however, explore the character of this rule or the conditions under which it functions. These are matters to which we now turn.

Our hypothesis about clauses like (2) can be made more precise. *Do* is an auxiliary, and all auxiliary verbs are, in initial structure, intransitive verbs taking subject complements. It follows that underlying examples like (2) will be a common structure along the lines of:[1]

(4)

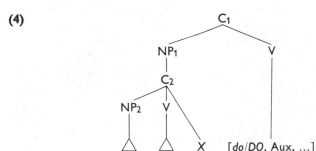

This will be converted to

(5)

by the application of s-Raising, which is obligatory with all auxiliaries. Such structures are in effect the appropriate surface structures for those examples in (2) which preserve an occurrence of *do*.[2] To derive (2a), Do Erasure must function. We now want to explore the conditions under which this rule operates. These conditions determine which examples derived from structures like (4) end up with inflected *do* and unmarked verbs like *fire*, as in (2b–e), and which end up with no *do* and inflected nonauxiliaries, as in (2a).

Paradigms like (2) suggest initially the following about the conditions for loss of *do*. First, it does not happen when the negative marker, *not* (or its contracted variant *n't*), are present. That is, (2a) contains no negative and the following are ill-formed:

(6) a *Jim not fired them.
 b *Jim fired not them.

Second, *do* appears to be preserved in interrogatives, (2d,e).[3] Third, although not illustrated yet, *do* is also preserved by the emphatic form *so*:

(7) a Jim did so fire them.
 b *Jim so fired them.

With respect to *do*, *so* patterns exactly like the negative marker. Finally, the major gap in the paradigm of examples with *do*, that illustrated by examples like (3), involves unstressed or noncontrastive *do*. We conclude that in the case of negatives, emphatics with *so*, and interrogatives, Do Erasure is blocked, preserving auxiliary *do* in the relevant surface structures.

One might try to formulate Do Erasure so that it does not delete *do* in interrogative clauses, negative clauses, or emphasized clauses with *so*. However, such a description ignores one crucial aspect of the erasure of auxiliary *do*. Compare an existing example like (2a) and a nonexisting but "expected" structure like (3):

(8) a Marilyn loved Jack.
 b *Marilyn did love Jack.

If the former is to be derived from the structure underlying the latter, it is necessary not only for *do* to be deleted, but also for an adjustment to be made with respect to tense. Simple removal of the auxiliary verb would yield the ill-formed:

(9) *Marilyn love Jack.

Here the V has, wrongly, no tense marker. What is evidently required in addition is an operation to place on its complement V the tense which *do* originally has. Derivations of examples like (2a) and (8) involve not only Do Erasure but another rule, which we call *Tense Extraction*.

How are these two rules related? We suggest that Tense Extraction operates *before* Do Erasure. Moreover, this operation creates the proper environment for Do Erasure. Tense Extraction will create *tenseless* occurrences of *do*. Our claim is that there is, independently, a general rule in English which deletes tenseless auxiliary *do*. What is the basis for this view?

Recall (from Chapter 26) the parallelism between *do* and the auxiliary *be*. In the analysis presented here, the status and function of *do* in examples like (10a) is identical to that of *be* in examples like (10b):

(10) a Melvin **does** not bore me.
     b Melvin **is** not boring to me.

In other words, where *be* functions in effect as an empty or meaningless verb which bears the tenses for adjectives, *do* has a similar function for the inflectable verbs in those cases where the latter cannot bear tenses.[4] However, adjectives can never inflect, while inflectable verbs sometimes can. This difference arises because there is no analogue of Tense Extraction and Do Erasure for *be*. The base structures of clauses like (10a,b) are formally identical, differing only in the choice of auxiliary and the subcategory to which the main verb of the complement belongs.

Previously, we distinguished as subcategories of V, adjectives (Adj) (like *fat*), and auxiliaries (Aux). Let us elaborate the analysis further by distinguishing those auxiliaries which can inflect (*have, be, do*) from those which cannot (the modals, *will*, etc.) and by referring to inflectable nonauxiliaries as *Pure Verbs* (PV). We now recognize the following categories in the verbal system:

(11) a [V, Adj, ...]   Adjectives (*thin, courageous,* etc.)

      b [V, Aux, Modal, ...]   Modals (*must, can, will,* etc.)

      c [V, Aux, Nonmodal, ...] Inflectable Auxiliaries (*have, be, do*)

      d [V, PV, ...]   Inflectable Nonauxiliaries (*exist, love, pinch,* etc.)

Auxiliaries (b and c)

In Chapter 26, we stated a principle that all adjectives, that is, all [V, Adj, . . .], occur in initial structures directly below the auxiliary *be*. There is an analogous principle for PVs. Every inflectable nonauxiliary verb must be embedded directly below *do*. That is, such verbs must occur in the initial configuration in (4). This simply makes more explicit the view that the initial structure relation between *do* and PVs is formally the same as that between *be* and *Adj*.

If everything else were the same, one would therefore expect occurrence of *do* in the following examples, parallel to *be*:

(12) a   Jack is interesting to you.
  a′ *Jack does interest you.
  b   Jack must be interesting to you.
  b′ *Jack must do interest you.
  c   Jack has been interesting to you.
  c′ *Jack has done interest you.

But the cases with *do* are all ill-formed. We have already decided that those like (12a′) are a function of Do Erasure. It would also be natural to assume that structures like (12b′,c′), which arise automatically from the general assumption that all PVs start out embedded directly below *do*, are converted to the actually found

(13) a   Jack must interest you.
  b   Jack has interested you.

by application of Do Erasure.

Moreover, such examples offer an important clue to the conditions for Do Erasure application. The *do*'s in (12b′, c′) occur in positions where no tense is possible. Note the untensed forms of *be* in the parallel positions in (12b,c). It seems that the deletion of unstressed *do* is connected to tenselessness. In fact, the following is a general property of the auxiliary *do* in English:

(14) The auxiliary *do* cannot occur in untensed clauses.

Beyond examples like (12b′,c′), which already support this claim, note the following examples of standard gerundive, infinitival, and subjunctive constructions, in which auxiliary *do* is impossible:

(15) a   Joan's being sad worries me.
  b   *Joan's doing become sad worries me.
  c   Joan's becoming sad worries me.

(16) a   For him to be sick would be tragic.
       b   *For him to do become sick would be tragic.
       c   For him to become sick would be tragic.

(17) a   It is mandatory that the candidates be seated.
       b   *It is mandatory that the candidates do stay seated.
       c   It is mandatory that the candidates stay seated.

That is, in superficially untensed clauses of all varieties,[5] the *do*'s expected under our analysis never occur.

    This strongly suggests that Do Erasure removes an auxiliary *do* which is a bare stem. Such a rule will automatically convert examples like (12b') to (13a).[6] But now return to pairs like:

(18) a   *Jack does like Sally.
       b   Jack likes Sally.

These involve both Tense Extraction and Do Erasure. It should now be clear how the former creates the conditions for the latter. For a rule which removes the tense from *does* in (18a) will leave a bare stem *do*. And then the same rule which functions for other untensed clauses will erase the *do* here. In other words, a treatment in which Tense Extraction creates the conditions for Do Erasure subsumes the deletion of *do* in cases like (18) under a more general phenomenon of the *do* loss which is typical of untensed environments.

    We have now decided in effect that Do Erasure can be stated as follows:

(19)   Do Erasure

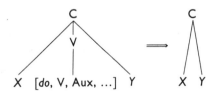

This means that the various conditions associated with *do* loss in main clauses and the presence of *not*, *so*, or interrogativeness are *not* part of Do Erasure. The natural assumption is that *they are restrictions on the operation of Tense Extraction*. Therefore, the claim is that Do Erasure operates on at least two types of tenseless auxiliary *do*'s: those which never have tense (e.g., that in (12b')) and those which have a tense at one stage but lose it because of the operation of Tense Extraction (e.g. that in (18a)).

How can one formulate the conditions under which a tense is removed from unstressed *do* and placed on the complement V of this auxiliary? These conditions involve negation, *so*, and interrogatives,[7] which we reillustrate:

(20) a Johnson $\begin{Bmatrix} \text{did not} \\ \text{didn't} \end{Bmatrix}$ call.

      b Johnson did so call.

      c Did Johnson call?

Observation of such examples suggests for the first time why these three processes might block loss of *do*. In each case, something intervenes between the auxiliary *do* and its complement verb. In (20a), it is the negative; in (20b), the form *so*; and in (20c), the subject NP. It is tempting therefore to formulate Tense Extraction in such a way that it is blocked by any of these intervening elements. This we can do as follows:

(21)

TENSE Extraction

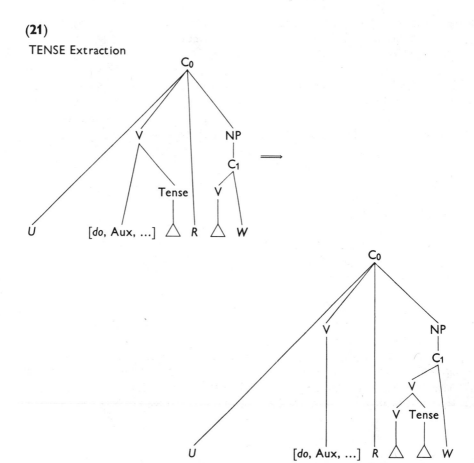

Conditions: a   *do* is unstressed

b   R does not contain[8] any of:

(i)   *not*

(ii) *so*

(iii) subject NP (of *do*)

This rule requires a number of comments. First, since the complement of *do* is assumed to follow it, Tense Extraction must be ordered after s-Raising. For the order in question is not the initial structure order, but that generated by application of s-Raising. Second, the rule only applies to unstressed *do*[9] and is thus properly not inconsistent with examples like (22a).

(22) a   They DO own a Packard.

b   *They do own a Packard.

even though nothing intervenes between *do* and its complement verb. Third, for (21) to be blocked properly in the interrogative cases with unstressed *do*, something must guarantee the presence of the subject NP after *do*. This is a word order not produced by any rules so far. It deviates from the order imposed by the base rules, which permit subjects only in front of their verbs. (This word order is discussed in detail in Chapter 28.) Finally, Tense Extraction refers to a constituent Tense, which can be assumed to dominate one of the two tense inflections, present or past. However, none of our rules so far introduce such a constituent. Therefore, literally, there is no way for structures of the sort which (21) operates on to be generated in our grammar. Unfortunately, the description of tense is too involved to permit treatment in an introductory work. We shall simply assume therefore that some satisfactory way of providing the proper inputs to Tense Extraction exists.[10]

We have thus proposed a description of clauses containing PVs with the following properties. In initial structures such verbs must be embedded immediately below the auxiliary *do*. In some environments, these *do*'s do not receive tense inflections. In this case, they are uniformly removed by Do Erasure. In other environments, the *do*'s are inflected. Here there are two possibilities. If the conditions for Tense Extraction are met, this rule applies, placing the tense on the complement verb. This makes Do Erasure applicable to *do*. If, however, the conditions for Tense Extraction are not met, the tense stays on *do*, Do Erasure is blocked, and an inflected form of *do* shows up in the surface structure. We illustrate with a typical derivation

(23)   Initial Structure

a
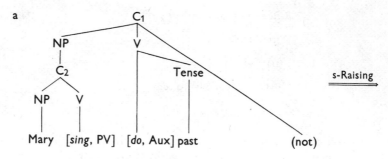

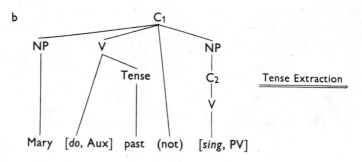

s-Raising ⟹

b

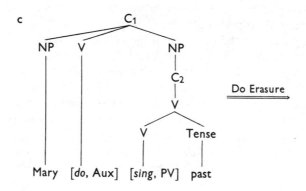

Tense Extraction ⟹

c

Do Erasure ⟹

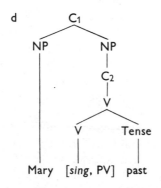

d

The optional *not* in (23) permits us to compress two different derivations into a single set of diagrams. Of course, if *not* is actually present, then Tense Extraction would not apply. Example (23b) with *not* would then be essentially the surface structure.

We have now sketched an analysis of the English verbal system in which each of the two major lexical subtypes of verbs, adjectives (Adj) and pure verbs (PV), occur in initial structures only in a single type of configuration. Adj must occur embedded directly below the auxiliary *be*; PV, directly below *do*. In the case of Adj, this pattern is essentially realized in surface structures. But the existence of Tense Extraction and Do Erasure provides a far more complicated situation for PVs. As a function of these rules, PVs in some contexts end up with the tense which would otherwise go on *do*. Those *do*'s not in association with a tense ending are erased.

We have thus proposed two new constraints on initial structures. These restrictions on Adj and PV are, in effect, an illustration of a new type of grammatical rule. They amount to formal conditions which must be met by structures at a certain level. Structures which are otherwise well-formed (according to the base rules, principles of lexical insertion, etc.) are nonetheless ill-formed if they fail such conditions.[11] Such rules are sometimes referred to as *filters*. The two principles illustrated so far are only a small sample of the role which such conditions seem to play in the English verbal system. The scope of the present discussion does not permit us to deal with other such filters. However, it is necessary to consider the way the filters which have been stated relate to earlier descriptions of passivization.

The analysis just given of the relation between PVs and *do* is not really consistent with certain other suggestions made earlier. In particular, in Chapter 25 we argued that the verb *be* which occurs with passive clauses is an independent auxiliary. It thus starts out in initial structure as an intransitive, taking the clause which undergoes Passive as its subject complement. Later, it obligatorily triggers s-Raising. Hence, in these terms, underlying a passive sentence like (24a) will be the structure (24b):

(**24**) a The bomb was dismantled by Ted

b

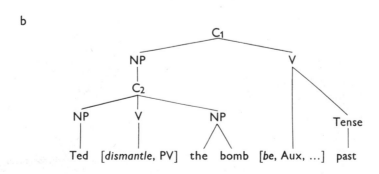

Here, it is C_2 which undergoes Passive. Later, it is the derived subject produced by Passive which undergoes s-Raising to become the derived subject of *was*.

But now the inconsistency in our analysis appears. We claimed earlier in this chapter that all PVs must be embedded in initial structure below the auxiliary *do*. Dismantle in (24) is a PV. But it is embedded below *be* and not *do*. That is, with respect to choice of meaningless auxiliary, verbs of clauses which undergo Passive behave like Adjs and not like other PVs. This fact is so far not accounted for in our treatment.

There is, however, a way to refine our analysis so that it is consistent with all of the facts. Since our claim is that all PVs start out below the auxiliary *do*, let us assume that (24b) is incorrect as an initial structure. It should be changed to a configuration in which *do* replaces *be* as the main clause verb stem. This makes the initial structure consistent with the filter holding for all PVs. But now the initial structure does not contain the auxiliary which actually shows up in the surface structure. We can then add a rule which changes the auxiliary *do* to the auxiliary *be* under certain conditions. Call this rule *Do Replacement*. Under what circumstances will Do Replacement operate? Clearly, just when the complement clause of *do* undergoes Passive. It will be convenient to refine the formulation of Passive slightly as follows. Assume that when Passive applies to a clause it assigns to the main V of that clause the syntactic feature [...Passive...]. Thus, after Passive applies to C_2 in (24b), the verb will have the form:

(25) [*dismantle*, V, PV, Passive, ...]

We can then formulate Do Replacement as follows, under the assumption that this rule is ordered *after* s-Raising:

(26) Do Replacement

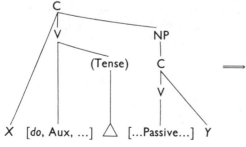

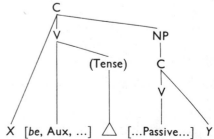

The feature [...Passive...] which we now assume to be added by the rule Passive, thus serves to trigger the action of the rule which shifts the auxiliary associated with passive clauses from *do* to *be*.

This feature can do one other job as well. As noted earlier, the verbs in passive clauses are assigned the past participle ending, for example, *-ed* in (24a). We can now assume that there is a further rule, call it *Past Participle*, which functions as follows:

(**27**)   Past Participle

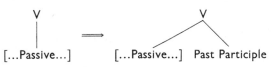

The feature [...Passive...] restricts this operation to just those verbs which are the main verbs of clauses which have undergone Passive.[12]

We have now refined the analysis of passivization as follows. The rule Passive itself inverts the order of NPs and adds the preposition *by* to the former subject. It also adds the feature [...Passive...] to the transitive verb which determines its application. This in turn triggers a shift of the higher auxiliary from *do* to *be* by way of Do Replacement, and triggers the addition of an ending to the passive verb, by way of Past Participle.

We have now given as full a description as is feasible in a work like this of the English verbal system. The chief features of our analysis, begun in Chapter 25, can be summarized in the following claims:

(**28**)   a   The categories of adjective, modal, inflectable auxiliary, and inflectable nonauxiliary are all subtypes of V.
   b   Each auxiliary is, in initial structure, an Intransitive V taking a complement clause subject.
   c   Each auxiliary obligatorily triggers s-Raising.
   d   Adjectives (Adj) are restricted to initial configurations in which they are the main verbs of the complements of *be*.
   e   Inflectable nonauxiliaries (pure verbs: PV) are restricted to initial configurations in which they are the main verbs of the complements of *do*.
   f   *Do* is converted to *be* (by Do Replacement) when its complement verb is marked [... Passive...].
   g   In certain cases, Tense Extraction switches the tense from auxiliary *do* to the complement.
   h   When Tense Extraction functions, the conditions for Do Erasure are created.
   i   Do Erasure deletes all occurrences of untensed *do*, both those created by Tense Extraction and those which never receive tense because, for instance, they are embedded directly below a modal. Do Erasure also deletes the tenseless *do* found in the variety of other untensed clauses (infinitives, etc.). Our fragmentary

description has not included any account of how this tenseless status arises. In fact, we have not given any account of the origin of untensed clauses in general.

j The existence of inflected nonauxiliaries is totally a function of the operation of Tense Extraction. If this rule did *not* exist, English would have only three inflected verbs, the inflectable auxiliaries *have*, *be*, and *do*. Without Tense Extraction, PVs would only occur as the main verbs of untensed, unmarked infinitives, those directly below *do*.

To complete our extremely limited description of the verbal system of English clauses, we treat one further question: the superficial constituent structure of clauses (with respect to their basic constituents, subject NPs, Vs, object NPs, etc.) According to a widely held view, English clauses, in general, have a *binary* or two-constituent structure. One immediate constituent is the subject NP, the other a phrase type usually called Verb Phrase (VP). According to this view, the following sentences, for instance, would have bracketings as indicated:

(29) [Mary] [died].

(30)
a	[Mary] [has died].	f	[Mary] [must have been dying].
b	[Mary] [is dying]	g	[Mary] [is sick]
c	[Mary] [has been dying].	h	[Mary] [has been sick].
d	[Mary] [will die].	i	[Mary] [must be sick].
e	[Mary] [must have died].	j	[Mary] [must have been sick].

In each case, the second bracketed sequence would be regarded as a VP. Within such an approach, the fundamental base rule of English is taken to be something like:

(31) C $\longrightarrow$ NP VP

This is evidently different from any rule in this manual, since our base grammar recognized no VP constituent.

We can now make explicit our view that the analysis represented in (29)–(31) is largely mistaken. This is already implied by the sketchy treatment of the grammar of the verbal system we have given. According to our description of the constituent structures given in (29) and (30), only that in (29) is correct. None of the examples in (30) would receive binary derived structures from our rules.

Let us see how our rules distinguish (29) and (30) and, more generally, how they assign derived constituent structure. Our base rule for introducing clause structure insofar as NPs and Vs are concerned was:

(32) C $\longrightarrow$ NP V (NP) (NP)

This recognizes no internal bracketing for clauses. In particular, it does not bracket the V and everything else in a constituent separate from the subject

NP. It follows that any such bracketing in derived structures must, in our terms, *be a function of transformational operations*. Moreover, (32) permits only a single verb per clause, while, according to our descriptions, all of the examples of (30) have more than one verb in surface structure. Some, for example (30j), have as many as four. Only two of the many transformational rules we have discussed are relevant for determining the derived bracketings of clauses like those in (29) and (30), namely, s-Raising and Do Erasure.

The relevance of s-Raising is clear. Every example in (29)–(30) involves at least one initial auxiliary verb. Such verbs obligatorily trigger s-Raising. In every case, the initial structure main verb of clauses like those in (29) and (30) is an auxiliary. This V triggers s-Raising. The derived bracketing of such examples is therefore not that of the initial structure, but at best that which s-Raising generates. What is the form of derived structure which s-Raising produces? This rule takes the subject of a complement clause, makes that the new subject, and postposes the remnants of the complement after the main verb. Operating on an intransitive structure of the form

(33)

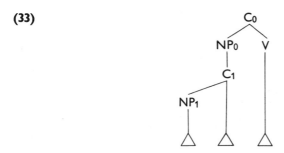

s-Raising yields, as we recall from Chapters 20 and 21:

(34)

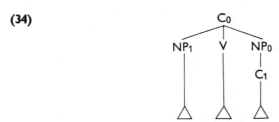

That is, the output of s-Raising is a ternary structure. It follows that any highest clause of the form C_0 in which s-Raising is the only relevant bracketing rule to operate will end up with a ternary structure.

Turning to (30), we find that every example would have the initial form in (33) since the main verb of each is an auxiliary verb. Therefore, since s-Raising obligatorily applies in all such cases, the derived structure of each example in (30) would have the form in (34). Thus all such examples have ternary rather than binary bracketings.

This leaves (29). In our terms, such examples are also derived from initial trees with the main verb an auxiliary, namely, *do*. Thus (29) differs from the examples in (30) chiefly in that it has undergone Do Erasure, triggered by the functioning of Tense Extraction. Since Do Erasure operates after s-Raising, it operates on the ternary structure created by s-Raising. It operates on the kind of ternary structure which is *maintained* in cases like the following, containing stressed *do*:

(35) Mary DID die.

This would have the derived structure:

(36)

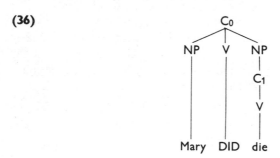

Do Erasure removes the main verb of C_0 in unstressed cases. But, if one immediate constituent is erased from a ternary bracketing structure, the result is necessarily binary. That is, Do Erasure (preceded by Tense Extraction) will convert a structure like (36) (but containing unstressed *do*) to:

(37)

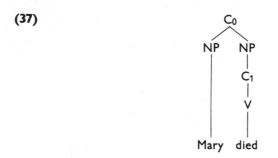

In this case, the second immediate constituent of C_0 is a single V because the original C_1 was intransitive. Regardless of whether C_1 contains direct objects, indirect objects, adverbs, etc., all of its elements other than its subject NP (which is raised by s-Raising into C_0), will form part of the second immediate constituent in cases analogous to (37). Thus s-Raising and Do Erasure will also combine to impose binary surface structures on examples like:

(38)   a   [Jim] [sang the lullaby].
           b   [She] [sold the beanbag to Charley yesterday]
           c   [They] [sent the money to the bank in a truck]

It follows that our approach to English clause structure makes the following claim about superficial constituent structure:

(39) The only binary bracketed clauses are those formed through operation of Do Erasure. Other main clauses will have the basically ternary structure [Subject NP—V—Everything else] produced by s-Raising.

We suggest that the view that binary bracketing is typical of English clauses is an overgeneralization based on the properties of a minority of clauses like (30).

What then of the so-called VP constituent, which is supposed to characterize the nonsubject constituent in the binary bracketing? Our rules assign structures which make it possible to claim that there is something *partly like* the VP constituent of binary grammars.

One of the typical configurations created by the rules proposed in our account of the English verbal system is a C node which has lost its subject NP. For instance, in the surface structure of (30j), there are several such nodes:

(40)

C_1, C_2, and C_3 have this property. To a certain extent, such subjectless C nodes correspond to what are called VPs in many other descriptions. The difference though is that the highest verb, here V_0, is not part of any such phrase, since the C which it is attached to has its subject NP.

To the limited extent it is possible to find grammatical phenomena which are stateable in terms of a notion of VP, these involve C nodes without subjects in our sense. Consider:

(41) a John will go and so will Bob.
      b John is sick and so is Tom.
      c John ate the meat and so did Harry.

The anaphoric process involving the word *so* here is such that the *so* corresponds to a C node without a subject, namely, the remnants of the underlying complements of *will*, *be*, and *do*, respectively. There are similar rules. What is not found, we claim, are anaphoric rules which group the highest verb and everything else after it together as a single unit. Thus there is no anaphoric process of the form

(42) a   Bill will go and Tony X.
      b   Bill is sick and Tony X.
      c   Bill went and Tony X.

where an identical superficial sequence *X* is interpreted to mean respectively 'will go', 'is sick', and 'went', One would expect an element like *X* if there were a VP constituent corresponding to the main V plus everything else.

Similarly, there are rules which can reposition complex constituents headed by V, for instance that involved in such constituent frontings as those in the second conjuncts of:

(43) a   They told Ted to pay up and pay up he did.
      b   They said he would pay up and pay up he will.
      c   They said he was sick and sick he was.

But in each case the fronted sequence, *pay up*, *sick*, etc.,[13] corresponds in our terms to a C node which has lost its subject. Note the impossibility of fronting a sequence corresponding to the VP whose existence is *not* recognized by our rules:

(44) a   *They told Ted to pay up and DID pay up he.
      b   *They said he would pay up and will pay up he.
      c   *They said he was sick and was sick he.

We conclude that, insofar as there is any reality to the notion of VP, it is properly reconstructible in terms of C nodes which have lost their subject NPs. Thus, from a formal point of view, in:

(45)

it is the lefthand configuration that frequently corresponds in our trees to the symbol VP used by other grammarians. More generally, we conclude that the commonly appealed-to VP corresponds to two different sorts of things. On the one hand, it corresponds to C nodes which have lost their subjects through operations like s-Raising, o-Raising, and Equi. In this usage, the concept of VP is, according to the description in this manual, real. But there is no obvious need to mark it with a special node label.[14] On the other hand, some uses of the term VP involve recognition of a constituent dominating the main V of a clause plus everything else, but excluding the subject NP. This usage is, we claim, incorrect. There simply is no such constituent. Those cases of surface structures which appear to have this form, like (29) above, obtain it only through the operation of Do Erasure. Clauses with actually present auxiliary verbs have ternary structures. We conclude that in this second sense, VP is an incorrect overgeneralization from the class of structures generated by Do Erasure. It follows that there is no need for base rules to impose a binary structure on clauses, no need for them to introduce any nodes labeled VP.

SUMMARY

In this chapter, three separate but related topics were dealt with. The first concerned the behavior of the auxiliary verb *do*. It was shown that its absence from simple declaratives and its presence in interrogatives, negatives, tag questions, *so* emphatic clauses, and truncated clauses is linked to two rules, Tense Extraction and Do Erasure. The generalization these rules embody is that unstressed *do* may not appear tenseless in English. The operation of the former renders *do* tenseless in apparently simple declaratives and thereby triggers Do Erasure. The environments where Do Erasure fails to apply are those where Tense Extraction has failed to apply. The failure of Tense Extraction is linked to the occurrence of some constituent between *do* and its main verb.

The implications of the analysis of *do* required modification of the accounts given earlier of passivization. In particular, all PVs require a higher *do*. Passive constructions appear to conflict with this. Passive verbs are PVs and yet they appear under *be*. We accounted for this by introducing Do Replacement, which replaces *do* by *be* when Passive has applied to the complement of *do*.

Finally, we show that given the *do* analysis, there is no need to postulate a separate VP node. In terms of the present framework, Cs which have lost their subjects through operations like s-Raising, o-Raising, Equi, etc., correspond to one class of constituent often referred to as VPs. Thus, the concept of VP is partially real, but there is no need to recognize a special node label. Other uses of VP have no counterpart in the system described in this manual.

NOTES

1. In the structures presented in this chapter, we ignore the marking of tense, except where it is explicitly relevant. See note 10.

2. This comment ignores the special word order of the auxiliary verb and subject NP in the interrogative examples. This is treated in detail in Chapter 28, where it is shown to be a consequence of a rule called Subject-Auxiliary Inversion.

3. In Chapter 28, it is seen that this is a simplification.

4. The marking of tense is intimately connected with the phenomenon of subject-verb agreement, as follows. Only verbs inflected for tense can show agreement. However, the English agreement system is rather impoverished. Except with *be*, it only distinguishes third person singular from everything else. Further, even this distinction is only drawn in the present tense:

(i) a   Jack sings.
    b $\left\{ \begin{matrix} \text{I} \\ \text{They} \\ \text{you} \\ \text{we} \end{matrix} \right\}$ sing.

    c   Jacked worried.
    d $\left\{ \begin{matrix} \text{I} \\ \text{they} \\ \text{you} \\ \text{we} \end{matrix} \right\}$ worried.

We assume that there is an agreement rule, placing certain features on verbs dependent on the features of their subject NPs. But this rule operates at best only when the verbs in question have tense inflections.

5. There is one class of exceptions to this, namely, imperatives like

(i) a   Don't be silly.
    b   Do be careful.

in which there is no basis for assuming the presence of any tense (any more than in any other imperatives). We do not understand this and our rules do not account for it. We suspect that the *be* in sentences like (ia,b) is a late replacement for a distinct underlying verb, something like *act*. Semantically for instance, (ib) is not the imparative of (iia) but of something like (iib):

(ii) a   You are careful.
    b   You act careful(ly).

6. The derivation of (13b) from a structure like that of (12c') is more complicated. For not only must *do* erase, but its aspect ending must go on the complement verb of *do*. This process is remarkably parallel to that stated in

Tense Extraction for tense endings. In a fuller treatment, we would suggest an extension of Tense Extraction to cover aspect endings as well. There is, though, a difference between the aspect endings and tense endings with respect to *do*. As we have seen, stressed *DO*'s generally, and unstressed *do*'s sometimes, can occur with tense endings. But auxiliary *do*'s can never occur with aspect endings. Therefore, where Tense Extraction operates only under certain conditions for the tense endings, a more general rule would operate under all circumstances for the aspect endings. This is a further contrast between the auxiliaries *be* and *do*, since the former takes both aspect endings:

(i)   a   Melvin has been arrested (by the FBI).
       b   *The FBI has done arrested Melvin.
(ii)   a   Melvin is being interrogated by the guards.
       b   *The guards are doing interrogate Melvin.

7. There is at least one other set of conditions under which Tense Extraction must be blocked, illustrated by such cases as:

(i)   Jack didn't go but Bill did.
(ii)   Jack went and so did Bill.
(iii)   Jack didn't go, did he?

These all involve *anaphora*, that is, deletion of a portion of sentence structure which is identical to some other portion. Hence, (i) would seem to derive from a fuller structure of the form:

(iv)   [Jack didn't go but Bill did go]

A glance at our formulation of Tense Extraction in (21) in the text suggests that this rule can be blocked if it is ordered to follow all the deletion rules operative in cases like (i)–(iii). For, under those conditions, the V on which the extracted tense would be placed would no longer exist. The conditions for Tense Extraction would then not be met.

8. We have introduced no method of formally indicating stress. This is a weakness of the present description which it is not possible to overcome in an introductory work.

     Condition (b) of (21) says "contain any" because, in certain cases, for instance, negative questions like

(i)   Does he not know Spanish?

there will be both a *not* and a subject NP between *do* and its complement verb.

9. We noted earlier that no *do*'s at all occur in untensed surface clauses. We proposed to explain this by the fact that Do Erasure would delete all such occurrences. But this would not by itself explain the absence of stressed *do* in such clauses. However, there seems to be a general principle blocking stressed nonmodal auxiliaries in untensed clauses. So the problem seems to be solvable by a general constraint on the distribution of all stressed nonmodal auxiliaries:

(i) Melvin is believed to $\left\{ \begin{array}{c} \text{be} \\ \text{*BE} \end{array} \right\}$ sick.

(ii) Joan seems to $\left\{ \begin{array}{c} \text{have} \\ \text{*HAVE} \end{array} \right\}$ gone.

10. A natural way to treat tense in the present grammar is to assume that present and past, like the "future" *will*, are verbs in initial structure. They would also take the clauses in which they ultimately appear as their complements. So, in these terms, the initial structure of

(i) Bob was sick.

would be:

(ii)

Bob   [*sick*, Adj] [*be*, Aux] Past

There would then have to be affixation rules which attach Vs like Past to the main verb of their complements (in (ii), to *be*; see note 2 of Chapter 26). Note that in some languages, for example, French, the future forms, which in English show up as verbal words, are also affixed. Note also that Tense Extraction, like Affixation, Chomsky-adjoins (see note 3 of Chapter 17) the relevant affix to its V node.

An analysis like (ii) permits the insertion of tenses in initial structures without expanding the base rules. All that is required is entries for the particular items recognized. Present and Past will then be inserted just as other verbs listed in the lexicon. The difference is that Present and Past will trigger an affixation rule.

A parallel analysis can be suggested for the aspect endings. Therefore, an example like

(iii) Joan has been singing.

would have an ultimate initial structure along the lines of:

(iv)

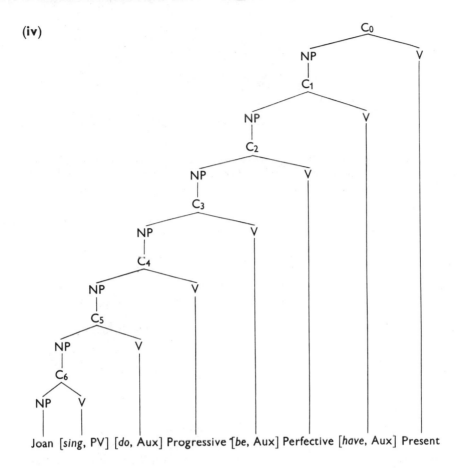

Joan [*sing*, PV] [*do*, Aux] Progressive [*be*, Aux] Perfective [*have*, Aux] Present

In such a treatment, all of the elements Present, Past, Perfective, and Progressive would have to undergo affixation rules. Moreover, these rules would apply before the obligatory application of s-Raising.

It is not hard to develop a formal analysis of tense and aspect along the lines of this note, one which is consistent with other assumptions we have made. But this lies beyond the scope of an introductory work. It is only fair to note, however, that such a treatment differs from that which is found in almost all current works on the transformational grammar of English. In these, tense and aspect endings are usually introduced directly as affixes by special base rules.

11. For example, the base rules and lexicon we have suggested would permit the derivation of the initial structure:

(i)

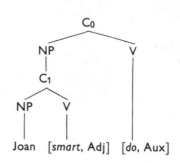

But, according to what we are now saying, (i) is nonetheless ill-formed, because it does not meet the conditions of the filter requiring Adj to be embedded directly below *be*. Thus, the filter accounts for the ill-formedness of examples like

(ii) *Joan does smart.

which are well-formed in terms of base rules and lexical insertion alone.

12. It may be possible to extend the rule in (27) to also introduce the past participle ending in those cases where it marks perfective aspect, as in:

(i) Jack has eaten. (Compare the passive: Jack was eaten by the boa constrictor.)

In such cases, it would be triggered not by the feature [... Passive ...] but by some mark of the aspect involved.

13. The fact that phrases like *pay up* and *sick* on the one hand, and *do* and *be* on the other, behave the same under this process is an argument for the treatment of this manual. For, in our terms, *do* and *be* are both members of the same category, nonmodal Aux V, and PVs and Adjs like *pay* and *sick* have common structure as Vs.

14. If it is necessary to refer to VPs in the existing sense as a group, this can be done without recognizing a special label. One can simply add to linguistic theory a *definition*, specifying a VP as a C node which has lost its subject NP in one of several ways. In these terms, VP would be a derivative concept reducible to more primitive notions like C, subject NP, etc.

PROBLEMS

1. What accounts for the ungrammaticality of:

(i) *It would be terrible for her to *do lose.

2. Describe the surface structure of:

(i) Priscilla must be ill.

3. Account for the ungrammaticality of the following:

 (i) *John do lost.
 (ii) *John did lose.

CHAPTER 28 INTERROGATIVES AND SUBJECT-AUXILIARY INVERSION

PREVIEW

In the preceding chapter, a fact about English word order was touched on; namely, in yes-no questions a surface word order appears which is different from the word order of declarative sentences. In these questions, the auxiliary verb associated with the sentence occurs before the subject. The base rule

(i)   C $\longrightarrow$ NP V (NP) (NP)

introduces an order with the subject first. There is no base rule of the form:

(ii) C $\longrightarrow$ V NP (NP) (NP)

Moreover, subject-creating rules like Passive and s-Raising help to generate a surface [Subject NP—V] word order. In order to account for the "inverted" word order of yes-no questions, we postulate a rule called *Subject-Auxiliary Inversion*. This chapter is devoted to specifying the conditions under which this rule operates. The account given reveals that the principles involved in yes-no questions are the same as those underlying the inverted order in information questions such as *Who did John invite to the party?* or *Who did Mary marry?*

The majority of English clauses containing subjects have a surface word order in which the subject NP precedes the main verb of the clause. There are, however, a number of types of clause in which this is not the case. Primary among these are standard interrogative clauses. We now consider the origin of the contrast between [Subject NP—V] (SV) and [V—Subject NP] (VS) word order in these cases.

The typical word order of English main clauses is shown in such *declarative* sentences as:

(1) a Melvin is sick.
    b Melvin has gone.
    c Melvin DOES like Patricia.
    d Melvin must call his aunt.

Here the main clauses, corresponding to the sentences as wholes, have main verbs which are auxiliaries. In each case, the subject NP, *Melvin*, precedes the auxiliary verb. However, as noted in Chapter 26, in yes-no questions, the standard word order has the auxiliary verb before the subject:

(2) a Is Melvin sick?
    b Has Melvin gone?
    c DOES Melvin like Patricia?
    d Must Melvin call his aunt?

This feature of verbs like *is, has, must*, etc., was seen to be one of the characteristic properties distinguishing auxiliaries from PVs like *eat, go*, etc.

In the grammatical description sketched in this manual, SV order in derived structures is a reflection of two factors. First, the order of elements generated in base structures by (3) gives all initial structure clauses SV order:

(3) C $\longrightarrow$ NP V (NP) (NP)

This rule guarantees that all surface structure clauses will have SV order *if* the surface subjects of these clauses correspond to their initial subjects. However, in almost all cases, the surface subjects of clauses in the present grammar are derived subjects, derived by such subject-creating rules as s-Raising, Passive, etc. Thus, in a case like (4a)

(4) a Melvin was kidnapped by the terrorists.
    b Was Melvin kidnapped by the terrorists?

Melvin is the surface subject of *was* as a result of an application of Passive and an application of s-Raising triggered by the auxiliary *be*. But note that, in our grammar, all subject-creating transformational rules place NPs in the position of initial structure subjects, that is, preverbally. Consequently, structures like (4a) derived by subject-creating rules are also predicted to end up in all cases with SV order. It remains unexplained how the order found in cases like (4b) is derived.

Since the grammar sketched up to this point will yield SV order for all clauses, it is evidently necessary to add at least one further statement to account for the VS order of those clauses which manifest it. For the range of cases under discussion here, we will assume that VS order is a function of the operation of a rule, called *Subject-Auxiliary Inversion*. This rule will interchange the positions of subject NPs and auxiliary verbs in some clauses. We now must determine the contexts in which it should operate.

Subject-Auxiliary Inversion must function in interrogative clauses but not in declarative clauses. The grammar will have to impose a formal categorization of this difference on clauses. This aspect of the grammar suggests new motivation for the traditional categorization of clauses into declarative, interrogative, imperative, etc. There would seem to be at least two different ways to mark such categorizations formally. One could assume that C nodes themselves are associated with syntactic features which mark these distinctions. Or, one could assume that different types of clauses are distinguished by morphemic-type markers, present in initial structures but later deleted. We shall make the latter choice. Suppose we assume the existence of such clause markers as $Q?$ (interrogative), D (declarative), and I (imperative). We can then replace rule (3) by the rules in (5a), which collapse into (5b):

(5) a $\quad$ C $\longrightarrow$ D NP V (NP) (NP)

$\qquad$ C $\longrightarrow$ Q? NP V (NP) (NP)

$\qquad$ C $\longrightarrow$ I NP V (NP) (NP)

$\quad$ b $\quad$ C $\longrightarrow$ $\begin{Bmatrix} D \\ Q? \\ I \end{Bmatrix}$ NP V (NP) (NP)

A fuller account would include further markers for exclamations, suggestions, etc. We have decided to generate these clause marker morphemes initially, because their effects tend to be toward the beginning of clauses. We thus are now assuming that every C^1 in trees initially contains one or another of the clause markers.

Subject-Auxiliary Inversion will have an environment which refers to the presence of the marker Q?, accounting for the fact that it does not apply in declarative clauses.[2] This is the first element determining the domain of its operation.

We have said that Subject-Auxiliary Inversion functions in interrogative clauses, by which we now mean those containing a Q?. This is, however, at best true only when the clauses in question are *main clauses*. There are a wide range of *embedded* interrogative clauses and, in standard English,[3] Subject-Auxiliary Inversion never functions in these:

(6) a $\quad$ I learned $\begin{Bmatrix} \text{when Gladys screamed} \\ \text{what Gladys ate} \\ \text{what he was proud of} \\ \text{who Gladys had hired} \\ \text{where we can move to} \end{Bmatrix}$.

b *I learned

when did Gladys scream
what did Gladys eat
what was he proud of
who had Gladys hired
where can we move to

.

In other words, we have so far ignored the fact that English has interrogative complements, that is, question C in the configuration:

(7)

NP
|
C
|
△

In terms of the rule (5b), these complements would begin with the morpheme Q?, whereas those complements considered up to this point, which were declarative, would have initial structures beginning with D. It can be seen from (6), though, that interrogative complements have the SV order typical of declarative clauses. In (6b), where all the complements have the form of well-formed independent clauses, the examples are ill-formed. It follows that Subject-Auxiliary Inversion does not apply in all clauses beginning with a Q?. The proper restriction would seem to be that the rule does not function when the Q?-containing clause is in the configuration in (7). This is the second feature of the environment we have determined.

We may now assume that Subject-Auxiliary Inversion operates uniformly[4] on main clause interrogatives of the yes-no variety. We have also illustrated that it operates in many cases of nonyes-no questions, those beginning with one of the interrogative words *who, what, when, where, why,* etc. However, among the latter type, there is a systematic exception, a class of examples where, *even in main clauses,* Subject-Auxiliary Inversion does not function. Contrast:

(8) a When did Bob give the apple to Martha?
     b Who did Bob give the apple to?
     c What did Bob give to Martha?
     d Who gave the apple to Martha then?
     e *Did who give the apple to Martha then?

The existence of (8d) and the impossibility of (8e) is perfectly regular for all types of interrogative clauses. That is, whenever the questioned NP, *who, what, which man,* etc., is the *subject* of the clause, Subject-Auxiliary Inversion does not function, and the clause is treated, with respect to the order of subject NP and V, like a declarative clause.

Why should inversion work for all yes-no questions and all information questions, except those where it is the subject NP that is being questioned?

What is it that all yes-no questions and all information questions except those with questioned subject NPs have in common? Our answer is that inversion is correlated with the existence of a certain kind of element *occurring in front of the* subject NP at the point where Subject-Auxiliary Inversion operates.

A glance at cases like (8) supports this view initially. In each case where Subject-Auxiliary Inversion does operate, a special kind of element is found in presubject position, namely, one of the question forms *who, when*, etc. Suppose any such form is referred to as a *WH phrase*. One hypothesis then is that the functioning of Subject-Auxiliary Inversion in interrogatives is connected to the existence of a WH phrase *in front of the subject*. This view would immediately explain the failure of inversion in cases like (8d,e), where it is the subject that is questioned. This follows since, in these, there is never a WH phrase in front of the subject. Rather, the subject itself is a WH phrase.

The problem which this proposal immediately raises is why Subject-Auxiliary Inversion works in yes-no questions, where there appears to be no WH phrase at all. A possible answer is provided when one considers the systematic relations between unembedded interrogative clauses and those which are embedded as complements. All of the cases of embedded clauses so far illustrated have been embedded information question clauses. Note though that, just as example (9b) corresponds to (9a)

(9) a Who did you hypnotize?
    b He knows who you hypnotized.

so does example (10b) correspond to (10a):

(10) a Did you hypnotize Fred?
     b He knows whether you hypnotized Fred.

In this case, the embedded yes-no interrogative clause contains a special element, *whether*, in front of the subject. Suppose one claims both (i) that this element is present in the remote structures of unembedded as well as embedded yes-no interrogative clauses; and (ii) that *whether* is a WH phrase, that is, a member of the same category of constituents as *who, what, when, which man*, etc. This would imply the existence of a rule to delete *whether* when it is not in a complement. Call this rule *Whether Deletion*. If Whether Deletion is ordered *after* Subject-Auxiliary Inversion, the presence of *whether* explains why yes-no questions behave exactly like information questions in which nonsubjects are questioned. That is, at the relevant stage, questions like

(11) a Will he come?
     b Is he sick?
     c Has he died?
     d Do you like him?

will have structures of the form:

(12) a [Q? whether he will come]
b [Q? whether he is sick]
c [Q? whether he has died]
d [Q? whether you do like him]

Thus all yes-no questions, like all those information questions in which non-subjects are questioned,[5] will have a WH phrase in front of their subject NPs. We have now determined the third necessary feature of the environment of Subject-Auxiliary Inversion: the presence of a presubject WH phrase.

Overall then, Subject-Auxiliary Inversion shifts the order of subject NP and V in a clause which:

(13) a Begins with a Q?;
b Is not a complement;
c Has a presubject WH phrase.

Before actually stating Subject-Auxiliary Inversion, it is worth describing one other detail of English clause structure. Although we are not attempting to deal with negation in this manual,[6] it has at several points been necessary to say a few words about negative elements (for instance, when noting in Chapter 27 how *not* blocks Tense Extraction and preserves auxiliary *do*). Now, as is well known, there are two different ways in which the basic negative *not* can appear in surface structures, as a separate word or *as a contraction* attached to a preceding auxiliary:

(14) a Melvin is not sick.   a′ Melvin isn't sick.
b Melvin has not left.   b′ Melvin hasn't left.
c Melvin does not read Spanish. c′ Melvin doesn't read Spanish.
d Melvin can not fly.   d′ Melvin can't fly.

We can assume that there is an optional rule, call it *Not Contraction*, which accounts for the shortened forms.[7]

Contracted negatives behave differently than noncontracted ones with respect to the inversion of subject NP and auxiliary V:

(15) a Is Melvin not sick?   a′ Isn't Melvin sick?
b Has Melvin not left?   b′ Hasn't Melvin left?
c Does Melvin not read Spanish? c′ Doesn't Melvin read Spanish?
d Can Melvin not fly?   d′ Can't Melvin fly?

(16) a Who did Jack not call?   a′ Who didn't Jack call?
b Why will you not resign?   b′ Why won't[8] you resign?

The examples in the left column of (15) and (16) sound formal and pedantic today. Nonetheless, they are no doubt still to be regarded as well-formed.

When Subject-Auxiliary Inversion operates, a contracted negative ends up in front of the subject NP. A noncontracted one does not. It is simple to account for these possibilities by adding to the description of Aux in Subject-Auxiliary Inversion a symbol for contracted *not*. If it is assumed that contracted *not*'s are incorporated under the V node, then the presence of such a symbol will specify that a contracted *not* is carried along to the new position by the rule. Hence we state:

(17) Subject-Auxiliary Inversion

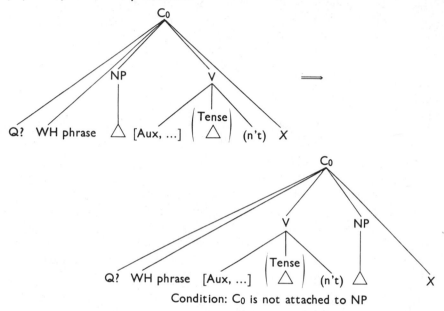

Condition: C_0 is not attached to NP

The optionality of Tense (indicated by parentheses around the Tense node) is due to the fact that the uninflectable auxiliaries, the modals, do not take tense though they do undergo Subject-Auxiliary Inversion. (We have said nothing about how the fact that modals do not take tense is to be dealt with. This would take us beyond the scope of this manual. The requisite mechanism involves the filters mentioned in Chapter 27 and in note 11 of that Chapter.)

If Not Contraction, operating before Subject-Auxiliary Inversion, contracts the *not* onto an auxiliary which undergoes the latter rule, the negative will end up on that auxiliary in front of the subject. If, however, the *not* is not previously contracted, it will be unaffected by the rule in (17) and hence maintain its position. It will thus end up after the subject NP, which is placed immediately after the auxiliary by (17).

Our description of Subject-Auxiliary Inversion in interrogative main clauses is based crucially on the presence of a WH phrase in a position in front of the subject NP. We have not, however, said anything about the origin of these WH phrases, how they are generated, or how they obtain presubject position. The case of *whether*, which we have taken to be the WH phrase underlying inversion in yes-no questions, is most recalcitrant. It is not even clear what category of constituent it belongs to. The problems concerning *whether* are so intricate[9] and so poorly understood that we cannot even attempt to say anything further in an introductory treatment of this kind.

What about the other WH phrases, *who, which (dog), when, why*, etc.? Two questions in particular are of relevance. How do such elements originate in base structures, and how do they achieve presubject position? Let us consider the latter first:

(18)   a   Shirley tossed the grenade to Bob in the garage.
      b   Who did Shirley toss the grenade to in the garage?
      c   What did Shirley toss to Bob in the garage?
      d   Which garage did Shirley toss the grenade to Bob in?

Example (18a) contains a subject NP, a direct object NP (*the grenade*), an indirect object NP (*Bob*), and a locative NP (*the garage*). In each of (18b–d), (i) one of these three NP types is absent from its standard position, and (ii) the clause-initial WH phrase is understood as the NP functioning like an NP in the empty position. Hence, in (18b) *who* is understood as the indirect object of *toss*, etc. This range of facts can be accounted for by positing a rule, call it *WH Fronting*, which relocates a certain class of NPs to clause-initial position in interrogative clauses. Which class of NPs? The answer is WH phrases.

Our assumption is that the grammar must somehow characterize a certain subset of NPs (as well as *whether*) as WH phrases. We will not delve here into how this might be done, whether by the presence of a particular morpheme, *wh*, by the presence of a syntactic feature [Wh] associated with the relevant NP nodes, or what. It is only clear that there must be a formal demarcation of this set of NPs.[10] Then, WH Fronting will move WH-phrase NPs to the front of clauses containing Q?. Observe that WH Fronting, unlike Subject-Auxiliary Inversion, operates in interrogative complements as well as in main clauses. It will thus be defined in terms of clause-initial Q?'s and WH phrases, with no analogue of the condition on Subject-Auxiliary Inversion precluding application when the C_0 is attached to a higher NP.

We will not attempt to actually state WH Fronting, whose fomulation involves many difficulties.[11] One problem is whether this rule is to be identified with the rule which operates to relocate many of the same types of phrases in *relative clauses*, both restrictive and appositive:

(19)   a   ... the guy who Shirley tossed the grenade to in the garage ...
      b   ... the grenade which Shirley tossed to Bob in the garage ...
      c   ... the garage which Shirley tossed the grenade to Bob in ...
      d   ... the garage where Shirley tossed the grenade to Bob ...

Another problem involves the possibility for certain, but not all, prepositions to accompany WH phrases when they are fronted. This accompaniment is sometimes optional, sometimes banned, and sometimes obligatory:

(20)   a   Which garage did you sleep in?
      b   In which garage did you sleep?

(21) a   Who are you fond of?
     b   *Of whom are you fond?

(22) a   *Which performance did she faint during?
     b   During which performance did she faint?

These and related questions make a productive study, on which there is already a rich literature. But space does not permit a further development here.

We limit ourselves to observing that Subject-Auxiliary Inversion depends crucially on the presence of presubject WH phrases. It is therefore necessary for WH Fronting to apply before Subject-Auxiliary Inversion. This raises the general question of the way the rules introduced in this chapter are ordered with respect to each other and how they are integrated with previous rules relevant to the verbal system. We will consider this matter briefly.

The crucial connection between Subject-Auxiliary Inversion and previous rules involves Tense Extraction. This rule removes tense suffixes from the auxiliary *do* and places them on the main verb of the complement of *do*, under certain conditions. In Chapter 27 we saw that Tense Extraction had to be blocked in certain cases. Among these are examples where Subject-Auxiliary Inversion applies with unstressed *do*:

(23) a   Do you understand medieval logic?
     b   Does Cynthia trust them?

Blockage of Tense Extraction preserves auxiliary *do* in these examples, permitting it to survive into surface structure. We claimed in Chapter 27 that the extraction of a tense suffix from unstressed *do* was blocked when this auxiliary is separated from its complement V by any of the elements *not, so,* or subject NP. But we now know that a subject NP in this position is a function of the operation of Subject-Auxiliary Inversion. The latter rule must therefore *precede* Tense Extraction to block extraction of tense in questions with inversion. Thus, the deletion of unstressed *do* in declaratives like (24a) and interrogatives like (24b) is a function of the fact that Tense Extraction is not blocked:

(24) a   He dove.
     b   Who dove?

In particular, in (24b), it is not blocked because Subject-Auxiliary Inversion did not apply (because there was no presubject WH phrase).

It seems then that we are led to the following overall ordering of rules relating to Subject-Auxiliary Inversion:[12]

(25)   WH Fronting
       Subject-Auxiliary Inversion
       Tense Extraction, Whether Deletion
       Do Erasure

WH Fronting must precede Subject-Auxiliary Inversion since it sometimes creates the conditions for the latter. Subject-Auxiliary Inversion must precede Tense Extraction since its operation prevents the former from applying incorrectly in certain cases. Similarly, Whether Deletion must follow Subject-Auxiliary Inversion because the *whether* must be present to trigger inversion in yes-no interrogatives. As indicated by their presence on the same line in (25), however, Tense Extraction and Whether Deletion have no necessary ordering relations with regard to each other. Finally, Do Erasure follows Tense Extraction for reasons discussed extensively in Chapter 27.

To conclude this brief description of interrogative clauses, we shall go over two characteristic derivations to illustrate the combined application of the different rules. Let us treat the examples:

(26) a Did Frank threaten Sue?
     b Who will Sue call?

After the application of s-Raising, (26a) will have a structure of the form:

(27)

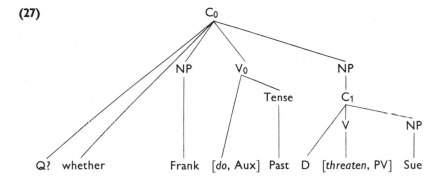

At this point, the rules in (25) would be checked and applied if applicable. WH Fronting is not applicable. Subject-Auxiliary Inversion will apply, since C_0 is not a complement, C_0 begins with Q?, and there is a presubject WH phrase, *whether*. Only at this stage can Tense Extraction be checked for application. But it is blocked, since the subject NP, *Frank*, now intervenes between *do* and its complement verb, *threaten*. Whether Deletion, which we have not stated,[13] will then remove this element, and Do Erasure is reached. But this is blocked since *do* has retained its tense suffix. All that is necessary to turn the result into the ultimate output, or at least the right input for the spelling rules, is removal of the type markers. Clearly, a special rule is required for just this purpose, since none of D, Q?, or I shows up as a morpheme in surface structure.

After the application of s-Raising, (26b) will have a structure of the form:

(28)

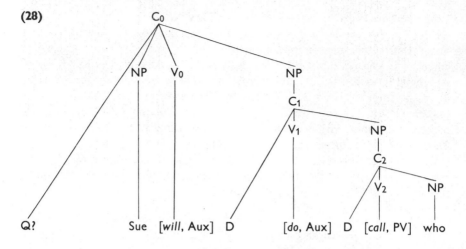

Here, WH Fronting is applicable, since there is a WH phrase, *who*, in an overall clause beginning with Q?. The NP *who* is thus reattached to C_0 next to Q?. The derivation moves to Subject-Auxiliary Inversion. Each of the crucial conditions for this is met. There is a Q?, a main verb which is an Aux (*will*), a presubject WH phrase, namely, *who* (which reached that position because of the previous operation of WH Fronting), and, finally, C_0 is not a complement. The rule then will place *will* in front of the NP *Sue*. Tense Extraction and Whether Deletion cannot apply and Do Erasure is reached in the ordering of rules. Since there is an auxiliary *do* with no suffix, this rule is applicable. The *do* will be deleted. Deletion of the type markers then essentially completes the derivation.

SUMMARY

This chapter has been devoted to specifying the rule Subject-Auxiliary Inversion. This rule is responsible for the VS word order which appears in yes-no questions and in those information questions in which constituents other than the subject NPs are questioned. The account specifies that Subject-Auxiliary Inversion is triggered by remote structure clauses which have three properties:

(i) They begin with a Q? marker.
(ii) They are not complements.
(iii) They have a presubject WH phrase.

These properties presuppose a certain amount of analysis. The Q? mentioned in (i) is part of a system of markers postulated to distinguish the three types of sentences encountered thus far; questions, declaratives, and imperatives. In a fuller treatment, more types would have to be distinguished. In standard English, inversion does not take place in complements; for example, *I wonder who John invited* but not **I wonder who did John invite*. Therefore, it is necessary to impose the restriction (ii). The failure of inversion to operate in information questions in which the subject is questioned was taken to show that inversion in information questions depends on the occurrence of a WH phrase in presubject position. This is the force of (iii). In this treatment, interrogative words and phrases like *who, what, when, which (man), what (story)*, etc., are members of a subcategory of NPs called WH phrases. The analysis involves postulation of a rule which moves WH phrases to clause-initial (and hence presubject) position. Such a rule was mentioned but not formulated.

The postulation of a WH phrase (namely, *whether*) in the presubject position of the initial structures of yes-no questions enables the inversion in these to be treated in the same way as that in information questions. Evidence in favor of this analysis is provided by the surface occurrence of *whether* in complement question clauses such as *I wonder whether John will come*. Whether Deletion is then required to erase *whether* from non-complement clauses.

Finally, the interaction of these phenomena with negative contraction was considered as was the relative ordering of the various rules postulated in this chapter with Tense Extraction and Do Erasure.

NOTES

1. The grammar must somehow impose restrictions on the types of clauses which can be embedded in various positions. For instance, it will have to guarantee that relative clauses, both restrictive and appositive, involve only D initial clauses, that a verb like *believe* takes D complements, but that *wonder* takes Q? complements. The best way to impose this class of restrictions is open. In particular, auxiliaries, which require obligatory subject complements, require in addition that these complements be declarative. Some earlier rules may have to be modified slightly to take account of the presence of the relevant clause markers. But we shall ignore this detail.

2. Actually, either Subject-Auxiliary Inversion or other rules with the same function operate in *some* declarative clauses:

(i) a   Never have I seen such nonsense.
      b   Seldom will all of them agree on any proposal.

Certain adverbs like *never* and *seldom* appear to be the crucial triggering elements for this inversion, but only when occurring in certain positions:

(ii) a   *Have I never seen such nonsense.
      b   I have never seen such nonsense.

Moreover, in certain conditional clauses, a similar inversion takes place:

(iii) a   If I were immortal, I would cancel my insurance.
       b   Were I immortal, I would cancel my insurance.
(iv) a   If he had two heads, his dentist bills would be higher.
      b   Had he two heads, his dentist bills would be higher.

It seems that there is a rule permitting *if* to delete from such clauses in a formal style, and that this obligatorily requires inversion. Similarly, examples of the following sort

(v) a   Don't you dare kiss my daughter.
      b   *You don't dare kiss my daughter (Well-formed only as a declarative.)

suggest that some inversion rule also operates in imperatives which preserve the subject pronoun. In this introductory work, we restrict attention to inversion linked to interrogative clauses.

3. There are dialects, normally regarded as substandard, in which inversion takes place in *some* embedded interrogative clauses. Where standard English has (ia), these dialects have (ib) as well-formed:

(i) a   I $\begin{Bmatrix} \text{want to} \\ \text{wanna} \end{Bmatrix}$ know who he dated.
     b   I wanna know who did he date.

For these variants, the condition on Subject-Auxiliary Inversion to be described in the text must be replaced by a weaker restriction.

4. We are ignoring here various types of interrogative clauses with declarative word order in which interrogation is marked only by intonation:

(i) You're happy?

On the assumption that these have initial structures containing Q?, we have no way to distinguish them from cases where inversion is obligatory. This indicates that there are subvarieties of interrogative clauses, but we have little understanding of this range of phenomena at the moment. It is thus not taken account of in our rules.

5. The question arises as to what guarantees that questioned nonsubjects are in presubject position at the relevant point. This is discussed in the text after Subject-Auxiliary Inversion is described further.

6. In particular, we have given no base rules to introduce negative forms.

7. For the most part, every auxiliary form has a contracted negative variant, with a few spelling irregularities:

  (i) *willn't = won't

However, *shall*, which has become increasingly marginal in modern American English, has no contracted variant for most speakers, *shan't* being archaic.

  A major gap in the system of contractions is that involving *am*:

  (ii) *amn't

This form, though widely used by young children, does not exist in the standard language. This has been the source of one of the traditional bugaboos of prescriptive grammatical instruction. The gap in (ii) is often filled by:

(iii) ain't

For some reason, however, *ain't* became a (mildly) tabooed form, associated with illiteracy and lack of education. The amount of energy which has been expended attempting to stamp out *ain't* is remarkable. For speakers for whom *ain't* is truly not part of the language system, the gap created by the lack of *amn't* is unfilled. The actual use of *ain't* is not limited to filling the gap noted in (ii). It is also used as a contraction for all of the forms of *be*, regardless of person or number.

8. See note 7 for the origin of this form.

9. The word *whether* is actually related to the disjunction *either*, in roughly the way *who* is related to *someone*, and *what* to *something*. Thus, the study of *whether* leads into the realm of coordination. Note such parallelisms as:

  (i) I said that either he came or (he did) not (come).
  (ii) I know whether he came or (did) not (come).

And note the possible manifestation of these disjunctive elements even in unembedded clauses:

(iii) Did he come or not?

These reinforce our confidence that it is proper to recognize *whether* in examples like (iii). But they show that a serious treatment is not possible independent of a general consideration of disjunction.

10. In view of such parallelisms as

  (i) $\begin{Bmatrix} \text{some} \\ \text{what} \end{Bmatrix}$ man

  (ii) $\begin{Bmatrix} \text{someone} \\ \text{who} \end{Bmatrix}$

(iii) $\begin{Bmatrix} \text{something} \\ \text{what} \end{Bmatrix}$

(iv) $\begin{Bmatrix} \text{somewhere} \\ \text{where} \end{Bmatrix}$

it seems likely first, that membership in the category of WH phrases is determined by the type of article that an NP has and second, that the one-word WH phrases like *what, who, where*, etc., are a function of the same operation creating one-word pronouns like *someone, somewhere*, etc., alongside the typical two-word constructions *some object, some person*, etc.

11. One problem of relevance concerns cases like

(i) Who called who?

in which more than one NP is questioned. Quite regularly in such cases Wh Fronting does not apply:

(ii) *Who did who call?

Although representing this fact is a difficulty for the formulation of the WH fronting rule, note how it supports the claim that Subject-Auxiliary Inversion is dependent on a presubject WH phrase. For, as illustrated by (i), when WH Fronting fails to apply, so does Subject-Auxiliary Inversion.

12. Not Contraction is not mentioned in (25) since we know of no necessary ordering relations between this operation and other rules of relevance here. It must simply be able to apply before Subject-Auxiliary Inversion. But this is accounted for by having it unordered with respect to all rules. Such an unordered status means that the rule can freely apply whenever its conditions are met.

13. It would seem that *whether* is deleted whenever it appears as a constituent of a noncomplement clause.

PROBLEMS

1. What aspect of our treatment of Subject-Auxiliary Inversion is supported by the following examples:

(i) You went where?
(ii) She married who?
(iii) You learned to do what with whom?

(The rising lines indicate rising intonation, used to express incredulity.)

2. Explain the position of the *n't* in:

(i) Isn't that a giraffe?

3. Give the initial tree for the sentence:

(i) Was it discovered by the police who Gladys called?

PART V CONCLUSION

CHAPTER 29 **THE PRINCIPLE OF CYCLIC APPLICATION**

PREVIEW

In previous chapters, we have recognized a number of particular rules. These can interact in many possible ways. At points in earlier discussions (see Chapter 21, (6)–(10), for example), it became crucial to consider the way different rules interacted in a single derivation. At such points, we often assumed that the rules involved would apply in some needed order. We did not ask, however, whether anything guaranteed that they applied in the required order and only that. Though we have dealt with only a handful of cases of rule interactions in this manual, there are, in fact, enormous numbers of sentences in which complex rule interactions occur. In many of these, problems of rule application order can arise unless general principles guarantee the proper application sequence.

In this chapter, we first examine sentences involving a single relevant rule, Equi. We show that in derivations in which Equi applies more than once, it is necessary to impose a specific constraint on the way it applies. Namely, it must apply to more deeply embedded Cs before higher level Cs can be operated on. Moreover, successive applications of Equi must apply to successively less deeply embedded Cs. This process iterates up remote trees until the highest C has been reached and no further applications are possible. This principle of application is called the *cyclic principle*.

We then examine cases where one or more of the following rules are involved: Reflexivization, s-Raising, o-Raising, Passive, Quantifier Floating. We show that potential problems of rule ordering do not arise if all these rules apply according to the cyclic principle. In particular, the cyclic principle is shown to be absolutely crucial to guarantee that the clause mate constraint functions as necessary in the operation of Reflexivization. The discussion of cyclic application is thus the final improvement of the description of reflexive marking which played such a central role in the beginning of this work.

In this chapter, we consider an important principle which controls the interaction of a subset of the transformational rules we have discussed. This is called the principle of the transformational cycle, or the *cyclic principle* for short. The cyclic principle is to a significant extent implicit in many of the discussions of earlier chapters. Our goal is to make it explicit and to show how it explains the way several of the rules we have recognized interconnect when applying in the same derivation.

Recall that in Chapter 11 we introduced a controlled deletion rule which works on complements. Equi erases the subject pronoun of a complement clause when this is coreferential to the subject of the next most inclusive clause. This rule is at work in:

(1) a Jack wants her to go.

   b *Jack$_i$ wants him$_i$ to go. $\xrightarrow{\text{Equi}}$

   c Jack wants to go.

(2) a Martha arranged for me to win.

   b *Martha$_i$ arranged for her$_i$ to win. $\xrightarrow{\text{Equi}}$

   c Martha arranged to win.

These schematic derivations ignore certain complexities underlying the infinitival complements, in particular, the fact that each involves an occurrence of the auxiliary *do*. Since these are marginal to present concerns, we will not pay attention to them for the moment.

It is worth reiterating that the deletion performed by Equi is only possible when the complement subject to be deleted is coreferential with the subject in the *immediately higher* clause. Call this the *Immediacy Condition*. Thus the example

(3) Martha$_i$ wanted Bob to arrange for her$_i$ to win.

is well-formed and cannot be converted by Equi to:

(4) Martha wanted Bob to arrange to win.

For, although (4) is well-formed, it is not related to (3). Rather it derives from:

(5) *Martha wanted Bob$_j$ to arrange for him$_j$ to win.

And (5) meets the Immediacy Condition.
Consider now:

(6) Martha wanted to arrange to win.

A comparison with (1)–(5) as well as a consideration of the meaning of (6) shows that it involves *two* applications of Equi. Example (6) is understood in such a way that both *win* and *arrange* have underlying subjects coreferential with the NP *Martha*. Therefore, the initial structure of (6) would have to be along the following lines, ignoring questions of tense and auxiliary:

(7)

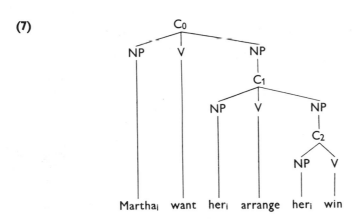

To derive (6) from (7), Equi must apply twice: once to the subject of *win*, and once to the subject of *arrange*. However, if Equi applies first to the subject of *arrange*, it will never be able to apply to the subject of *win* because the Immediacy Condition would never again be met. A grammar with such an order of rule applications would wrongly predict the well-formedness of examples like:

(8) *Martha$_i$ wanted to arrange for her$_i$ to win.

Thus, in a proper grammar of English, some principle must guarantee that, given a structure like (7), Equi applies to the subject of *win* before it applies to subject of *arrange*. Because the situation in (6) and (8) is the regular one, there is a general problem here. Since only a single rule is involved, there is no possible solution in terms of rule ordering.

However, there is a general principle which will perform the function required. In a configuration like (7), there are Cs embedded within Cs embedded within Cs, that is, more and more inclusive embedding. This can continue without bound, as illustrated in earlier discussions of recursion and the infinitude of the set of sentences. In such structures, it is possible to identify the most deeply embedded C, the nextmost, etc.[1] In (7), for instance, C_2 is the most deeply embedded structure, C_1 the next, and C_0 the next. We assume that for any language, English included, there is a group of transformational rules, called *cyclic rules*. With respect to successively embedded structures like (7), cyclic rules apply as follows:

(9) The cyclic rules are applied first to the most deeply embedded structure, only then to the next most, and so on. Once all applicable cyclic rules have been applied to a particular level, operation passes to the next higher C, and never returns. Within each level, optional rules may or may not apply and obligatory rules must, as expected.

Principle (9) is referred to as the *principle of cyclic application,* or the *cyclic principle.*

Suppose we assume that Equi is a cyclic rule. Return to (7). Given principle (9), Equi will be applied first in the lowest or most deeply embedded structures, and only then in higher ones. Thus, it will apply first in C_1 and only then in C_0. In general, therefore, one application of Equi could never block another in a lower part of a tree.

Given the cyclic principle, all that need be said to make the original description of Equi in Chapter 11 work properly for complex trees like (7) is the specification that Equi is one of the cyclic rules. It is reasonable to say that the cyclic principle explains the behavior of Equi in cases like (7). However, this explanation would be more profound if it did not simply assert a brute fact about Equi—that it is a cyclic rule. That is, the explanation would be more profound if the membership of Equi in the class of cyclic rules followed from some general principle. One possible principle which would have this effect is:

(10) All (controlled) coreferential deletion rules are cyclic.

If a principle like (10) is valid,[2] then the presence of the English rule Equi among the set of cyclic operations is not something which has to be learned by speakers of English. Rather, it is a predictable consequence of (10), given the kind of formal operation Equi performs.

It is worth going over in detail how the derivation of (6) proceeds, given a fuller underlying structure in which the auxiliaries required by the discussions in earlier chapters are present. The more complete remote structure of (6) would be:

(11)

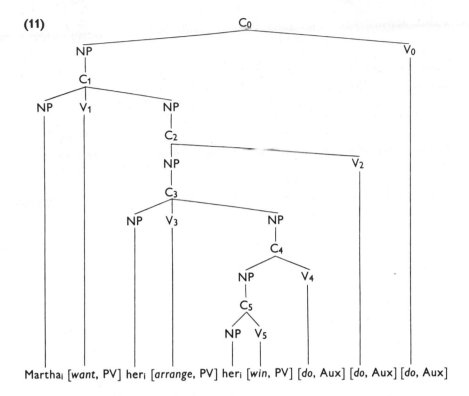

Martha$_i$ [*want*, PV] her$_i$ [*arrange*, PV] her$_i$ [*win*, PV] [*do*, Aux] [*do*, Aux] [*do*, Aux]

In (11), the cycle will begin at C_5. But no rule of relevance can apply. At C_4, s-Raising will work, and her$_i$ rises to become subject of C_4. At C_3, Equi can be checked for application and there are two coreferents. One is the main clause subject, the other the subject of the complement, due to the previous application of s-Raising. Hence the Immediacy Condition holds within the derived C_3. Equi can apply, deleting the derived subject of the complement of *arrange*, that is, the derived subject of C_4. On the C_2 cycle, the subject of the complement of V_2, her$_i$, is raised by s-Raising to become the new subject of C_2. At the level of C_1, Equi is again potentially applicable. The Immediacy Condition is met, since the original subject of *arrange* is now subject of V_2, *do*, and hence subject of the complement of *want*. Equi will then apply to delete this occurrence of her$_i$ also. Finally, on the C_0 cycle, *Martha* is lifted to be subject of C_0 by s-Raising. The derivation thus proceeds as required, even when auxiliary verbs are taken into account, given the necessary assumption that s-Raising is cyclic. This will be further supported below.

In describing the derivation of (6) from (11), we did not mention the need for Do Erasure to apply to all three occurrences of *do*. And not marking tense obscures the fact that Tense Extraction would also have to apply prior to that application of Do Erasure which removes the highest *do*. In introducing the principle of the cycle, we allowed for the existence of noncyclic transformations. There is evidence that many transformations fall into a block of postcyclical rules, which only apply after the cyclic transformations have operated at every level. Our guess is that rules like Tense Extraction and Do Erasure are postcyclic. In any event, we know of no reason to assume they are cyclic. We will not discuss postcyclic rules in the present work.

We have shown that the cyclic principle explains the way Equi applies to complex structures which meet its conditions at several different levels. So far, this is the only basis offered for the cyclic principle. It is easy to show, however, that the same principle is required for other rules given earlier, when these interact in complex cases.

Earlier discussions isolated the following four operations:

(12) a Passive
      b s-Raising
      c o-Raising
      d Reflexivization

Indeed, much of the early part of this manual was devoted to elaborating and refining the description of Reflexivization, whose final statement is found in Chapter 17. These rules have largely been considered in isolation. At this point, it is of importance to analyze some of the ways they interrelate. For this reveals in another way the role of the cyclic principle in the overall operation of grammatical rules.

Following are *some* of the crucial features of the rules in (12):

(13) a Passive turns objects of clauses into new derived subjects of those clauses.
      b s-Raising turns subject complement subjects into main clause subjects.
      c o-Raising turns object complement subjects into main clause objects.
      d Reflexivization determines the particular reflexive shape *self* for pronouns with coreferential antecedents, provided that antecedent and pronoun meet the clause mate condition.

Now let us turn to an example:

(14) $Jack_i$ considered $himself_i^1$ to have proved $himself_i^2$ to have been slandered by the *News*.

If one wishes pronouns in the positions of the two reflexive NPs in sentences such as (14) to be coreferential to $Jack_i$, they *must* be reflexive in form. We are interested in determining how and why these two NPs are reflexivized, given the general principles governing reflexives.

Taking account of what has been previously established about Reflexivization, $himself_i^2$ must have $himself_i^1$ as its antecedent, while the latter must have $Jack_i$ for an antecedent. It follows from (13d) that $himself_i^1$ and $himself_i^2$ must be clause mates at the point when Reflexivization applies to them and that $Jack_i$ and $himself_i^1$ must be clause mates at the point when Reflexivization applies to them. Something in the grammar of English must guarantee that these conditions are met in the derivation of (14) from its initial structure. Let us consider what can be determined about this structure.

Consider is a verb like *believe*, that is, a trigger of o-Raising. Thus, everything after the word *considered* in (14) was *originally* part of the single complement of *considered*. The derivational ancestor of $himself_i^1$ got lifted out of that clause and made a constituent of the main clause by an application of o-Raising. This made it the derived object of *considered*. Next, the complement of *considered* is itself a complex structure with a main verb *proved*, which also takes a complement object. Further, *prove* is also a trigger for o-Raising. Thus, everything after the word *proved* in (14) was originally part of the complement clause of *proved*. However, the NP which ends up as $himself_i^2$ ceased to be part of that clause as a result of a distinct application of o-Raising. After this, it became the derived object of *proved*.

Finally, consider the complement of *proved*. The element which is raised out of this clause by o-Raising had to be a subject of the complement at the point of o-Raising application. That is, $himself_i^2$ in (14) had to be the complement subject at that point. However, the complement of *proved* is passive in form. Consequently, $himself_i^2$ only became subject of that complement as a function of the application of Passive within the complement of *proved*. If this had *not* happened, then the NP *the News* would have stayed subject of that clause. And, if everything else remained the same, one would have derived, instead of (14):

(15) $Jack_i$ considered $himself_i$ to have proved the *News* to have slandered him_i.

In this, him_i and not a reflexive form is required:

(16) *$Jack_i$ considered $himself_i$ to have proved the *News* to have slandered $himself_i$.

In this description of sentence (14), we have ignored what was established in Chapters 25–27 about the origin of auxiliaries like *have*, the role of *do*, etc. If we wish to specify an initial structure for (14) which is as complete as possible given our understanding to this point, these factors have to be included. The most complete initial structure of (14) in terms of earlier descriptions, ignoring tense and aspect endings, is (17).

(17)

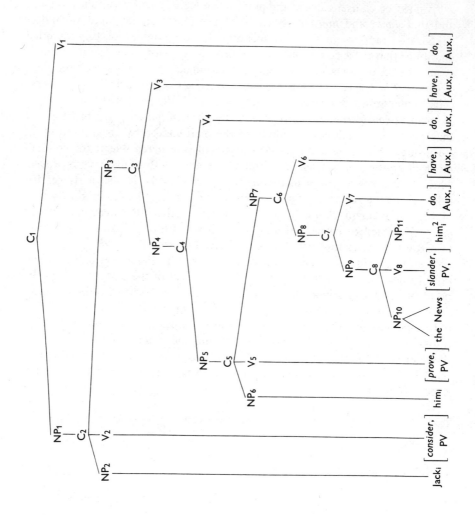

A good deal of the complexity of (17) is due to those structures underlying the auxiliaries *have* and *do* (the latter delete). Since we have already
considered auxiliaries in earlier chapters, it is convenient to approach the
structure of (14) by abstracting away from them temporarily. Let us therefore
suppress from (17) all of those structures involving auxiliaries. This permits
suppression of five of the eight Cs and five of the eight Vs in (17). We emerge
with a more manageable structure:

(18)

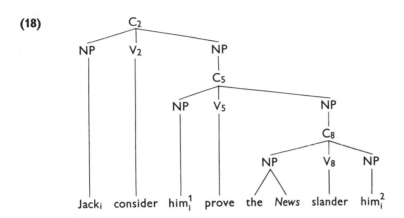

Note that those structures of (17) which remain in (18) have kept the same
numbering. This brings out the fact that (18) is merely a device to simplify
our exposition.

Previous discussion shows that, to derive (14) from (18), several applications of o-Raising, one of Passive, and several of Reflexivization are required.
We claimed that Passive applied in C_8, making him_i^2 the derived subject of
C_8. This then underwent o-Raising, and hence was lifted into C_5, where it
becomes a clause mate of him_i^1. Similarly, at some point, o-Raising must
apply to him_i^1, the subject of C_5, and make it a derived object of C_2 and
hence a clause mate of $Jack_i$.

One must say that it is the raising of him_i^2 into C_5 and the raising of him_i^1
into C_2 that permits (in fact, requires) the reflexivization of these NPs. It is
only these applications of o-Raising that bring about the clause mate status
of antecedent and pronoun which Reflexivization is known to require. There
is, however, a problem lurking in an account of the derivation of (14), which
depends on two separate applications of o-Raising. In (18), none of the three
coreferential NPs are clause mates. Thus, Reflexivization is not determined
by the initial structure configurations. Similarly, none of the three NPs are
clause mates in the surface structure of (14). This structure would be, taking
into account all of the rules, all of the structure of (17), the role of Do Erasure,
etc., as follows (where the numbering of C nodes again corresponds to that
in (17)):

(19)

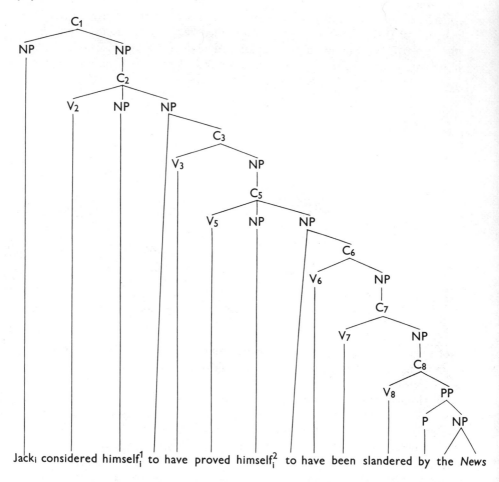

We have discovered the following significant and perhaps surprising fact. Two NPs which function as antecedent and pronoun for an application of the rule Reflexivization, which requires such pairs to be clause mates, are clause mates *neither* in initial structure *nor* in surface structure. The only possible conclusion is that these NPs are clause mates *at some intermediate stage in the derivation.*

Let us consider the structure of (18) again to determine whether this is the case, or, rather under what conditions it will or will not be the case. With respect to (18), we have seen that o-Raising triggered by *prove* cannot possibly apply until Passive has applied within C_8. In other words, it cannot apply until a stage, like the following which is the output of Passive, has been derived:

(20)

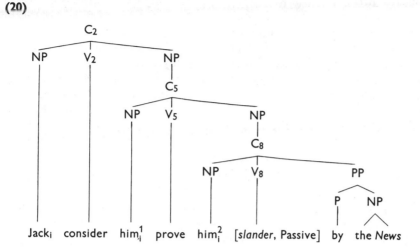

We know that in order to derive (19), it is necessary that both him_i^2 and him_i^1 undergo separate applications of o-Raising. Now the key point is reached. If one is going to explain the facts in (14) and (15), it must be (i) possible for the two NPs which end up as reflexives to become clause mates during some intermediate stage of derivation and (ii) impossible for them not to become clause mates at some intermediate stage. If only (i) were met, the grammar could derive (14), but it would also wrongly permit the impossible:

(21)   *Jack$_i$ considered himself$_i$ to have proved him$_i$ to have been slandered by the *News*.

Therefore, a correct grammar must somehow meet both of the conditions (i) and (ii).

Condition (i) will be met if o-Raising applies to him_i^2 in (20) before it applies to him_i^1. That is, it will be met if, in general, with respect to structures like (20), o-Raising applies in C_5 before it applies in C_2. If this is the case, the two NPs in question will be clause mates in C_5, before o-Raising applies again at the higher level to extract him_i^1 from C_5 and make it a constituent of C_2. If, however, o-Raising applied at the higher level first, there would be no stage at which the relevant NPs were clause mates. It follows that for conditions (i) and (ii) above to be met, something must provide the following guarantee. In a derivation where multiple applications of o-Raising occur, the application in a clause like C_5 necessarily precedes that in a clause like C_2.

Significantly, the cyclic principle appealed to in the discussion of examples with multiple applications of Equi provides the needed guarantee here, if it is assumed that o-Raising and Reflexivization are cyclic rules. The cyclic principle guarantees with respect to (20) and analogous derivations that there is an intermediate structure in which $him_i{}^1$ and $him_i{}^2$ are clause mates. Given that principle, the application of o-Raising triggered by *consider*, which is in a higher level of structure than *prove*, cannot precede the application of o-Raising triggered by *prove*. Therefore, in any such derivation, the correspondent of $him_i{}^2$ in surface structure must be reflexive in form, accounting for the occurrence of (14) and the ill-formedness of (16). The implications of the cyclic principle for cases like (20) can be expressed in a slightly different way as follows. In such derivations, a single rule, o-Raising, moves one NP *into* a certain clause, C_x, from a lower clause, and moves another NP *out of* C_x, into a higher clause. Given the cyclic principle, these operations must always take place in such a way that the NP entering C_x enters before the NP leaving C_x leaves. The two NPs will then be clause mates at an intermediate stage.

The cyclic principle says that for a specified class of transformational rules, operations on embedded structures can effect those on higher structures, but not conversely. For instance, operation of Passive in the lowest C, C_8 of (20), determines that o-Raising at the next level will raise what was originally the object NP of C_8 rather than its original subject. The claim is that the opposite sort of thing will never happen. That is, there are no cases where, for instance, application of Passive on a main clause determines which NP o-Raising operates on when applying in a subordinate clause embedded in that main clause. Put differently, there are rules like o-Raising, s-Raising, etc., which refer to certain properties of an embedded clause, such as "subject of that clause." The cyclic principle correctly predicts which subjects will be extracted by these rules. They will be those NPs which are subjects after application of all the cyclic rules to the embedded clause. Hence, it is really the cyclic principle which predicts that o-Raising, s-Raising, etc., necessarily operate on the derived subjects produced by Passive and similar rules.

The principle of cyclic application thus guarantees that, for sentences like (14), those NPs which must be clause mates for Reflexivization to operate correctly go through a stage where they are clause mates. This stage is neither at the level of initial structure nor at the level of surface structure. Among other things, such an account provides one of the most striking kinds of argument for the existence of intermediate levels of remote structure.

The argument for the cyclic principle based on the interaction of o-Raising and Reflexivization was given in terms of (18). This, however, is not a real initial structure in our terms but only a simplification of the genuine structure found in (17). The question is whether our description carries over to the complex structure. The fact that it does depends on two key assumptions:

(22) a Every V of (17) suppressed to get (18) is an obligatory s-Raising trigger.

        b s-Raising, like o-Raising, Reflexivization and Passive, is a cyclic rule.

The cyclic principle insists that all cyclic rules must be applied from bottom to top in tree structures. It is easy to see that the structure C_1 in (17),[3] which would only be reached at the end of the cyclic part of the derivation, is really irrelevant to questions of reflexives. This is so since it is superordinate to those levels which contain coreferential elements. The suppression of this aspect of (17) thus surely did not distort the account of what takes place. However, elements like V_1, V_3, V_4, V_6, and V_7 are within the domain where Reflexivization must apply, since some of them intervene between structures containing coreferents. They thus cannot be ignored in a description of how Reflexivization applies to such complex structures.

So, let us briefly sketch what will happen to (17), given (22). The derivation will commence in the most deeply embedded C, which is C_8. Passive is applicable, and will apply. This makes him_i^2 the new subject of C_8. At this point, the cycle moves to the next most inclusive C, C_7. Here the only rule of relevance which can apply is s-Raising. This is obligatory with the auxiliary do^4 and hence must make him_i^2 the new subject of C_7. At this point, the cycle moves to C_6. Again the only rule of relevance is s-Raising. This again applies obligatorily, making him_i^2 the new subject of C_6. Now, only at this point is the cycle of C_5 reached. This clause is headed by an o-Raising trigger, *prove*. The rule o-Raising raises the subject of the complement of the trigger. The complement of C_5 is C_6. And we have just seen that at the point where o-Raising can apply on the cycle of C_5, the subject of C_6 is him_i^2, due to several previous cycles on which s-Raising applied. Hence on the cycle of C_5, it is him_i^2 which becomes the derived object of C_5 and a clause mate of the subject of *prove*. But since at that stage these clause mates are coreferential, Reflexivization will apply on the cycle of C_5. This ultimately has the effect of turning him_i^2 into $himself_i^2$, as required. On the next, or C_4 cycle, the main V is auxiliary *do*, which is an s-Raising trigger. So the subject of C_5 is turned into the new subject of C_4. On the C_3 cycle, the same thing happens and him_i^1 becomes the subject of *have*. On the C_2 cycle, the main V is an o-Raising trigger, and the subject of the complement of that V is raised. But previous s-Raising applications have determined that at the C_2 stage of the cycle, that complement subject is him_i^1. Hence this rises up to become the derived object of *consider*, long *after* it served as the antecedent for Reflexivization during the C_5 cycle. Then, on the following C_1 cycle, $Jack_i$ will undergo application of s-Raising, triggered by the highest *do* in (17).

It follows that the simplification of our description of the interaction of Reflexivization and o-Raising, which led to the introduction of the artifact in (18), had no erroneous effects. It simply served to eliminate a number of cycles on which particular NPs undergo s-Raising. None of the results of the discussion were distorted.

The cyclic principle also plays a role in accounting for the interaction of s-Raising and Reflexivization in cases where the former is triggered by Vs like *seem.* This was discussed in Chapter 21 at a point where we could not appeal to the cyclic principle.

Consider:

(23) Joan$_i$ seems to me to understand $\left\{ \begin{array}{l} \text{me} \\ \text{*myself} \\ \text{herself}_i \\ \text{*her}_i \end{array} \right\}$.

(24) I seem to Joan$_i$ to understand $\left\{ \begin{array}{l} \text{*me} \\ \text{myself} \\ \text{*herself}_i \\ \text{her}_i \end{array} \right\}$.

We explained such facts earlier (see (6)–(10) of Chapter 21) simply by saying that Reflexivization applied in such cases before s-Raising. But we could not say at that point what prevented s-Raising from applying first, wrongly destroying the clause mate relationship before Reflexivization applied. It is now clear that it is the cyclic principle which guarantees that Reflexivization applies first in such cases. This principle requires that all cyclic rules be checked for application and applied on more deeply embedded structures first. But, in the initial structure of examples like (23), *Joan$_i$* is the complement subject. Therefore, the conditions for Reflexivization are met on the cycle of *understand*. But s-Raising only becomes applicable on the cycle defined by *seem*. Since the two occurrences of *me* never get to be clause mates, Reflexivization can never apply to them. Example (24) illustrates essentially the same points. The only difference is that in (24), a first person form was subject of the underlying complement of *seem*.

A final note on Reflexivization is in order. In our earlier accounts of this process, before we had worked out the analysis of auxiliaries as main Vs triggering s-Raising, before the discussion of Do Erasure, and before the introduction of the cyclic principle, we frequently claimed that particular pairs of NPs were clause mates. Thus, we would have said that the italicized NPs were clause mates in:

(25) *Harriet* is overly critical of *herself*.

We gave the impression at that point that such NPs were surface structure clause mates. This is incorrect. It can now be seen that in all such cases, the relevant NPs are actually only clause mates before s-Raising applies. Notice that in the description we have developed here, even the italicized NPs in

(26) *Harriet* understands *herself*.

are not *surface* clause mates. *Harriet* is a surface constituent of the main clause, whose main verb has been erased by Do Erasure. *Herself* is a constituent of the complement of *do*. Of course, they were clause mates during the cycle determined by *understand*, so the specification of reflexive form is perfectly regular. Thus, the distortion in our earlier discussion, necessitated by a lack of theoretical development at that stage, is benign.

We have illustrated the need for the cyclic principle with derivations involving multiple applications of Equi, interactions between o-Raising and Reflexivization, and interactions between Reflexivization and s-Raising. The cyclic principle, which we believe to be one of the major theoretical insights of transformational grammar, also plays a critical role in the description of the rule Quantifier Floating, given in Chapter 24 and heavily relied on in Chapter 25. We will conclude our account of the cyclic principle by considering the need for such a principle in this domain.

The basic generalization about the floating Qs *all*, *both*, and *each* is that they can be extracted from a complex NP and attracted to a particular verb, only if the complex NP is a subject of that verb. In a variety of cases like (27)–(29) a floating Q can occur in more than one position:

(27)   a   The boats all have sunk.
        b   The boats have all sunk.

(28)   a   The boats all will sink.
        b   The boats will all sink.

(29)   a   The boats all seem to have sunk.
        b   The boats seem to all have sunk.
        c   The boats seem to have all sunk.

We took distributions like these to be evidence that the complex NPs underlying such cases had been subjects of different verbs at different stages. This was due to the functioning of s-Raising. However, this formulation remained relatively vague since we did not specify explicitly how Quantifier Floating interacted with s-Raising to produce the alternative positionings of Q. Given the cyclic principle, however, it is easy to do this if it is assumed that Quantifier Floating is a cyclic rule.

Moreover, one must assume that Quantifier Floating is ordered after certain rules, in fact, after every rule capable of creating derived subjects. The reason is this. Derived subjects are suitable sources for floating Qs, and NPs which were subjects but cease to be are not suitable sources with respect to a particular clause. Compare the following examples in which application of Passive is critical:

(30)   a   All of the hawks saw the armadillo.
        b   The hawks all saw the armadillo.
        c   The armadillo was seen by all of the hawks.
        d   *The armadillo was all seen by the hawks.

(31)   a   The cook peeled both of the onions.
        b   *The cook both peeled the onions.

c   Both of the onions were peeled by the cook.
d   The onions were both peeled by the cook.

In (30d), the derivational ancestor of *the hawks* was originally a subject of *see*, just as in (30a). But it ceases to be such when Passive operates. And the Q cannot float away from this ex-subject. Thus Quantifier Floating should be ordered after Passive. In (31b), the ancestor of *the onions* is not part of a subject, but of an object. Quantifier Floating is thus blocked. But Passive makes this NP part of a subject. And then, as (31d) shows, Quantifier Floating can apply. Therefore, what acts as a subject with respect to Quantifier Floating is again determined by the output of Passive, even within a single cycle. This is accounted for if Quantifier Floating is ordered after Passive. In the same way, one can show that Quantifier Floating must follow other subject-creating rules, including s-Raising.

The alternative positions of Q, as in (27)–(29), turn out to involve nothing more than differences as to what cycles the optional rule of Quantifier Floating is applied on. To see this, consider (28a,b), which would have the initial structure:

(32)

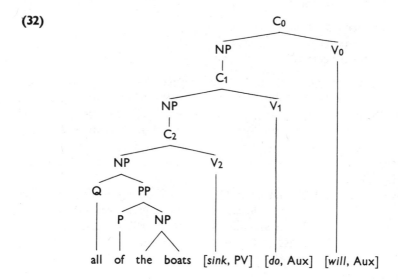

The relevant rules are s-Raising and Quantifier Floating. The cycle will begin at the deepest level, C_2. If Quantifier Floating, which is optional, applies, *all* will become a constituent of C_2, being attracted to *sink*, and (28b) will be derived. At the level of C_1, s-Raising is obligatory. If Quantifier Floating did not apply on the first cycle, it can do so on the second cycle *only* after s-Raising, which it follows in the ordering of rules. The Q would then become a constituent of C_1.[5] At the level of C_0, s-Raising is once more obligatory. As before, if Quantifier Floating did not apply on previous cycles, it becomes applicable at this last cycle. If it applies, the Q will be attracted to *will* and become a constituent of C_0. Example (28a) results. The alternative positions in sets like (27)–(29) are thus a natural function of rules like s-Raising and Quantifier Floating, if these apply cyclically. As s-Raising creates new subjects, it creates new environments for Quantifier Floating.

To conclude this discussion, recall a remark made earlier about Equi. We stressed that a more profound explanation of the facts would exist if some principle guaranteed that English Equi was a cyclical rule. Such a principle was tentatively proposed. Obviously, the analogous remark holds for other rules we have argued to be cyclical, s-Raising, o-Raising, Passive, Reflexivization, and Quantifier Floating. For these rules also, one must search for principles which would make it unnecessary to say that English speakers *learn* that such rules apply cyclically.[6]

SUMMARY

This chapter presented one of the major theoretical insights of transformational grammar: that a subset of transformational rules apply in derivations according to the cyclic principle. This states:

(i)   The cyclic rules are applied first to the most deeply embedded structure, only then to the next most, and so on. Once all applicable cyclic rules have been applied to a particular level, operation passes to the next higher C, and never returns. Within each level, optional rules may or may not apply and obligatory rules must, as expected.

The cyclic principle was supported by showing how it explains a number of facts about the interaction of several rules introduced earlier both with themselves and with each other. These are Equi, Passive, s-Raising, o-Raising, Reflexivization, and Quantifier Floating.

We explicated how the cyclic principle correctly prevents one operation of Equi from destroying the environment for others. We showed how it accounts for the alternate positions of floating Qs. Most importantly, we showed how the cyclic principle guarantees in certain derivations that pairs of NPs go through a stage at which they are clause mates, even though they neither start out in initial structure nor end up in surface structure with this status. The cyclic principle is thus a further necessary refinement of the major descriptive task of the first part of this manual—

accountIng for the distribution of reflexives. Finally, we argued that more profound explanations of cyclic behavior of individual rules can only be obtained by discovering principles which predict that particular rules are cyclic. Two such principles were tentatively offered. The first claims that all coreferential deletion rules are cyclic, the other that rules which create new subjects and direct objects are cyclic.

NOTES

1. This is a simplification. Actually, many structures will contain separate sets of clauses involving separate echelons of embedding, between which there is no relation relevant for rule application. Hence in a case like

(i) The car *which I bought* is near the car *which you bought*.

the italicized relative clauses are both embedded, but neither more than the other. The principle to be described in the text will thus really refer to maximal sets of successive embeddings. The set in (i) has two members. Thus in such a case there are, in effect, two first cycles, etc.

2. Principle (10) predicts that the following deletion rules in English are also cyclical:

(i) Melvin$_i$ entered the room and then he$_i$ fainted
$$\Downarrow$$
$$0$$

(ii) Melvin$_i$ is too mean for Mary to marry him$_i$
$$\Downarrow$$
$$0$$

(iii) a America's$_i$ defense and that of nations related to her$_i$ . . . $\Longrightarrow$
$$\Downarrow$$
$$0$$

  b America's defense and that of related nations . . .

This prediction is supported by all of the known evidence.

3. To follow the discussion at this point, the reader should draw (17) on a separate piece of paper and have it available for line-by-line reference.

4. This auxiliary is *do* because of the general conditions on all PVs. Since Passive applies to the directly lower clause, this *do* is ultimately converted to *be* by the rule Do Replacement introduced in Chapter 27.

5. When the V_1 of C_1 is deleted by Do Erasure, the result of floating on this cycle becomes identical with the result of floating on the C_2 cycle.

6. In the case of the first three rules, one promising principle seems to be that any rule which creates new subjects or objects is cyclical.

PROBLEMS

1. Consider the sentence:

(i) Joe wanted to be loved.

In the derivation of (i), the rule Passive must apply before the rule Equi since Passive creates the subject which Equi deletes. Does this show that Passive must precede Equi in an ordering of the rules of English?

2. Consider the sentence:

(i) Mary wanted to express herself clearly.

Account for the occurrence of the reflexive pronoun *herself.*

3. Omitting tense, construct the initial structure for the sentence:

(i) The gorillas were believed by the director to all be rabid.

Number the clauses from *bottom to top.* In the cycle of which clause does Quantifier Floating apply? Include all auxiliary verb cycles in your answer.

EPILOGUE

In this book, we have attempted to motivate and to formulate a number of generalizations about English grammar. These generalizations took the form of specific rules. It was stated at the outset that our account was doomed to be fragmentary, not only because of limitations of space, but also because of limitations of contemporary knowledge. Now we are in a position to see another sort of limitation.

In the concluding chapter of this book, we encountered a generalization of a higher level than those represented by particular grammatical rules. We found it possible to recognize a general principle of cyclic rule application governing some of the rules of English grammar. This kind of *metaprinciple* has the status of a linguistic universal. In other words (if it ultimately proves correct), it is a fragment of linguistic knowledge which predicts properties of individual rules of English grammar (and all other grammars as well). Such a principle exemplifies the truth that speakers of a language can, and almost certainly do, possess linguistic knowledge *that they have not learned.* They possess it simply by virtue of having the innate intellectual equipment which comes from being a human being. If the theory involving the cyclic principle is correct, English speakers need not, for example, learn the way Equi applies in complex derivations where its conditions are met at various levels of embedding. (This assumes also the existence of some principle predicting that Equi lies in the set of cyclic rules.)

It follows from these considerations that even if we had been more successful in proposing and justifying particular generalizations (rules), the results of our inquiry would still have fallen far short of providing an ultimate account of the nature of English grammar. For the existence of particular generalizations (rules) about individual languages only sets the stage for a still more profound inquiry which characterizes theoretical linguistics, namely, the search for metaprinciples which predict and hence explain as many properties as possible of individual rules. Our discussion of cyclic application is simply a first indication that such a more profound inquiry is not merely abstractly possible but is to a significant extent feasible even today. Moreover, the discussion of cyclic application shows that, in the absence of such meta-principles, particular rules frequently will not function properly. Ultimately, no real separation can exist between the study of the grammar of an individual language like English and the study of universal grammar.

Our book thus ends where a deeper study of English begins.

ANSWERS TO PROBLEMS

Chapter 2

1. The first occurrence. The reason is that the replacement of the first occurrence by *I* yields a well-formed sentence. However, no replacement of the second occurrence of *myself* improves the example, as the following show:

(i) *Myself likes $\begin{Bmatrix} me \\ I \\ Sally \end{Bmatrix}$.

2. For 2(i), *John* is the antecedent for *he*.
For 2(ii), *Mary* is the antecedent for *she* and *John* for *he*.
For 2(iii), *John* is intuitively the antecedent of *his*.
   The dictionary definition of antecedent is too narrow. In fact, antecedents sometimes follow as well as precede pronouns.

Chapter 3

1. Example (i) is compatible with 1D and (ii) is not. Since *I think you know him better than Melvin does* is a clause, it follows that (i) contains internal clause boundaries and is not a minimal clause, by definition. Therefore, *I* and *me* are not in the same minimal clause, and it is correctly predicted that no *myself* form should occur. In (ii) the sequence *it is better to die for one's country than to live forever in ignominy* is an internal clause. Therefore, 1(ii) as a whole is not a minimal clause. Therefore, *I* and *myself* are not in the same minimal clause, and it is wrongly predicted that *myself* cannot occur.

2. #Greta said #that everyone knew #that it was unwise #for her to hire people #who eat gravel# # # #.

(i) #What James is# is unspeakable# #.

It is possible to do this because the two occurrences of *is* are in separate clauses. The first occurrence is part of a so-called headless relative construction (*What James is*) which forms the subject of the entire sentence.

A sentence with three consecutive occurrences of *is* is:

(ii) Melvin's nose isn't plugged up, and what the man whose is is is a doctor.

Chapter 4

1.

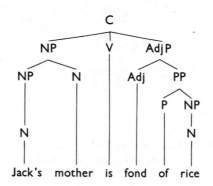

Jack's mother is fond of rice

2.

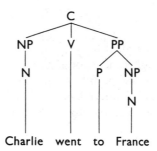

Charlie went to France

3.

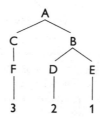

Chapter 5

1. The second *I* and *myself* are clause mates because they are both in the complement clause which is the object of *said*. Neither is therefore a clause mate of the first *I*, which is in the main clause.

2. *Me* is required because a form in the italicized position is not a clause mate of the first *me* in the sentence. They are not clause mates because the first is in one restrictive relative clause and the second is in another.

Chapter 6

1.

  (i) a She told Mary$_i$ that her$_i$ mother was sick.

       b She$_i$ told Mary that her$_i$ mother was sick.

  (ii) a The possibility that Bob$_i$ has cancer doesn't worry him$_i$, but it does worry his$_i$ mother.

       b The possibility that Bob$_i$ has cancer doesn't worry him$_i$, but it does worry his mother.

       c The possibility that Bob$_i$ has cancer doesn't worry him, but it does worry his$_i$ mother.

       d The possibility that Bob has cancer doesn't worry him$_i$, but it does worry his$_i$ mother.

(iii) a The realization that Bob$_i$ has cancer doesn't worry him, but it does worry his$_i$ mother.

       b The realization that Bob has cancer doesn't worry him$_i$, but it does worry his$_i$ mother.

If you are interested in the difference between the way the words *possibility* and *realization* in (ii) and (iii) contrast with respect to coreference possibilities, see Ross (1969) in the bibliographical references to Chapter 29.

2. In (i) the pronoun is the subject of a tensed clause; namely, [*that they were arrested*]; in (ii) the pronoun is the subject of an untensed clause; namely, [*for them to be arrested*]. Thus Rule 1G(b) predicts the occurrence of a subject form in the former and an object form in the latter.

Chapter 7

1. Example (i) is ill-formed because the pronoun after *about* is not reflexive. This is impossible since in the remote structure the sentence, being an imperative, has a *you* subject. Therefore, there are clause mate coreferents and the object of *about* should be reflexive in form. In (ii), there being no second person antecedent for *you*, no reflexive is required.

2. The account suggests that these curses do *not* have second person subjects in remote structure. For if they did, the reflexive pronouns would be well-formed and the nonreflexive pronouns would be ill-formed, according to Rule 1G.

3. Example (i) is well-formed because the reflexive pronoun has a clause mate antecedent; namely, the subject of *argue*. Example (ii) is ill-formed because there is no coreferential antecedent for *myself*, even in remote structure. The remote structure subject of *argue* must be *you* since (ii) is an imperative, and *you* cannot be coreferential with a first person pronoun.

Chapter 8

1. The regularity in nonimperative sentences is that the pronoun in the expression *on X's own* must agree with the subject of the clause containing that expression. Thus, the paired well-formedness of

(i) You cut the grass on your own.

and

(ii) Cut the grass on your own.

shows that only the postulation of remote structure second person subjects for imperatives can permit imperative sentences to be subsumed under exactly the same regularity.

2. In our analysis of imperative clauses, these have second person subjects in remote structure. Under that assumption the ill-formedness of (iii) is automatically predicted by whatever principle turns out to be relevant to block (ii), and this principle is needed no matter how one describes imperative clauses. Thus (iii) shows in another way that imperative clauses behave as if they had second person subjects.

3. The regularity is that the pronoun before *best* in the expression *do X's best* must agree with the subject of that expression. Therefore, the distribution in

(i) Do ⎧ your ⎫ best.
⎪ *my ⎪
⎨ *his ⎬
⎪ *her ⎪
⎪ *their⎪
⎩ *our ⎭

shows that imperative clauses are behaving as if they had second person subjects.

4. A group of such expressions includes:

- **(i)** hold *X*'s breath
- **(ii)** go *X*'s own way
- **(iii)** be beside *X*'s self with anger
- **(iv)** have bats in *X*'s belfry
- **(v)** have ants in *X*'s pants
- **(vi)** have a frog in *X*'s throat
- **(vii)** have butterflies in *X*'s stomach
- **(viii)** have a hole in *X*'s head
- **(ix)** have a charm all *X*'s own
- **(x)** be out of *X*'s mind
- **(xi)** be out of *X*'s depth
- **(xii)** be in over *X*'s head

Chapter 9

1. For (i) the initial argument is that without postulating a remote structure subject, the presence of the reflexive form is exceptional. However, if it is claimed that such sentences have remote structures which *can* contain first person plural subjects, the presence of *ourselves* is correctly predicted by Rule 1G. Moreover, postulation of such subjects also regularizes a range of other phenomena, as illustrated by:

- **(i)** a How about criticizing our own mothers.
- b How about craning our necks.
- c How about going there by ourselves.

The distribution in

(ii) How about criticizing
$$\left\{ \begin{array}{l} \text{myself} \\ \text{yourself} \\ \text{yourselves} \\ \text{ourselves} \\ \text{oneself} \\ \text{*himself} \\ \text{*herself} \\ \text{*itself} \\ \text{*themselves} \end{array} \right\}.$$

seems to suggest that the underlying subject must be nonthird person. However, this apparently predicts that *oneself* should be starred in (ii) above. This ignores the fact that the peculiar pronoun *one* is broad enough in reference to include the speaker and hearer. Thus, it is not an *exclusively* third person element. The regularity thus seems to be that the deleted subject in this construction *must* include reference to first and/or second person. The form of answer for (ii)–(iv) is similar to the above.

2. The arguments consist of showing that a range of phenomena known to require antecedents can occur in this construction type. So:

   (i)   Why improve yourself.
  (ii)   Why improve your own mother.
 (iii)   Why do it by yourself.
  (iv)   Why do your best.
   (v)   Why crane your neck.

3. The regularity illustrated in (i) is that the sequence *you both* does not occur in a well-formed clause structure containing a previous second person pronoun. Therefore, the ill-formedness of

(i)   *Why not analyze you both.

is an argument for such a sentence having a second person subject at a remote structure stage. This is necessary to subsume the ill-formedness in (i) above under the same principle operative for the examples in the question.

Chapter 10

1. The post-*and* clause contains a reflexive pronoun. It can only have such if at a remote stage there is a coreferent antecedent for that reflexive in the clause. Since the antecedent is not present in surface structure, it must have been deleted. The only rule which could delete an NP in the appropriate position is CCS Deletion. However, the only NP in the initial conjunct which is co-referential to *herself* is *Betty*. But *Betty* is not the subject of the initial conjunct. Thus (i) is ill-formed because CCS Deletion has applied to a structure in which the requirement that the controller NP be a subject is not met.

2. *Do X's best* requires a subject which agrees with the pronoun that occurs in the *X* position before *best*. This pronoun must thus have been deleted from the second clause of (i) and CCS Deletion is the only rule that could do the job. This requires that the subject deleted be coreferential with the subject of the preceding clause. In surface structure, the preceding clause has a null subject. Therefore, the CCS Deletion controller must have itself been deleted. There is, however, a rule that can accomplish this in such a case as (i), namely, Why Not Deletion, which can delete second person pronouns. Example (ii) is ill-formed because CCS Deletion could only have deleted *he*, which does not agree with *your*. Thus, the requirement on the idiom *do X's best* is not met.

3. The regularity is that the subject of the *before* clause is deleted if its co-referent in the main clause subject acts as controller (by means of what is evidently an additional controlled deletion rule). The second conjunct in (iii) reveals the operation of this same rule. However, there is no explicit controller in the surface structure. One must thus be posited in remote structure. Fortunately, then, the posited controller of the deletion in *before* clauses will automatically be erased by CCS Deletion. Thus, the facts in (i) and (ii) support a CCS Deletion analysis because only such a CCS Deletion rule permits postulation of the controller NP required by the other deletion rule.

Chapter 11

1. The subject of *improve* must be deleted by Equi. Therefore, it must be a coreferent of the subject of *promise*. Since the latter is not present in surface structure, it must have been deleted, and only CCS Deletion could do the job. Therefore, the subject of *promise* must be coreferential to *Sally*, because CCS Deletion only works between the coreferential subjects of conjoined clauses. Replacing all the deleted pronouns, then, yields a structure that can be schematically represented as follows:

(i) [Sally$_i$ won the lottery and then she$_i$ promised Martin

she$_i$ to improve $\begin{Bmatrix} \text{herself}_i \\ \text{*himself} \\ \text{*yourself} \end{Bmatrix}$]

We thus see that the facts in (i) are due to the same basic principles which account for the distribution in

(ii) She improved $\begin{Bmatrix} \text{herself} \\ \text{*himself} \\ \text{*yourself} \end{Bmatrix}$.

that is, to the principle that a reflexive pronoun agrees with its clause mate antecedent.

2. *Do X's best* requires a pronoun in the X position which agrees with the subject of its clause. Since the required antecedent is not present in surface structure, it must have been deleted. Only Equi could have done the job. However, the controller of Equi is also not present in surface structure. Therefore, it too must have been deleted. Only I Deletion could have done the job. Since I Deletion can only delete second person pronouns, only a second person pronoun could ultimately occupy the X position in the *do X's best* phrase.

3. The remote structure is:

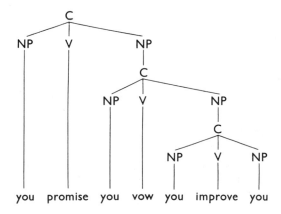

Since the subject and object of *improve* are coreferent clause mates, reflexive form for the object is predicted by Rule 1G. The subject of *improve* must be deleted, and only Equi is available to do the job. The subject of *vow* must also be deleted and, again, only Equi can do the job. Finally, the subject of *promise* must be deleted. This can only be accomplished by I Deletion.

Notice that in this description there are two applications of Equi. It is crucial that the one which applies to the lowest clause subject apply first. For a discussion of the principle that gurantees this order of application, see Chapter 29.

Chapter 12

1. Rule 1G(a), which determines reflexive form, must apply before CCS Deletion. If CCS Deletion applied first, then there would be no antecedent clause mate to determine the need for a reflexive pronoun.

2. A sentence in the superficial sense is simply the string of words forming the bottom line of a surface structure tree. If, therefore, the number of sentences is infinite, the number of surface structures is infinite. But each surface structure is simply the last stage of a derivation. Thus, if there are an infinite number of surface structures, there are an infinite number of derivations. But the initial stage of each derivation is an initial tree. Therefore, if there are an infinite number of derivations, there are an infinite number of initial trees.

Chapter 13

1. The rules are:

(i) A $\longrightarrow$ B C
     C $\longrightarrow$ D E

(ii) V $\longrightarrow$ Q X W R
     Q $\longrightarrow$ F
     R $\longrightarrow$ G H

(iii) A $\longrightarrow$ B C
      C $\longrightarrow$ A
      C $\longrightarrow$ D E

2. The italicized NP *Sally* is an indirect object in the initial structure but a direct object in all structures after the point in the derivation where Indirect Object Shift applies.

3. Under the assumption stated, the NP *price* originates as a subject. Subject NPs are not associated with prepositions by base rules. Therefore, *in* would have to be transformationally inserted after the operation of the transformation which derives structures like (ii).

Chapter 14

1. They can do so by being embedded successively one within the other, as in:

(i) Joan called Sally, who called Ruth, who called Claudia, who called Doris, . . .

2. The source of the ambiguity is that the restrictive relative clause *who had rabies* can arise either stacked on the head *the sailor* or else embedded in the larger *who visited the nurse who had rabies*. The expression could be derived from either of the following two structures:

(i) Stacked Structure

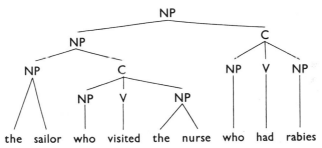

(ii) Embedded Structure

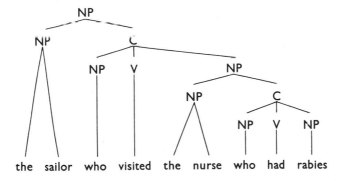

3. The two different types are:

(i) Clauses
Joan sang and Martha grunted and Betty hummed . . .

(ii) Verbs
Bill ate, drank, belched, sighed, . . . and yawned.

These facts indicate that the base rules need to be expanded to include the possibility of conjunction in Cs and Vs as well as NPs. Other major categories such as Adj and Adv will have to be included as well. Indeed, the facts suggest that all major syntactic categories in English can participate in conjunction and the base rules need to reflect this.

Chapter 15

1. First, the corresponding pairs have essentially the same meaning. Second, they involve the same stem morphemes. Both (40b) and (41b) involve the stems *Turk*, *build*, and *missile*. Third, the number of compound forms is open-ended. For example, *built* occurs with thousands of proper forms like *Turkish*. Fourth, as soon as one learns a new proper stem, one can use it in the compound with no further learning. Hence upon learning that there is an inhabited planet named *Zarkon*, one can immediately speak of *Zarkonese-built missiles*, *Zarkonese-backed takeovers*, etc. Finally, there is a relatively natural rule to derive forms like (40) from forms like (41), namely, a rule which compounds the participle with the head noun of the following NP.

2. Yes. All of the kinds of arguments given in the text to show that other complex words are not lexically listed apply here as well. Thus, *builder* is related to *one who builds*; *home-builder* to *one who builds homes*; *sharpener* to *something which sharpens*; and *knife-sharpener* to *something that sharpens knives*.

3. All of the words on the right begin with the same negative prefix morpheme. However, the shape of this morpheme differs in each case. This reveals the following general feature of morphemes: their shapes may be differentially determined by the shape of the stem to which they are affixed. For another example of this, listen carefully to the different pronunciations of the plural morpheme in the three words *cats*, *dogs*, and *foxes*.

Chapter 16

1. The ungrammaticality of (i) is due to the fact that *sigh*, an intransitive verb, has been inserted into a ditransitive configuration.

2. The lexical entries are:

  (i) [*cauterize*, V, Transitive, . . .]
 (ii) [*hand*, V, Ditransitive, . . .]
(iii) [*faint*, V, Intransitive, . . .]

3. There are twelve possibilities:

 (i) NP V
    Melvin grunted.
(ii) NP V NP
    Melvin painted the cabinet.

(iii) NP V NP NP
Melvin handed the letter to Sally.
(iv) NP V PP
Melvin grunted under the table.
(v) NP V NP PP
Melvin painted the cabinet in the hall.
(vi) NP V NP NP PP
Melvin handed the letter to Sally on the bus.
(vii) NP V PP PP
Melvin grunted under the table in the morning.
(viii) NP V NP PP PP
Melvin painted the cabinet in the hall on Sunday.
(ix) NP V NP NP PP PP
Melvin handed the letter to Sally in the hall in the morning.
(x) NP V PP PP PP
Melvin grunted in the hall on Thursday for the monkey.
(xi) NP V NP PP PP PP
Melvin painted the cabinet in the hall on Thursday for the monkey.
(xii) NP V NP NP PP PP PP
Melvin handed the letter to Sally in the hall on Thursday for the postman.

Chapter 17

1. The rule in (i) does not apply to the tree in (ii). The rule requires that postparticle NPs have the analysis *the* N. But in (ii) the postparticle NP has the analysis *some* N.

2. The problem is how to constrain the base rules in such a way that imperative clauses with nonsecond person subjects are not generated. In other words, how can the base rules be blocked from yielding examples like:

(i) *Please they go away!
(ii) *Kindly we sit down!

3. The analysis is:

my		[Pro, Gen, I, An, Sing]
your	a	[Pro, Gen, II, An, Sing]
	b	[Pro, Gen, II, An, Pl]
	c	[Pro, Gen, II, III, An, Pl]
his		[Pro, Gen, III, An, Masc, Sing]
her		[Pro, Gen, III, An, Fem, Sing]
its		[Pro, Gen, III, Neu, Sing]
our	a	[Pro, Gen, I, II, An, Pl]
	b	[Pro, Gen, I, III, An, Pl]
	c	[Pro, Gen, I, II, III, An, Pl]

their a [Pro, Gen, III, An, Pl]
        b [Pro, Gen, III, Neu, Pl]

Chapter 18

1. They are both passives and thus manifest the same selectional restrictions as their corresponding actives, which are:

(i) !Bob tasted the sum of 3 and 3.
(ii) !The butter impeached the rolls.

Taste is a verb requiring its object to designate a physical object while *the sum of 3 and 3* refers to an abstraction. This clash is the source of the unacceptability of (i). *Impeach* requires a subject referring to mind-possessing beings or their institutions and an object NP designating an individual holding a certain office. Thus, (ii) involves violations of the conditions on both subject and object of *impeach*.

2. Example (i) shows that among the subject NPs that CCS Deletion erases are subjects created by Passive. Since CCS Deletion can only remove subjects, and since the removed NP was not a subject before Passive made it such, it follows that Passive must apply before CCS Deletion.

3. The core operation of Passive turns a direct object into a subject. Intransitive clauses contain no direct objects and thus cannot undergo Passive.

Chapter 19

1. The formulation of Extraposition in the text erroneously predicts that (ii) and (iv) are well-formed. These examples suggest that the appropriate restriction is that Extraposition is inapplicable within a clause containing more than one complement of the infinitival or *that* clause type.

2. The clause which is extraposed in (ii) only became a subject in (i) as a result of the application of Passive. Thus both (i) and (ii) have a remote structure corresponding to

(i) The director argued *that Edward was a Martian.*

in which the italicized portion is the direct object. Therefore, Passive must apply before Extraposition.

3. Example (ii) is derived by Extraposition. This is the only way the infinitive which is the underlying subject can get to extraposed position. However, Extraposition leaves behind the element *it*. Therefore, (iii) could only be derived if Extraposition left behind the element *this*, which it never does.

Chapter 20

1. There must be a special principle to assign the figurative meaning to clauses like:

(i) [the cat has X's tongue]

In the simple clauses the idiomatically interpreted material is contiguous. Given a Raising analysis of *seem* complements, the principle needed for the simple clauses also suffices for examples like (i) *in the question*. Such examples thus support a Raising analysis.

2. Given a grammar containing Raising, the contrast between (i) and (ii) is an automatic consequence of the independently existing contrast between:

(i)   Now is a good time for wheat.
(ii)   *Now produces a lot of wheat.

3. It predicts that the contrast will be manifested in the complements of *seem* as follows:

(i)   The important thing to him seems to be money.
(ii)   *The important thing to him seems to bother me.

Chapter 21

1. The clearest evidence is that *apt* occurs with highly restricted subject NPs.

(i)   The cat is apt to be out of the bag by then.
(ii)   Now is apt to be a poor time for wheat.
(iii)   There is apt to be trouble in Mongolia.
(iv)   Little heed is apt to be taken of your suggestion.

2.

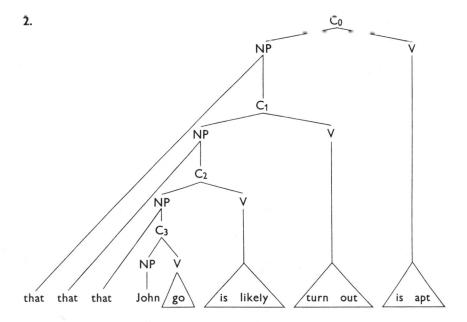

3. The rules apply in the order Reflexivization, Raising. The reason is that Raising destroys the clause mate relation between *Melvin* and *himself*. Hence, if the order were reversed, Reflexivization would, wrongly, not apply.

Chapter 22

1. *Now* is a highly restricted NP which normally only occurs as a subject of predicate nominals. In (i), it occurs as the subject of a passive clause. Passive only applies to sisters of the verb. Therefore, since *now* must have started out in the subordinate clause, but must have entered the main clause before Passive could apply, some rule must exist to lift NPs into main clause object position.

2. Sentence (i) is a passive clause. Therefore, it is derived by the rule Passive. Hence, at a remote stage, *Joe* must be the object of *believe*. However, *Joe* is the antecedent of *himself*. And the antecedent of a reflexive must be its clause mate at some stage. Therefore, at one point, *Joe* must have been in the complement of *believe*. The initial tree for (i) would be:

(i)

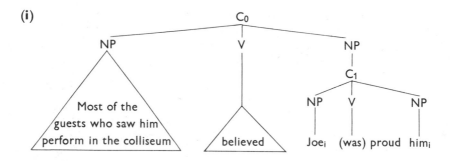

The rules Reflexivization, o-Raising, and Passive must apply in that order.

3. Sentence (i) is ill-formed because it can only be derived by Complex NP Shift. But the shifted NP is a subject. And Complex NP Shift does not apply to subjects.

Chapter 23

1. In a grammar containing Active, *now* would have to be the initial structure subject of the main clause. But it is a highly restricted NP, normally constrained to occur as the subject of predicate nominals, as in:

(i) Now is a poor time to invest in gold.

Postulation of Active would thus make it extremely difficult to account for such violations as:

(ii) *Now is believed by most authorities $\left\{\begin{array}{l}\text{to be crummy} \\ \text{to worry the President} \\ \text{to resemble then}\end{array}\right\}$.

In a grammar based on Passive and o-Raising, such restrictions follow automatically from the constraints needed independently in simple clauses containing *now* as subject.

2. The initial tree is:

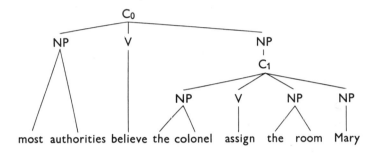

In C_1, *Mary* is an indirect object. It undergoes Indirect Object Shift, becoming the direct object of *assign*. Then it undergoes Passive, becoming the subject of *assign*. Next, it undergoes o-Raising, becoming the direct object of *believe*. Finally, it undergoes Passive in C_0, becoming the subject of (*was*) *believed*.

Chapter 24

1. The second clause in (iii) contains a floating Q. These can only be generated by Quantifier Floating if there is a subject NP. Therefore, underlying the second clause of (iii) must be the structure:

(i) [and then all of them$_i$ ran away]

This would be converted to:

(ii) [and then they$_i$ all ran away]

by Quantifier Floating. But since the *they*$_i$ does not show up in surface structure, something must delete it. CCS Deletion is the needed rule.

2. Both *tend* and *turn out* are s-Raising triggers. Therefore, the most deeply embedded clause in the initial structure of (i) is:

(i) [all of the candidates be incompetent]

Quantifier Floating applies to this structure, positioning the Q and making *the candidates* the derived subject of *be*. Then *the candidates* successively undergoes s-Raising twice, becoming the subject of *turn out* and finally, the subject of *tend*.

3. In (i), *all of the men* is not a subject. Hence Quantifier Floating cannot apply. There is no rule to generate (ii). In (iii), *all of the men* is a derived object of *believe* (as a result of the operation of o-Raising). Therefore, it was a remote subject of *be*, and Quantifier Floating was applicable at that stage, producing (iv).

Chapter 25

1. The remote tree for (i) would be:

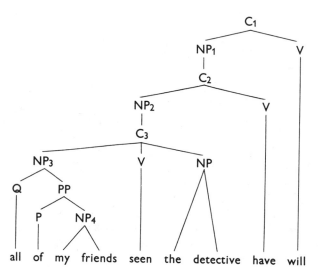

First, NP_3 would undergo s-Raising, becoming subject of C_2. Then Quantifier Floating places the Q next to *have* and makes NP_4 the subject of *have*. NP_4 is then promoted by s-Raising to subject of *will*.

2. Like all auxiliary verbs, *have* requires its initial subject NP to be clausal (that is, a complement).

3. In (ii), Quantifier Floating applies before s-Raising creates the subject of *have*. In (i), Quantifier Floating applies after this application of s-Raising.

Chapter 26

1. For the requisite derivations (that is, (i) from (ii), etc.), rules are required which delete relative pronouns like *who* and *which* and a form of the the verb *be*. In addition, a preposing rule is required which preposes the remaining elements once the deletions have taken place. This rule need only refer to the single category V if adjectives and participles are assigned to this category.

2. Since rule (i) does not introduce any prepositions on objects, examples like (ii) show that there must exist a transformational rule to create the PP node which occurs in surface structure over the object NP of adjectives.

3. Some sentences that show that *dare* can occur as an auxiliary are:

(i)   Dare we do that? (*compare* Can we do that?)
(ii)   We dare not do that. (*compare* We cannot do that.)
(iii) *I want to dare do that. (*compare* *I want to will do that.)

Chapter 27

1. Sentence (i) is ill-formed because it contains an auxiliary *do* which is tenseless. This is a violation of the obligatory application of Do Erasure.

2. The surface structure tree is:

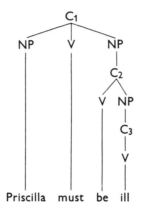

This tree is the result of two applications of s-Raising. One is triggered by *be* and one by *must*.

3. Sentence (i) is ill-formed because Do Erasure has, wrongly, failed to apply even though the conditions for its application have been created by the prior operation of Tense Extraction.

Sentence (ii) is ill-formed because, although the conditions for the obligatory application of Tense Extraction are met, that rule has failed to apply.

Chapter 28

1. These examples support the claim that inversion is only triggered when there is a presubject WH phrase. They support it because they do not have presubject WH phrases, and this is compatible with the absence of inversion.

2. The *n't* achieves its terminal locus as follows. First, it becomes part of the auxiliary verb by way of Not Contraction. Then, it travels to presubject position along with the rest of the auxiliary verb when Subject-Auxiliary Inversion applies.

3.

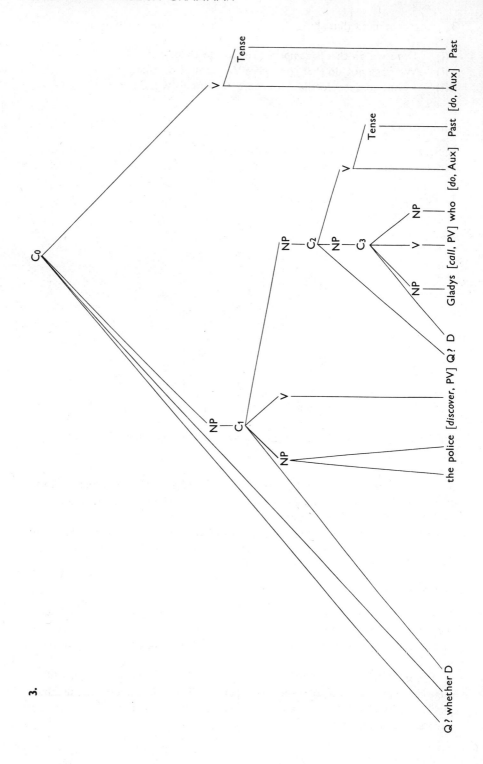

Chapter 29

1. No. In the derivation of (i), Passive applies on the cycle of the complement, while Equi cannot apply before the cycle determined by *want*. Therefore, regardless of the order of these two rules, the cyclic principle guarantees
that Passive will apply first in the derivation of (i). Consequently, the order of
application in such a derivation is explained without any appeal to the relative
order between the rules themselves, and it cannot support the assumption
of any particular order.

2. Ignoring auxiliaries, the most deeply embedded clause in the initial structure corresponding to (i) is the clause:

(i) [Mary express herself clearly]

In this clause, *Mary* and *herself* are clause mates and Reflexivization correctly
predicts the occurrence of the reflexive pronoun *herself*. However, (i) is embedded in a higher clause whose main verb is *want* and whose subject is coreferential with the complement subject. Thus, Equi can apply in the derivation of the problem sentence. The application of Reflexivization to it must
precede that of Equi. Otherwise the latter will delete the clause mate coreferent
of the ancestor of *herself* before Reflexivization has applied. However, there
is no need to express this ordering specifically. It is guaranteed by the cyclic
principle, just as in the previous problem the order is guaranteed between
Passive and Equi.

3. The initial structure is:

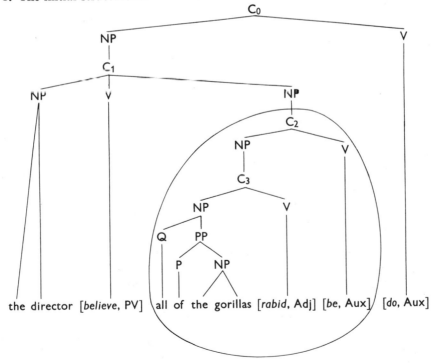

Quantifier Floating applies on the cycle of C_2, accounting for the fact that the Q is attracted to the verb *be*. The appropriate cycle is circled in the above tree.

BIBLIOGRAPHY

Chapter 1

Akmajian, A. and F. W. Heny (1975) *An Introduction to the Principles of Transformational Syntax*. Cambridge, Mass.: M.I.T. Press.

Cattell, R. N. (1969) *The New English Grammar*. Cambridge, Mass.: M.I.T. Press.

Chomsky, N. (1966) "The Current Scene in Linguistics: Present Directions." *College English* 27: 587–595; reprinted in Reibel, D. A. and S. Schane, eds. (1969) *Modern Studies in English*. Englewood Cliffs, N.J.: Prentice–Hall.

Chomsky, N. (1969) "Generative Grammars as Theories of Linguistic Competence." in Reibel and Schane, eds. (1969); excerpted from Chomsky, N. (1965) *Aspects of the Theory of Syntax*, secs. 1.1, 3–9. Cambridge, Mass.: M.I.T. Press.

Curme, G. O. (1931) *Syntax*. Lexington, Mass.: Heath.

Halle, M. and S. J. Keyser (1968) "What We Do When We Speak." in Kolers, P. A. and M. Eden, eds. (1968) *Recognizing Patterns: Studies in Living and Automatic Systems*. Cambridge, Mass.: M.I.T. Press.

Jespersen, O. (1940–49) *A Modern English Grammar on Historical Principles*, 7 vols. Copenhagen, Denmark: Munksgaard.

Langacker, R. W. (1968) *Language and Its Structure*. New York: Harcourt Brace Jovanovich.

Langendoen, D. T. (1969) *The Study of Syntax*. New York: Holt, Rinehart & Winston.

Postal, P. M. (1964) "Underlying and Superficial Linguistic Structure." *Harvard Educational Review* 34: 246–266; reprinted in Reibel and Schane, eds. (1969).

Postal, P. M. (1969) Review of A. McIntosh and M. A. K. Halliday, *Papers in General, Descriptive and Applied Linguistics. Foundations of Language* 5: 409–426.

Poutsma, H. (1904) *A Grammar of Late Modern English*. Groningen: P. Noordhoff.

Chapter 2

Curme, G. O. (1931) *Syntax*. Lexington, Mass.: Heath.

Chapter 3

Langacker, R. W. (1968) *Language and Its Structure.* New York: Harcourt Brace Jovanovich.

Strang, B. M. H. (1963) *Modern English Structure.* New York: St. Martin's Press.

Chapter 4

Akmajian, A. and F. W. Heny (1975) *An Introduction to the Principles of Transformational Syntax.* Cambridge, Mass.: M.I.T. Press.

Bach, E. (1974) *Syntactic Theory.* New York: Holt, Rinehart & Winston.

Chomsky, N. (1965) *Aspects of the Theory of Syntax.* Cambridge, Mass.: M.I.T. Press.

Chomsky, N. (1972) *Language and Mind.* New York: Harcourt Brace Jovanovich.

Jacobs, R. A. and P. S. Rosenbaum (1968) *English Transformational Grammar.* Waltham, Mass.: Ginn/Blaisdell.

Langacker, R. W. (1968) *Language and Its Structure.* New York: Harcourt Brace Jovanovich.

Lees, R. B. (1957) Review of Chomsky (1957). *Language* 33: 375–407.

Postal, P. M. (1964) "Underlying and Superficial Linguistic Structure." *Harvard Educational Review* 34: 246–266; reprinted in Reibel, D. A. and S. Schane, eds. (1969) *Modern Studies in English.* Englewood Cliffs, N.J.: Prentice-Hall.

Chapter 5

Jacobs, R. A. and P. S. Rosenbaum (1968) *English Transformational Grammar.* Waltham, Mass.: Ginn/Blaisdell.

Langacker, R. W. (1969) "On Pronominalization and the Chain of Command." in Reibel, D. A. and S. Schane, eds. (1969) *Modern Studies in English.* Englewood Cliffs, N.J.: Prentice-Hall.

Lees, R. B. and E. Klima (1963) "Rules for English Pronominalization." *Language* 39: 17–29; reprinted in Reibel and Schane, eds. (1969).

Postal, P. M. (1969) Review of A. McIntosh and M. A. K. Halliday, *Papers in General, Descriptive and Applied Linguistics. Foundations of Language* 5: 409–426.

Postal, P. M. (1971) *Cross-Over Phenomena.* New York: Holt, Rinehart & Winston.

Chapter 6

Langacker, R. W. (1969) "On Pronominalization and the Chain of Command." in Reibel, D. A. and S. Schane, eds. (1969) *Modern Studies in English.* Englewood Cliffs, N.J.: Prentice-Hall.

Lees, R. B. and E. Klima (1963) "Rules for English Pronominalization." *Language* 39: 17–29; reprinted in Reibel and Schane, eds. (1969).

Postal, P. M. (1969) Review of A. McIntosh and M. A. K. Halliday, *Papers in General, Descriptive and Applied Linguistics. Foundations of Language* 5: 409–426.

Chapter 7

Bach, E. (1974) *Syntactic Theory.* New York: Holt, Rinehart & Winston.

Bolinger, D. L. (1967) "The Imperative in English." in *To Honor Roman Jakobson.* The Hague: Mouton.

Langendoen, D. T. (1969) *The Study of Syntax.* New York: Holt, Rinehart & Winston.

Lees, R. B. and E. Klima (1963) "Rules for English Pronominalization." *Language* 39: 17–29; reprinted in Reibel, D. A. and S. Schane, eds. (1969) *Modern Studies in English.* Englewood Cliffs, N.J.: Prentice-Hall.

Postal, P. M. (1964) "Underlying and Superficial Linguistic Structure." *Harvard Educational Review* 34: 246–266; reprinted in Reibel and Schane, eds. (1969).

Thorne, J. P. (1966) "English Imperative Sentences." *Journal of Linguistics* 2: 69–78.

Chapter 8

Bach, E. (1974) *Syntactic Theory.* New York: Holt, Rinehart & Winston.

Jacobs, R. A. and P. S. Rosenbaum (1968) *English Transformational Grammar*. Waltham, Mass.: Ginn/Blaisdell.

Langacker, R. W. (1968) *Language and Its Structure*. New York: Harcourt Brace Jovanovich.

Lees, R. B. and E. Klima (1963) "Rules for English Pronominalization." *Language* 39: 17–29; reprinted in Reibel, D. A. and S. Schane, eds. (1969) *Modern Studies in English*. Englewood Cliffs, N.J.: Prentice-Hall.

Postal, P. M. (1964) "Underlying and Superficial Linguistic Structure." *Harvard Educational Review* 34: 246–266; reprinted in Reibel and Schane, eds. (1969).

Postal, P. M. (1969) Review of A. McIntosh and M. A. K. Halliday, *Papers in General, Descriptive and Applied Linguistics. Foundations of Language* 5: 409–426.

Chapter 9

Bach, E. (1974) *Syntactic Theory*. New York: Holt, Rinehart & Winston.

Chomsky, N. (1792) *Language and Mind*. New York: Harcourt Brace Jovanovich.

Jacobs, R. A. and P. S. Rosenbaum (1968) *English Transformational Grammar*. Waltham, Mass.: Ginn/Blaisdell.

Langacker, R. W. (1968) *Language and Its Structure*. New York: Harcourt Brace Jovanovich.

Chapter 10

Langacker, R. W. (1969) "On Pronominalization and the Chain of Command." in Reibel, D. A. and S. Schane, eds. (1969) *Modern Studies in English*. Englewood Cliffs, N.J.: Prentice-Hall.

Lees, R. B. and E. Klima (1963) "Rules for English Pronominalization." *Language* 39: 17–29; reprinted in Reibel and Schane, eds. (1969)

Postal, P. M. (1969) Review of A. McIntosh and M. A. K. Halliday, *Papers in General, Descriptive and Applied Linguistics. Foundations of Language* 5: 409–426.

Postal, P. M. (1971) *Cross-Over Phenomena*. New York: Holt, Rinehart & Winston.

Chapter 11

Bach, E. (1974) *Syntactic Theory*. New York: Holt, Rinehart & Winston.

Burt, M. K. (1971) *From Deep to Surface Structure, An Introduction to Transformational Syntax*. New York: Harper & Row.

Jacobs, R. A. and P. S. Rosenbaum (1968) *English Transformational Grammar*. Waltham, Mass.: Ginn/Blaisdell.

Postal, P. M. (1969) Review of A. McIntosh and M. A. K. Halliday, *Papers in General, Descriptive and Applied Linguistics. Foundations of Language* 5: 409–426.

Postal, P. M. (1970) "On Coreferential Complement Subject Deletion." *Linguistic Inquiry* 1: 439–500.

Rosenbaum, P. S. (1967) *The Grammar of English Predicate Complement Constructions*. Cambridge, Mass.: M.I.T. Press.

Stockwell, R. P., P. Schachter and B. H. Partee (1973) *The Major Syntactic Structures of English*. New York: Holt, Rinehart & Winston.

Chapter 12

Akmajian, A. and F. W. Heny (1975) *An Introduction to the Principles of Transformational Syntax*. Cambridge, Mass.: M.I.T. Press.

Bach, E. (1974) *Syntactic Theory*. New York: Holt, Rinehart & Winston.

Chomsky, N. (1957) *Syntactic Structures*. The Hague: Mouton.

Chomsky, N. (1965) *Aspects of the Theory of Syntax*. Cambridge, Mass.: M.I.T. Press.

Chomsky, N. (1966) "The Current Scene in Linguistics: Present Directions." *College English* 27: 587–595; reprinted in Reibel, D. A. and S. Schane, eds. (1969). *Modern Studies in English*. Englewood Cliffs, N.J.: Prentice-Hall.

Chomsky, N. (1972) *Language and Mind*. New York: Harcourt Brace Jovanovich.

Chomsky, N. (1969) "Generative Grammars as Theories of Linguistic Competence." in Reibel and Schane, eds. (1969); excerpted from Chomsky, N. (1965) *Aspects of the Theory of Syntax*, secs. 1.1, 3–9. Cambridge, Mass.: M.I.T. Press.

Langendoen, D. T. (1969) *The Study of Syntax*. New York: Holt, Rinehart & Winston.

Postal, P. M. (1964) "Underlying and Superficial Linguistic Structure." *Harvard Educational Review* 34: 246–266; reprinted in Reibel and Schane, eds. (1969).

Chapter 13

Akmajian, A. and F. W. Heny (1975) *An Introduction to the Principles of Transformational Syntax*. Cambridge, Mass.: M.I.T. Press.

Bach, E. (1974) *Syntactic Theory*. New York: Holt, Rinehart & Winston.

Burt, M. K. (1971) *From Deep to Surface Structure, An Introduction to Transformational Syntax*. New York: Harper & Row.

Chomsky, N. (1965) *Aspects of the Theory of Syntax*. Cambridge, Mass.: M.I.T. Press.

Fillmore, C. J. (1965) *Indirect Object Constructions in Engish and the Ordering of Transformations*. The Hague: Mouton.

Jacobs, R. A. and P. S. Rosenbaum (1968) *English Transformational Grammar*. Waltham, Mass.: Ginn/Blaisdell.

Langacker, R. W. (1968) *Language and Its Structure*. New York: Harcourt Brace Jovanovich.

Lees, R. B. (1957) Review of Chomsky (1957). *Language* 33: 375–407.

Lees, R. B. (1960) *A Grammar of English Nominalizations*. The Hague: Mouton.

Rosenbaum, P. S. (1967) *The Grammar of English Predicate Complement Constructions*. Cambridge, Mass.: M.I.T. Press.

Chapter 14

Akmajian, A. and F. W. Heny (1975) *An Introduction to the Principles of Transformational Syntax*. Cambridge, Mass.: M.I.T. Press.

Bach, E. (1974) *Syntactic Theory*. New York: Holt, Rinehart & Winston.

Burt, M. K. (1971) *From Deep to Surface Structure, An Introduction to Transformational Syntax*. New York: Harper & Row.

Chomsky, N. (1965) *Aspects of the Theory of Syntax*. Cambridge, Mass.: M.I.T. Press.

Dougherty, R. C. (1970) "A Grammar of Coordinate Conjoined Structures: I." *Language* 46: 850–898.

Dougherty, R. C. (1971) "A Grammar of Coordinate Conjoined Structures: II." *Language* 47: 298–339.

Fillmore, C. J. (1963) "The Position of Embedding Transformations in a Grammar." *Word* 19: 208–231.

Langacker, R. W. (1969) "On Pronominalization and the Chain of Command." in Reibel, D. A. and S. Schane, eds. (1969) *Modern Studies in English*. Englewood Cliffs, N.J.: Prentice-Hall.

Langendoen, T. D. (1970) *Essentials of English Grammar*. New York: Holt, Rinehart & Winston.

Lees, R. B. (1960) *A Grammar of English Nominalizations*. The Hague: Mouton.

Postal, P. M. (1970) "On Coreferential Complement Subject Deletion." *Linguistic Inquiry* 1: 439–500

Rosenbaum, P. S. (1967) *The Grammar of English Predicate Complement Constructions*. Cambridge, Mass.: M.I.T. Press.

Stockwell, R. P. , P. Schachter and B. M. Partee (1973) *The Major Syntactic Structures of English*. New York: Holt, Rinehart & Winston.

Chapter 15

Chomsky, N. and M. Halle (1968) *The Sound Pattern of English*. New York: Harper & Row.

Halle, M. and S. J. Keyser (1971) *English Stress: Its Form, Its Growth and Its Role in Verse.* New York: Harper & Row.

Lees, R. B. (1960) *A Grammar of English Nominalizations.* The Hague: Mouton.

Marchand, H. (1969) *The Categories and Types of Present-Day English Word-Formation.* Munich: Beck.

Siegel, D. (1973) "Non-sources of Unpassives." in Kimball, J. P., ed. (1973) *Syntax and Semantics*, vol. 2. New York: Academic Press

Sloat, C. (1969) "Proper Nouns in English." *Language* 45: 26–30.

Chapter 16

Bach, E. (1974) *Syntactic Theory.* New York: Holt, Rinehart & Winston.

Chomsky, N. (1965) *Aspects of the Theory of Syntax.* Cambridge, Mass.: M.I.T. Press.

Jacobs, R. A. and P. S. Rosenbaum (1968) *English Transformational Grammar.* Waltham, Mass.: Ginn/Blaisdell.

Stockwell, R. P., P. Schachter and B. M. Partee (1973) *The Major Syntactic Structures of English.* New York: Holt, Rinehart & Winston.

Chapter 17

Akmajian, A. and F. W. Heny (1975) *An Introduction to the Principles of Transformational Syntax.* Cambridge, Mass.: M.I.T. Press.

Bach, E. (1974) *Syntactic Theory.* New York: Holt, Rinehart & Winston.

Burt, M. K. (1971) *From Deep to Surface Structure, An Introduction to Transformational Syntax.* New York: Harper & Row.

Chomsky, N. (1957) *Syntactic Structures.* The Hague: Mouton.

Langendoen, D. T. (1969) *The Study of Syntax.* New York: Holt, Rinehart & Winston.

Lees, R. B. and E. Klima (1963) "Rules for English Pronominalization." *Language* 39: 17–29; reprinted in Reibel, D. A. and S. Schane, eds. (1969) *Modern Studies in English.* Englewood Cliffs, N.J.: Prentice-Hall.

Lester, M. (1971) *Introductory Transformational Grammar of English.* New York: Holt, Rinehart & Winston.

Stockwell, R. P., P. Schachter and B. M. Partee (1973) *The Major Syntactic Structures of English.* New York: Holt, Rinehart & Winston.

Chapter 18

Akmajian, A. and F. W. Heny (1975) *An Introduction to the Principles of Transformational Syntax.* Cambridge, Mass.: M.I.T. Press.

Bach, E. (1974) *Syntactic Theory.* New York: Holt, Rinehart & Winston.

Burt, M. K. (1971) *From Deep to Surface Structure, An Introduction to Transformational Syntax.* New York: Harper & Row.

Chomsky, N. (1957) *Syntactic Structures.* The Hague: Mouton.

Chomsky, N. (1972) *Language and Mind.* New York: Harcourt Brace Jovanovich.

Hasagawa, K. (1968) "The Passive Construction in English." *Language* 44: 230–244.

Jacobs, R. A. and P. S. Rosenbaum (1968) *English Transformational Grammar.* Waltham, Mass.: Ginn/Blaisdell.

Lees, R. B. (1957) Review of Chomsky (1957). *Language* 33: 375–407.

Lees, R. B. (1960) *A Grammar of English Nominalizations.* The Hague: Mouton.

Rosenbaum, P. S. (1967) *The Grammar of English Predicate Complement Constructions.* Cambridge, Mass.: M.I.T. Press.

Siegel, D. (1973) "Non-sources of Unpassives." in Kimball, J. P., ed. (1973) *Syntax and Semantics*, vol. 2. New York: Academic Press.

Stockwell, R. P., P. Schachter and B. M. Partee (1973) *The Major Syntactic Structures of English.* New York: Holt, Rinehart & Winston.

Chapter 19

Akmajian, A. and F. W. Heny (1975) *An Introduction to the Principles of Transformational Syntax*. Cambridge, Mass.: M.I.T. Press.

Bach, E. (1974) *Syntactic Theory*. New York: Holt, Rinehart & Winston.

Burt, M. K. (1971) *From Deep to Surface Structure, An Introduction to Transformational Syntax*. New York: Harper & Row.

Higgins, R. F. (1973) "On J. Emonds' 'Analysis of Extraposition'." in Kimball, J. P., ed. (1973) *Syntax and Semantics*, vol. 2. New York: Academic Press.

Jacobs, R. A. and P. S. Rosenbaum (1968) *English Transformational Grammar*. Waltham, Mass.: Ginn/Blaisdell.

Kuno, S. (1973) "Constraints on Internal Clauses and Sentential Subjects." *Linguistic Inquiry* 4: 363–386.

Langendoen, D. T. (1966) "The Syntax of the English Expletive 'It'." in Dineen, F., ed. (1966) *Monograph Series on Languages and Linguistics*, No. 24. Washington, D.C.: Georgetown University Press.

Postal, P. M. (1974) *On Raising*. Cambridge, Mass.: M.I.T. Press.

Rosenbaum, P. S. (1967) *The Grammar of English Predicate Complement Constructions*. Cambridge, Mass.: M.I.T. Press.

Stockwell, R. P., P. Schachter and B. M. Partee (1973) *The Major Syntactic Structures of English*. New York: Holt, Rinehart & Winston.

Chapter 20

Akmajian, A. and F. W. Heny (1975) *An Introduction to the Principles of Transformational Syntax*. Cambridge, Mass.: M.I.T. Press.

Bach, E. (1974) *Syntactic Theory*. New York: Holt, Rinehart & Winston.

Burt, M. K. (1971) *From Deep to Surface Structure, An Introduction to Transformational Syntax*. New York: Harper & Row.

Jacobs, R. A. and P. S. Rosenbaum (1968) *English Transformational Grammar*. Waltham, Mass.: Ginn/Blaisdell.

Langendoen, D. T. (1970) "The 'Can't Seem To' Construction." *Linguistic Inquiry* 1: 25–36.

Perlmutter, D. M. (1970) "The Two Verbs *Begin*." in Jacobs, R. A. and P. S. Rosenbaum, eds. (1970) *Readings in Transformational Grammar*. Waltham, Mass.: Ginn/Blaisdell.

Postal, P. M. (1974) *On Raising*. Cambridge, Mass.: M.I.T. Press.

Rosenbaum, P. S. (1967) *The Grammar of English Predicate Complement Constructions*. Cambridge, Mass.: M.I.T. Press.

Stockwell, R. P., P. Schachter and B. M. Partee (1973) *The Major Syntactic Structures of English*. New York: Holt, Rinehart & Winston.

Chapter 21

Akmajian, A. and F. W. Heny (1975) *An Introduction to the Principles of Transformational Syntax*. Cambridge, Mass.: M.I.T. Press.

Bach, E. (1974) *Syntactic Theory*. New York: Holt, Rinehart & Winston.

Burt, M. K. (1971) *From Deep to Surface Structure, An Introduction to Transformational Syntax*. New York: Harper & Row.

Jacobs, R. A. and P. S. Rosenbaum (1968) *English Transformational Grammar*. Waltham, Mass.: Ginn/Blaisdell.

Langendoen, D. T. (1970) "The 'Can't Seem To' Construction." *Linguistic Inquiry* 1: 25–36.

Perlmutter, D. M. (1970) "The Two Verbs *Begin*." in Jacobs, R. A. and P. S. Rosenbaum, eds. (1970) *Readings in Transformational Grammar*. Waltham, Mass.: Ginn/Blaisdell.

Postal, P. M. (1974) *On Raising*. Cambridge, Mass.: M.I.T. Press.

Rosenbaum, P. S. (1967) *The Grammar of English Predicate Complement Constructions*. Cambridge, Mass.: M.I.T. Press.

Stockwell, R. P., P. Schachter and B. M. Partee (1973) *The Major Syntactic Structures of English*. New York: Holt, Rinehart & Winston.

Chapter 22

Akmajian, A. and F. W. Heny (1975) *An Introduction to the Principles of Transformational Syntax*. Cambridge, Mass.: M.I.T. Press.

Bach, E. (1974) *Syntactic Theory*. New York: Holt, Rinehart & Winston.

Burt, M. K. (1971) *From Deep to Surface Structure, An Introduction to Transformational Syntax*. New York: Harper & Row.

Jacobs, R. A. and P. S. Rosenbaum (1968) *English Transformational Grammar*. Waltham, Mass.: Ginn/Blaisdell.

Postal, P. M. (1974) *On Raising*. Cambridge, Mass.: M.I.T. Press.

Rosenbaum, P. S. (1967) *The Grammar of English Predicate Complement Constructions*. Cambridge, Mass.: M.I.T. Press.

Stockwell, R. P., P. Schachter and B. M. Partee (1973) *The Major Syntactic Structures of English*. New York: Holt, Rinehart & Winston.

Chapter 23

Akmajian, A. and F. W. Heny (1975) *An Introduction to the Principles of Transformational Syntax*. Cambridge, Mass.: M.I.T. Press.

Bach, E. (1974) *Syntactic Theory*. New York: Holt, Rinehart & Winston.

Burt, M. K. (1971) *From Deep to Surface Structure, An Introduction to Transformational Syntax*. New York: Harper & Row.

Fillmore, C. J. (1965) *Indirect Object Constructions in English and the Ordering of Transformations*. The Hague: Mouton.

Jacobs, R. A. and P. S. Rosenbaum (1968) *English Transformational Grammar*. Waltham, Mass.: Ginn/Blaisdell.

Postal, P. M. (1964) "Underlying and Superficial Linguistic Structure." *Harvard Educational Review* 34: 246–266; reprinted in Reibel, D. A. and S. Schane, eds. (1969) *Modern Studies in English*. Englewood Cliffs, N.J.: Prentice–Hall.

Rosenbaum, P. S. (1967) *The Grammar of English Predicate Complement Constructions*. Cambridge, Mass.: M.I.T. Press.

Stockwell, R. P., P. Schachter and B. M. Partee (1973) *The Major Syntactic Structures of English*. New York: Holt, Rinehart & Winston.

Chapter 24

Hudson, R. A. (1970) "On Clauses Containing Conjoined and Plural Noun-Phrases in English." *Lingua* 24: Number 2.

Postal, P. M. (1974) *On Raising*. Cambridge, Mass.: M.I.T. Press.

Chapter 25

Akmajian, A. and T. Wasow (1975) "VP Constituency and the Shifty Verb 'be'." *Linquistic Analysis* 1.

Postal, P. M. (1974) *On Raising*. Cambridge, Mass.: M.I.T. Press.

Ross, J. R. (1969) "Auxiliaries as Main Verbs." *Studies in Philosophical Linguistics* 1: 77–102.

Chapter 26

Akmajian, A. and F. W. Heny (1975) *An Introduction to the Principles of Transformational Syntax*. Cambridge, Mass.: M.I.T. Press.

Akmajian, A. and T. Wasow (1975) "VP Constituency and the Shifty Verb 'be'." *Linguistic Analysis* 1.

Chomsky, N. (1957) *Syntactic Structures*. The Hague: Mouton.

Langendoen, D. T. (1970) "The 'Can't Seem To' Construction." *Linguistic Inquiry* 1: 25–36.

Postal, P. M. (1974) *On Raising*. Cambridge, Mass.: M.I.T. Press.

Ross, J. R. (1969) "Auxiliaries as Main Verbs." *Studies in Philosophical Linguistics* 1: 77–102.

Chapter 27
Akmajian, A. and F. W. Heny (1975) *An Introduction to the Principles of Transformational Syntax*. Cambridge, Mass.: M.I.T. Press.
Akmajian, A. and T. Wasow (1975) "VP Constituency and the Shifty Verb 'be'." *Linguistic Analysis* 1.
Chomsky, N. (1957) *Syntactic Structures*. The Hague: Mouton.
Klima, E. S. (1964) "Negation in English." in Fodor, J. A. and J. J. Katz, eds. (1964) *The Structure of Language*. Englewood Cliffs, N.J.: Prentice–Hall.
Ross, J. R. (1969) "Auxiliaries as Main Verbs." *Studies in Philosophical Linguistics* 1:77–102.
Stockwell, R. P., P. Schachter and B. M. Partee (1973) *The Major Syntactic Structures of English*. New York: Holt, Rinehart & Winston.

Chapter 28
Bach, E. (1974) *Syntactic Theory*. New York: Holt, Rinehart & Winston.
Baker, C. L. (1970) "Notes on the Description of English Questions: The Role of an Abstract Question Morpheme." *Foundations of Language* 6: 197–219.
Bresnan, J. W. (1970) "On Complementizers: Toward a Syntactic Theory of Complement Types." *Foundations of Language* 6: 297–321.
Klima, E. S. (1964) "Negation in English." in Fodor, J. A. and J. J. Katz, eds. (1964) *The Structure of Language*, Englewood Cliffs, N.J.: Prentice-Hall.
Kuno, S. and J. J. Robinson (1972) "Multiple Wh Questions." *Linguistic Inquiry* 3: 463–468.
Live, A. N. (1967) "Subject-Verb Inversion (in English)." *General Linguistics* 7: Number 2.
Postal, P. M. (1972) "On Some Rules that Are Not Successive Cyclic." *Linguistic Inquiry* 3: 211–222.
Stockwell, R. P., P. Schachter and B. M. Partee (1973) *The Major Syntactic Structures of English*. New York: Holt, Rinehart & Winston.

Chapter 29
Akmajian, A. and F. W. Heny (1975) *An Introduction to the Principles of Transformational Syntax*. Cambridge, Mass.: M.I.T. Press.
Bach, E. (1974) *Syntactic Theory*. New York: Holt, Rinehart & Winston.
Burt, M. K. (1971) *From Deep to Surface Structure, An Introduction to Transformational Syntax*. New York: Harper & Row.
Chomsky, N. (1965) *Aspects of the Theory of Syntax*. Cambridge, Mass.: M.I.T. Press.
Fillmore, C. J. (1963) "The Position of Embedding Transformations in a Grammar." *Word* 19: 208–231.
Jacobs, R. A. and P. S. Rosenbaum (1968) *English Transformational Grammar*. Waltham, Mass.: Ginn/Blaisdell.
Postal, P. M. (1970) "On Coreferential Complement Subject Deletion." *Linguistic Inquiry* 1: 439–500.
Postal, P. M. (1972) "On Some Rules that Are Not Successive Cyclic." *Linguistic Inquiry* 3: 211–222.
Postal, P. M. (1974) *On Raising*. Cambridge, Mass.: M.I.T. Press.
Rosenbaum, P. S (1967) *The Grammar of English Predicate Complement Constructions*. Cambridge, Mass.: M.I.T. Press.
Ross, J. R. (1969) "The Cyclic Nature of English Pronominalization." in Reibel and Schane, eds. (1969).
Stockwell, R. P., P. Schachter and B. M. Partee (1973) *The Major Syntactic Structures of English*. New York: Holt, Rinehart & Winston.

Other Recommended Reading
Bach, E. (1971) "Syntax since Aspects." *Monograph Series on Languages and Linguistics*, No. 24. Washington, D.C.: Georgetown University Press.

Dineen, F., ed. (1966) *Monograph Series on Languages and Linguistics*, no. 19. Washington, D.C.: Georgetown University Press.

Fodor, J. A. and J. J. Katz, eds. (1964) *The Structure of Language*. Englewood Cliffs, N.J.: Prentice–Hall.

Jacobs, R. A. and P. S. Rosenbaum, eds. (1970) *Readings in Transformational Grammar*. Waltham, Mass.: Ginn/Blaisdell.

Kimball, J. P., ed. (1973) *Syntax and Semantics*, vol. 2. New York: Academic Press.

Kruisinga, E. (1931–32) *A Handbook of Present-Day English*, Part II, 5th ed. Groningen: P. Noordhoff.

Lasnik, H. and R. Fiengo (1975) "Some Issues in the Theory of Transformational Grammar." *Linguistic Inquiry* 6: 4.

Lester, M. (1970) *Readings in Applied Transformational Grammar*, New York: Holt, Rinehart & Winston.

McCawley, J. D. (1970) Review of O. Jespersen, *Analytic Syntax*. *Language* 46: 442–449.

Postal, P. M. (1975) "Avoiding Reference to Subject." *Linguistic Inquiry* 6: 4.

Quirk, R. and S. Greenbaum (1973) *A Concise Grammar of Contemporary English*. New York: Harcourt Brace Jovanovich.

Reibel, D. A. and S. Schane, eds. (1969) *Modern Studies in English*. Englewood Cliffs, N.J.: Prentice-Hall.

Ross, J. R. (1969) "A Proposed Rule of Tree-Pruning." in Reibel and Schane, eds. (1969).

Thomas, O. (1966) *Transformational Grammar and the Teacher of English*. New York: Holt, Rinehart & Winston.

INDEX

Accent. *See* Stress
Active sentences, 217, 225fn. 3
Active verbs, 75fn. 3
Adjective, 30, 161–163
    and modals, 328–329
    as modifiers of nouns, 332–333fn. 1
    productive formation of, 161
    and raising, 260
    and *un-*, 177–178fn. 12
    as verbs, 307–309, 326
Affixation, rule of, 333–334fn. 2
Agent
    definition of, 70–71
    and imperatives, 71–72
Agreement, 16fn. 5, 55–56, 65fn. 14
Anaphora, 354, 357fn. 7
and. See Coordination
Antecedent, 11, 17fn. 7, 18 prob. 2. *See
    also* Agreement
    extrasentential, 63fn. 7
    and imperatives, 68
Articles, 148, 168–169, 176fn. 5, 177fn. 8
Auxiliary, 307–316
    and interrogative clauses, 327
    and negation elements, 327
    and *so,* 328
    subcategorization of, 322–331
    and tag-clause questions, 327–328
Auxiliary, rule of, 326

Bare stem, 329. *See also* Stem
Base component, 139–155
Base grammar. *See* Base rules
Base rules, 127–134
Be
    and adjectives, 307–310
    and passive constructions, 310–312
    and predicate nominals, 81, 319–
        320fn. 8
    and progressive constructions, 310–312
    and raising, 308–309, 311
Binding of quantifiers, 292–293. *See also*
    Quantifiers

Bitransitive clause. *See* Ditransitive clause
Boundary symbols, 156fn. 1
Brackets, 31–32. *See also* Tree
by. See Passive constructions

Case, 52–53. *See also* Inflectional endings
Case markings, 52
Causatives
    and passive constructions, 225fn. 1,2
Center embedding, 157fn. 5
Chomsky, N., 211fn. 7
Chomsky-adjunction, 210fn. 3
Clausal idioms, 250
Clause, 20, 27fn. 4, 29–33
    appositive, 23
    main, 24
    minimal, 21, 42–46
    non-restrictive relative. *See* Clause, ap-
        positive
    restrictive relative, 23, 144–149
    and sentence, 40fn. 1
Clause boundary, 20–21, 156fn. 1
    internal, 20, 137
Clause mate, 45–46
Collapsing of rules, 130
Complement, definition of, 143
Complementizer, 26fn. 2
Complex NP shift, rule of, 273
    and extraposition, 269
    and raising, 276
Complex symbols, 204–208
Compound nouns, 163–172
Conjoined coreferential subject deletion,
        96–100, 194, 198–199, 252fn. 2
    and imperative deletion, 98–100
    and why not deletion, 99–100
Conjunction copy, rule of, 152–153, 194–
        195, 210fn. 3. *See also* Initial con-
        junct erasure, Optional erasure
Constant, 63fn. 9
Constituent, 34–36. *See also* Tree
    immediate, 37